INSIDERS' GUIDE® TO

HAMPTON ROADS

Virginia Beach, Norfolk, & Newport News

FIRST EDITION

TONY GERMANOTTA

INSIDERS' GUIDE

GUILFORD, CONNECTICUT
AN IMPRINT OF GLOBE PEQUOT PRESS

All the information in this guidebook is subject to change. We recommend that you call ahead to obtain current information before traveling.

INSIDERS' GUIDE ®

Editor: Amy Lyons
Project Editor: Lynn Zelem
Layout Artist: Kevin Mak
Text Design: Sheryl Kober
Maps: Design Maps, Inc. © Morris Book Publishing, LLC

Library of Congress Cataloging-in-Publication Data is available on file.
ISBN 978-0-7627-6017-6

Printed in the United States of America
10 9 8 7 6 5 4 3 2 1

CONTENTS

CONTENTS

Directory of Maps

ABOUT THE AUTHOR

Tony Germanotta has spent 30 years living in, and writing about, Hampton Roads as an award-winning reporter and editor for *The Virginian-Pilot* and *The Ledger-Star* newspapers.

He has paddled the local waterways and sailed the bays, accompanied Coast Guard rescue missions, and catapulted off aircraft carriers.

He even backseated with the Air Force Thunderbirds and the Navy's Blue Angels as they tried their best to turn him inside out practicing for air shows over Virginia Beach.

A passion for the quirky led him to explore the joys of living in a lighthouse, took him to honky-tonks and concert halls, and lured him behind the scenes at the area's many historic attractions.

He's covered presidential elections and royal visits, epic trials and everyday struggles. *Pilot* editor Denis Finley once said Tony not only knew where the bodies were buried but "who dug the holes and where they bought the shovels."

ACKNOWLEDGMENTS

This book would not have been possible without the support and inspiration of my wife Marcy and son Alex, who always help me find joy in the moment; and my Aunt Kass, who never let me settle for a 99. I'd also like to thank all the friends and colleagues who endured my endless questions and shared their personal secrets.

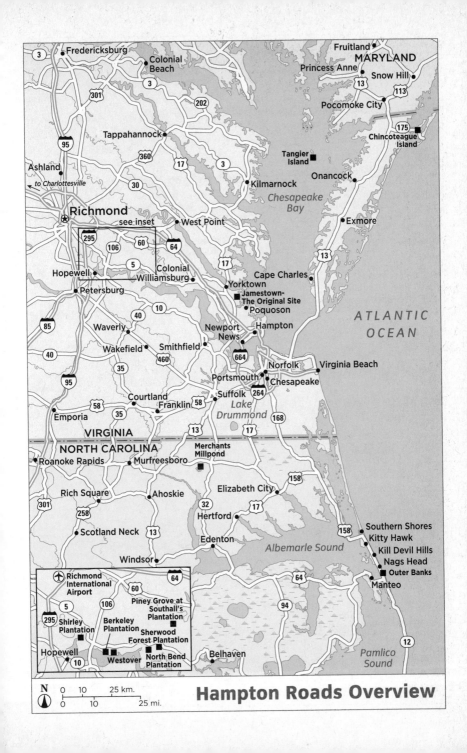

Hampton Roads Overview

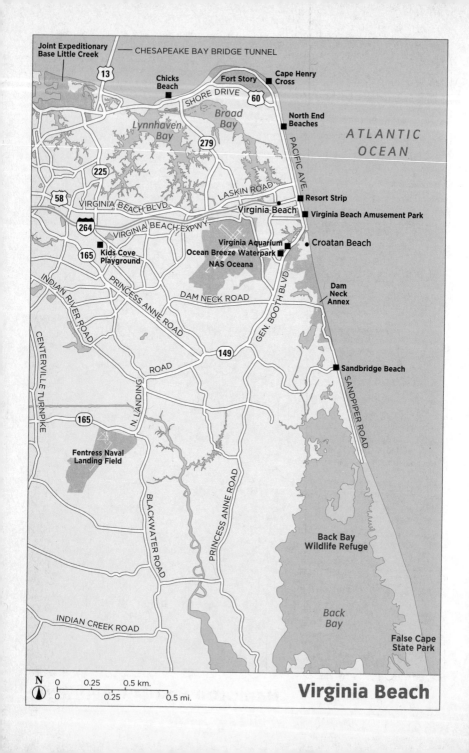

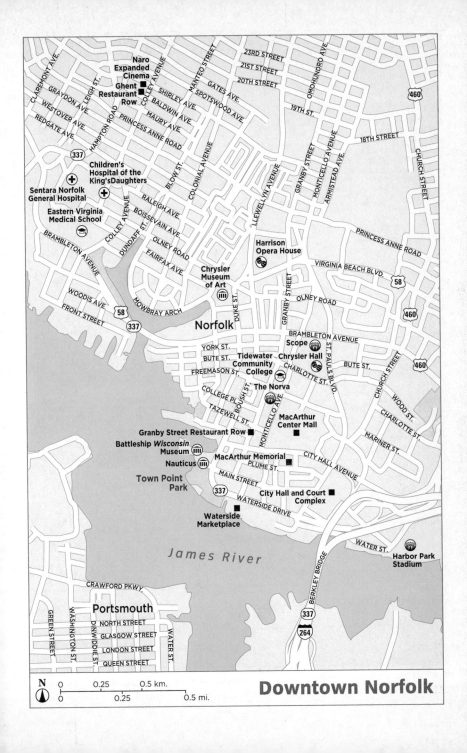

Downtown Norfolk

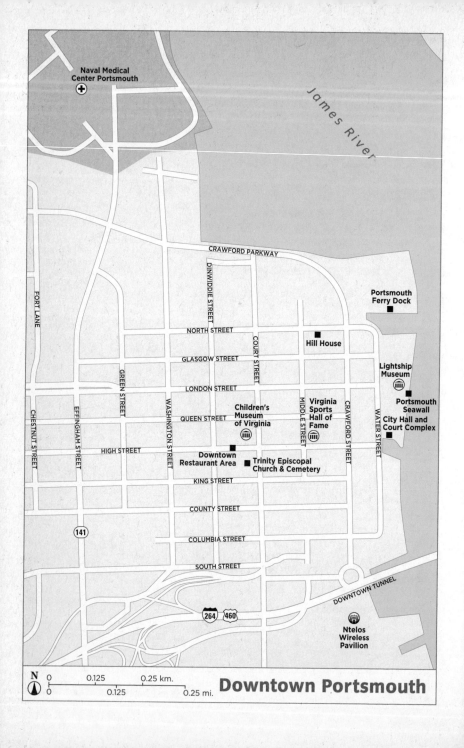

Downtown Portsmouth

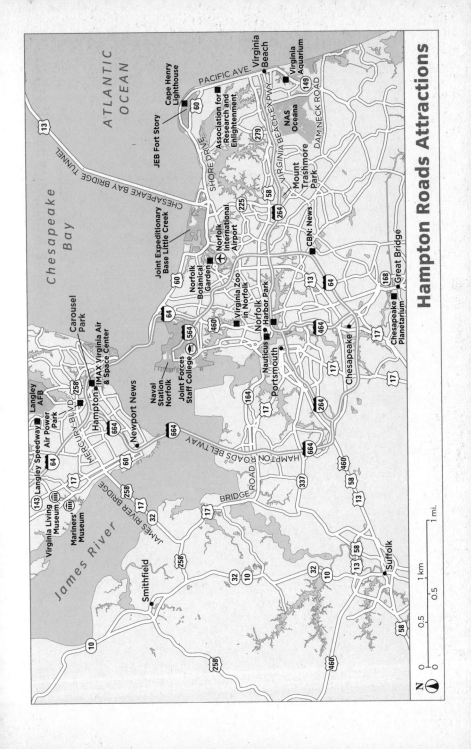

Hampton Roads Attractions

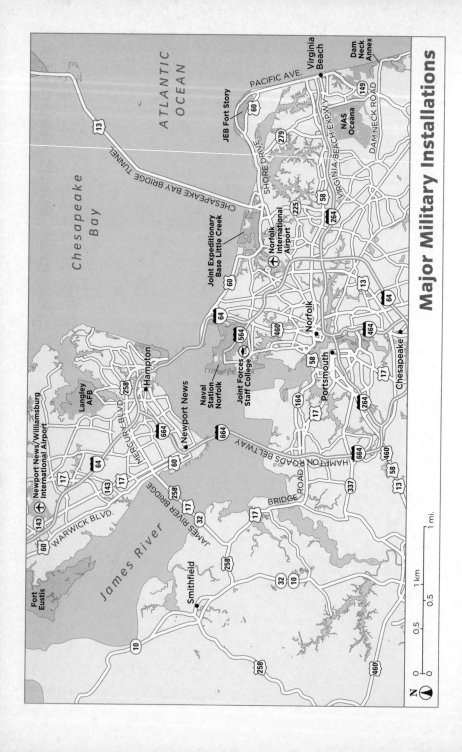

Major Military Installations

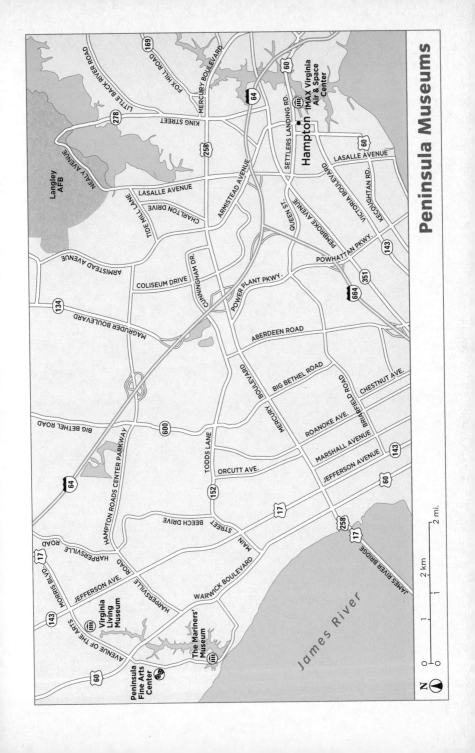

Peninsula Museums

PREFACE

Welcome to Hampton Roads, the nation's 33rd largest metropolitan area, a place where nature and industry rub shoulders with the military and summer vacationers.

Here you can watch the sun rise over the Atlantic and set behind Back Bay, all within the borders of Virginia Beach, the state's most populous city. You can paddle a canoe along the pristine Northwest River in Chesapeake or practice your archery in a municipal park in Newport News.

Feeling a little more urban? Explore Norfolk's resurgent downtown, with its bustling night scene. Enjoy gawking at the restored Colonial homes in Portsmouth's Olde Towne, catch an art flick at the Naro Expanded Cinema, or an aria at the Harrison Opera House.

Hampton Roads is a place with deep historic roots. The first English settlers landed at Cape Henry in 1607, on their way to establish the Jamestown settlement and a relationship with Pocahontas. An obscure skirmish at the Great Bridge bridge (one local columnist used to call it the great, Great Bridge, bridge battle) chased the British out of Hampton Roads and eventually led to the Revolutionary War's end at nearby Yorktown. It was in full view of locals that the future of naval warfare took root when the ironclads *Monitor* and *Merrimack* pounded each other into a Civil War standoff. And it was from here that millions of Americans shipped out to fight for freedom in World Wars I and II.

Seven of Virginia's top 10 cities are located here—and the military population would form another if split out. Some 3 million tourists flock to the region every year, swelling the population not only in summer but also in what are now known as the shoulder seasons of late spring and early fall.

There was a time when Norfolk's downtown was notorious for tattoo parlors and the boozy joints that preyed on sailors. But all that is gone now, replaced by family-friendly restaurants, a waterfront marketplace, and an upscale mall dropped right into the heart of the city.

I came to Hampton Roads in 1980 looking to enrich my newspaper resume and move on. I fell in love with the area and with its diversity of activities and wound up staying at that same newspaper for nearly 30 years. I'm no longer working for the newspaper, but I am still enjoying the area, and most importantly, the people who call it home.

HOW TO USE THIS BOOK

When I was about 13, you could get a new volume of an encyclopedia every week or so at the local supermarket until you had accumulated a complete "standard reference" set. I'd wait anxiously for my mother to come home from shopping, grab the latest book, and start devouring it from cover to cover.

I think of this Insiders' Guide in much the same way as those Funk & Wagnalls. You can certainly read it from front to back. And if you do, I hope you get as much joy in the journey as I did moving from Aachen (a city in Germany) to Zyrian (a Finno-Ugrian tribe also known as Syryenian) in my still-cherished 25-volume set.

But it's also designed for skimming and cherry picking.

Like an encyclopedia, I crafted this book also to be a quick reference, a place to look things up, to plan the next trip, to see what's nearby and what might be worth a longer journey.

In just minutes, you can tap my 30-plus years living, working, and reporting in Hampton Roads. And explore with me some of the new treasures I discovered while researching and writing this guide.

I think it will be pretty self-evident as you go along, but here's how I have organized this book.

Since this community is divided into two regions, and within them eight individual cities, I break up the chapters that way wherever it makes sense. So if you are thinking about a meal, you'll find that chapter divided by locality since you probably want to know what's closest as well as the overall best.

On the other hand, if you are considering a museum, watching a game, or exploring a wetlands, it's more about the destination's charms than the neighborhood. So in chapters like the one on our wildly varied parks, I just roll out the biggest guns and what you'll find there. Even in that chapter, though, when I look at dog parks, I break that up by location, since you probably don't want to drive halfway to Richmond with a panting puppy on your neck.

That drive and any others will be easier if you check out the tips in the Getting Here, Getting Around chapter. As a newspaper reporter, I spent countless days in strange cities, often stuck in traffic. I'd tune into the radio and be completely lost when the announcer listed the snarls. The names and shortcuts locals used didn't make it to my map, I found. Here, I'll let you in on what that helicopter reporter actually calls the highway you're on when he doesn't refer to it by its official numbers. And if you have to take a train out of town, I'll show you how to find the area's single stealth station, which seems to have been planned by a military expert in camouflage.

Every chapter has a number of Insiders' tips, things you just won't find anywhere else. And there's usually a Close-up that focuses on something extra special. Everywhere, you'll find context.

One thing about a place like Hampton Roads, with its constant influx of new residents and tourists, is it's so easy to lose track of the area's history and the things that gave it shape. The History and Area Overview chapters will fill in those blanks and help you understand why things are, even when it doesn't make obvious sense.

You can't consider moving to or exploring Hampton Roads without examining the military. I've given it a separate chapter. The military is more than an economic machine, the factory in this factory town. It has helped the area grow from a sleepy farm community into a sophisticated urban center. Soldiers and sailors from far and wide have augmented the region's Southern charm with an influx of Midwestern simplicity and New England frugality.

The military's impact is everywhere. They are your Girl Scout leaders. Their spouses teach in the local schools, and their children are your kids' best friends. Once-exotic cuisine has become our takeout dinners. In many areas of Hampton Roads, it's easier to find a good bagel for breakfast than grits and red-eye gravy. We may be 100 miles from the Capital of the Confederacy, but without such a military presence, Richmond remains several states and at least a century more Southern.

Take a look at the performing arts scene or even the radio dial here. There's a diversity of offerings that few similar sized localities can claim. In fact, the only area where we lag is in professional sports. Hampton Roads is the largest metropolitan area without a major league team. Perhaps it's because those sailors and soldiers who come here and settle still root for their hometown heroes.

Still, there's plenty to do and see. Check out the chapter on the Performing Arts, and the ones on Parks and Recreation and Spectator Sports. Maybe we just don't have the time or energy left to commit our souls to a major league team.

You can spend years just exploring our many museums, with offerings that range from one of the world's finest collections of art glass to the turret of the mighty ironclad *Monitor*. I'll give you the Cliff's Notes in the Museums chapter.

If you have children, we have stuff to keep them busy as well as educated. Check out the Kidstuff chapter for the inside scoop on everything from playgrounds to major attractions.

The Shopping chapter will show you the best Insider flea markets and thrift shops, boutiques, and specialists selling everything from fashion to high end audio and kayaks.

If you have a limited time to spend in Hampton Roads, this book points out the stuff you shouldn't miss in the Attractions chapter.

And if you are lucky enough to be moving here, either as part of a military transfer or because so many media lists rank the area so highly, be sure to check out the blue-tabbed pages at the back of the book, where you will find the **Living Here** appendix. This section gives you a feel for the various neighborhoods you might consider, the school systems, the health care options, and even the real estate agents and builders you might want to explore.

Even a book of this size can only touch on the best. Keep an open mind and open eyes. I've been here for more than half my life and I am still finding new favorites. I hope I always will.

Also, businesses come and go, sometimes very quickly. There's a phone number attached to every location in this book. I've tried to focus on the perennial bests, those with staying power and a reputation earned over time. But even the most cherished places sometimes call it quits. So phone and confirm before you head out. Prices are also always in flux. In some chapters we give a range, while in others, such as the one on golf, there are actual fees. Those were accurate up to publication. And even if they change, they still serve as a guide to the relative breakdown between various courses. Still, you'll want to ask about the cost when you call to reserve your tee time.

If you discover something has changed or find something you think should be included in updates of this book, let us know. Your feedback will help us improve the next edition. Write to *Insiders' Guide to Hampton Roads*, GPP, P.O. Box 480, Guilford, CT, 06437-0480 or by e-mail to editorial@globepequot.com.

Enjoy your explorations of Hampton Roads. If you're lucky, you might wind up calling it home the way I did.

AREA OVERVIEW

Hampton Roads, once known as Tidewater, Virginia, is actually two distinct regions divided by the broad mouth of the James River. Locals refer to them as the Southside and the Peninsula.

Once kept apart by ferries and tolls, they have grown increasingly isolated as the area's population swells and traffic congestion on interstate bridges and tunnels again makes the river a regular choke point.

Seven of the state's largest 10 cities are located here, and the region's 1.6 million population is 20 percent of Virginia as a whole. There's a third distinct but dispersed community—the military. Hampton Roads has the nation's largest concentration of uniform personnel at its numerous Navy, Air Force, and Army installations. Those service members and their families, if singled out, would form another top-10 Virginia city. If you add the military members who have retired in this area, the impact gets even more impressive. The Navy alone counts 84,000 active duty members in Hampton Roads with another 97,000 family members and 44,000 retirees and surviving spouses.

CLIMATE

The weather in Hampton Roads isn't perfect. For that you'd need to live in Tahiti or Hawaii. But it can often come close.

Winter blizzards usually track to the north, perhaps steered away by the moderating effects of the Atlantic Ocean and Chesapeake Bay. Hurricanes usually stay to the south, and when they do threaten, it is generally the nearby Outer Banks of North Carolina that take it on their jutting chin.

This region is officially regarded as humid subtropical. What that means is you will experience all four seasons here but generally without extremes. Winters tend to be sunny, and the average high temperature in January, the coldest month, is a bearable 48 degrees. Extended cold snaps are almost as rare as snowfalls. You can go years without seeing any flakes stick. And when they do,

the winter wonderland effect doesn't usually outlast its charm.

Summers can get sticky. That humid moniker isn't misleading. July is the sultriest month, with an average high of 85. But spring comes early here, with glorious warming snaps even in January and February. And fall lingers with shirtsleeve days often right up to Christmas. In short, you'll need a coat here, but rarely earmuffs, and for most of the year you'll be comfortable in T-shirts and sandals.

GEOGRAPHY

The first thing you need to know about this area is there are no counties until you get out in the boonies. Virginia has an unusual governance system in which cities can exist without being part of a corresponding county. And in the 1960s, those cities were in a feeding frenzy, annexing outlying land at a rate that alarmed their surrounding communities. So several of those counties decided to incorporate into their own independent suburban cities, setting the stage for decades of decline in the now-hemmed-in urban centers and creating some enormous land masses that are cities only in name.

As a result, today there is no All-American central core here surrounded by suburbs, which is reflected in the Census Bureau's decision last decade to no longer identify this as the Norfolk Metropolitan Statistical area.

Virginia Beach is now the state's biggest city, with nearly double Norfolk's population, and Chesapeake is closing in as well. So the government now refers to us as the Virginia Beach, Norfolk-Newport News, VA-NC Metropolitan Statistical area. Quite a mouthful, and it still leaves a ton of large cities out of the title.

The diffusion of power and influence left a dismal legacy. State funding doesn't begin to match the population or financial impact of the region, and Hampton Roads remains the largest metropolitan area in the country without a major league sports franchise. Our last near miss was an attempt to woo the Expos before MLB settled on Washington, D.C. It has also stranded the state's largest population centers without a decent passenger rail link to the East Coast corridor. (See the Getting Here, Getting Around chapter.)

Here's a thumbnail sketch of the major cities and counties in the region:

Norfolk

With a population of 235,092, Norfolk remains the cultural and commercial center of the region and seems to be getting a second wind as people and restaurants move back to its downtown. Norfolk is home to the world-ranked Chrysler Museum; the Virginia Opera; the Virginia Symphony; the Norfolk Tides, a AAA baseball affiliate of the Baltimore Orioles, and the Norfolk Admirals, the Tampa Bay Lightning's top minor league hockey affiliate. Its waterfront bustles with coal terminals, commercial shipyards. and international port facilities.

History abounds here, from the cannonball that remains lodged in the brick wall at St. Paul's Church, the only structure to survive the destruction of the city ordered by Lord Dunmore on New Year's Day in 1776, to the tomb of that old soldier who promised to return and then was forced to fade away, Gen. Douglas MacArthur.

Norfolk is host to Old Dominion and Norfolk State universities and Virginia Wesleyan College, as well as the Eastern Virginia Medical School with its history making in-vitro fertilization center. It boasts the region's small financial district and the world's largest Navy base, with piers bristling with warships of every type.

In recent years, redevelopment on large sections that had lain fallow since the Urban Renewal demolitions of the 1960s was finally finished, resulting in a number of vibrant downtown neighborhoods, an upscale pedestrian-friendly mall, a festival marketplace, and a riverfront park that hosts cruise lines and annual tall ship gatherings. Downtown is also home to fine restaurants, new condos, and apartments that offer a chic urban living experience.

Norfolk Southern railroad is the only Fortune 500 Company based here, but Norfolk is also known as the headquarters of People for the Ethical Treatment of Animals, which has forged an international reputation by flamboyant campaigns against wearing fur and eating meat.

Virginia Beach

Now the state's most populous city, with 431,451 residents in 2009, it was born in the 1960s as America embraced suburbia. The Beach is much more than the resort area that provided its name in the 1963 merger of the little town and what was once Princess Anne County. There are 35 miles of Atlantic and Chesapeake Bay beaches in this vacation destination, but when it began, the new city was mostly farmland and small towns. Over the decades, though, the open acres have sprouted suburban developments.

Once, those who didn't work at the Navy's Oceana Master Jet Base probably commuted to defense-related jobs in Norfolk or Portsmouth. But a skyline and employment hub has grown at Town Center. The woods and fields that once formed the geographic center of this city have given way to office towers and a dining and shopping Mecca. A civic center and city hall was built in the southern farmlands, which residents complained was equally inconvenient to all population centers. Strip malls and communities were being built so quickly throughout the city in the 1980s that civic leaders drew a Green Line in the sandy soil designed to preserve the bucolic charm of the southern half of the city.

Even so, pressure persisted, and developments now ring Oceana. The encroachment of housing just outside the fences nearly cost the city the vital base and all of its jobs. The city won a reprieve by promising the Navy it would limit any new development around the air station and remove any deemed too close for safety. Another innovative program pays farmers not to sell their acreage for development, thereby preserving green space while allowing the landowners to be compensated for the potential value they have volunteered to forfeit.

Amerigroup, the health insurance giant, is a Fortune 500 company based in Virginia Beach. So is the Christian Broadcasting Network, which pioneering televangelist Pat Robertson grew from a low-powered UHF station in Portsmouth to a cable giant with international reach and its own university, Regent, complete with law school.

Chesapeake

Not long ago, Chesapeake was struggling to cope with being one of the fastest-growing communities in America. The latest estimate put the population at 216,622, but like Virginia Beach a decade earlier, Chesapeake was failing to keep pace with the influx of newcomers and the demands they placed on roads and schools. The boom slowed as civic leaders installed tighter development guidelines and builders moved on to the open land of adjacent Suffolk. Chesapeake also was born in 1963 with the merger of South Norfolk and Norfolk County. The result is a city with an unusual shape, wrapping its arms around Norfolk and Portsmouth. It is a city with no downtown, but two distinct population centers. The Great Bridge/Greenbrier corridor is home to the civic center and the bulk of the population. Western Branch, which closes the loop around Portsmouth, is the other suburban center. Each has its own large indoor mall and surrounding concentration of shops and restaurants.

Chesapeake shares the Great Dismal Swamp National Wildlife Refuge, which a young George Washington helped survey, with its western neighbor, Suffolk.

Chesapeake also has one of the area's most unusual city parks, Northwest River, a vast wooded stretch along that waterway that offers camping and canoeing, star gazing, and an equestrian center.

Dollar Tree Inc. got its start here and is the city's only Fortune 500 Company.

Portsmouth

This city along the Elizabeth River grew in step with the nation's first Naval Shipyard, ironically called the Norfolk Naval Shipyard although it is entirely in the city of Portsmouth. Portsmouth residents, a proud breed, have always been miffed by this slight, but it's not likely to be changed any time soon. There is already a Portsmouth Naval Shipyard. It's in Kittery, Maine, across the harbor from Portsmouth, New Hampshire, which makes just about as much sense to the slighted residents in Kittery. A correction, however, is no simple mission. It would involve millions of defense dollars in just sign and letterhead changes, let alone a lot of industrial confusion, so the Navy prefers to keep it all historically, if not geographically, pure.

Portsmouth is a city that struggles to pay its bills. It's not just that the suburban revolt cost any chance at expansion and caused an exodus of the most affluent residents. More than half of Portsmouth's potential real estate tax revenue is off limits to the community because the lucrative land is owned by federal and state facilities or tax-exempt churches.

Still, there has been a renaissance underway along the downtown riverfront, with a new hotel/convention center, outdoor amphitheater, and fashionable people returning to live in Olde Towne and Park Place. When a Walmart opened in Midtown, on land where the old Mid-City Shopping Center once thrived, it signaled the business community was ready to bet again on Portsmouth.

There is lots of history in Portsmouth. Olde Towne boasts the largest collection of historic homes between Alexandria and Charleston. The Cradock community near the Norfolk Naval Shipyard is one of the first planned developments in the nation, put up by the government, like many other Portsmouth neighborhoods, to house workers rushing to answer the nation's need for shipbuilding. This one was built in 1918 for World War I and included schools, shopping, and homes all within walking distance, with a streetcar line right to the gates of the yard.

That shipyard was the focus of the city's occupation by the British and the Union armies, but before being taken by the Yanks, it built the ironclad *Merrimack*, which the Confederate Navy renamed the *Virginia*, and which fought the Union's *Monitor* to a stalemate in the Battle of Hampton Roads, ushering out the era of wooden warships.

Portsmouth is home to the Coast Guard's Atlantic Command, responsible for all Coast Guard operations on the eastern half of the world, from the Rocky Mountains to the Arabian Gulf. That involves more than search and rescue these days, since the Coast Guard is now a military force under the Department of Homeland Security.

Suffolk

The largest city in land area in Virginia, Suffolk sprawls over 430 square miles. It is also one of the nation's fastest growing communities, with defense-oriented technology and simulation companies thriving in the northern area while agriculture still dominates in the south. Suffolk, too, is the creation of a merger, in 1974 between the city of the same name and Nansemond County. There is a small downtown, with restaurants and a new Culture Center that books national acts.

Suffolk is the place Italian immigrant Amedeo Obici settled and where he turned his Planters Peanuts into a food giant. There are still peanut farms here, their tubers growing under sandy mounds, and Suffolk remains a major peanut processing center with an annual Peanut Festival to celebrate its heritage. There are a few cotton fields to be found as well. But Suffolk is on its way to its suburban future.

The city is home to the wide Nansemond River and a bevy of lakes, including Lake Drummond in the Great Dismal Swamp National Wildlife Refuge. It is one of only two natural lakes in all of Virginia. The other, Mountain Lake, is in the Appalachians far to the west. The rest of the lakes here and in the state are man-made reservoirs.

The main public road to the Great Dismal Swamp refuge is on the Suffolk side, and its trails are open for hiking and biking during daylight hours. Walk where Washington trod and take a look at the swamp, which was part of the Underground Railroad for escaping slaves who hid in its dense woods and used the marsh and water to throw dogs off their trails.

Newport News

Another urban city with its history and fortunes tied to the water, Newport News stretches, far and narrow, like Chile, along the western spine of the Peninsula. It is 23 miles long and just 3 miles wide. All that frontage along the James River led to a history of shipbuilding and commerce. Northrop Grumman Newport News, once known as Newport News Shipbuilding, is the largest

shipyard, and it's the only place in the nation that can build and refuel nuclear aircraft carriers. The city also has a marine terminal and a busy port in its downtown.

Newport News was first settled by English colonists in 1622, and the name is thought to come from Capt. Christopher Newport, who brought news and supplies to the settlers up river at Jamestown. It became an independent city in 1896 and merged with Warwick County in 1958.

Hilton Village was begun in 1918, the prototype for approximately 100 wartime government housing communities. Like in Portsmouth's Cradock and Truxtun neighborhoods, there were paved streets, curbs, gutters, and streetlights. The planned community also featured four churches and several stores. It was bought from the government by the chairman of the shipyard. Eventually, the shipyard sold the homes, turning it into a privately owned neighborhood. It's on the National Register of Historic Places and has a state-empowered village architectural review board that works to maintain its character.

Newport News has a great museum district just north of Hilton Village along the river, including the Mariners' Museum and USS *Monitor* Center, designated by Congress as America's national maritime museum. The museum is a treasure of nautical memorabilia, including paintings, artifacts, figureheads, ship models, and small craft from around the world. The *Monitor* Center features the turret of this unique ship and a full-scale replica of the ironclad where visitors can walk the decks.

The Virginia Living Museum and Peninsula Fine Arts center round out the offerings on Avenue of the Arts.

Farther north and a world away from the city's tough East Side neighborhoods lies Newport News Park, the second largest municipal park in America, where you can camp, canoe, fish, and even practice archery on a wooded course. There are 30 miles of hiking and biking trails, an arboretum, and two public golf courses.

Newport News is also home to the Thomas Jefferson National Accelerator Facility, exploring atomic physics at the quark level, and Fort Eustis, the Army's component of the newly minted Joint Base Langley-Eustis. Eustis is the headquarters of the Army's Transportation Corps and the service's Transportation School. The base also hosts the U.S. Army Transportation Museum where you can see the history of military vehicles and other memorabilia.

Hampton

Capt. John Smith first set foot on Hampton's soil in 1607 when he and fellow members of the Jamestown settlement stopped in the Kecoughtan Indian village for several days. The English built a fort at Old Point Comfort two years later, establishing the roots of the city at this strategic bay overlook.

Hampton is home to Langley Air Force Base, that service's component of Joint Base Langley-Eustis. It also can claim a hand in the exploration of space. The initial astronaut group trained at NASA's Langley facility, and the center is still in the forefront of research that ranges from space flights to improving the fuel economy and safety of passenger airliners.

It's also the location of Hampton University, a privately endowed, historically black school that was founded just after the Civil War, and Fort Monroe, the last fortification at Old Point Comfort and the final American military base with a moat. It is in the process of being returned to civilian use.

The Casement Museum on the fort tells the story of runaway slaves who sought sanctuary behind its walls and of a young soldier, Edgar Allan Poe, who was stationed there. The fort also was the prison of former Confederate President Jefferson Davis.

Downtown Hampton has seen a resurgence since the opening of the Virginia Air and Space Center, which combined the visitors centers for the NASA Langley Research Center and the Langley Air Force Base. It has hands-on exhibits and an IMAX theater. Nearby you can ride an antique outdoor carousel, one of only 200 in the country.

Poquoson

The smallest city in Hampton Roads, Poquoson is often overlooked or assumed to be a neighborhood in Hampton. But Poquoson is its own entity, a bedroom community on the eastern tip of the Peninsula. Surrounded by water and wetlands, the city boasts 84 miles of shoreline. In fact, more than 80 percent of the city's surface is covered by water.

A 20-square-mile peninsula forms the heart of the city with the Poquoson River on the north, the Back River and Wythe Creek on the south, and the Chesapeake Bay on the East.

GETTING HERE, GETTING AROUND

There are countless ways to get into Hampton Roads. But the most breathtaking has to be via the Chesapeake Bay Bridge-Tunnel. Billed as an engineering wonder, the 18-mile span is the world's longest bridge-tunnel complex, crossing the point where the Atlantic meets the Bay. You can look over the guardrails as you cruise a few feet over the swells and watch fleets of sports fishermen, scads of sailboats, and an ever-present parade of freighters. If you get really lucky, you might catch the eerie specter of a submarine beginning one of its secret missions, the dark conning tower seeming to float above fog-socked seas as it spends its final few minutes on the surface. Keep an even sharper eye out in the summer for pods of porpoises, which will occasionally parallel your car for miles, their backs arching in and out of the water as they frolic.

When you finally get to Virginia Beach, Shore Drive is the link to the resort strand, and it's one of the most beautiful approaches to any vacation destination. Thick woods, some laced with Spanish moss, line both sides of the roadway for miles, providing a lush counterpoint to the half hour you just spent over the bounding main. You'll pass the wooded entrances to First Landing State Park and historic Fort Story before, suddenly, you emerge at the Oceanfront's North End, home to luxurious beach "bungalows" tucked just behind the dunes.

Atlantic Avenue gets progressively more commercial as you head south along the strand, and when you pass the stately Cavalier Hotel you enter the tourist zone, where hotels in a steady line tower over fine sandy beaches.

Arriving by air has its own rewards. On a clear day—and this area tends to be clear and sunny even in the midst of winter's grip—you'll likely bank over the Navy piers as you fly into Norfolk International. The array of aircraft carriers, destroyers, frigates, and amphibious assault ships that stretch out below give testimony to the might of the Atlantic Fleet that calls this world's largest Navy base home. Some of those piers will always be empty, their ships off protecting the peace in far-away lands.

BY CAR

Like Philadelphia and New York City, Hampton Roads sits at the southeastern-most corner of its state, essentially at the end of the road. It was once dubbed "Tollwater," a play on its former Tidewater moniker that mocked the tolls needed to cross the bridges and tunnels that connected it to the rest of Virginia. Those booths are gone now, but there's lots of talk about new public-private partnerships being needed to relieve congestion and provide another hurricane evacuation route, with the return of tolls a necessary evil.

Hampton Roads has a public transit system, but it can be difficult to master, especially if you are traveling between cities or from Southside to the Peninsula. So most residents commute by car. That creates a lot of congestion, especially at bridge and tunnel choke points. And there are lots of bridges and tunnels. In fact, the region is a world leader in using tunnels to span waterways (see Close-up). And the rush hour here tends to be earlier—and longer—than in most metropolitan areas. That's the result of the military, which reports to work at what they term "zero dark thirty" and leaves its bases early as well. The industries that rely on defense work tend to mirror their customers' hours. Then, just when the roads seem ready to clear of uniformed drivers, the non-military employers empty out, extending the commuter crunch. In short, there is often a lot of traffic on a road network that is handicapped by all the region's rivers and wetlands and which developed haphazardly over the years, as each city stubbornly took an independent path.

Since there is no simple grid here, a GPS unit can really help, especially when you bore down into suburban neighborhoods with all their cul-de-sacs, circles, and sound-alike addresses. And a good street map, with a detailed index, is a must if you'll be here long.

i Even if you intend to stay in downtown Norfolk or Portsmouth, you'll probably want to rent a car. This is a vast area, with a wide range of cities and a lot of ground between civic centers and attractions.

i The Chesapeake Bay Bridge-Tunnel Commission now has mp3 tours you can download that provide 20-minute narrations to the trip. The tour includes a history of the facility, facts about how it was engineered, and points of interest along the way. It's available for free at www.cbbt.com/ipodtour.html.

The Roads

There are several main thoroughfares connecting and traversing the region. Most are adjuncts to I-64 that connects Hampton Roads to the rest of Virginia, and their names reflect that.

Interstates 664, 464 and 264 feed off of I-64, and together they reach into all sections of the area, completing at the Monitor-Merrimack Bridge-Tunnel what is tantamount to a beltway around the region.

I-64: This road stretches nearly 300 miles across the center of the state, from the West Virginia line down through Charlottesville, Richmond, Williamsburg, and then Newport News and Hampton before crossing the mouth of the James River at the Hampton Roads Bridge-Tunnel to the Southside. It passes through each of the area's seven main cities, forming the backbone of the highway network, although it doesn't actually pass through any of the Southside's downtowns.

The section of I-64 in Hampton, connecting to the then-new Hampton Roads Bridge-Tunnel, was the initial segment, opening in 1957 as a toll road. The first tunnel tube, by the way, was the first underwater link ever built between man-made islands. The highway remains the main connector between Southside and Peninsula, and is routinely clogged, especially on weekend getaways—often leading to miles-long traffic jams on either side of the tunnel and again up where the road abruptly narrows to two lanes near the Newport News/Williamsburg International Airport exit. Morning and evening commutes can be a bear here too. The Monitor-Merrimack tunnel on I-664 is an alternate route that may add miles to the trip, but can be shorter in time and much less stressful—unless there is an accident there.

i Be careful when navigating on I-64. Like many names in the area, the locations can be confusing. For example, South Norfolk is actually in Chesapeake, while Port Norfolk and West Norfolk are in Portsmouth. And Chesapeake is the only city without a sniff of that historic bay. So it probably makes some twisted sense that in much of Hampton Roads, what used to be signed as I-64 East actually heads in different compass directions, including due west. It's the result of the road not simply continuing to the Oceanfront when it was built in 1958. To be fair, when it was designed, there was no city of Virginia Beach, just a quaint resort village. So once it crossed the Hampton Roads-Bridge Tunnel, I-64 spun off in a 35-mile arc, sort of a semi-beltway through Norfolk, what would eventually become Virginia Beach, and Chesapeake, finally ending in Suffolk.

I-264: This is the highway that connects Virginia Beach to Norfolk and then over the Berkley Bridge and through the Downtown Tunnel to Portsmouth and on to Chesapeake. Part of it was once a toll road known as the Virginia Beach-Norfolk Expressway. And the tunnel also had its toll collectors.

Now they are all free, and since it is the main route between two of the most populous cities in Virginia, it is often crowded, especially at rush hours. It does have HOV lanes in some of the most congested stretches, and like all Hampton Roads HOV lanes, they only require two people to be in the car. There are parallel roads, such as Virginia Beach Boulevard, that can be quicker during rush hours, despite the stoplights and slower speed limits. And the Midtown Tunnel provides an alternative link between Norfolk and Portsmouth, although it is often more crowded, holding the distinction of being the busiest two lane road east of the Mississippi, with more than a million motorists funneling through every month.

I-464: This road spins off the Berkley Bridge in Norfolk and into Chesapeake, eventually connecting with the last toll road in the region, the Chesapeake Expressway, a 10-mile route opened in 2001 to get Outer Banks-bound cars through this southern stretch of Virginia without jamming up local roads. As Chesapeake has grown as a bedroom community, traffic has increased on 464. Where once it only slowed across the bridge, thanks to cars waiting to get into the adjacent Downtown Tunnel into Portsmouth, it now can be pretty crowded at rush hours all the way through the city. Still, it always seems to move once you clear the bridge area, barring an accident.

I-664: This is the last leg of the spur roads, connecting Suffolk and Portsmouth through the Monitor-Merrimack Bridge-Tunnel to Newport News and Hampton. It completes the Hampton Roads Beltway and is usually a good alternate route to the much busier Hampton Road Bridge-Tunnel, with only half the three million vehicles per month of its older sibling.

Traffic Alerts

There's a traffic advisory radio station on AM-610 that is a must check for those attempting a crossing and is a wise option for scoping out other potential snarls. The highway department also offers Web cams of area choke points at VirginiaDOT.org, if you have Internet access, or you can dial 511 for a telephone rundown of local traffic problems. As in most areas, media traffic alerts will use local names that often don't appear on maps. So here's a short rundown of the area's drawbridges: The Gilmerton Bridge crosses the Southern Branch of the Elizabeth River on Rte. 13, known as Military Highway in Chesapeake. Just up the river from it is what is known as the High Rise Bridge, carrying I-64 traffic. Also in Chesapeake is something called the Steel Bridge, a narrow swing draw that routinely stops traffic on Dominion Boulevard. The Berkley Bridge is in Norfolk connecting the downtown and Berkley's shipyard areas. It's a busy connector on the I-64, I-464 path. And just a bit downriver is the Campostella Bridge, a much less traveled roadway between Norfolk and Chesapeake that insiders often use when the Berkley is jammed.

U.S. Route 13, referred to on traffic updates as Military Highway: This historic road begins in Philadelphia and runs south, bisecting the Delmarva Peninsula, and over the Chesapeake Bay Bridge-Tunnel into Virginia Beach where it then crosses over into Norfolk near the airport and on through Chesapeake and Suffolk before heading into North Carolina. It's one of those belly-of-a-region roads, with strip shopping centers, industrial parks, junkyards, and other blue-collar attractions along its Hampton Roads path. It's a route with plenty of red lights and a couple red light districts, as well. But it often offers a less congested north-south or east-west path than the interstates.

U.S. Route 17: This road winds through Newport News as Jefferson Avenue and Mercury Boulevard, over the James River Bridge into Isle of Wight County and then through northern Suffolk as Bridge Road and as High Street through the Churchland area of Portsmouth, changing over to Frederick Boulevard as it heads into the city's downtown. In Chesapeake, it becomes Dominion Boulevard where it crosses the often-clogged two-lane Steel Bridge and tracks beside the Dismal Swamp Canal into North Carolina. There it widens into a major highway that runs to Elizabeth City. In Virginia, it's another blue-collar highway that handles a lot of overflow traffic. The bridges along the way are often bottlenecks, though.

VA Route 168: This road begins in Norfolk near the Chesapeake Bay and runs south along Tidewater Drive to the Campostella Bridge, crossing into Chesapeake and eventually becoming Battlefield Boulevard. It continues as the Chesapeake Expressway into North Carolina, where it meets NC Route 168 and heads on to the Outer Banks. Battlefield Boulevard also heads to North Carolina as Route 168-Business. Since there is no toll on Battlefield, most locals use it and leave the tolled expressway to out-of-towners who don't know better.

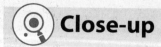

Close-up

Some Other Streets to Know

Norfolk: Granby Street runs the entire length of the city, the historic heart of town. Here is where the famous World War II red light district that gave Norfolk its rough-and-ready reputation was once located. All that's gone now. And recent years have seen a rebirth of the street in downtown, with loads of restaurants and clubs and an upscale urban mall making it a popular destination again. Virginia Beach Boulevard and Princess Anne Road go east-west. Ocean View Avenue serves the bay beaches.

Virginia Beach: Atlantic Avenue is the tourist strip with the requisite souvenir stores, pancake houses, hotels, and motels. It's a busy parade on a summer evening of families looking for fun and teenagers on the prowl. Parking is pretty much limited to city and private lots, but Beach residents get a break in municipal lots if they want to visit the Oceanfront their taxes support. Other busy thoroughfares include Kempsville Road, Lynnhaven Parkway, and Laskin Road, all homes to shopping centers.

Portsmouth: High Street bisects this town, and it is a broad avenue that was designed to impress when plotted by the city's founding father, Col. William Crawford. There are shops and restaurants downtown and museums galore near the end where the street meets the Elizabeth River. But the truly amazing discoveries are located in the small streets of Olde Towne off High near Court, where residents still live in homes in which Washington, Benedict Arnold, and Lord Cornwallis are said to have slept. Check out the graveyard at Trinity Episcopal Church at Court and High for some historic markers.

Suffolk: Main Street is the main street here, but most traffic sweeps by downtown on the Route 58 bypass. The busy and growing Northern suburbs are served by Routes 10 and 17.

Newport News: Warwick Boulevard is an industrial route that runs by the giant Northrop Grumman Newport News Shipyard and is paralleled by Jefferson Avenue as the major north-south routes. Mercury Boulevard runs east-west.

Hampton: Mercury Boulevard is a main thoroughfare heading from the James River in Newport News all the way to Fort Monroe on the mouth of the bay. And Settlers Landing Road winds past Hampton University, the Virginia Air and Space Center, and all sorts of downtown attractions.

Parking

This varies by city. Urban areas usually have a very limited on-street parking, and they respond with meters and aggressive ticket patrols. So pack a tube of quarters if you think you might get lucky. All areas have plenty of public parking lots, and some shops will validate your parking slip, so ask.

In the more suburban cities, even monsters like Virginia Beach, parking tends to be free, downtown included. But if you are heading for the Oceanfront, be prepared to pay or be ticketed. In downtown Hampton, you also might need to feed a meter. Daily rates in parking garages here are nothing like those in big cities. Norfolk municipal lots average about $1 per hour with a maximum of

$12 a day. Virginia Beach public lots on the Oceanfront run between $5 and $7 a day for non-residents.

BY AIR

Hampton Roads is a busy aviation destination. With the largest concentration of uniformed service men and women in the country, there are always people flying in and out, and they need to get here from all necks of the nation and world. There are two commercial airports serving the region. The largest, by far, is Norfolk International. Although there are currently no scheduled international flights out of either airport, Norfolk has a separate international terminal ready with customs and immigration services for charters. The Peninsula is served by Newport News/Williamsburg International, which largely hosts economy carriers. Chambers Field on the Norfolk Naval Station is another bustling airport, with an ongoing array of passenger and cargo flights strictly for supporting military missions.

Norfolk International Airport

Norfolk International Airport, designated ORF, is served by six major airlines and their half dozen regional carriers. It hosts 340 arrivals and departures daily and is open around the clock, although no airlines currently schedule flights after midnight.

The airport is located on the Norfolk–Virginia Beach line, just south of the Little Creek Amphibious Base on the Chesapeake Bay and adjacent to the historic Norfolk Botanical Gardens. The airport is a mile east of I-64 off the Norview Avenue exit. That makes it an easy drive from any of the area's cities. It's about 11 miles by interstate from downtown Norfolk, 18 miles from the Oceanfront in Virginia Beach,

30 miles from downtown Suffolk, 17 miles from Chesapeake City Hall, 10 miles from Olde Towne Portsmouth, 15 miles from downtown Hampton, and 21 miles from Newport News City Hall. Of course, travel times will all depend on traffic and whether tunnels and bridges are flowing or at a standstill.

Norfolk International has two concourses in the main terminal, with 24 gates. It was recently modernized with new parking garages and baggage pickup areas and a pedestrian bridge with a moving sidewalk to connect the ground terminal to the main arrival and departure areas. To serve the military, there is a USO/Armed Services YMCA lounge.

The airport has 10 restaurants and lounges on site, mostly your typical travel fare, but there is a Phillips Seafood Restaurant in the main lobby, an offshoot of the famous Baltimore Inner Harbor eatery, and a Wolfgang Puck To-Go offering gourmet sandwiches and salads in each of the concourses.

The airport also boasts a currency exchange, a military and visitors' information center, and a barbershop/shoeshine parlor in the departures terminal. There's even a Kids Works interactive play area and toy store to keep the children occupied.

The airport has seven rental car companies on site and conference rooms available for those who would prefer never to leave the facility.

A shuttle service, Carey VIP Airport Connection–Norfolk, is located outside baggage claim at the booth marked Airport Connection. The price for a single rider to get to downtown Norfolk is $23 and to the Virginia Beach Oceanfront it's $40.

For information or to make a reservation, call (757) 963-0433 or toll free at (866) 823-4626.

Serving ORF

Airlines:

American/American Eagle	(800) 433-7300	www.aa.com
Continental/Continental Express	(800) 525-0280	www.continental.com
Delta/Delta Connection	(800) 221-1212	www.delta.com
Southwest	(800) 435-9792	www.southwest.com
United Express	(800) 241-6522	www.united.com
US Airways/US Airways Express	(800) 428-4322	www.usairways.com

Rental Car Companies:

Alamo	(800) 462-5266	www.alamo.com
Avis	(800) 831-2847	www.avis.com
Budget	(800) 527-0700	www.drivebudget.com
Dollar	(800) 800-4000	www.dollar.com
Enterprise	(800) 736-8227	www.enterprise.com
Hertz	(800) 654-3131	www.hertz.com
National	(800) 227-7368	www.nationalcar.com
Thrifty	(800) 367-2277	www.thrifty.com

Taxis:

Andy's Cab Co.	(757) 461-8880, (866) 840-6573	www.andystaxigroup.com
Black and White Cabs	(757) 855-4444	www.norfolkblackandwhitecabs.com
City Wide Cabs	(757) 622-2227	
Duke Cab Co.	(757) 583-4079	
East Side Cabs	(757) 718-0937	
Eden Cab Co.	(757) 235-3333	
Waterside Taxi Co. Inc.	(757) 328-1250	
Norfolk Checker	(757) 855-3333	www.norfolkcheckertaxi.com
Oceanside Executive	(757) 455-5996	
Southside Cab Co.	(757) 423-0154	

Newport News/
Williamsburg International Airport

Newport News/Williamsburg International Airport, designation PHF, is located in northern Newport News and is served by four budget airlines: USAirways, Delta, AirTran, and Frontier. It was once known as Patrick Henry Field, hence that puzzling luggage tag code, and has been growing steadily over the years as people from both sides of the water drive the extra distance for its relaxed atmosphere, cheap extended parking, and low fares. There's one terminal with eight gates, although for some reason they skip gates 7 and 8 and go straight to 9 and 10. Most of the direct flights head to East Coast destinations such as Philadelphia, Washington, D.C., Orlando, Jacksonville, New York City, and Charlotte. Frontier joined the party in 2010 with non-stops to Denver and connecting flights to other western destinations including LA, Phoenix, and Las Vegas. The downside to this airport's quaint charm is there is very little to do in the single terminal building. One restaurant, the Blue Sky Cafe, and the adjacent TK's Pub offer deli menu items, and Hudson News has a shop that sells its typical array of magazines and gifts in the terminal atrium. Taxis park in a holding area at the west end of the terminal near the AirTran Airways ticket counter.

Serving PHF

Airlines:

US Airways	(800) 428-4322	www.usairways.com
Delta	(800) 221-1212	www.delta.com
AirTran	(800) 247-8726	www.airtran.com
Frontier	(800) 432-1359	www.frontierairlines.com

Rental Car Companies:

Avis	(800) 331-1212	www.avis.com
Enterprise	(800) 261-7331	www.enterprise.com
Budget	(757) 874-5794	www.drivebudget.com
National	(800) 227-7368	www.nationalcar.com
Hertz	(800) 654-3131	www.hertz.com

Taxis:

Associated Cabs	(757) 887-3412	
Yellow Cab	(757) 855-1111	www.yellowcabofnewportnews.com
North End Cab	(757) 244-4000	
Independent Cab	(757) 245-8378	
Orange Cab Co.	(757) 369-8977	
Hops Cabs	(757) 245-3005	
All City Taxi	(757) 380-8300	

BY TRAIN & BUS (OR BOTH)

Amtrak

There is an Amtrak station in Hampton Roads, but only the most persistent will be able to find it. It's a small ticket counter and waiting room located next to a ground level track in Newport News at 9304 Warwick Blvd. There's a tiny blue and white Amtrak sign on the Warwick road, and the low brick station is set back behind some trees and a small parking lot at the end of a long driveway that's very easy to miss, even when you've been here before. This is no Grand Central. It's basically a spur line with just a couple of departures and arrivals a day. You can make it work, but if you need to get to or from Norfolk or Virginia Beach instead of this fairly desolate section of Newport News, you will actually begin and finish your trip by charter bus. The good news is: if you drive, you can park for free. But the station closes at 8 p.m. so you might not want to leave anything expensive in plain view.

If you'd like to give it a go, or just want to explore the arcane art of reading a railroad schedule, drop by www.amtrak.com and look around. It's far from user friendly, though. The station is coded NPN, which will help when you try to find a train or a fare. A train ride to Philadelphia from Newport News runs $83 in the morning and $58 if you can wait until afternoon or evenings. Most folks are probably on their way to D.C., a $60 morning route, and $42 in afternoons or evenings. From there, you can switch trains and head just about anywhere.

By the way, the "train station" Amtrak lists in Virginia Beach is a bus stop at 19th Street and Pacific Avenue and in Norfolk you can hear your "All aboard" in the Bus Shelter at Monticello Avenue and Virginia Beach Boulevard. There's no ticket window at either location, of course, so you need to reserve your seat ahead of time online or by phone, at (800) USA-RAIL.

Greyhound

The bus giant has stations in Norfolk, at 701 Monticello Ave., and Virginia Beach, at 1017 Laskin Rd. (which is nearly a mile from the surf,) and stops in Hampton at C More Travel Corp, 2 West Pembroke Ave., and in Suffolk at the Red Apple Restaurant, 1139 Carolina Rd. For schedule information, call (800) 231-2222 or go to www.greyhound.com.

There are a bunch of charter bus companies in Hampton Roads that offer Saturday excursions to visit the casinos in Atlantic City, and Apex Bus, (202) 449-9758, www.apexbus.com, offers cheap fares on regular red-eye runs between Norfolk and New York City's Chinatown.

Public Transit

Hampton Roads Transit was formed in 1999 by the merger of Pentran and Tidewater Rapid Transit, the first voluntary marriage of two transit agencies in the country. The resulting agency serves the seven large Hampton Roads communities, but not all are equal partners. The agency explains that each city determines how much service is to be provided in its area. There are 70 fixed regular routes, and pickup services are available for those with disabilities. HRT also operates a free shuttle service in downtown Norfolk and a $2 all-day Virginia Beach resort area fare.

The best bargain, though, is HRT's paddlewheel ferry between downtown Norfolk and Portsmouth. It's a pedestrian ferry that gets you out on the water for a 15-minute crossing of the Elizabeth River that doubles as a short sight-seeing trip. The ferry costs

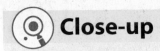 **Close-up**

Driving Underwater

It's an impressive list of underwater highways: Four tubes form a pair of tunnels connecting Virginia Beach to the Eastern Shore Peninsula at the Chesapeake Bay Bridge-Tunnel. Another two tubes span the mouth of the James River between Norfolk and Hampton at the Hampton Roads Bridge-Tunnel. A pair crosses the Southern Branch of the Elizabeth River from Norfolk to Portsmouth at the Downtown Tunnel, and another tube does the same farther up the river at the Midtown Tunnel. Then there's the newest of the links, the two tubes of the Monitor-Merrimack Bridge-Tunnel linking Portsmouth and Newport News. That's a lot of very expensive submarine road surface.

As you sit in tunnel traffic waiting for another breakdown to be cleared, you might wonder why there are so many of these engineered choke points around Hampton Roads. It's a matter of national defense.

Look at where those tunnels are located: The Chesapeake Bay Bridge-Tunnel crosses the mouth of the estuary, the point where the bay joins the Atlantic Ocean. Every one of the Atlantic Fleet's Norfolk-based ships is berthed behind that potential barrier. Had the Navy allowed the cheaper and easier construction of bridges across the bay, a few well-placed bombs might be all it would take to trap the fleet in port, where it would be useless and pretty much sitting ducks.

The other tunnels were demanded for exactly the same reason: to ensure that vital maritime traffic is never interrupted across the mouth of Hampton Roads or in the Elizabeth and James Rivers where there are coal piers and shipyards essential to our national interests.

The Navy also keeps a fleet of minesweepers around to make sure those above-tunnel channels aren't booby trapped, and during World Wars I and II, when German submarines and U-boats roamed along the Atlantic Coast sinking ships, special steel submarine nets were erected to keep the marauders out of the harbor.

The busiest local tunnel is the Hampton Roads Bridge-Tunnel, which carries nearly three million vehicles a month and in the tourist season can see more than 100,000 a day. How does that compare? The world's busiest vehicular tunnel is New York's Lincoln Tunnel, with an average of 3.5 million vehicles each month—or a mere 20,000 more per day. And the Lincoln has three tubes to handle its crunch, the world's only three-tube tunnel.

Other local tunnels are also crammed. The Downtown Tunnel also carries about three million vehicles a month but doesn't suffer from the same tourist surge. The Monitor-Merrimack Tunnel carries 1.5 million vehicles each month, and the Midtown Tunnel does 1 million vehicles per month through its single tube.

$1.50 and lets you sail past all those cars stuck on the Berkley Bridge waiting to get through the Downtown Tunnel. HRT also has a network of Park-and-Ride lots and helps put potential ride sharers together.

For information on routes or fares, call HRT at (757) 222-6100 or visit www.gohrt.com.

HISTORY

How many Virginians does it take to change a light bulb?

Six, a twist on the old joke goes. One screws the new one in, and the other five sit around and reminisce about how great the old bulb was.

There's a lot of truth to this bit of humor. The Old Dominion worships its heritage, and Hampton Roads is the place it all started. If you enjoy putting context to the contemporary, take some time and explore the many places here that gave our country its start. Here's a primer to put you in the mood.

PREHISTORY

The history of Hampton Roads didn't begin on April 26, 1607, when the first English settlers set foot on Cape Henry in Virginia Beach. There were thousands of Native Americans already living, fishing, hunting, and farming in the region. In fact, Powhatan, the famous father of Pocahontas, ruled over an empire of 30 tribes and some 10,000 indigenous people. Unfortunately, these first Virginians didn't leave any written records.

What largely survives are the colorful place names that dot the area. Some, such as Chesapean, Kecoughtan, Nansemond, or Croatan, recall tribes that were here long before the first Europeans arrived.

The natives lived in a host of villages located along the area's waters, which served as the supermarkets and superhighways of their time. Archeologists are still learning details about the cultures and histories of these people. Eleven of the tribes that survived European extermination efforts, punishing race laws, and punitive census policies aimed at wiping out their heritage have earned state recognition. No Virginia tribe has the federal recognition that in other states has permitted Indian gaming casinos, partly because of those state census tricks that arbitrarily reclassified Indians as "coloreds." Two tribes, the Pamunkey and Mattaponi, still show up in Richmond every November to pay an annual tax tribute of fish or game called for in a treaty that predates American independence.

i You can explore living tableaus of a Powhatan Indian Village at the Historic Villages at Cape Henry, or take a day trip to the Jamestown Settlement and see how the natives went about their daily lives and how they helped the English survive their first years in Virginia.

EUROPEANS COME

Old World sailors had visited the Chesapeake Bay long before the Jamestown Settlers arrived to exploit area resources. Spaniards explored the area nearly a century earlier, calling it Bahia de Santa Maria. They even brought a local chief's son, Paquiquino, back to Spain in 1561 in hopes he would help them convert his people. He learned their language and religion and returned with an expedition that established a settlement on the York River. But Paquiquino abandoned the Spaniards and later led an attack that killed all but one child. The Spanish came back to rescue the boy, but would never again try to settle this far north. The French also had sailed into the area before the English, but they, too, didn't stay.

Thus, the modern history of Hampton Roads harkens to those persistent Jamestown settlers. The first bunch arrived in 1607 on three ships, the *Susan Constant*, the *Godspeed*, and the *Discovery*. The Virginia Company, a group of London entrepreneurs who hoped to settle Virginia, find gold, and seek a water route to the Orient, funded the expedition.

Although the English first landed at Cape Henry, they had been instructed to sail on and settle in more protected waters. So they claimed a beach bluff in the name of the king, ate oysters that had been left roasting by some surprised natives, and eventually beat back a small hostile band that crept up on them in the evening, bows in mouths.

Although the English planted a cross in thanks at Cape Henry, they didn't linger in Hampton Roads. Sailing up the James River to what would become Jamestown, they passed forests and fields off the Lynnhaven and Elizabeth Rivers that had been the domain of the Chesapean or Chesapeakes. The tribe had either been eradicated by Powhatan's forces before the English arrived or were reduced to that small band that were the first to attack the settlers. In either case, the Chesapeakes were soon gone, their villages, including a large one on the Elizabeth River where Norfolk now stands, abandoned.

The English also showed no interest in Southside Hampton Roads for another couple decades. They had enough trouble upriver.

Jamestown

After the ships dropped them off, almost half of the 104 initial colonists died within four months. Their settlement was set in a swamp, with water that became brackish and unhealthy in the summer. It was infested with disease-carrying mosquitoes and surrounded by natives who attacked often enough that the English hunkered down behind wooden fortifications. There were periods of peace and cooperation. In fact, the first shared Thanksgiving feast in the New World probably happened in Jamestown, not Plymouth Rock. Peace, however, would always be tenuous.

Powhatan captured Capt. John Smith, a military man who soon took command of the settlement, when he was exploring the James River in 1607. According to the story Smith later told, that's when the chief's 10-year-old daughter, Pocahontas, saved him from being executed. Most historians now believe it was just a tale, or that Smith misread an initiation ceremony. But Smith was set free and allowed to return to a starving Jamestown.

Relations with Powhatan's tribes waxed and waned, but improved after tobacco entrepreneur John Rolfe married a then-teenage Pocahontas in 1614. The English never found their gold or that elusive passage to Asia. But Rolfe's work with tobacco would set the foundation for Virginia's economy and Hampton Roads future. The colonists were struggling to find an export commodity until Rolfe produced a plant that could compete with the preferred Spanish-grown tobacco in Europe.

Over the years, more English settlers arrived, establishing plantations where they could grow tobacco, which became the basis for the entire economy. Fines were levied in pounds of tobacco, debts paid and brides purchased by the same measure.

Rolfe exported his first crop of improved tobacco in 1612. By 1629 the colony was sending 1.5 million pounds to market in England. Tobacco wore out the land, so new fields were always being tilled. And it required a lot of labor, leading to the import of slaves from Africa and the West Indies.

Hampton Roads

The first European settlement to take root in Hampton Roads proper was in what is now Hampton. In 1610, some of the English settlers moved 35 miles south to the prosperous Indian village of Kecoughtan, which had a panoramic view of the bay where supply ships or Spanish marauders could be spotted. Their settlement was named Port Comfort and later Old Port Comfort.

The first African slaves arrived at Port Comfort in 1619 on a privateer that traded them for provisions. It's unclear if they were considered slaves in the colony at the time, or just indentured servants able to earn their freedom through work. By 1640, the colony had slaves who could be bought and sold and had no right to work off their servitude. By 1700, Virginia was importing huge numbers of African slaves for the tobacco fields.

All that commerce required vessels, and a shipping village known as Hampton sprouted around Port Comfort. Coastal Virginia was full of old timber, perfect for shipbuilding and repairs. So yards were founded. Other settlements sprang up along local waterways where plantation owners could load their crops on shallow draft tobacco boats to be taken to port for export. Eventually, a real town emerged in Norfolk, which also had deepwater access and was more convenient for the planters shipping from the Southside. Across the Elizabeth River from Norfolk, a shipyard was built in Gosport, and the town of Portsmouth developed along with it.

A REGION SHAPED BY WAR

In Boston, they had a Tea Party. In Virginia, the anger was over more than just the tax on their favorite beverage. All Colonial tobacco had to be shipped to England, where it was resold, at a profit the planters never saw.

It was a Virginian, Thomas Jefferson, who penned the Declaration of Independence and another, George Washington, who led the Colonial Army. But Norfolk, by now the largest town in Hampton Roads, still had many Royalists among its trading families. They wanted to keep their prosperity by maintaining their biggest market.

In June, 1775, Virginia's Royal Governor, Lord Dunmore, was forced to flee the capital in Williamsburg, then a revolutionary hotbed, and took refuge on the British frigate *Otter* on the Elizabeth River. A day's march to the south, an obscure trestle would prove a pivot in the American Revolution.

The small wooden bridge over the Southern Branch of the Elizabeth River gave the village of Great Bridge its name. Swamps flanked the road here, and this bridge was the choke point through which any Colonial army had to march to free Norfolk. Dunmore built a fortification on the north and stationed about 100 men there.

When the advance guard of the Colonial forces arrived, they threw up breastworks on their side of the river and waited for reinforcements from North Carolina. Dunmore underestimated their numbers, mustered his troops, and launched an attack. The colonists not only held, but their fierce fusillade forced the British to retreat. The actual battle, on Dec. 9, 1775, lasted less than 30 minutes. The British lost 40 men, while the colonists suffered one small hand wound. The incident emboldened the colonists and shook the British.

With the bridge lost, Dunmore didn't try to hold Norfolk. His forces retreated to their ships. After warning that women and children should be evacuated from the city, the British fleet began bombarding the city about 4 p.m. on New Year's Day, 1776, and British shore parties set fire to the wharves. But their efforts were nothing compared to the devastation wrought by Colonists, angry at the Royalist sentiments of Norfolk and eager to leave nothing to support the British should they return. More than 800 buildings were burnt that day, and a city of chimneys was all that remained from what had been a bustling town. Nearly all trace of the pre-Revolutionary Norfolk was gone.

One of Dunmore's cannonballs struck the brick wall of Old Saint Paul Church. In 1848, a cannonball was discovered covered by dirt beneath a hole in that wall, which, unlike the church itself, had survived the shelling and burning. In 1901, the ball was cemented back into its hole, and it remains there today, the namesake of the city's self-guided walking tour.

The British would return to occupy Portsmouth and make it their headquarters. But the Battle of Great Bridge, known at the time as the 2nd Bunker Hill, effectively ended royal authority in Virginia. Six months later, Jefferson's Declaration of Independence would ring out across a new nation

convinced by the wholesale destruction of Norfolk, now blamed exclusively on the British, that there could be no compromise with the king.

i Norfolk's Cannonball Trail takes you on a stroll through its four centuries of history. Call (757) 664-6620 for info. And Portsmouth offers its own Path of History walking tour that includes 45 sites in its historic district. You can also enjoy an Olde Towne Lantern Tour in Portsmouth with a guide in period attire, Tues and Sat from June through Sept. Information is available at (757) 393-5111.

YELLOW FEVER

It took decades, but Hampton Roads was rebuilt after the Revolutionary War. The nation's first naval yard was established at the Gosport yard, abandoned by its Royalist owner. It is home to the first dry dock in the New World, which opened in 1833. Drydock Number 1, as it was called, is still in service at what is now the Norfolk Naval Shipyard. The adjacent town of Portsmouth grew in support and later to include that shipyard.

By 1855, Norfolk, too, was a bustling town, although it had yet to resume its former position as a preeminent port.

The two cities were soon to be hit hard by the scourge of Yellow Fever.

The steamboat *Benjamin Franklin*, on its way from St. Thomas to New York, was forced into Norfolk on June 7, 1855 by sickness aboard ship. It was held in quarantine for 12 days before being allowed to a Portsmouth shipyard for repairs. The captain, who had sworn his crewmen had not died from the fever, also disobeyed orders and emptied his disease riddled, mosquito-infested bilges when he got to Portsmouth.

Soon the fever was spreading from ship-yard workers into the adjacent tenements. The disease crossed the river into Norfolk with fleeing slum residents. Those who could abandoned the city. But there were few places willing to take them in. One boat-load was turned back at bayonet point at Point Comfort. The epidemic ended with the frosts of late October. Some 2,000 had died, one in three residents at the time, including the mayor and 25 doctors who came to help.

OCCUPIED AGAIN

When the Civil War erupted at Fort Sumter, Norfolk and Portsmouth once again found themselves on the strategic front lines. Union forces, fearing a militia uprising, burnt the Navy Yard and scuttled the ships there before withdrawing to Fort Monroe, which would never fall into Confederate hands. The so-called "Freedom Fort" became a des-tination for runaway slaves after Maj. Gen. Benjamin F. Butler declared that any slave that came onto Union territory would not be returned to slave owners. By the end of the war, some 10,000 blacks had found liberty there. Their story is told in exhibits at the fort's Casemate Museum.

The two armies fought a battle on the Peninsula at Big Bethel, halfway between Yorktown and Newport News, with the Con-federates beating back the Union troops.

At the Navy Yard, Southerners managed to save the cannons of those scuttled ships and turned a decrepit steamship, the U.S.S. Merrimack, into the ironclad they called The C.S.S. Virginia.

For one day, it seemed as if the Vir-ginia alone would break the crippling Union blockade. On Mar 8, 1962, C.S.S. Virginia steamed into battle for the first time. It attacked the Union's wooden fleet off Fort Monroe, ramming and sinking the much larger Cumberland and forcing the Congress to surrender under a rain of cannonballs. Return fire from Union ships and shore bat-teries bounced off the Virginia's thick iron armor. It seemed the Virginia was invincible, able perhaps to take the fight right up the Potomac to the White House itself.

The next day, when the Virginia returned to finish off the Union fleet, it encoun-tered an equally strange-looking vessel, the Union's own ironclad, the U.S.S. Monitor. The two vessels fired on each other for hours, but it was a draw. The era of wooden warships was over. The Monitor's two guns couldn't dent the Virginia, and the Virginia was too slow to ram the agile Monitor.

The stalemate over Hampton Roads ended when President Lincoln arrived at Fort Monroe and personally ordered the capture of Norfolk and Portsmouth. Troops landed at what is now Ocean View, but found lit-tle resistance. The Confederate forces had already retreated on their way to Petersburg. First, though, the Confederates again razed the Navy Yard rather than leave it in Union hands. Norfolk and Portsmouth would now be occupied for the rest of the war.

The Virginia sailed out of the harbor as well, but it couldn't get past the shallows to Richmond. So it was burned off Craney Island and its powder magazines exploded by the retreating Confederates. Its guns were taken to shore batteries, and they helped hold the Union fleet south of Richmond. Some of the Virginia's iron plating was later salvaged and turned into souvenirs or displayed in muse-ums. One piece was melted down and cast into a bell for the Jamestown Exposition of 1907, but numerous expeditions have not found the ship's final resting place.

The *Monitor* also quickly became history. It sank in a storm off the Outer Banks of North Carolina on New Year's Eve, 1862. Its wreckage, discovered in 1973, is a National Marine Sanctuary. The *Monitor*'s innovative turret was raised and preserved and is the centerpiece of the USS *Monitor* Center at the Mariners' Museum in Newport News. (See entry in the Museums chapter.)

When the war finally ended, Confederate President Jefferson Davis was captured in Georgia and imprisoned at Fort Monroe for nearly two years. The cell in Casemate No. 2, where he spent the first 4 ½ months, is preserved as part of the fort's Casemate Museum. It contains a reproduction of the cot he slept on, the shelf where he kept his pipe, a Bible, a table, and chair. When Davis was a prisoner there, one wall was decorated with a large American flag. That 35-star flag is under glass in the museum.

A NAVY TOWN

Norfolk grew as a port after the war. With better rail service, it was a natural for exporting cotton and peanuts and really came into its own when the first load of coal rolled down from the mountains in 1883.

Railroads helped Norfolk rebound. But the Chesapeake and Ohio Railroad pretty much gave birth to the city of Newport News. The line ran from Richmond to a deep-water terminal along the James River in Newport News. The railroad's president, Collis P. Huntington, extended the line to Hampton Roads so he could to ship his company's coal. He also founded what would become the Newport News Shipbuilding and Dry Dock Company to repair and build colliers, tugs, and later, warships. Combined, these industries put thousands to work on the Peninsula and gave rise to a city.

Hampton Roads soon became the world's largest coal port, with loading facilities at Norfolk's Lamberts Point and Sewells Point as well. It also became a Navy institution.

It was from Norfolk that Commodore Matthew Perry sailed in 1852 with a squadron that would open the ports of Japan to the United States two years later. The nation's modern Navy was born in 1883 when Congress appropriated money for four steel warships. Much of the fleet was built at the government shipyard and through contracts with the Newport News yard, which would become Virginia's largest private employer.

When President Teddy Roosevelt decided to show America's new muscle, he assembled his Great White Fleet in Hampton Roads in 1907 and sent it on its around-the-world cruise. Seven of the 16 battleships in that fleet had been built at Newport News. But it was a failed celebration that really made Norfolk a Navy town. To mark the 300th anniversary of the Jamestown Settlement, a world's fair was staged on the Norfolk waterfront. The exposition opened on Apr 26, 1907, with a naval review hosted by President Roosevelt. States and territories erected exhibition displays, with Pennsylvania building a mini Independence Hall that still stands. But attendance was disappointing, and the company that backed the fair went bankrupt, throwing the land into limbo. Efforts to sell it to Washington were either ignored or put on hold.

OVER THERE

Hampton Roads was no stranger to uniforms, but the two World Wars would turn this region into the military juggernaut it remains today. Not only would Hampton Roads become the world's largest Navy center, but Air Force and Army buildups, combined with the Coast Guard, would lead to the largest concentration of service members in the nation. And that doesn't count the civilian economy that would flourish on defense dollars for the next century.

Once the kaiser's submarines started sinking American ships, it was clear we would be going to war in Europe. Extra shifts were added to local shipyards, and Americans began flooding into the area from all over to build the fleet. At Newport News Shipbuilding, the workforce jumped from 7,600 to more than 12,000 by war's end. At the Naval shipyard in Portsmouth, 11,000 workers made their way through the gates.

The main cities in the area, Norfolk, Portsmouth, and Newport News, struggled to find housing for the influx. So the nation got into community building for the first time. Hilton Village outside Newport News, then Cradock and Truxton in Portsmouth, were planned and homes built. Many still stand today. On bases, the military scrambled to increase its own housing stock. And throughout the area, private housing went up and people rented out rooms to pitch in.

Less crowded than the commercial waters off Norfolk, Newport News became one of two ports of embarkation, shipping 750,000 troops to France. Air aces Eddie Rickenbacker and Billy Mitchell got their training at the private Curtiss Flying School established just east of Newport News, and the Army set up Camp Eustis and Langley Field on the Peninsula as well. At Fort Monroe, artillery battalions were trained to man shore guns. Fort Story, where the Jamestown settlers landed in Virginia Beach, was outfitted with troops and cannon from Fort Monroe.

In Norfolk, the day after war was declared, Congress pulled the trigger, finally buying the Jamestown Exposition site. President Woodrow Wilson signed a proclamation establishing there what was called the Naval Operating Base Hampton Roads, and construction began almost immediately. Barracks, mess halls, storehouses, and a roadway were thrown together, and the base grew to be home to 34,000 personnel. Those stately exhibition halls were turned into officers' quarters and remain to this day as an opulent Admirals' Row.

When the war ended 17 months later, the local shipyards shrank and people returned to their home states, but the Navy was here for good. It was in Hampton Roads, today home to all East Coast aircraft carriers, that Naval aviation got its start. Eugene Ely flew a biplane off a temporary platform on the light cruiser USS *Birmingham* off Newport News on Nov 14, 1910. The wheels dipped into the water before he got fully airborne, and he landed on the Willoughby beach rather than try to get the rest of the way to the Norfolk Navy Base. He would also be the first to land a plane on a Navy ship, but that happened in San Francisco two months later. Starting with his experiments here, Ely proved the potential of naval aviation and set the stage for the Navy's air force.

Workers at the Norfolk Naval Shipyard took the efforts farther, slapping a wooden runway on a former collier in 1920 and creating the world's first carrier, the CV-1 Langley. Like the ironclads, it would forever change Naval history.

With war raging in Europe and Asia, there was a rush to re-arm the officially neutral America.

By 1940, the Portsmouth shipyard was adding about 1,000 workers a month, and the operating base in Norfolk was talking about doubling its personnel. The Navy also bought land in Princess Anne County for an auxiliary airfield that would grow to become Oceana, the nation's premier Naval Jet base. The Naval Air station in Norfolk was expanded, and the Army leased a state compound for Camp Pendleton.

When the Japanese, using aircraft carriers, attacked Pearl Harbor on Dec 7, 1941, Hampton Roads was overwhelmed overnight, becoming what Norfolk's official historian later described as a "Conscripted City."

Norfolk's population more than doubled from 137,500 in 1939 to 305,121 in 1943. In Portsmouth, temporary quarters were erected outside the shipyard that would linger for generations beyond their design, turning eventually into substandard housing for the poor.

In Norfolk, the Navy Operating Base would swell from 30,000 sailors at the start of the war to a peak of 168,000 uniformed and 200,000 civilians in December of 1943. The shipyard in Portsmouth doubled in size to 43,000 workers and built 101 new ships.

Red light districts in Norfolk and Portsmouth became notorious for servicing and fleecing those sailors. The area's reputation as a sin city would last for decades, reinforced by the wartime stories of the more than 1.7 million who funneled through Hampton Roads on their way to and from the battlefields of Europe.

Among them would be a group of Norfolk men who had joined the National Guard's 111th Field Artillery unit here, many for a few extra dollars' spending money, and found themselves storming Normandy's beaches on D-Day. Most would fight as infantry after their guns and ammo sank in the English Channel when their amphibious landing trucks, known as Ducks, were overloaded and swamped.

One man, Bill Halstead, would hit the shore in a borrowed Navy pea coat. He picked up a rifle dropped by a dead comrade and fought over the dunes and through the hedgerows of Normandy. Halstead carried that blue coat right through France and into Germany and finally presented it to the captain of the USS *Normandy*, where it was displayed with honor on the 50th anniversary of D-Day. Halstead built a monument to the "boys" who died in Europe. He never married or had children, and when he died in 2003 Halstead was buried next to the monument at Forest Lawn Cemetery. The remaining D-Day survivors still gather there every Memorial Day and place a wreath at Halstead's monument.

The military continues to be the lifeblood of this region, with nearly half of the local economy dependant on defense dollars. And world history continues to be made by the 101,000 servicemen and women stationed here.

The failed mission to rescue the hostages being held in Iran was launched from the Norfolk-based Nimitz aircraft carrier. The planes and Tomahawk missiles that began both wars with Iraq came from this port.

And it was here that the worst breach of national security occurred since Ethel and Julius Rosenberg sold the secrets of the atomic bomb to the Soviet Union.

In 1985, a retired Navy communications expert was picked up in Maryland after trying to pass a bag full of secrets to the Soviets. John A. Walker Jr. had run a family-and-friend spy ring out of Norfolk for decades, giving our Cold War enemies the ability to read every coded message and to know how we would react to any attacks. He was uncovered when his ex-wife blew the whistle after he tried to recruit their daughter into the ring. Walker agreed to cooperate with authorities in exchange for a reduced sentence for their son, who had been groomed for the job and was caught with boxes of top-secret documents hidden aboard his ship. Everything JAWS, as he fancifully called himself, had touched or seen while in the service was probably sold to the Soviets, Walker told debriefers. Since he had the highest clearance and was in several sensitive positions, that flood of information was so considerable the KGB had to open a separate division just to handle Walker's espionage. Walker continued long after retiring by recruiting a brother, a son, and a best friend into the ring. The son served his sentence and was paroled, but the others are likely to die in prison.

MODERN ERA

After the war, Hampton Roads' cities were in an expansive mood. Norfolk annexed a region known as Tanner's Creek and asked state permission to absorb the nearby Princess Anne County town of Kempsville, as well. Portsmouth was also picking up land, and there was even talk that the two cities should combine, perhaps with their neighbors to the north and create a true metropolis. Norfolk's Wards Corner was already known as the Times Square of the South.

But times were changing, and veterans were looking for more than a city apartment on a trolley line. The American dream was no longer just a home, but one on a suburban plot with a nice picket fence. And it increasingly called for racial equality.

Blacks had fought valiantly for their country in World War II, but in the South they remained sequestered by race and limited in the jobs they could do. Harry Truman ordered the military fully integrated in 1947.

But though they might be considered equal on local bases, when blacks left for home they were heading into a still-segregated Hampton Roads.

Virginia had a poll tax to discourage black voting until a 1966 Supreme Court decision tossed it out. Interracial marriage was illegal, the Ku Klux Klan active, and schools operated under the "separate but equal" doctrine that was always separate but never equal. Black teachers earned much less than their white colleagues, no matter their credentials, and minority schools never got the supplies or books that went to their white counterparts.

All that was supposed to end with the 1954 U.S. Supreme Court decision known as *Brown vs. Board of Education*, which also incorporated a Virginia NAACP lawsuit involving Prince Edward County public schools.

Instead, in 1956, U.S. Sen. Harry F. Byrd Sr., whose political machine ran Virginia, called for what became known as Massive Resistance to the Supreme Court's desegregation orders.

There were a number of provisions to Massive Resistance, but the key was a law that threatened to cut off state funds and close any public school that agreed to follow the order to desegregate.

Norfolk's six all-white public junior and senior high schools were closed in 1958 rather than obey the federal court order to admit black students. *The Virginian-Pilot* newspaper in Norfolk opposed the action, and its editor, Lenoir Chambers, won a Pulitzer Prize for his anti-segregation editorials. The paper's only other Pulitzer to that time was for opposing the lynching of blacks.

Nearly 13,000 students were locked out of schools in Norfolk, Charlottesville, and Front Royal while state and federal court rulings were appealed. Both decisions came down on Jan 19, 1959, and each found the closings unconstitutional. The governor, who had ridden into office on the back of Massive Resistance, relented. On Feb 2, 1959, 17 black students in Norfolk enrolled in formerly all-white schools, with network cameras rolling.

The postwar period also brought the beginning of urban redevelopment projects across America. Norfolk was a frontrunner in the fight against blight, with a Redevelopment and Housing Authority determined to create the first city without slums. It was the initial city in the nation to undertake redevelopment under the Housing Act of 1949. What that translated to, however, was often the condemnation of large swaths of the city, including many traditional black communities. Much of that land would remain undeveloped until the end of the 20th century.

Annexation

Today, the borders in Hampton Roads are fixed. It wasn't always that way. The maps had been changing almost from the first Royal Charter as counties split, towns formed, cities developed and then declared themselves independent of their counties.

In the 1960s, Hampton Roads cities were looking at suburbanization and an exodus of their wealthiest residents. They reacted by taking advantage of Virginia's annexation laws. Essentially, cities were permitted to petition the state to absorb surrounding land, so long as it wasn't part of another city.

Hampton merged with the historic remnants of Elizabeth City County to form the current city of Hampton in 1952. Warwick County, that same year, became the City of Warwick in an attempt to prevent annexation by Newport News. Six years later, the

two cities merged into the current Newport News.

Norfolk had used annexation to grow from 50 acres in 1682 to nearly 62 square miles after seizing part of Princess Anne County in 1959. The biggest jump came in 1923 when Norfolk added 20 neighborhoods and nearly quadrupled in size.

Portsmouth was also grabbing adjacent land and had filed paperwork to add adjacent portions of Norfolk County known as Western Branch and Churchland.

County leaders there took their only recourse. In 1963, the city of South Norfolk merged with the rest of Norfolk County and they declared themselves the new city of Chesapeake. To the east, Princess Anne County, worried about Norfolk's expansion, declared itself the new city of Virginia Beach.

Portsmouth sued and was eventually allowed to add Churchland to its borders, but the city and Norfolk were now effectively locked in place.

Farther west, Nansemond County became a city in 1972 and merged with the smaller city of Suffolk in 1974 to form the present city of Suffolk in 1974. And Poquoson became an independent city in 1975. In 1979, the Virginia General Assembly passed a law that would allow counties to petition courts for immunity from annexation by large cities, and in 1987 legislators placed a moratorium on future annexations that was due to expire in 2010. No matter here, though. With nothing but cities in Hampton Roads, these borders, like the *Monitor* and *Virginia*, are ironclad.

MODERN MARVELS

Little by little, Norfolk began filling in the open areas created when downtown neighborhoods were razed. A medical school. An arena and concert hall. A hotel on the Elizabeth River. A waterfront park with an annual festival next door. A new federal office building. A central library. A festival marketplace. An upscale mall. A downtown community college campus. A new baseball stadium. Business towers. At some point, the downtown area reached critical mass, the point when people wanted to return to live and play.

Soon, condos were growing along the busy roads and shops opening on streets that used to echo with lonely footsteps. Downtown was once again a destination, with restaurants and nightlife. Tough neighborhoods along the bay were cleared and high-end homes replaced them.

Across the river, Portsmouth was also experiencing a renaissance, with its own waterfront hotel and convention center, an amphitheater, and restaurants drawing people back to High Street.

In Virginia Beach there was no urban core to revitalize, so they built one from scratch at the intersection of Virginia Beach and Independence boulevards. Town Center became the downtown the city never had.

In Suffolk, merchants returned to Main Street and the city opened a Cultural Arts Center in what had once been a high school, with nationally known entertainment to draw back the crowds.

In Chesapeake, once best known for farm silos and the Great Dismal Swamp, a giant community was planned and grew on what was once a tree nursery known as Greenbrier and another shopping district emerged in Western Branch.

In Hampton, downtown decay was stemmed when the Air and Space Museum opened along the historic waterfront and in Newport News tired old malls and replaced by new style outdoor shopping centers.

As Hampton Roads moves into the second decade of the 21st century, there are plans for a high-speed rail line linking Norfolk and Virginia Beach and an effort to bring passenger rail service again to the Southside, connecting us once again with the entire Eastern Corridor.

The military continues to be the lifeblood, and area politicians who earlier succeeded in saving Norfolk Naval Shipyard and the Naval Air Station Oceana from budget cutters are battling Navy plans to move one of our nuclear aircraft carriers to Florida, a move that would drain half a billion dollars from the local economy. The Navy contends it would be wise to again have two carrier ports on the East Coast. Hampton Roads leaders argue that the nation can't afford the upgrades that would be necessary to make Mayport Naval Station a suitable home.

The Secretary of Defense also recently decided to eliminate the Joint Forces Command, which employs 6,300 and has been the driving force behind the high-tech modeling and simulation region in northern Suffolk. Local leaders are fighting the order, hoping to save as many as 10,000 jobs connected with the command.

Also news that China has been developing a long-range cruise missile that might be able to neutralize the power of an aircraft carrier, perhaps even making them obsolete, has local leaders wondering whether it's time to rethink the area's reliance on a defense industry that may be at the start of radical changes. Still, it's unlikely the military will ever be a historic footnote in Hampton Roads. So long as we are a shipping nation, there will always be a need for a Navy, and this community will remain its major homeport.

MILITARY

You can't overstate the importance of the military to Hampton Roads. Nearly half of the local economy is based on Department of Defense money. In 2009, that amounted to $18.9 billion the services spent right here.

The annual flood of federal funds, which nearly doubled over the last decade, helps cushion the area during recessions. The constant relocation of personnel keeps housing markets moving. The influx of dependents provides a steady stream of potential employees as well as new customers to area merchants.

The services are so ingrained that it often takes a major conflict, with mass deployments, to really get a sense of their daily impact. Suddenly, clogged roads are empty, and malls seem abandoned. There's an eerie emptiness in the quiet when the background roar of practicing jets vanishes with the squadrons. And the rows of empty piers along the waterfront give silent testimony to conflicts half a world away.

There are nine major military bases in Hampton Roads proper, and another pair just up the road in Yorktown, for a total of more than 101,000 men and women in uniform stationed here.

OVERVIEW

One third of the Navy's entire fleet and a quarter of its planes and people are home-ported in Hampton Roads. Naval Station Norfolk is the world's largest Navy base, with 68 ships, 16 aircraft squadrons. and 386 tenant commands. Some 54,000 sailors serve there, making it second only to Fort Hood's 65,000 soldiers in U.S. military base population. But where Fort Hood is a city virtually unto itself in the middle of Texas, Naval Station Norfolk is just the biggest of Hampton Roads' many military facilities.

Little Creek Amphibious Base is home to 18 ships and some 12,000 sailors and Marines. Naval Air Station Oceana is the Navy's East Coast Master Jet base, with nearly 8,000 sailors and 300 aircraft. Its annex at Dam Neck is home to another 4,000 sailors, including several SEAL teams and training schools.

That's just the Navy. The Army has some 5,000 personnel up at Fort Eustis in Newport News, another 800 wrapping up business at historic Fort Monroe, and nearly 2,000 at Fort Story. The Air Force has almost 13,000 in uniform at Langley Air Force Base in Hampton, and the Coast Guard has another 1,700 personnel in the region.

Each facility also has a cadre of civilians who make the base function or provide support services. That's another 31,000 Hampton Roads residents drawing paychecks from the Department of Defense.

Add to that the nation's largest government shipyard, and an assortment of private shipyards, from the massive Northrop

Grumman Newport News Shipbuilding, the state's largest private workplace, to smaller specialty yards—all relying either entirely or to a great degree on Navy work—and you get a sense of what Uncle Sam means to Hampton Roads.

Security has become much tighter on all area bases since the attacks on the World Trade Center and Pentagon on Sept 11, 2001. (Fighters from Langley and ships from Norfolk were dispatched immediately that morning to ensure there were no additional acts of terrorism.) As a result, it's not usually possible to wander onto area bases. But there are official tours and a few places locals know to scope out the action.

Here's a look at the major installations.

NAVAL STATION NORFOLK

Naval Station Norfolk is the world's largest Navy base. It was born at the start of World War II when Congress authorized purchasing a large swath along the northern tip of Norfolk known as Sewells Point that had gone begging since it hosted the failed Jamestown Exhibition in 1907.

The Norfolk station was called the Naval Operating Base, and some old salts—and radio traffic reporters—still refer to it by its military abbreviation: NOB. Next door is Chambers Field, which eventually became the Naval Air Station Norfolk. Eventually, they were folded together into the giant Naval Station Norfolk, which is the hub of the entire Atlantic Fleet.

In manpower, the station is, by far, the largest military base in the region. If you factor in the people it supports, as well as those actually on base, it is the largest military installation of any service. Even in land area, Naval Station Norfolk is huge, covering 4,400 acres. Its 17 piers along the Elizabeth River feature

everything from submarines to aircraft carriers. The 15 aircraft hangars here shelter 148 planes. And the station is home to the country's largest military supply facility.

Essentially, anything the Navy has afloat, in the air, or underwater you are likely to spot here or at nearby Little Creek Amphibious Base at one time or another.

In times of peace, aircraft carrier strike groups set off from Norfolk on six-month cruises to the Mediterranean Sea or Persian Gulf, with routine swings into other waters for humanitarian missions or just to show the flag. Much of the Navy's mission is to have troops pre-deployed in hot spots, ready to react should something happen. It's said that when a president is awakened to the news of another crisis, his first question is always, "Where are my carriers?"

Departures of the battle groups are dismal affairs, with loved ones hugging final goodbyes, then watching as the ships head off on their way to the Atlantic. Homecomings, however, are something special, with limos waiting in the lots, and spouses in their finest impatiently scanning for the first sight of Navy gray on the horizon. The centuries have produced a standard ritual, with one wife winning a first-aboard contest, babies born during the deployment in a special new mothers' tent, and a band playing in celebration as the sailors in their white uniforms line the rails hoping to spot a lover or a face from home.

During wars, those deployments last longer and come more frequently, putting additional strain on the families left behind.

The base is an actual home to many sailors, offering everything from clinics and a pharmacy to a commissary and exchange mall just outside the gates. The McDonalds just off the carrier piers is one of the busiest fast food restaurants in the nation, always full of sailors looking for a break from their normal mess hall or galley meals.

You'll need a special pass to get on base if you go it alone, but there are guided bus trips that leave from the Tour and Information Office off Hampton Boulevard every day that offer a flavor of what goes on here. Before 9/11, there would often be a ship open to the public on weekends, but security is a lot tighter and the service stretched a lot thinner these days. There are also water tours that will bring you past the piers. Before 9/11 you could pull your motorboat right up to a carrier. Now there is a keep-away zone that is strictly enforced. You may not see the sailor with the loaded gun, but he or she is there and determined to protect ship and shipmates.

ℹ️ Be warned, the Navy loves its abbreviations. In fact, there's a DICNAVAB to keep track of them. If you open that book to the D chapter, you can find its own entry in the ciphers: the Dictionary of Naval Abbreviations. The U.S. Navy is often credited with the longest abbreviations in the English Language, such as its ADCOMSUBORD-COMPHIBSPAC. It stands for Administrative Command, Amphibious Forces, Pacific Fleet Subordinate Command. Live here long enough, and all these letters jumbled together will start making perfect sense to you. The service also tends to give its names by function first, then location. So it isn't the Norfolk Naval Station, it is Naval Station Norfolk. But when the facility isn't where it seems, they scrub that system. So the naval shipyard in Portsmouth is known as the Norfolk Naval Shipyard. It keeps you on your toes.

NAVAL AMPHIBOUS BASE LITTLE CREEK

These days, the base that begins at the Norfolk–Virginia Beach border on the Chesapeake Bay is known as Joint Expeditionary Base Little Creek-Fort Story, but the Navy portion of this two-service operation is the largest in land and personnel. In fact, Little Creek is the world's largest naval amphibious base.

Little Creek is home to the ships that carry Marines and their gear into war. Those are known as Expeditionary Forces, hence the new name. The base was established in 1945 from four World War II bases. It hosts 18 amphibious ships and has an estimated annual payroll of $821 million and a force of nearly 12,000 sailors and Marines. It also is home to 35 LCACs (Landing Crafts Air Cushion), which are hovercraft able to speed troops over water right up a beach, and 34 conventional LCUs (landing craft units) and other smaller boats. The base employs some 5,000 civilian workers.

It is also home to several of the Navy's highly secretive SEAL teams. (That acronym stands for Sea, Air, and Land because these Special Forces, once known as Navy Frogmen, are no longer just underwater experts.) Some of the Amphibious Assault Ships here are almost as large as an aircraft carrier and are often referred to by civilians as helicopter carriers. They and their sister amphibious assault ships can haul entire fighting forces, tanks, trucks, and the close-in support aircraft needed for establishing a beachhead.

If you take Shore Drive, the 4,000-acre base seems to run on forever behind its cyclone fence walls and above-ground steam pipes. In addition to the amphibious troops, the base is home to explosive ordnance disposal teams and the Navy's resurrected riverene squadrons. There are also training commands on the sprawling base.

The most unusual is the Navy School of Music, which serves as the first stop for instrumentalists and singers trying to join the military bands of all the branches. Once again, this is the largest facility of its kind in the world. There are nine rehearsal areas, each linked by closed circuit televisions, and more than 100 studios for practice and instruction. Here, the service members upon arrival are issued an instrument rather than a rifle. The school also has the largest instrument repair shop in the military.

NAVAL AIR STATION OCEANA

Another area installation born during World War II, Oceana grew from an auxiliary field carved out of a swamp to the East Coast's Master Jet Base. Oceana is now Virginia Beach's largest employer, with some 14,600 military and another 2,000 civilians working there.

There are more than six miles of runways at Oceana, and 19 fighter/attack squadrons who fly the Navy's premier fighter-bombers, the FA/18 Hornets and Super Hornets, are constantly buzzing over the beaches and neighborhoods.

This is where neighbors coined the phrase "Sound of Freedom" to describe the near constant roar of jets flying overhead or practicing their carrier landing techniques on specially marked runways here or at nearby Fentress Auxiliary Field in Chesapeake. (Many aren't so fond of the roar, which got louder when the Navy moved from F-14 Tomcats to Super Hornets. Some homeowners have filed lawsuits seeking damages for the stress and property value loss they say were caused by the din.)

Every year, the 250 aircraft based at Oceana make more than a quarter million takeoffs and landings trying to perfect what is the most dangerous act in aviation, putting a huge jet full of fuel, and often weapons, down on a moving strip of deck, in total darkness and in storms that can make that deck heave—and doing all this after completing a dangerous mission through antiaircraft fire. If a jet misses the mark, it can overshoot one of the three arresting cables designed to snag the tailhook. The pilots are taught to gun their engines just in case, so they can get back into the air for another try. But come in on a bad angle, and you can crash into other planes on the crowded deck or just plunge a $55 million jet into the ocean and hope to eject to safety.

Oceana is another base that is like its own city. It has a commissary, shopping mall, bank, post office, golf course, and gym.

The area around Oceana has developed so much since its inception that the pilots have had to change some of their procedures during practice to avoid disturbing homeowners. And they now deal with streetlights where there should, ideally, be darkness leading to an array of guide lights, known as the Meatball, that a pilot uses to plot his course and speed onto the deck.

The Navy nearly decided to close Oceana a few years back and move to a less developed environment, but local officials promised to end commercial encroachment around the base and have been working to move away some of the most inappropriate buildings, such as elementary schools, within high noise and potential crash zones.

Just outside the gates is a Jet Observation Park, where you can sit at picnic tables and watch the nation's best pilots at work.

NAVAL AIR STATION OCEANA DAM NECK ANNEX

Located right on the Atlantic about 5 miles south of the Virginia Beach main resort area, Dam Neck is a support center with a number of schools as well as additional SEAL teams. This is home of the Fleet Combat Training Center for the Atlantic Fleet, the Naval Special Warfare Development Command, the Naval Guided Missile School, the Navy and Marine Corps Intelligence Training Center, and the Naval Surface Warfare Center. There are 4,000 service personnel stationed or going to school here and another 1,500 civilians who keep the base running.

NORFOLK NAVAL SHIPYARD

Another in the area's litany of largest and oldest, the Norfolk Naval Shipyard (which is located in Portsmouth; see explanation in Area Overview) dates back to 1767. Drydock 1, the first ever built in America, is still in use. The shipyard employs some 7,000 people and another 8,000 crewmen can usually be found stationed aboard the vessels here for repair.

The shipyard was enlarged several times as it geared up for various war production periods. Before the Navy opened its base in Norfolk, the shipyard in Portsmouth was known as the Norfolk Naval Yard, serving as both repair facility and the local naval base.

It now has more than 4 miles of waterfront. A drive on I-464 across the Southern Branch of the Elizabeth River will give a good view of that industrial area. Here, you can see cranes of every size, from a massive hammerhead that can lift entire ship sections, to the normal one on its back that seems like a Tonka toy in comparison.

Inside are shops that can handle the latest electronic weapons and forges where blacksmiths can make any part needed to get a ship back into the fight.

A shipyard cannon that was fired every evening became the curfew call on which generations of Portsmouth children relied. Businesses set their clocks and gents their pocket watches to the nine o'clock gun. It was silenced in recent years, first by the departure of the Marines who used to perform the chore, then by the economy. There are often nostalgic calls to bring it back. Then again, the sound of gunfire in the night is no longer so comforting.

The shipyard can handle any of the Navy's vessels, including nuclear aircraft carriers. When one makes the 12-mile sail for repairs from Naval Station Norfolk it provides a great opportunity to get up close to the world's most massive war machine. Even though the carrier remains well out in the Elizabeth, fidgeted over by a passel of tugs, its flight decks seem to arch over the Portsmouth Seawall promenade, nearly blocking out the sun. Standing under that eclipse is an experience hard to forget.

i There's a free Naval Shipyard Museum & Lightship Museum a few miles from the shipyard on the seawall at the base of High Street. Inside, you'll find a wealth of artifacts from uniforms to models of the historic ships built here.

THE ARMY

Fort Eustis, on the northern reaches of Newport News, is home to the Army's Transportation Corps, the most deployed branch of the nation's largest service. In 2010, the fort got a new name when its management was merged with nearby Langley Air

Force Base. They're now called the Joint Base Langley-Eustis.

Eustis began as a camp in 1917 but dates all the way back to Pocahontas's days because it was here that her husband, tobacco farmer John Rolfe, had his plantation. The army bought the property, known as Mulberry Island, in 1918. The camp became Fort Eustis in 1923. But it left military life briefly and served as a federal prison for bootleggers from 1931 until the end of Prohibition.

The fort reopened in August 1940 as the Coast Artillery Replacement Training Center and, after World War II, it was home of the new Transportation School.

To this day, soldiers come and learn how to operate rail, marine, amphibious, and other modes of transportation. It is now under the Training and Doctrine Command.

Soldiers from Fort Eustis have been involved in ensuring the troops and supplies arrived for both Gulf Wars, as well as serving in Somalia, Rwanda, Haiti, and Bosnia.

The fort has nearly 5,000 soldiers and about as many civilian workers on its 8,000 acres. Here, you'll find soldiers training to operate the Army's Navy, a fleet of boats designed to put troops on the beach. Are these vessels ships? Depends on whom you ask. Navy regulations say a ship is a vessel that can carry boats. Submarines, for instance, are considered boats, not ships. Well, these Army craft carry landing boats. Makes them ships, right? Well, not quite. Another determinant in the Navy is who is at the helm. All Navy ships have commissioned officers in charge. The Army takes a different tact. Its drivers are non-commissioned warrant officers. Call them vessels and you'll be on solid ground.

The fort has computerized simulators that train all services in how to deploy units and gear; how to drive those "vessels" without hitting anything; how to control the damage if you do hit something; how to use cranes; and even realistic trainers for learning to drive the Army's trucks and other supply vehicles.

The base is also home to the U.S. Army Transportation Museum. Here you can work your way through the military history, examining the vehicles that were used, ranging from mules and Conestoga wagons of the Revolutionary War to the most modern Humvees and armored personnel carriers still traveling in Afghanistan and Iraq. There are about 100 land, water, and rail vehicles on display as well as plenty of other interesting diversions. Did you know the U.S. operated its own Camel Corps from 1855 to 1866? You will once you visit here. You'll have to check in at the guard station and get a visitor's pass. Don't bring anything you'd be ashamed having discovered in a search, since all vehicles are potential subjects.

FORT MONROE

The last American military installation with a moat, Fort Monroe is in the process of being closed and will be turned over to the state of Virginia in September 2011.

This is a place steeped in history, and the historic buildings will be preserved when the state takes control.

The first slaves in the colonies landed here on a privateer, and were traded for provisions. The fort, the largest built of stone in the United States, was a key Union stronghold throughout the Civil War and became the goal of runaway slaves seeking liberty, earning its nickname, Freedom's Fortress.

President Lincoln came here to supervise the war in Hampton Roads and order the capture of Norfolk. Off these shores, the

Monitor and *Merrimack*, actually known as the CSS *Virginia* at that time, fought the first battle of the ironclads.

Inside the fort, Edgar Allan Poe wrote while pulling Army duty and Confederate President Jefferson Davis was imprisoned after his capture in Georgia.

The fort served as the protector of the local harbor, with cannons that could sink invading ships far out to sea. After World War II, it became home to the command that oversaw the training of the nation's soldiers. That branch is now called the Training and Doctrine Command.

Every time Congress looked around for bases to close, Fort Monroe seemed the most likely, thanks to its moat and its valuable waterfront location. But centuries of military use left a legacy of countless buried armaments. Periodically, some kid or weekend gardener would dig up an unexploded bomb that dated back to the Civil War. It was often determined it would cost too much to clear all of this, a requirement for transfer back to civilian use. That reprieve finally ran out in the 2005 Base Realignment and Closure process. Military planners can do their work anywhere, the cost cutters decided. It was time to return the fort to the state and save the federal government some money.

These days, the base only has about 800 soldiers and 1,600 civilians, but they are some of the top military minds. And those who live on this installation truly walk with ghosts.

FORT STORY

The second half of the new Joint Expeditionary Base, Fort Story is a developer's dream. It is on the Chesapeake Bay where it meets the Atlantic Ocean. Here the beaches are not reserved for tourists but host soldier, SEAL, and amphibious assault training.

The fort is also the only U.S. Army location that has the deepwater sea anchorage and natural beach to train soldiers in getting troops and gear from ships to shore. And it is the Army's sole site for training reverse osmosis water purification units who convert salt water into fresh.

The 1,500-acre base is also home to Cape Henry Lighthouse and the nearby Cape Henry Memorial Cross, a monument that marks the location where the Jamestown settlers first set foot on American soil.

The fort, now technically known as the East Campus, has 1,800 soldiers and another 1,000 civilians. Visitors can get a pass to see the lighthouse and cross.

AIR FORCE
Langley Air Force Base

Hope you're not tired of the firsts, because Langley is the oldest continually active Air Force base in the world. It started in 1916 and was named Langley Field for aviation pioneer Samuel Pierpont Langley.

Over the years, Langley-based pilots have flown everything from blimps to the new F-22A Raptor. It is home to the Air Combat Command, the Air Forces largest major command, and the 1st Fighter Wing and 480th Intelligence Wing.

The base has about 9,000 uniformed personnel and another 2,800 civilians. It occupies 3,167 acres.

Langley is where the concept of air power was developed when Brig Gen. Billy Mitchell flew bombing runs over captured German warships anchored off the Virginia coast, proving that aircraft could sink such ships.

It was home to the Army Air Corps and many of the base's buildings date back to before World War II.

During that war, Langley units helped develop submarine detection gear that broke the U-Boat scourge off the Atlantic coast. After the war, Langley was home to the new Tactical Air Command and base for the latest jets.

Langley pilots have been flying those jets ever since, deploying to Saudi Arabia to fly missions in the first Gulf War. They flew no-fly zone missions over Iraq after that war and were there to patrol the skies during the second Gulf War.

When terrorists attacked the World Trade Center and Pentagon on 9/11, three jets from Langley were scrambled, and when all commercial traffic was ordered to the ground, they flew guard over the nation's capital.

And a demonstration team flying the stealth Raptor based at Langley has been traveling the nation showing what this most advanced jet can do.

COAST GUARD

We don't tend to think of the Coast Guard as a military unit, but after 9/11 the Coast Guard moved from the Department of Transportation to the Department of Homeland Security. And it has always fallen under the Department of Defense during wars.

Hampton Roads is home to the Coast Guard's Atlantic Command, with offices in downtown Portsmouth, as well as the Base Portsmouth near Craney Island and a training center up the road in Yorktown.

The Coast Guard is the smallest of the services, and even here, where all operations from the Mississippi River to the Middle East are overseen, there are only about 2,200 resident Coasties and some 800 civilians.

They operate a search and rescue base in Virginia Beach as well as out of the support center. The support center is home to six of the service's largest and most modern cutters.

ACCOMMODATIONS

Lodging is where this place really shows its split personality, with a huge resort hotel and motel industry in Virginia Beach serving the Oceanfront and the more obvious chains offering plenty of places to stay in the other cities.

Obviously, prices are highest right on the beach in the heart of the tourist season. But those Boardwalk resorts can be bargain getaways in the winter, when you can appreciate the warm, indoor view of a stormy winter Atlantic. Most area hotels provide free parking for registered guests, but you'll want to check their policy before inviting friends to visit or if using more than one vehicle on your vacation.

Like any major metropolitan area, you'll find a wide range of amenities and prices to match in Hampton Roads. But this area isn't known for super bargains, so you'll want to do some research before staying in a place that seems really cheap—it might not meet your standards or be in a safe location. And like any city, convenience comes at a price. If you want to be right in any of the downtowns or in the middle of the resort strip in Virginia Beach, you'll pay for it. The trade-off is the time, aggravation, and parking fees you'll wind up saving.

One final proviso: I wouldn't recommend staying on the Peninsula if your main interest is enjoying the Southside beaches. The tunnels are too often backed up in summer, and you'll wind up spending more time seething in traffic than sizzling on a towel.

Since nearly 3 million of the folks who visit here every year are heading for the beaches, we'll look at the resort area separately. In addition to the 20,000 rooms for rent there, you'll find many of the area's bed and breakfasts, the only youth hostel, and the bulk of the commercial campgrounds serving this market. The beach also has plenty of summer rentals and cottages in Sandbridge that go by the week or season. Check with some of the realtors in the relocation chapter for listings.

Then I'll break down the lodging situation for each of the other cities. Obviously, this is no comprehensive listing, just a good sample of well-respected facilities to get your search going. Most places here are non-smoking, handicapped accessible, and accept major credit cards. Very few welcome pets.

Price Code

$.................... Under $100
$$ .... $100 to $200
$$$ .... $201 to $300
$$$$ .... Over $300

Prices are based on a one-night stay in a standard room during the full-price summer season. Many hotels will have higher-priced options, such as suites, and the codes were based on May 2010 rates. Rates can be higher here on weekends and for special events and do not include taxes, which total 13 percent, plus a $1 per night room occupancy charge.

VIRGINIA BEACH

Oceanfront

The resort strip basically follows the 3-mile Boardwalk's path, with the bulk of the hotels and motels towering over the beach down here. Other, smaller and less opulent places are tucked on the streets farther from the surf. If you like action, you'll want to consider the area around 21st Street—that's about the center of the real touristy area. If you prefer a little more relaxed environment, head for the northern end of the Boardwalk. There are many different rates down here, not only between the different hotels and motels but also by the season. The midsummer is the highest priced, but there is also a lot of demand here in what are known as the shoulder seasons, the glorious early fall when the ocean water remains warm but the days aren't so humid, and late spring when the southern location gives us a jump on summer. Since kids are in school then, highest demand and costs tend to be on weekends, especially any three-day holidays, and for special events like the Neptune Festival. You can get a feel of what is happening here throughout the year in the Annual Events & Festivals chapter.

Based on a summer visitors' study and tourism impact research in 2009, the typical Virginia Beach tourist is between 35 and 54 years old, married with children, and middle class. Most come from the mid-Atlantic region, especially from Northern Virginia, Maryland, West Virginia, and Washington, D.C., but Canadians love the place, representing more than a tenth of the area's tourists every year.

The same studies showed that more than three quarters of the tourists had been here before and 93 percent felt it was a great or good place to visit.

The **Virginia Beach Hotel-Motel Association,** (757) 428-8015, counts 89 members, so there are plenty of rooms available. The **Virginia Beach Convention and Visitors Bureau,** (757) 385-4700, has information to help you pick a place, but neither will make outright recommendations.

Here are a few places to consider in a range of offerings, from luxurious to efficiencies, brand new to turn of the 20th century, resort to basic beach cottage.

ANGIE'S GUEST COTTAGE $–$$
302 24th St.
Virginia Beach
(757) 491-1830
www.angiescottage.com
Angie's is the area's only hostel. It is located in a beach cottage built in the early 1900s that once housed the families of Coast Guard surf men who were on duty at the old Coast Guard Station that is now a museum. The original Angie bought it and turned it into a traditional beach guesthouse. The Yates family came aboard in 1978 and added the dorm hostel in the back and bed and breakfast accommodations in the main house. The cottage itself offers six private guest rooms, all updated in 2007 and some with private entrances. They no longer offer breakfasts, though. The hostel has five dorm rooms

with 34 bunks. There is no age limit on the hostel. Angie's is also affiliated with Ocean Cove Motel and offers Ocean Cove Cottages, three-bedroom, two-bath cottages that can be rented by the week. The rates vary by week and day of week. Beds in the hostel are $31 a night weekends in the peak season, a few dollars cheaper on weekdays or for members of Hostelling International-USA, and there's a two-day minimum during the week and three days over a weekend. You'll need your own pillowcases and sheets if you're staying in the dorms.

BARKLEY COTTAGE BED
AND BREAKFAST $$
400 16th St.
Virginia Beach
(757) 422-1956
www.barclaycottage.com

Appreciate history? Well, this small bed and breakfast is one of only two remaining original beach cottages in the city. It has been welcoming guests since 1917. The home was built in 1895 by Norfolk and Virginia Beach Railroad as the clubhouse for a golf course on Lake Holly that was never built. Miss Barkley, as her guests called her, moved in with her parents in 1916 and ran it as a seasonal guesthouse and also operated a primary school in the building for 50 years. Mystic Edgar Cayce, a friend, held several of his readings here. After she died, her estate sold the property to developers. It was purchased in the 1980s by a retiree who put in such amenities as heat and air-conditioning. He later sold it to the current owners and innkeepers Stephen and Marie-Louise LaFond. There are five themed rooms now, all filled with family and Victorian era antiques. Look for Marie-Louise's quilts, which are hung throughout. Three

of the rooms have queen-sized beds and private baths; two have jetted-air spa tubs. The other rooms share a bath, which is a bit cheaper. One of these has a king sized bed; the other has two twins that can be combined into a Euro King. This is an adult-only place; you'll have to leave your kids and pets at home if you want to be pampered. Snacks and cold beverages are always available. If you want to get up and watch the sunrise over the beach a few blocks away, early coffee service will be waiting for you. In the afternoons, there's fresh-baked cookies and evenings they serve wine. And of course there's the breakfast, an hour and a half affair with multiple courses and interesting twists and conversations at a communal table that seats 10. You also get fresh beach towels every day and free beach chairs, umbrellas, boogie boards, and bicycles. Off-street parking is included in the price. Because the home was built so long ago, the doors to the bathrooms are too narrow for wheelchairs, so it's probably not a great choice for folks who require one.

BEACH SPA BED AND BREAKFAST $$
2420 Arctic Ave.
Virginia Beach
(757) 422-2621
www.beachspabnb.com

The Beach Spa has been voted the top bed and breakfast in America. This is another historic home—the cottage was built around 1937—that opened in 2007 as a mini-spa resort. There are 8 rooms, each named for a historic beach hotel. Four have king beds, four have queen—all offer private bathrooms, and one is ADA certified. This is a place with a historic feel but a modern heart. There are spa showers in every room, a spa tower where you can watch the sunrise, and a year-round heated outdoor spa pool. You can bring your children—it costs $15 each—or an adult guest for $30 a night. There's Wi-Fi here and flat-screen TVs with cable, should you want to stay in touch. But there are no phones in the rooms to disturb you. In afternoons, you get a cordial snack and then there are the gourmet breakfasts. If you really want to relax, you can order up one of their special massages, but you need to schedule 48 hours in advance. They range from $75 for a 45-minute head and neck massage to $210 an hour for a couple's private full-body Swedish massage.

BREAKERS RESORT INN $$
1503 Atlantic Ave.
Virginia Beach
(757) 428-1821
www.breakersresort.com

This is a family-owned and operated hotel right on the southern end of the tourist strip, at 16th Street. It opened in 1984 but was completely renovated in 2006. There are 56 rooms here running from the standard with a refrigerator, coffee maker, and two queen beds to efficiency suites that have a separate bedroom, living room, and kitchenettes. Rooms with king sized beds also have Jacuzzi tubs. Every room offers a private oceanfront balcony. A cafe serves breakfast and lunch here, and this is one of the places where smokers can find lodging. There are two wheelchair-accessible rooms; one is a suite. There's an outdoor pool and free bicycles for guests to roam the Boardwalk.

THE CAPES HOTEL $$
2001 Atlantic Ave.
Virginia Beach
(757) 428-5421
www.capeshotel.com

This is another of the smaller, locally owned Oceanfront hotels, with 59 rooms and private balconies overlooking the surf. There's a range of rooms, from standard to king suites. The standard offers a pair of double beds, coffee maker, refrigerator, microwave, and free HBO and expanded cable for those rainy days. They also offer value weeks, with steep discounts on a limited number of rooms. You can find the weeks on the website. Just follow the directions there. Some rooms have whirlpool tubs, and there's an indoor pool overlooking the ocean that's heated in the winter. You can add extra guests to a room for $10 each per night.

COURTYARD BY MARRIOTT
OCEANFRONT SOUTH $$$
2501 Atlantic Ave.
Virginia Beach
(757) 491-6222

Marriott operates two courtyard inns at the Oceanfront. The Courtyard South has 141 rooms with either a pair of double beds or a single king. There are also suites. There's no charge for extra residents. All rooms are oceanfront and all have private balconies. There's an indoor pool and a whirlpool and some rooms are wheelchair-accessible. There's a full restaurant here and free Wi-Fi. What sets it apart from its sibling is location. This Marriott is right in the middle of all the Oceanfront action.

COURTYARD BY MARRIOTT
OCEANFRONT NORTH $$$
3737 Atlantic Ave.
Virginia Beach
(757) 437-0098
www.courtyardoceanfrontnorth.com

The other Courtyard is located at the calmer north end of the Boardwalk. There are 11 floors here with 100 rooms, each with an oceanfront balcony. The outdoor pool has a tropical theme and a tiki bar, open until 7 p.m., so you can relax with a drink by the pool. There's also an indoor pool for the colder months. There's a restaurant that serves breakfast and even room service for evening meals, which is rare in a Courtyard property. This facility was completely renovated in 2009.

CUTTY SARK MOTEL EFFICIENCIES AND HISTORIC COTTAGES   **$$**
3614 Atlantic Ave.
Virginia Beach
(757) 428-2116
www.cuttysarkvb.com
Step into this small motel on the North End and you step back in time. The calendar at the Cutty Sark stopped flipping at 1969, which is when this 13-room place opened. It was built by a contractor who thought he wanted to be an innkeeper, then went back to his building career. "It's basically the same as it was in those days," longtime owner Ms. Jimmie Koch said. "We kind of cherish our vintage." This is one of the oldest motels at the beach and draws a loyal crowd. Ms. Koch has seen children of guests grow up and bring their own children to recapture their beach magic. These are all efficiencies and cottages, with full stoves and ovens as well as microwaves and coffee makers. Families usually eat breakfast in, enjoying coffee on their balconies in their PJs. The ocean is just across Atlantic Avenue, and you can even see it from those private balconies. They don't accept American Express here, but any other card is welcome. You can smoke out on the balconies, where there are ashtrays, but not in the rooms. Since this place is seasonal, open only during pleasant weather, that shouldn't be an ordeal. One room is

wheelchair-accessible. Additional guests are $10 per night, but children 10 and under are free. Ms. Koch, who has been running the motel for more than 30 years with her husband, is proud of keeping it true to its history. "We have maintained the retro, and we're coming back in style," she said.

ECONO LODGE OCEANFRONT   **$$**
2109 Atlantic Ave.
Virginia Beach
(757) 428-2403
There are 56 rooms here, most with two double beds, and this is another of the rare places where smokers are still welcome. One room is handicapped accessible; all are oceanfront with private balconies or patios. A continental breakfast is included in the rate with the fixings to make your own waffles if you're so inclined. The building opened in 1990, and there is a small indoor pool. There is also an indoor parking garage for the guests. There's another Econo Lodge, a few blocks down at 2707 Atlantic Ave. (757-428-3970), called Econo Lodge on the Ocean. It's a 38-bed, three story motel with no elevator, which also offers all oceanfront rooms and a continental breakfast. It has a heated outdoor pool and rooms for smokers.

FAIRFIELD INN & SUITES   **$$$**
1901 Atlantic Ave.
Virginia Beach
(757) 422-4885
This is another Marriott property with 114 rooms that opened in 2006. There's an indoor pool, fitness room, and a whirlpool and a complimentary continental breakfast. There's no charge for additional guests, and rooms feature either king or double beds. All rooms have an ocean view, private balcony, and free Wi-Fi.

HILTON VIRGINIA BEACH
OCEANFRONT $$$$
3001 Atlantic Ave.
Virginia Beach
(757) 213-3000

This hotel rises 21 stories over the beach, with a breathtaking infinity pool on the roof. That's one of those pools with glass sides that seem to fall right off the edge of the world, or in this case, right into the Boardwalk below. The hotel is home to two award-winning restaurants, Catch 31, with its outdoor fireplaces, and Salacia, the only AAA 4-diamond steakhouse in Virginia. Just outside is Neptune Park, with its impressive statue of the Greek god, and the upscale Shoppes at 31 Ocean. There are 289 rooms here, and a stay doesn't come cheap. The hotel opened in 2005, built on one of the last remaining open areas along the Boardwalk. There is a single floor here set aside for smokers, and there are wheelchair-accessible rooms. Folks love the seasonal Sky Bar—it's on the roof with that pool.

HOLIDAY INN & SUITES
NORTH BEACH $$$
3900 Atlantic Ave.
Virginia Beach
(757) 428-1711

This resort recently underwent a $19 million renovation. There are 238 rooms at this Holiday Inn, but what sets it apart is the water amenities. Not only is this right on the beach at 39th Street in the North End, but it has its own aquatic wonders. There are five pools here, one on the oceanfront, two lazy rivers, and two water slides to frolic in. And there's a spa and state-of-the-art fitness center. If you want to stay in your room, they have flat-screen TVs with free Wi-Fi and even iPod docking stations. And there's a

complimentary Splash Camp where you can leave your 4- to 12-year-olds in the summer months to play while you head out to have your own fun. There's a restaurant and even a 48-seat movie theater that shows G to PG family films.

OCEAN BEACH CLUB $$$
3401 Atlantic Ave.
Virginia Beach
(757) 213-0601
www.vboceanbeachclub.com

One of the newest resorts on the beach, having opened in 2008, this 19-floor hotel has 347 rooms, all with queen-sized beds. Ocean-view suites have private balconies. There's a stunning indoor pool and an outdoor pool, with a tiki bar, as well as a pool for kids. The sky fitness center on the top floor is a real lure for those who love to exercise. Here you can work out on state-of-the-art equipment with the Atlantic Ocean as a backdrop. They also offer oceanfront yoga sessions and instruction and a game room for rainy days. The hotel won Expedia's Insiders Select award of excellence in 2009, putting it in the top 1 percent of the site's hotels and resorts.

Rest of Virginia Beach

FOUNDERS INN & SPA $$
5641 Indian River Rd.
Virginia Beach
(757) 424-5511

The Founders Inn is a 240-room hotel and spa located on the Christian Broadcasting Network and Regent University campus off Centerville Turnpike and Indian River Road. The grounds are sculpted like an English garden, the architecture is Georgian, and there are many antiques and period furnishings throughout. There's a Jacuzzi tub

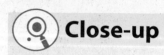 **Close-up**

Timeless Luxury

Want to stay where seven U.S. presidents and countless celebrities and robber barons once vacationed? The **Cavalier Hotel** (4201 Atlantic Ave., Virginia Beach, 757-425-8555, www.cavalierhotel.com, $$) is the destination that put Virginia Beach on the map. It opened during the Roaring 20s, a magnificent concrete, steel, and brick edifice on a small bluff overlooking the Atlantic. Back then, heading to the beach was an arduous affair, but Norfolk & Western Railroad soon installed tracks and a new gasoline-powered train named "The Cavalier" that ran from Chicago to the hotel's private depot. The Cavalier also had a fleet of limousines that ferried guests from local steamship lines and railroad stations. And during Prohibition, they were used to take guests to area speakeasies and gambling establishments.

This was the time of gentlemen's sporting clubs, and the Cavalier's Hunt Room served the purpose and even offered kennels for hunting dogs. This was luxury living, with salt water taps in the bathrooms for sea bathing in private and even sinks with an ice-water spigot before refrigeration, fed by a wooden cask on the roof filled with ice and water.

A separate dining room catered to chauffeurs. And a radio station, WSEA, operated from the hotel, broadcasting coast to coast and welcoming Charles Lindberg home as he passed on his way back to Washington D.C. after his solo trans-Atlantic flight.

There were barbers and druggists and a doctor in residence, and a stockbroker's office with a ticker tape connected to the New York Stock Exchange that got the breaking news of Black Friday and the end of the Gilded Age that had kept this place so profitable.

A few weeks before the crash that ushered in the Great Depression, the fabled Cavalier Beach Club opened. Every major big band of the time would play here, including Benny Goodman, Cab Calloway, and Glen Miller. Folks came out to hear Frank Sinatra, Bing Crosby, and Xavier Cugat. In fact, in the two decades that were the peak of the Big Band era, no other place in the world hired as many fabled acts.

overlooking a lake and an outdoor pool with a beach-like, gently graded entry. There are also fountains throughout the pool area and a 25-foot enclosed circular slide for kids, as well as an indoor pool for cooler weather. There are several restaurants here, and a breakfast spot called the Muffin Pan. Many people come specifically for the spa, where you can enjoy manicures, pedicures, facials, and complete massages. There are packages that combine the spa with a room rate. It's also a conference center and has been

designated a green hotel and convention center by the state.

HILTON GARDEN INN VIRGINIA BEACH TOWN CENTER $$
252 Town Center Dr.
Virginia Beach
(757) 326-6200

Some folks prefer to stay in the center of town, in the Town Center area. The Hilton Garden Inn offers 176 rooms with king or a pair of queen beds. There are suites, suites

Even after the market collapsed, the Cavalier kept going, becoming the beach's largest employer. F. Scott Fitzgerald, Judy Garland, Will Rogers, Bette Davis, Jean Harlow, Mary Pickford, and Betty Grable stayed here. Fatty Arbuckle, famous for his excesses, would rent an entire floor when he came. During World War II, the Navy commandeered the hotel as a radar training school. The direct train service to the Cavalier ended after World War II, but the hotel continued on. Some of the "Dennis the Menace" cartoons drawn by Hank Ketchum were based on his family's visits to the Cavalier.

Progress almost did what hurricane winds and the Great Depression failed to accomplish. A new Cavalier opened on the Oceanfront in 1973, and the old building was slated for demolition. In fact, all of its contents were sold in a public auction. But the people wouldn't accept the Cavalier's closure, and they saved the historic hotel. The original building, now known as the Cavalier on the Hill, reopened in 1976.

The Cavalier is now a complex of the two hotels on 18 acres at 42nd Street and Atlantic Avenue. The Cavalier Oceanfront has kept up with all the modern changes; the Cavalier on the Hill just across the street preserves its history and luxury. There are 400 bedrooms in the combination with rates that range from $200 to $500 a night. You can't bring your hunting dogs anymore, but those sporting days can be relived in the Hunt Room Grille, which remains as one of four restaurants on the property.

There's a 1,500-square-foot health club in the complex and two Olympic-sized pools. Most importantly, there's that history, which includes Calvin Coolidge, Herbert Hoover, Harry Truman, Dwight Eisenhower, John Kennedy, Lyndon Johnson, and Richard Nixon as presidential guests.

Folks even say there are ghosts roaming the Hill's halls. Adolph Coors mysteriously fell to his death from a sixth-floor window there in 1929 when his Colorado brewery was forced out of the beer business by Prohibition, and some say his spirit is still here, joined by the specter of a cat that fell into a pool and the little girl who drowned trying to save it. That makes the old Cavalier a favorite haunt around Halloween.

with whirlpools, and wheelchair-accessible rooms. The hotel opened in 2003, and there's plenty of free public parking in the area for families who are coming with more than one vehicle.

VIRGINIA BEACH RESORT HOTEL & CONFERENCE CENTER $$$
2800 Shore Dr.
Virginia Beach
(757) 481-9000
www.virginiabeachresort.com

This resort is located right on the beach, but it's the Chesapeake Bay outside the door, and here you can watch a dramatic sunset over the bay from any of the 295 suites. You can also see the sun rise over the nearby Atlantic from here. The hotel is a few miles from the Oceanfront strip. It's been open since 1986 and offers a private beach. Another unusual feature is a heated saltwater pool that goes from indoor to outdoor and you can swim between the two. Smokers are welcome here, and there are wheelchair-accessible rooms including one with a roll-in shower. Guests here get three hours free bike rentals and can even go on a Segway tour down to the nearby First Landing State Park and the Oceanfront. And you get 90 minutes of free tennis at the award-winning Virginia Beach Tennis Club for every night you stay here. The front desk will reserve your court for you. They also offer special whale watching packages with a suite, a boat trip, admission to the Virginia Aquarium, and an IMAX movie for a family of four, starting at $225 a night.

WESTIN VIRGINIA BEACH TOWN CENTER $$
4535 Commerce St.
Virginia Beach
(757) 557-0550

The Westin that towers over Town Center is a combination condo and hotel and is the tallest building in all of Virginia. It has 236 rooms, a heated indoor pool, a whirlpool, and a gym. Some rooms have their own treadmill for an extra charge, so you don't have to travel any farther to get a workout. They offer up to 20 percent off if you reserve 21 days in advance as well as discounts for AAA members. These suites all feature two queens or one king bed.

Campgrounds

Virginia Beach offers several resort-style campgrounds for those who'd rather sleep in their motor home or pitch a tent. Most sites are located south of the resort area before you get to Sandbridge. Here are a couple of the largest.

HOLIDAY TRAV-L-PARK $
1075 General Booth Blvd.
Virginia Beach
(757) 425-0249

A large camping resort, this has four playgrounds and five pools, including one for younger kids. There are bands and DJs every night by the pool or pavilion and cartoon movies as well. They have a free parking lot at the beach for the guests who'd rather not use the city trolleys.

NORTH LANDING BEACH RIVERFRONT CAMPGROUND & RESORT $
161 Princess Anne Rd.
Virginia Beach
(757) 426-6241

This one is a lot farther from the resort bustle, nestled right on the North Landing River, a wide expanse of the Atlantic Intracoastal Waterway. Here, you can water ski, canoe, kayak, or just bask on the private beach or by the pool. It's only a 20-mile ride to the Oceanfront resort area, so you can easily trade your quiet for excitement. Again there are all kinds of sites and cabins available. You'll get free Wi-Fi here too, so you can surf the Web while toasting marshmallows over an open fire.

VIRGINIA BEACH KOA $
1240 General Booth Blvd.
Virginia Beach
(757) 428-1444

This large campground offers a 2-mile bike trail to the beach, and easy access to the city trolleys that take you to the resort area up the road. They offer tent and RV sites as well as cabins and lodges. You even get free Wi-Fi at most sites, and an outdoor cinema, so this is hardly roughing it. And there's a Kamp K9 interactive dog park.

NORFOLK

Norfolk has several areas with hotels. The best lodgings tend to be downtown. There's another group, though, that serves visitors to the Naval Base.

Downtown

COURTYARD MARRIOTT NORFOLK DOWNTOWN $$
520 Plume St.
Norfolk
(757) 963-6000

This recently renovated hotel near MacArthur Center offers free Wi-Fi and views of downtown Norfolk. There's a fitness center and a restaurant serving breakfast and dinner. There are 137 rooms in this eight-floor hotel, which has an indoor pool and whirlpool, and the bathrooms have Jacuzzi tubs. Parking is extra here, $12 a day off-site or $18 for on-site valet parking.

CROWNE PLAZA HOTEL $$
700 Monticello Ave.
Norfolk
(757) 627-5555

Another of the city's long-established hotels, this one is right across Brambleton Avenue from Scope and Chrysler Hall and just a short stroll from the Granby Street restaurants and clubs. The hotel was renovated in 2009 and offers 175 guest rooms and eight suites.

HAMPTON INN NORFOLK NAVAL BASE $$
8501 Hampton Blvd.
Norfolk
(757) 489-1000

If you have business on the base or you're in town to welcome home a loved one, you'll probably want to stay nearby to avoid the traffic. Well, you can't get much closer to the gates than this place. There are 117 rooms here with single king or two double beds. There are smoking rooms and wheelchair-accessible rooms as well. You also get complimentary breakfast and beverages and there's a fitness room and indoor pool.

HILTON NORFOLK AIRPORT $$
1500 North Military Hwy.
Norfolk
(757) 466-8000

This hotel is 2 miles from the airport, which is located adjacent to the Norfolk Botanical Garden's so there isn't the cluster of hotels associated with many big city airports. The Hilton offers free shuttle service to and from Norfolk International. There's complementary wireless Internet here, and the hotel's 247 guest rooms were recently renovated. There's also a new indoor pool and whirlpool and an outdoor pool for the warmer months. The hotel is just off I-64, which makes it an easy drive to many bases and businesses. Even the Oceanfront is only 11 miles away. This is one of the few pet friendly hotels in the area, but there is a $75 non-refundable fee, and any animal over 75 pounds must stay in a kennel.

NORFOLK WATERSIDE MARRIOTT $$
235 East Main St.
Norfolk
(757) 627-4200

This 24-floor, high-rise hotel is connected to the Waterside Convention Center just off the bustling Elizabeth River and in the area's financial district. It's near all the nightspots and an easy stroll to the MacArthur Center mall. Parking here is not free but $1 an hour or $19 per day. Every one of the 397 rooms and eight suites has a view of the working harbor where you never know what kind of ship will come by next, from sailing schooners to aircraft carriers. High-speed Internet is extra here, but you get unlimited free local and national calls. Shula's 347, legendary Miami Dolphins coach Don Shula's steakhouse, is located here and there is a dining room for breakfasts and a piano lounge for dinner.

PAGE HOUSE INN $$
323 Fairfax Ave.
Norfolk
(757) 625-5033
www.pagehouseinn.com

This bed and breakfast is the only AAA 4 Diamond rated lodging in Hampton Roads, an honor it has held for 15 consecutive years. The inn dates to 1899, and it's located next door to the Chrysler Museum of Art in the heart of Ghent and just a few blocks from Granby Street's nightlife. There are seven rooms to rent here, all furnished in period pieces, from brass canopy beds to rooms with gas log fireplaces and whirlpool tubs. They even have a fitness room so you can keep current with your exercise schedule as you relax in history. There's afternoon refreshments, including fresh-baked cookies in the informal parlor and, of course, a breakfast to remember in the dining room every morning. If you want to sleep in, you can pay extra for breakfast to be served in your room.

QUALITY INN NORFOLK
NAVAL BASE $$
8051 Hampton Blvd.
Norfolk
(757) 451-0000

Another hotel less than a mile from the Norfolk Naval Station's main gate, the Quality Inn offers free continental breakfast and Internet, a heated indoor pool and a hot tub. There are 119 rooms here. You can walk to the Tour and Information Office and board one of the bus tours of the world's largest Naval base. If you book in advance you can get a room for under $100 a night here.

SHERATON NORFOLK WATERSIDE $$
777 Waterside Dr.
Norfolk
(757) 622-6664

This hotel helped begin the downtown Renaissance, opening in 1976 as the area's premier lodgings. It's right on the Elizabeth River with wonderful views of the harbor. The entire hotel was recently upgraded in a $32 million renovation. There are 468 rooms and nine luxury suites and a brand new fitness facility that's open around the clock to fit your schedule. There's an outdoor pool and a sundeck where you can dine. You're near the action on Granby Street and also close enough to walk to a baseball game at Harbor Park.

PORTSMOUTH

Most of the places to stay in this historic city are located in or around Olde Towne, the original colonial area. Rates tend to be a little cheaper here in Portsmouth, on the lower end of the price code range, because it really isn't a tourist destination despite one of the best-preserved collections of antique homes in the nation.

COMFORT INN OLDE TOWNE   **$$**
347 Effingham St.
Portsmouth
(757) 397-7788

This Comfort Inn has 62 rooms, an exercise room, and a seasonal outdoor pool. It's 1 mile from the Naval Hospital and offers free continental breakfast and high-speed Internet.

**GLENCOE INN BED AND
BREAKFAST**   **$$**
222 North St.
Portsmouth
(757) 397-8128
www.glencoeinn.com

This home, built in 1890, overlooks the Elizabeth River in Olde Towne. It's won Best of Hampton Roads awards as best overnight stay, best breakfast, and best kept secret. There are four Scottish-themed rooms and a small formal garden, and you're right in the city's most historic area and an easy pedestrian ferry ride to downtown Norfolk as well.

**GOVERNOR DINWIDDIE HOTEL &
SUITES**   **$**
506 Dinwiddie St.
Portsmouth
(757) 392-1330
www.governordinwiddiehotel.com

This hotel was the center of action in the city from the end of World War II to the 1960s, and then fell on hard times. It's been completely restored and updated, and its location, on the corner of High and Dinwiddie Streets, puts it an easy stroll to all the city's best restaurants and nightlife. You get a complimentary hot breakfast buffet here and there's a fitness center with sauna. There are 60 rooms, including suites. You can bring up to two pets for $25 each per night. And there are some smoking rooms.

**THE PATRIOT INN BED
AND BREAKFAST**   **$$**
201 North St.
Portsmouth
(757) 391-0157
www.bbonline.com/va/patriot

A historic inn facing the Elizabeth River, this bed and breakfast was built in 1784 and still features hand-blown windowpanes. The basement here actually goes back to the 1750s. It was all that survived after the building was razed because its owner was a Tory loyal to the king. The four rooms are all decorated in period antiques and reproductions.

**RENAISSANCE PORTSMOUTH
HOTEL AND WATERFRONT
CONFERENCE CENTER**   **$$**
425 Water St.
Portsmouth
(757) 673-3000

This hotel is right on the Elizabeth River with spectacular views of the working harbor and downtown Norfolk. It's an upscale Marriott property with 244 rooms and five luxury suites on its 16 floors and the pride of this city's recent downtown resurgence, hence its name.

CHESAPEAKE

This is a working city, a suburb mostly, with lots of defense contractors in small industrial parks around the Greenbrier area. So most of its lodgings tend to be extended-stay type places or those that cater to the mid-range business traveler. Just about every chain you are familiar with will have a location in the city. Here are a few to get you started.

ALOFT CHESAPEAKE   **$$**
1454 Crossways Blvd.
Chesapeake
(757) 410-9562

One of the newer offerings in Chesapeake, this is a sleek, edgy place to stay just a few minutes from Greenbrier Mall. Every room has wired and wireless Internet and a connectivity station hooked to a 42-inch flat-screen TV. You get the feel of being in a loft, thanks to modern furniture, tall ceilings, and wide windows. There's an indoor pool, a lounge with a pool table, and a gym, and pets are welcome if under 40 pounds or with a special waiver if larger. They also offer a free shuttle to Norfolk International Airport.

CEDARTREE INN & SUITES $
721 Conference Center Dr.
Chesapeake
(757) 366-0100
www.cedartreeinnandsuites.com
This hotel by the Chesapeake Conference Center has 101 guest rooms, all recently remodeled. They all feature in-room DVD players, cable with HBO, and free high-speed Internet. The hotel is also near the Greenbrier Mall.

COURTYARD CHESAPEAKE GREENBRIER $$
1562 Crossways Blvd.
Chesapeake
(757) 420-1700
This Marriott offering is in the Greenbrier Business Park area near the Greenbrier Mall. It offers free shuttle service to Norfolk International Airport, flat-screen TVs, and free high-speed Internet throughout. The lobby and fitness center have been recently redone, and there's an indoor pool and whirlpool. You can print out your airline-boarding pass right in the lobby's 24-hour business center.

HILTON GARDEN INN CHESAPEAKE/ GREENBRIER $$
1565 Crossway Blvd.
Chesapeake
(757) 420-1212
This is another hotel near Greenbrier Mall in the Greenbrier Business Park with all the Hilton Inn amenities. There's a pool, whirlpool, and fitness center as well as free services that cater to traveling business people.

HYATT PLACE CHESAPEAKE/ GREENBRIER $$
709 Eden Way North
Chesapeake
(757) 312-0020
Every room has a 42-inch HDTV, with on-demand movies and DIRECTV SportsNet to tune in professional and college games. There's even a Hyatt Plug Panel that allows you to connect your laptop or other media devices to the HDTV. The fitness center is open around the clock, and there is an indoor pool and Wi-Fi free throughout the hotel.

WINGATE BY WYNDHAM $
817 Greenbrier Circle
Chesapeake
(757) 531-7777
www.wingatechesapeakeva.com
This Greenbrier-area hotel offers a free hot breakfast as well as the usual array of business-travel amenities such as free Internet service, an indoor pool, gym, and even a guest Laundromat.

SUFFOLK

HILTON GARDEN INN SUFFOLK RIVERFRONT $$
100 East Constance Rd.
Suffolk
(757) 925-1300

This hotel and conference center on the six-acre Constance Warf riverfront park opened a few years ago as part of Suffolk's effort to exploit the beauty of the Nansemond River and spark the renewal of the downtown area. The rooms here are all wired for the Internet and also offer Wi-Fi access and secure wireless printing. There's a fitness center, indoor pool and whirlpool. The Constant's Wharf Grill is open for breakfast, lunch and dinner, and room service is available.

HOLIDAY INN EXPRESS $
1018 Centerbrooke Lane
Suffolk
(757) 923-1010

This is typical of the Holiday Inn Express chain—clean, comfortable, and very economical if you book ahead of time. There are 79 rooms here, an outdoor pool, and a fitness center with a sauna. There's also a free hot breakfast bar.

TOWNEPLACE SUITES SUFFOLK $$
8050 Harbour View Blvd.
Suffolk
(757) 483-5177

Northern Suffolk, also known as Harbour View, has become a hotbed for military simulation and other defense industries. There are several hotels up here that provide extended-stay suites to serve this market. This one is part of the Marriott chain and within walking distance of Lockheed Martin's Center for Innovation as well as offices for Northrop Grumman, Raytheon, and General Dynamics. When you're not working, you can enjoy an outdoor pool and a fitness center. Pets are welcome here but smokers are not.

HAMPTON

CROWNE PLAZA HAMPTON MARINA HOTEL $$
700 Settlers Landing Rd.
Hampton
(757) 727-9700
www.hamptonmarinahotel.com

This hotel sits right on Hampton's historic harbor next to the Virginia Air and Space Center and Carousel Park and close to the Cousteau Society and Hampton University. It's the perfect place for a quick, romantic getaway with gorgeous views of the sailboats in the adjacent marina as well as plush accommodations. There are 173 rooms and suites in the hotel, each recently refreshed and overlooking either the water or downtown Hampton. You can pamper yourself with room service or head down to several restaurants, including Oyster Alley, which is open on the water in warm weather. There's a rooftop swimming pool, with a sun deck and concierge service to help with reservations. If you're traveling for the government or in the military, you get breakfast at the buffet for free. Parking here costs $3 a day. There are quiet zones where you are assured no maintenance worker or housekeeper will bother you between 9 p.m. and 10 a.m. and where children and boisterous groups won't be lodged.

EMBASSY SUITES HAMPTON ROADS $$
1700 Coliseum Dr.
Hampton
(757) 827-8200

This lavish hotel, spa, and convention center is located just off Interstates 64 and 664 and near the new Town Center downtown business and shopping area. You get cooked-to-order free breakfasts at a buffet and nightly manager's receptions in the 10-story open-air atrium. There are 295 suites here, each with two televisions, a private bedroom, a refrigerator, microwave, and coffee makers and a dining table. There are smoking and non-smoking rooms available. There's a pool, whirlpool, and fitness center, and a day spa offering massages, hydrotherapy rooms, facials, and other treatments for men and women. Wheelchair-accessible suites have roll-in showers.

HAMPTON INN
HAMPTON–NEWPORT NEWS $$
3101 Coliseum Dr.
Hampton
(757) 838-1400

Hampton Inns had to have a hotel in Hampton, didn't they? Well, they just built one near the new Peninsula Town Center shopping area. It accepts smokers as well as non-smokers, but keeps them in separate areas. Breakfast is free here, as is high-speed Internet access. There's a fitness room and a heated indoor pool as well.

MAGNOLIA HOUSE
BED & BREAKFAST $$
232 South Armistead Ave.
Hampton
(757) 722-2888

This bed and breakfast is located downtown in a Queen Anne Victorian building that is listed on the National Register of Historic Places and the Virginia Landmarks Register. There are two rooms and a suite here. Children are permitted, but those under 13 require innkeeper approval, and there are no pets allowed. Check for special last-minute weekend bargain rates or you can book the entire house for a girl's getaway.

NEWPORT NEWS

THE BOXWOOD INN $$
10 Elmhurst St.
Newport News
(757) 888-8854
www.boxwood-inn.com

This historic home once belonged to Simon Curtis, known as the boss man of Warwick County. It's in the historic Lee Hall area and is a Virginia Historic Landmark in its own right. The home opened as a bed and breakfast in 2000 but had a lot of history before then. General "Black Jack" Pershing is among the many military officers who called at this home, and there's a suite named in his honor. There are two suites and two rooms here, all with queen-sized beds and private baths, and furnished in antiques. Check the website for midweek or out of season specials. No pets, no smoking, and no children. There's a full breakfast every morning, plus an early bird basket for those who have to run and a sleepy head basket for those who would rather stay in their room.

COMFORT SUITES AIRPORT $–$$
12570 Jefferson Ave.
Newport News
(757) 947-1333
www.newportnewscs.com

Sometimes, you just want to stay near the airport so you'll have no trouble making a flight. This hotel is located less than a mile from Newport News Williamsburg International just off I-64, making it convenient if you have business on the Peninsula or just want to head 15 miles north to tour Williamsburg or stop at nearby Busch Gardens without trying to find a place to stay. There's a free shuttle to the airport. These are all suites with a complimentary hot breakfast. There's a heated indoor swimming pool and fitness center and free Internet, both wired and wireless.

COURTYARD BY MARRIOTT NEWPORT NEWS AIRPORT $$
530 St. Johns Rd.
Newport News
(757) 842-6212

Another option if you want to stay by the airport here. This is a newly built hotel with all the Courtyard features, including indoor pool, fitness center, free wireless Internet, and flat-screen TVs. It's close to the city's business district and 15 minutes from Colonial Williamsburg.

HOLIDAY INN HOTEL & SUITES NEWPORT NEWS $$
943 J. Clyde Morris Blvd.
Newport News
(757) 596-6417

A relatively small Holiday Inn, just 122 rooms and 19 suites, this is a recently built five-floor facility right off I-64. It's also close to the airport and an easy ride to Williamsburg or any of the area military bases.

MARRIOTT NEWPORT NEWS AT CITY CENTER $$
740 Town Center Dr.
Newport News
(757) 873-9299

This 250-room hotel is right at the city's upscale retail, restaurant, and business district. It has the largest Grand Ballroom in the area and has been named a Virginia Green Lodging award winner for its environmental efforts. Floor-to-ceiling windows look out on a five-acre fountain and the City Center complex. On-site parking is $6 per day, $12 for valet service, but there is free parking nearby. There are two special concierge levels, but all rooms have CD players, cable TV with HBO, and pay-per-view movies.

OMNI NEWPORT NEWS HOTEL $$
1000 Omni Blvd.
Newport News
(757) 873-6664

This luxury hotel is in a little oasis off I-64 at the heart of City Center. There are 181 rooms and suites here, an indoor swimming pool, whirlpool, and a recently spruced-up fitness center. All the modern conveniences, from free Wi-Fi to on-demand movies are offered. You can bring a small pet for a $50 nonrefundable deposit. There's an Italian restaurant here and a nightclub, Tribeca, which features live music and dancing until 2 a.m.

RESTAURANTS

Hampton Roads is in the South, but food wise it is far from a Southern city. Sure, if you search, you can find plenty of places dishing up grits and red-eye gravy, but that's not what we're noted for. Here, seafood is king. And why not? The Chesapeake Bay is the world's greatest estuary, a sanctuary and incubator for just about anything that swims. And when those fry mature, they head right out to the nearby Atlantic, where the parallel conveyor belts of the warm Gulf Stream and the cold Labrador Current ensure there's always lots to eat and no real reason for fish to migrate out of the reach of our watermen.

OVERVIEW

Not a fish eater? Don't despair. You can enjoy our many barbecue joints; in fact, you can pick between two local styles: Virginia barbecue sauce is red, rich, and tangy, while North Carolina makes its version nearly clear and heavy on vinegar and pepper flakes. Both states insist that barbecue means pork, slow roasted in smoky ovens over real hardwood. You can barbecue beef, they say, but that's why you buy a backyard grill.

There's also a diversity of dining few other Southern cities can boast. It comes from hundreds of years of military forces rotating in and out to local bases and bringing their local appetites and demand for the foods they left behind. So you'll find Philly cheesesteaks served on authentic Amoroso rolls trucked in from the Philadelphia bakery. The better Italian restaurants get their supplies directly from New York City's Little Italy.

Love Filipino food? There's a huge community here, thanks to the Navy. The same with Thai and other ethnic specialties.

Bottom line: if you hanker for some type of food, there's probably a place here that makes it, and makes it well. And if there's a national chain, you can bet it has outlets here. I won't spend lots of time on those, since you're probably familiar with their offerings. Instead, what follows are the local gems that keep us coming back.

In each listing you'll see a $ code. It's the Insider guide to relative pricing based on the cost of an average dinner for two, minus desert or alcoholic beverages. Of course, it should go without saying that things change. The restaurant business is very volatile. Chefs bounce between eateries, changing items or even entire menus. Places, even landmarks, close or change hands. So be sure to call before driving across the region.

So enough with the preliminaries. Here are the best, broken down into neighborhoods and then genres.

Price Code

Based on an average dinner for two, without drinks, appetizers, desserts, or tips. Unless it's a lunch only place, you can usually figure on one fewer $ for afternoon meals.

$.....................	**Under $20**
$$	**$20 to $40**
$$$	**$41 to $60**
$$$$	**Over $60**

Famous Uncle Al's Hot Dogs, Chesapeake/Norfolk/Virginia Beach, Hamburgers/Hot Dogs/Grill, $, 63, 74, 80

Fellini's Gourmet Pizza Cafe, Norfolk, Italian, $$, 75

58 Delicatessen, Virginia Beach, Deli/Sandwiches, $$, 62

Five Guys Famous Burgers and Fries, Chesapeake/Virginia Beach, Hamburgers/Hot Dogs/Grill, $, 63, 80

Forbidden City, Virginia Beach, Chinese, $$, 61

456 Fish, Norfolk, Seafood, $$$, 77

Frankie's Place For Ribs, Virginia Beach, Barbecue, $$, 61

Franks II Italian Restaurant, Chesapeake, Italian, $$, 81

Freemason Abbey, Norfolk, Seafood, $$$, 78

Gah Bua Kham, Hampton, Thai, $$, 85

George's Steakhouse, Suffolk, Steaks, $$, 84

The German Pantry Restaurant & Bierhaus, Norfolk, Germany, $$, 74

The Grate Steak, Norfolk, steak, $$$, 79

Great Bridge BBQ, Chesapeake, Barbecue, $, 79

The Grill at Great Bridge, Chesapeake, Hamburgers/Hot Dogs/Grill, $, 80

Guadalajara, Virginia Beach, Mexican, $$, 67, 76

Hayashi Sushi & Grill, Newport News, Japanese, $$, 86

The Heritage Cafe, Virginia Beach, Deli/Sandwiches, $, 62

Il Giardino Ristorante, Virginia Beach, Italian, $$$, 66

Jammin Jerk BBQ, Suffolk, Caribbean, $, 84

The Jewish Mother, Virginia Beach, Deli/Sandwiches $$, 62

Jewish Mother Backstage at the NorVa, Norfolk, American, $-$$, 72

Johnson's Barbecue, Chesapeake, Barbecue, $, 79

Kelly's Tavern, Chesapeake/Hampton/Newport News/Norfolk/Virginia Beach, Hamburgers/Hot Dogs/Grill, $-$$, 64, 74, 81, 84, 85

Kin's Wok, Norfolk, Chinese, $, 72

La Bella Italia, Virginia Beach, Italian, $$, 66

Luna Maya, Norfolk, Mexican, $$, 77

Lynnhaven Fish House, Virginia Beach, Seafood, $$$, 69

Machismo Burrito Bar, Norfolk, Mexican, $, 77

Mahi Mahs Seafood Restaurant & Sushi Saloon, Virginia Beach, Seafood, $$$, 69

Mary's Restaurant, Virginia Beach, American, $, 60

Mi Casita Mexican Restaurant, Virginia Beach, Mexican, $, 67

Mi Hogar Mexican Restaurant, Norfolk, Mexican, $, 77

Mizuno Japanese Restaurant, Virginia Beach, Japanese, $$$, 66

The Monastery Restaurant, Norfolk, Fine Dining, $$, 74

Nawab, Newport News/Norfolk/Virginia Beach, Indian, $$, 65, 75, 86

New York Deli, Portsmouth, Hamburgers/Hot Dogs/Deli, $, 83

99 Main Restaurant, Newport News, American, $$$, 85

No Frill Bar and Grill, Norfolk/Virginia Beach, American, $$, 60, 72

Old Hampton Seafood Kitchen, Hampton, Seafood, $, 85

Orapax Inn, Norfolk, Greek/Mediterranean/Middle Eastern, $$, 74

O'Sullivan's Wharf, Norfolk, Seafood, $$, 78

Pasha Mezze, Chesapeake, Greek/Mediterranean/Middle Eastern, $$, 80

P.F. Chang's China Bistro, Virginia Beach, Chinese, $$$, 61

Philly Style Steaks and Subs, Norfolk, Hamburgers/Hot Dogs/Grill, $, 74

Pho 78, Virginia Beach, Vietnamese, $, 71

Pho 79, Virginia Beach, Vietnamese $, 71

Pierce's, Williamsburg, Barbecue, $, 82

Plaza Azteca Restaurantes Mexicanos, Chesapeake/ Hampton/Newport News/ Suffolk/Virginia Beach, Mexican, $, 67, 81, 84, 85, 87

Primo 116 Bistro Italiano, Suffolk, Italian, $$$, 84

Queens Way Soul Cafe, Hampton, Soul Food, $$, 85

Rajput Indian Cuisine, Norfolk, Indian, $$, 75

Regino's Italian Restaurant, Norfolk, Italian, $$, 75

Rocky Mount Bar-B-Q, Newport News, Barbecue, $, 86

Rodman's Bones & Buddys, Portsmouth, Barbecue, $, 82

Sai Gai Traditional Japanese Steak House & Sushi Bar, Norfolk, Japanese, $$, 76

Saigon 1, Virginia Beach, Vietnamese, $, 71

San Antonio Sam's Cafe Saloon, Norfolk, Mexican, $$, 77

Schlesinger's, Newport News, Steak, $$$$, 87

Ship's Cabin, Norfolk, Seafood, $$, 78

Shogun Japanese Steakhouse, Virginia Beach, Japanese, $$, 66

Shorebreak Pizza, Virginia Beach, Hamburgers/Hot Dogs/Grill, $, 65

Simply Thai, Chesapeake, Thai, $$, 81

Sirena Cucina Italiana, Norfolk, Italian, $$$, 76

Smokehouse & Cooler, Virginia Beach, Barbecue, $$, 61

Steinhilbers, Virginia Beach, Seafood, $$$$, 69

Sumo Japanese Steak House, Virginia Beach, Japanese, $$, 66

Tabb's at Riverview, Norfolk, Seafood, $$, 78

Taste Unlimited, Newport News/Norfolk, Virginia Beach, Deli/Sandwiches, $, 62, 86

Tautog's Restaurant at Winston's Cottage, Virginia Beach, Seafood, $$, 70

Thaijindesu Thai & Sushi Bar, Newport News, Japanese/Thai, $$, 86

3 Amigos, Chesapeake/ Virginian Beach, Mexican, $, 67, 81

Tida Thai Cuisine, Virginia Beach, Thai, $$, 70, 82

Todd Jurich's Bistro, Norfolk, Fine Dining, $$$$, 73

Tony's Hot Dogs, Virginia Beach, Hamburgers/Hot Dogs/Grill, $, 64

Veneziano Restaurant, Norfolk, Italian, $$, 76

Vietnam Garden, Virginia Beach, Vietnamese, $$, 71

Vintage Kitchen, Norfolk, Hamburgers/Hot Dogs/ Grill, $, 75

Vintage Tavern, Suffolk, American, $$$, 83

Warriors Mongolian Grill, Virginia Beach, Chinese, $$, 61

Wilkes Barbeque, Hampton, Barbecue, $, 85

Willoughby Inn Seafood Restaurant, Norfolk, Seafood, $$, 78

Wood Chick's BBQ, Chesapeake, Barbecue, $, 79

Yanni's Casual Greek, Virginia Beach, Greek/ Mediterranean/Middle Eastern, $$$, 63

Zero's Subs, Virginia Beach, Deli/Sandwiches, $, 62

Zoe's, Virginia Beach, American, $$$, 60

Zushi Japanese Bistro, Virginia Beach, Japanese, $$, 66

VIRGINIA BEACH

Most of us locals don't venture past Lynnhaven Boulevard once the weather gets warm. We hate bucking the tourist traffic or paying for parking. Obviously the vacation strip has lots of places to eat, and a few are good enough to get us to brave the beach.

American

BEACH PUB $
1001 Laskin Rd.
Virginia Beach
(757) 422-8817

This is no fancy-pants place. But it's where you'll find blue-collar locals enjoying blue-plate specials. The seafood here is mostly fried, but it's fried well. And don't let the name throw you. It's nowhere near the beach and it's more diner than pub, unless your pub is known for crab omelets at breakfast. Bottom line: it's a good place to fill your tank without taking out a mortgage.

MARY'S RESTAURANT $
616 Virginia Beach Blvd.
Virginia Beach
(757) 428-1355
www.marys-restaurant.com

They may officially call it Mary's Restaurant, but for the past 40 years it's been known to locals as Mary's Country Kitchen. It's six blocks from the Boardwalk on 17th Street (that's what Virginia Beach Boulevard becomes down at the Oceanfront) so it's close enough to get the tourist trade. But they have to fight the regulars for seats for the $2.99 breakfast specials served daily from 6 to 9 a.m. This is strictly a breakfast and lunch place. It closes at 3 p.m.

NO FRILL BAR AND GRILL $$
1620 Laskin Rd.
Virginia Beach
(757) 425-2900
www.nofrillgrill.com

See the Norfolk location's review on page 72.

ZOE'S $$$
713 19th St.
Virginia Beach
(757) 437-3636
www.zoesvb.com

This is the beloved Zoe's second incarnation, and *Hampton Roads Magazine* voted it the region's best restaurant of any type in 2010 with a nearly perfect score by its judges. Here, you can watch chef Jerry Weihbrecht, who cooked at the James Beard House in NYC, whip up his special Blue Crab Mac-n-Cheese creation in the open-style kitchen.

Barbecue

THE BEACH BULLY $$
601 19th St.
Virginia Beach
(757) 422-4222
www.beachbully.com

This restaurant got its start at local outdoor festivals. The owners began with charcoal grills and frozen hamburgers, but soon moved to pulled pork and then beef, which is now the basis for the signature Beach Bully sandwich. They moved from a smaller location at the Oceanfront to their current one between the Atlantic and the Virginia Beach Convention Center. They still cater, by the way. The menu features barbecue chicken, pork and beef ribs and beef brisket in addition to their sandwich, as well as grilled tuna for those who want the surf experience.

FRANKIE'S PLACE FOR RIBS $$
5200 Fairfield Shopping Center
(Kempsville and Providence)
Virginia Beach
(757) 495-RIBS
www.frankiesribs.com

Yeah, they do pulled pork, but their name says it all. This is where you go for those baby back ribs. It's casual and that's good, because you'll probably get messy and want to lick your fingers a few times as you attack your rack. You can also get beef ribs and barbecue chicken here, or stop trying to decide and grab a combo. They've been going strong for nearly 30 years so they must be doing something very right.

SMOKEHOUSE & COOLER $$
2957 Shore Dr.
Virginia Beach
(757) 481-9737
www.smokehouseandcooler.com

For more than a decade, this restaurant in Chick's Beach has been cooking up multicultural barbecue in the Lynnhaven Beach Square Shopping Center. No, I don't mean it mixes Virginia and North Carolina approaches to pork. Chef Rob Murphy, who once worked at the Ritz-Carlton in Houston, uses international spices in his Asian, Caribbean, Cajun, and Creole inspired cuisine that makes it hard to categorize. The restaurant has been featured on the Food Network for "best of" barbecue bites. It annually gets nods as one of the region's best restaurants of any type by *Hampton Roads Magazine*. Here you'll find crispy beef eggrolls (the Food Network's winners) as well as dishes made with lamb, chicken, and even salmon.

Chinese

FORBIDDEN CITY $$
3333 Virginia Beach Blvd.
Virginia Beach
(757) 747-2388
www.forbiddencityvb.com

This isn't a corner Chinese takeout, but an upscale eatery that prepares Cantonese, Mandarin, and Szechuan delicacies. There are also vegetarian offerings and a dim sum menu. It's an annual best-of winner.

P.F. CHANG'S CHINA BISTRO $$$
4551 Virginia Beach Blvd.
Virginia Beach
(757) 473-9028
www.pfchangs.com

Okay, this is an international chain, but I'd be remiss not to include it here, since folks often line up out the door for a chance at a table. This is another upscale Chinese restaurant. You can order from a "for two" menu and get four courses for $40 or go exploring solo for potentially a lot more dough.

WARRIORS MONGOLIAN GRILL $$
401 North Great Neck Rd.
Virginia Beach
(757) 498-0323
www.warriorsgrill.com

This is an airy restaurant where you pick your components and let the chef stir it over a large, flat, iron plate. It's done with a long wooden stick as he or she walks in circles like a horse driving a mill stone. But the result is delicious and seasoned just like you want it. Genghis Khan's troops conquered the world using their shields as woks. It's one price for unlimited trips to the cookery.

Delis/Sandwiches

58 DELICATESSEN $$
4000 Virginia Beach Blvd.
Virginia Beach
(757) 227-5868

The sandwiches aren't cheap here, but they're stuffed New York style with real deli meats. You can satisfy your lox longing or indulge in some smoked whitefish salad.

THE HERITAGE CAFE $
314 Laskin Rd.
Virginia Beach
(757) 428-0500
www.theheritagecafe.com

This little cafe offers vegetarian and natural food items, including sandwiches, salads, fruit smoothies, organic vegetable juices, and daily lunch specials. Grab something then wander the adjacent health food and book stores. There's a plan to upgrade this block just off Atlantic Avenue so it's unclear how long this landmark will remain. Enjoy it while you can.

THE JEWISH MOTHER $$
3108 Pacific Ave.
Virginia Beach
(757) 422-5430
www.jewishmother.com

Back in 1975, Virginia Beach had no deli, so three partners got together and opened one, with a lot of help from the Jewish mother of one of the guys. Hence the name. The fame came with good food that cured the homesickness of displaced Northeasterners. It's not for nothing that they call the chicken soup here "penicillin soup." Soon the Mother was also getting famous for the musical acts that played the tiny venue. It's still one of the best places in the area to hear blues, up close and personal. And on Sunday afternoons, there's usually live classical guitar. But this restaurant too is in the crosshairs of that upgrade, so call before you head out.

TASTE UNLIMITED $
36th St. & Pacific Ave.
Virginia Beach
(757) 422-3399
www.tasteunlimited.com

This locally owned chain specializes in gourmet food items and sandwiches on fresh-baked bread with secret house dressings. Their motto is "Taste the Good Life," and their sandwiches live up to it. The offerings range from crab cake to a vegetarian sandwich known as the Princess Anne, Surry ham to curried chicken salad. Or you can mix and match any of their ingredients to make your own creation. And while you're in the store, check out one of their weekly free wine tastings. Two other Virginia Beach locations are at 4097 Shore Dr., (757) 464-1566 and Hilltop West Shopping Center, (757) 425-1858.

ZERO'S SUBS $
Two dozen area locations
www.zeros.com

This regional fast-food franchise got its start in Virginia Beach in 1967 with the idea that subs would taste a lot better if you baked them just before serving. They take good ingredients, put them together, and then place the sandwiches on a conveyor that pulls them through a super hot oven. The result is melted cheese and accentuated flavors. They also use the oven to make pizzas and offer wings, salads, and wraps. There are now 40 stores in nine states and franchises in China and New Zealand. In Hampton Roads you can find 5 restaurants in Chesapeake, 3 in Hampton, 4 in Norfolk, 1 each in Portsmouth and Suffolk, and 10 in their birthplace of Virginia Beach.

Greek/Mediterranean/Middle Eastern

AMMOS GREEK RESTAURANT $$
1401 Atlantic Ave.
Virginia Beach
(off the Boardwalk inside Sandcastle
Hotel Mall)
(757) 313-6083
www.ammosvb.com

This is a Greek experience on the Oceanfront, a restaurant offering a full range of Greek and Mediterranean meals as well as a Greek show, complete with belly dancing on some nights.

ATHENS PIZZA RESTAURANT $
1929 Centerville Turnpike
Virginia Beach
(757) 479-9873

This eatery across from the Woods Corner Shopping Center offers up gyros, subs, Greek salad, and spaghetti as well as pizza.

AZAR'S NATURAL FOODS $$
108 Prescott Ave.
Virginia Beach
(757) 486-7778

At Azar's two Hampton Roads locations, they don't limit themselves to any one country. Food and groceries sold here reflect the heritage of many locations, including Greek, Turkish, Lebanese, Moroccan, Spanish, and Italian. It's often voted the best restaurant for healthy eating by readers of *The Virginian-Pilot*. And when you leave, be sure to pick up one of their special dips and spreads.

YANNI'S CASUAL GREEK $$$
2101 McComas Way
Virginia Beach
(757) 689-2533

A relatively recent entry in the Greek genre, Yanni's is already winning a loyal base. It's family owned and operated and offers up a full range of traditional Greek meals and homemade desserts.

Hamburgers/Hot Dogs/Grill

FAMOUS UNCLE AL'S HOT DOGS $
3972 Holland Rd. #12D
Virginia Beach
(757) 486-8449

This is now a national chain, but it began right here in Virginia Beach when "Uncle Al" Stein of Brooklyn opened up a Coney Island–style restaurant like the ones he used to work at growing up. He imported his dogs from New York and the rest is history. Locals annually vote his the best hot dogs. The restaurants offer more than just grilled wieners. There's also a variety of deli sandwiches on the menu. Other Virginia Beach locations include: 1581 General Booth Blvd., (757) 333-3373; 5349 Kemps River Dr., (757) 420-7366; 3045 Shore Dr., (757) 481-2718; 2828 Virginia Beach Blvd., (757) 486-5727; and 928 Diamond Springs Rd., (757) 333-2660.

FIVE GUYS FAMOUS BURGERS AND FRIES $
5240 Fairfield Shopping Center
Virginia Beach
(757) 474-2222
www.fiveguys.com

This is a chain that started up the road in the Washington D.C. area. What you get here is what the name suggests: burgers, thick and plump and cooked to your order with all sorts of fixin's and fries that come in a large brown paper bag that sops up the peanut oil. Peanuts are part of the decor as well. Throughout the restaurant are stacks of large boxes of the goobers, the top one open with an invitation to dig in while you wait for your burger to be grilled. Don't fill up on the great

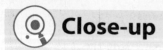

Close-up

The Norfolk Hot Dog

It all began off City Hall Avenue at **Bacalis' Hot Dog Place**, where the Greek-born George Bacalis carved out a living and a fanatical following making one product perfectly: thick-skinned Hormel wieners grilled just right, then slathered in a special chili with a squirt of yellow mustard and some chopped onions. Sure, you had a choice here. You could omit onions, mustard, or chili. But why would you? The combination was ethereal, a blend of snap and spice and bite and a lingering and delightful taste that made the humble frank something regal.

Over his 40 years in business, Bacalis hired a few fellow Greek immigrants to help keep up with the demand, and thus began a long tradition of Greek hot dog emporiums that continues to this day. The family resemblance is eerie: stark counter joints, the owner less-than-chatty, sometimes even hostile, as he works the grill. Hand lettered signs, and lawyers sitting elbow to elbow with construction workers, lost in the joy of an American classic. But we're getting ahead of ourselves.

Bacalis' begat Jimmy's. Jimmy Rellos, his long-time grill man, opened his own location on a back road in Virginia Beach. It didn't matter that this was a lunch-only place and nowhere near the tourist traps or Norfolk's employment centers. Jimmy's Formica counter was full every day for more than 35 years until he and his wife Effie, better known as Mrs. Jimmy, finally retired with a flourish in 2008—with people lined up out the door for a chance to get their last chili dog.

It also begat Tony's. Tony Mirabelle left in 1970 to open his own eatery on Lafayette Boulevard. After Tony died, his widow continued to operate the restaurant. One son went across the street and competed from a cart. Another son, Phil, carries on the tradition at **Tony's Hot Dogs** (412 Newtown Rd., 757-497-7850; $) in Virginia Beach, just over the Norfolk border.

Step in here, and you're back at Bacalis' dog joint. Phil isn't one for conversation, and you'd do well not to force the issue. But like Bacalis and his father and Jimmy before, he does his talking holding two buns in one hand while dressing them with some of that smooth, spicy all-meat Greek chili.

Does the final product taste just like George's or Jimmy's or even his father's? Regulars can argue for hours about the subtle differences. Who cares? It's still a Norfolk hot dog, done in a place where that's all that matters. Grab two and a drink, sit at the counter or one of the few tables, and take a bite. This is no ballpark frank, dependant on the surroundings for enjoyment. Nope, this is the American Dream on a plate, proof that one perfect product prepared with integrity can feed and educate a family for generations. Just don't ask for ketchup, it could get ugly.

peanuts, though, because even the small burger is plenty big enough. And if you order fries, one bag should do it for the entire table. Also located at 750 Independence Blvd., Virginia Beach, (757) 519-9001.

KELLY'S TAVERN $–$$
Hilltop
1936 Laskin Rd., Suite #201
Virginia Beach
(757) 491-8737
www.kellystavern.com

This is an 11-restaurant chain that stretches throughout Hampton Roads. The Ghent eatery opened in 1983 and quickly made its mark with huge burgers and a relaxed atmosphere. The restaurant annually wins best burger awards and has also gotten ribbons for its hot dogs, wings, and crab soup. But you can go fancier with entrees that can take the bill up a notch. They don't accept personal checks but are fine with credit cards. A few other Virginia Beach locations are 1830 Kempsville Rd., (757) 479-3940; Pembroke Mall, 4586 Virginia Beach Blvd., (757) 490-7999; and Strawbridge, 2131 General Booth Blvd., (757) 430-8999.

SHOREBREAK PIZZA $
2941 Shore Dr.
Virginia Beach
(757) 481-9393

These folks came in a tie for close second in the local newspaper's search for the area's best burger. And the addition of sweet potato chips to every plate didn't hurt.

Indian

NAWAB $$
756 First Colonial Rd.
Virginia Beach
(757) 491-8600
www.nawabonline.com

This is a small, family-run local chain of elegant Indian restaurants that began outside Military Circle Mall in 1992. The name is Punjabi for a man of means and the food is fit for such a discriminating palate. You'll find all of your favorites on the menu from fiery hot dishes to curries with subtle flavorings. The naan bread is freshly made, you can get tandoori specials or vegetarian offerings that won't leave you hankering for meat. The

best deal is the lunch buffet every afternoon where a single price buys unlimited trips to what amounts to a best-of sampler selection. Over the years, the family expanded to other areas, including Roanoke, West Virginia and North Carolina, but those restaurants are now independently owned and operated by friends and relatives so the original family can concentrate on the Hampton Roads area.

Italian

ALDO'S RISTORANTE $$
La Prominade Shopping Center
1860 Laskin Rd.
Virginia Beach
(757) 491-1111
www.aldosvb.com

A live pianist on Friday and Saturday nights sets the mood at this perennial favorite. The food also nets it annual Best of the Beach awards.

BELLA MONTE INTERNATIONAL MARKET PLACE AND CAFE $$
1201 Laskin Rd., Suite 100
Virginia Beach
(757) 425-6290
www.bellamontevb.com

It started as a little Italian grocery, importing fine cheese and olive oils from New York's Little Italy. Soon, people were crowding the place for the prepared foods and sandwiches. Eventually, Bella Monte moved to the Hilltop North shopping center and went upscale, complete with a piano bar. You can still buy imported meats and cheeses, fresh bread, and gourmet items, but there's also a romantic restaurant where you can indulge yourself in Italian delicacies.

IL GIARDINO RISTORANTE $$$
910 Atlantic Ave.
Virginia Beach
(757) 422-6464
www.ilgiardino.com

They have a wood-fueled oven at this Oceanfront restaurant where they bake their pizzas and fresh focaccia bread served with flavored olive oil. I shouldn't have to say it, but the sauces here are all home made. In the off season, they have a Sunday two-for-one special.

LA BELLA ITALIA $$
1065 Laskin Rd.
Virginia Beach
(757) 422-8536
www.labellaitalia.com

Another local favorite that started as a bakery and deli and then added a restaurant. When you walk in, you see a deli fully stocked with home-made foods, fresh mozzarella, pastries, breads, and cookies. You can buy the fixings for a meal or a meal ready to heat and eat, or just relax and enjoy a sit-down experience. It's a family-run operation that has attracted a loyal following in its dozen years and recently spawned a second restaurant at the Redmill shopping center. La Bella Italia Redmill (757-301-3603) is located at 2133 Upton Dr., Suite 128 in Virginia Beach.

Japanese

MIZUNO JAPANESE RESTAURANT $$$
1860 Laskin Rd.
Virginia Beach
(757) 422-1200
www.mizuno-sushi.com

Chef/owner Wataru Mizuno earned the title "master sushi chef" working in Tokyo, where he studied under fabled Master Chef Teruo Sato. Needless to say, the offerings here are made individually under his hand. The specialties of the house include toro tataki, calamari tempura, Mizuno roll, and tuna crunchy crunch. You can pick your own or let the chef put together a selection. You can even reserve your own Tatami room for parties of 10 to 12. The restaurant is closed on Monday.

SHOGUN JAPANESE STEAKHOUSE $$
550 1st Colonial Rd.
Virginia Beach
(757) 422-5150
www.shogunvabeach.com

Another longtime local hibachi steakhouse and sushi restaurant, Shogun has been around for more than 20 years and has been voted Best in the Beach by *The Virginian-Pilot*'s readers for 17 of them. Don't judge this place by its façade.

SUMO JAPANESE STEAK HOUSE $$
116 Independence Blvd.
Virginia Beach
(757) 497-6420
www.sumosteakhouse.com

Tucked away in the back of a small strip mall, this restaurant does the typical Japanese steakhouse hibachi show and does it well. It also has a following for its sushi offerings. It's a good place to take the family.

ZUSHI JAPANESE BISTRO $$
4540 Main St.
Virginia Beach
(757) 321-1495

One of the mainstays of Virginia Beach's new downtown, you can get your fresh sushi here while listening to smooth jazz.

Mexican

EL AZTECA $
314 Constitution Dr.
Virginia Beach
(757) 473-1746
www.elaztecamr.net
Not to be confused with Plaza Azteca, this is another family-run restaurant with several venues here in Hampton Roads. Quick, tasty food is the calling card here.

GUADALAJARA MEXICAN
CANTINA $$
200 21st St.
Virginia Beach
(757) 433-0140
www.guadalajaravb.com
A favorite that has been sprouting locations here since 1997, this is a more upscale Mexican eatery with a different feel at each of the restaurants. The Oceanfront store (200 21st St.) is casual, with a patio to enjoy the ocean breezes. The tropical cafe (2149 General Booth Blvd., 757-563-2926) has a Miami and Caribbean feel. The City Cafe in Norfolk (411 Granby St., 757-622-2489) has a New York vibe complete with sidewalk dining. And the Town Center restaurant on Columbus Street (4611 Columbus St., 757-493-8696) in Virginia Beach's "downtown" is glitzy, with fiber-optic bars that transforms into a dance venue after 10 p.m. on Fri and Sat. Other locations: 2272 West Great Neck Rd., (757) 481-5511 and 509 Hilltop Plaza Shopping Center, (757) 491-1613.

MI CASITA MEXICAN RESTAURANT $
3600 Bonney Rd.
Virginia Beach
(757) 463-3819
www.micasitamexican.com
Another local favorite, Mi Casita has been dishing up authentic Mexican fare since 1992 that's quick and tasty. They don't make anything super hot, though, so if you want to scald your taste buds, you'll need to ask or add hot sauce. They have a nice selection of Mexican-style seafood and vegetarian offerings.

PLAZA AZTECA RESTAURANTES
MEXICANOS $
5209 Providence Rd.
Virginia Beach
(757) 474-2698
www.plazaazteca.com
With 10 restaurants spread throughout Hampton Roads, you're always a short drive from this popular chain. The decor is rustic pine, the atmosphere family friendly, and the food is classic Mexican-American. They have vegetarian offerings on the menu as well as all your favorites in chicken, beef, and pork. Three other Virginia Beach locations are at 4292 Holland Rd., (757) 431-8135; 1824 Laskin Rd., (757) 425-1676; and 4501 Haygood Rd., (757) 363-7495.

3 AMIGOS $
1920 Centerville Turnpike
Virginia Beach
(757) 479-4100
This is a small local chain, with additional restaurants in Yorktown and Elizabeth City, N.C. The restaurants are located in neighborhood strip malls and offer the full standard Mexican fare. One treat is the "special dinner for two," a way to save a couple bucks and fill up by sharing what is essentially a Mexican sampler order. Don't tell them it's your birthday if you don't want the wait crew singing at your table.

Seafood

AWFUL ARTHUR'S OYSTER BAR $$
1630 General Booth Blvd.
Virginia Beach
(757) 426-7300
www.awfuls.com

This is a neighborhood raw bar and restaurant situated not far from the Oceana or Dam Neck naval bases where you can take your pick of southern or northern oysters or clams, raw or steamed, as well as steamed shrimp and New Zealand mussels, burgers, or fresh fish.

BLUE PETE'S $$$
1400 North Muddy Creek Rd.
Virginia Beach
(757) 453-6478
www.bluepetes.com

Talk about off the beaten path. Blue Pete's is located deep in the heart of Pungo, which is where Virginia Beach's beach and farm worlds collide. But the restaurant on Muddy Creek is legendary for good food and great service. You have to be special to stay in business this long this far from the tourist crowds or even local population centers. Blue Pete's is a destination dine, a romantic getaway. And it isn't open every day, so check, or better yet make a reservation, before heading out. Mention you're heading to Pungo and locals will ask if you're going to Blue Pete's. And if you are, be sure to pack a GPS or a good map. It's easy to get lost down there.

BUBBA'S SEAFOOD RESTAURANT & CRABHOUSE $$
3323 Shore Dr.
Virginia Beach
(757) 481-0907

Really like your fish fresh? Then wander over to Bubba's. Attached to the famous Bubba's Marina where local anglers line up on weekends to launch and retrieve their boats, this is dining at its most relaxed. From your table on the covered deck, you can enjoy the endless stream of vessels coming and going and even critique their captains while you eat. If the weather is bad, you can head inside for a bit of air-conditioning.

CAPTAIN GEORGE'S $$$
1956 Laskin Rd.
Virginia Beach
(757) 428-3494
www.captaingeorges.com

Now for a true change of pace, I offer up Captain George's Seafood Restaurant, the giant mother ship of a locally based chain of upscale seafood buffets. This restaurant is hard to miss, with its large neon sailboat sign and the bow of a square rigger protruding from the front of the building. The beach restaurant has become a tourist attraction and boasts a pair of the largest stained glass domes under one roof. (Each weighs more than five tons and took a year to complete.) If you eat your seafood by the pound, the all's-included buffet can be a bargain. The restaurant is only closed on Christmas Day. With outlets as well in Williamsburg, on the Outer Banks, and in Myrtle Beach, Captain George's is a seafood giant that claims to have booked 1/13th of the world's supply of crab legs in 2004. Every year, they go through a million pounds of the legs, 250,000 pounds of steamed or fried shrimp, and 10 tons of fryer oil.

CHARLIE'S SEAFOOD RESTAURANT $$
3139 Shore Dr.
Virginia Beach
(757) 481-9863
www.charliesseafood.com

Step inside this cinderblock building and you are transported half a century, to a time when Roy Rogers still rode the range, restaurants were built by families, and decor meant Formica, linoleum, and lots of simple wood. Charlie's has been operating this way for more than six decades. The only concession to time is the flat-screen TV now hung between the taxidermy fish at the end of the oyster bar. You don't need gimmicks when you make seafood as well as they do at Charlie's. The place's signature dish is she-crab soup; it's a thick, creamy concoction full of delicate lump crab meat with a hint of sherry that many combine with an appetizer and call it a meal. If you go that route, try pairing a bowl of the soup with an order of the barbecued oysters, delicate morsels on the half shell with bits of bacon and cheese and doused in a subtle barbecue sauce before being roasted under a broiler. They don't take personal checks, but usually have a discount coupon on their website and do give discounts to seniors and active duty military.

COASTAL GRILL $$$
1427 North Great Neck Rd.
Virginia Beach
(757) 496-3348
www.coastalgrill.com
A local favorite for two decades, this restaurant has won numerous awards for "classic, upscale cuisine." The menu is merely a guide here; check the blackboard for the chef's daily seafood creations. You can begin your meal with a pot of mussels steamed with thyme, onion, and tomato. Soft shell crabs are a specialty of the house.

LYNNHAVEN FISH HOUSE $$$
2350 Starfish Rd.
Virginia Beach
(757) 481-0003
www.lynnhavenfishhouse.net
Another long-time beach stalwart, this dressier casual bay-front restaurant has been voted "Best Seafood Restaurant" in Hampton Roads for 17 consecutive years by the local *Portfolio* magazine. The place is built right on the dunes with panoramic views of the Chesapeake Bay that are every bit as enticing as the fresh-caught menu offerings. She-crab soup is also a staple here and many think it's the best in the region.

MAHI MAH'S SEAFOOD RESTAURANT
& SUSHI SALOON $$$
615 Atlantic Ave.
Virginia Beach
(757) 437-8030
www.mahimahs.com
Rarely can a hotel restaurant boast being one of the favorites with locals, but Mahi Mah's, located on the water in the Oceanfront Ramada Inn, is just that. On the Boardwalk and overlooking the Atlantic Ocean, it's a place to see and be seen. This is a romantic restaurant to celebrate a special occasion or just to savor the award-winning seafood. There is a pair of outdoor patios and a stage that features local musicians. This is right on the strip, so be sure to make reservations during the season. And it's so popular reservations are probably a good idea even in the dead of winter.

STEINHILBERS $$$$
653 Thalia Rd.
Virginia Beach
(757) 340-1156
www.steinys.com

This is the area's most elegant seafood eatery. It's pricy, with appetizers running as much as many other place's entrees. And it's far from the tourist strip, which is no accident. Not too long ago, they closed down for the summer season rather than endure the crowds. Still, it consistently comes in among the top rated restaurants in the entire area. The atmosphere along the Lynnhaven River is romantic, the staff attentive, and the chef one of those locals follow from kitchen to kitchen.

TAUTOG'S RESTAURANT AT
  WINSTON'S COTTAGE   **$$**
205 23rd St.
Virginia Beach
(757) 422-0081
www.tautogs.com

This casual, oceanfront establishment located in the well-preserved 1920s Winston's beach cottage, emphasizes fresh seafood. There's a front porch for alfresco dining and the Wesley's "world-famous crab cakes" are the signature dish.

Steaks

ABERDEEN BARN   **$$$**
5805 Northampton Blvd.
Virginia Beach
(757) 464-1580
www.theaberdeenbarn.com

This restaurant has been in business since 1966, offering seafood and Sterling Silver Premium Beef aged at least 21 days.

BLACK ANGUS   **$$$**
706 Atlantic Ave.
Virginia Beach
(757) 428-7700
www.blackangusrestaurant.com

What are the odds that one of the best steakhouses in the region would be right on the Oceanfront? Well, the Black Angus has racked up dozens of best-of awards. The family-run business has been in operation since 1953 and isn't affiliated with the Black Angus Steakhouse chain out west. Look for discount coupons in those free tourist booklets. It may be just off the beach, but the dress is business casual. Bathing suits, cut offs, and other laid-back attire aren't welcome.

Thai

BANGKOK GARDEN   **$$**
4000 Virginia Beach Blvd.
Virginia Beach
(757) 498-5009
www.bangkokgardenva.com

This is an elegant Thai restaurant that matches its decor with the quality of its offerings. There are now four of the Gardens throughout Hampton Roads, with two in Virginia Beach (the other at 737 First Colonial Rd., Suite 307, 757-425-4909). They have a wide variety of offerings, including dishes from Northeastern Thailand.

TIDA THAI CUISINE   **$$**
336 Constitution Dr.
Virginia Beach
(757) 490-0515
www.tidathai.com

This little Thai restaurant, specializing in Thai seafood, is tucked behind the K-Mart near Pembroke Mall. It's very cozy, very pretty and, most important, very good. There are three branches of this restaurant with another in the Red Mill Commons shopping center in Virginia Beach (2133 Upton Dr., 757-301-6350) and the mother ship location in Chesapeake (1937 South Military Hwy., 757-543-9116).

Vietnamese

PHO 78 $
752 Timberlake Shopping Center
Virginia Beach
(757) 495-3007

Pho is a Vietnamese Noodle Soup, but lots more than that. It's a cheap, full meal and a culinary experience. This restaurant, one of several in the area with similar names, is expert at making the various permutations as well as other Vietnamese dishes. It probably says something about its authenticity that it's located next to a Vietnamese nail salon and grocery.

PHO 79 $
4816 Virginia Beach Blvd.
Virginia Beach
(757) 687-7844

This little restaurant off the boulevard may not look like much, but they know how to make pho.

SAIGON 1 $
448 Newtown Rd.
Virginia Beach
(757) 518-0307

Another small family place in a strip mall, Saigon 1 provides authentic Vietnamese fare and pho.

VIETNAM GARDEN $$
2404 Virginia Beach Blvd.
Virginia Beach
(757) 631-8048

Nestled in the London Bridge Shopping Center, this small Vietnamese restaurant has a strong local following.

NORFOLK

There are several dining hotspots in the city. Granby Street is the center of a downtown district, Ghent has a number of restaurants, and then there are local favorites scattered throughout the town. Here's a look at the best.

American

CHARLIE'S CAFE $
1800 Granby St.
Norfolk
(757) 625-0824

This diner in a small house on the corner of Granby in downtown Norfolk is best known for its Ultimate Omelets and killer Sunday brunches. For years this has been a place where local lawyers and beat cops felt at home. New owners a few years back saved it from falling into the hands of chains, degreased it a bit, added some vegetarian offerings, and hung art on the walls to keep pace with the gentrification of the neighborhood. But it's still Charlie's and still strictly cash and carry. Recently, Roadfood .com's Michael Stern visited, ate a potato omelet topped with habanero salsa, and pronounced Charlie's "worth planning a day around." Here, you can get some grits.

D'EGG DINER $
204 East Main St.
Norfolk
(757) 626-EGGS

Breakfast is the specialty, as it should be when "egg" is part of your name (and the last four digits of your phone number.) But this little restaurant across the street from the Marriott Hotel and Convention Center also serves up some amazing meatloaf.

DO-NUT DINETTE $
1917 Colley Ave.
Norfolk
(757) 625-0061

Another throwback is Ghent's Do-Nut Dinette. The small restaurant is a real diner, with green interior panels, a tile floor, and a long counter with about a dozen stools. They do breakfast the way a diner should. And they do buttery grits here to go with your country ham. Of course, as the name implies, they make their own donuts. But be warned. It's just one batch of these light, glazed gems made fresh every in the morning, so get there early or you'll be too late. One oddity is that it opens up again in the wee hours on weekends for those who need a breakfast after a late night on the town. Another cash only place and another that Michael Stern of Roadfood.com rates worth planning a day around.

JEWISH MOTHER BACKSTAGE
AT THE NORVA $–$$
320 Granby St.
Norfolk
(757) 622-5915
www.jewishmother.com

See the Virginia Beach location's review on page 62 and the tips box for getting in early at the NorVa theater on page 102.

NO FRILL BAR AND GRILL $$
806 Spotswood Ave.
Norfolk
(757) 627-4262
www.nofrillgrill.com

Don't let the name fool you, the No Frill Grill isn't a dive, it just operates on the principal that you'd probably rather put your money on your plate than in folks hovering around with a pepper mill. That's not to say that the service isn't good. It's just that people come here to eat, not for all the other frills. The menu is eclectic, running from a popular meatloaf to portabella pasta, with many adventurous stops along the way. The sandwich menu is extensive, with a variety of pita and burgers as well as creative deli offerings. The Ghent eatery spawned another in Virginia Beach (1620 Laskin Rd., 757-425-2900), which shares most of the menu and offers up some of its own specialties. They also make their own desserts and a wide variety of martini concoctions.

Chinese

KIN'S WOK $
222 West 21st St.
Norfolk
(757) 623-2933

This place always wins the best of Norfolk polls for its fast and affordable food. Folks drive across town for lunch knowing they will be served quickly and get something worth traveling for. There are lots of vegetarian items on the menu that are not done as an afterthought.

Deli/Sandwiches

BOBBIE B'S DELI $
433 Granby St.
Norfolk
(757) 623-7444
www.bobbiebsdeli.com

This downtown eatery offers up deli sandwiches and homemade deserts, and will even deliver if you can't leave your office. If you love fresh tomatoes, give the tomato mozzarella sandwich a try—juicy slices with slabs of cheese and whole basil leaves on a French roll drenched in balsamic vinegar and olive oil dressing. Breakfast and lunch only.

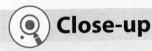

Close-up

Who Did You Say Invented the Ice-cream Cone?

Even if you don't believe that old Abe Doumar invented the ice-cream cone, it's fun to watch his nephew, Albert, whose been running **Doumar's** (1919 Monticello Ave., Norfolk, 757-627-4163, www.doumars.com; $) for more than 60 years, crank up that old waffle iron contraption that was certified by the Smithsonian as supposedly the first cone maker and whip up a fresh waffle cone for you.

This place is known for its ice cream, specially produced by a dairy in North Carolina, and its pork barbecue sandwiches still served by carhops. Flip on your headlights when you're ready to order and a server will swoop in. The food comes as it always has, wrapped in wax paper and held together with a toothpick. Go ahead, order two of the sandwiches. They go down so easily. It'll be served on a tray that attaches to your car window. You can get real limeades here and cherry Cokes from the fountain.

So what about that legend? Well, Abe arrived in America from Damascus, Syria, and went to work at the 1904 World's Fair in St. Louis. Supposedly, one night after selling paperweights filled with "water from the River Jordan," he bought a waffle from a vendor, rolled the waffle up the way Arabs do with pita bread, and added ice cream from another stall. He was soon selling more ice cream cones than holy water weights.

Abe eventually designed the four-iron waffle machine they still use here and was doing well enough to be able to bring his parents and brothers to America. The family came to Norfolk for the Jamestown Exposition of 1907, launching his ice-cream cone business at Ocean View Amusement Park, then the biggest attraction on the East Coast south of Atlantic City. One day, they sold nearly 23,000 ice cream cones.

The first stand was destroyed by a hurricane in 1933, so the family moved to the current location and it's been in constant operation ever since. They're closed on Sundays and don't take credit cards or checks. Remember, it's still 1950 here, at best. Inside the small restaurant there are pictures of the old days, charming signs that went up when they weren't intended to be charming, a few tables, and a counter that's usually filled by customers from all walks of life.

If you want to see Albert bake his cones, you should try to get there in the morning. But he's been known to fire up the iron at other times for kids. You can buy a jar of two dozen empty cones to take home and fill with your own ice cream, but you just can't recapture Doumar's, although Doumar's does a great job preserving the past.

Fine Dining

TODD JURICH'S BISTRO   **$$$$**
150 West Main St.
Norfolk
(757) 622-3210
www.toddjurichsbistro.com

Five-star dining presented by a chef who combined classical French education in Switzerland with classical Thai schooling in Bangkok. The result is a restaurant that has been featured in the *Washington Post*, the *New York Times*, *Southern Living*, *Food and Wine*, and *Travel and Leisure* magazines. The menu changes daily and features local produce. The "really good meatloaf and mashed potatoes" show the chef's skill, taking a comfort food and making it extraordinary.

THE MONASTERY RESTAURANT $$
443 Granby St.
Norfolk
(757) 625-8193

This is the place to get your goulash fix. The owners are Czech, so the menu is Central European. Every meal starts with homemade bread, cheese, and an apple. Roast duck is also a favorite of the regulars.

German

THE GERMAN PANTRY
RESTAURANT & BIERHAUS $$
5329 East Virginia Beach Blvd.
Norfolk
(757) 461-5100
www.thegermanpantry.com

Eat in or grab a wurst and go—you can't beat what they've been serving up here for nearly 40 years. They recently remodeled the restaurant, but the menu is still authentic Rhineland. And of course there's an extensive beer and wine list.

Greek/Mediterranean/Middle Eastern

AZAR'S NATURAL FOODS $$
2000 Colley Ave.
Norfolk
(757) 664-7955

See the Virginia Beach location's review on page 63.

ORAPAX INN $$
1300 Redgate Ave.
Norfolk
(757) 627-8041
www.theorapax.com

For more than 40 years, this has been the local's choice for Greek dining. Hey, they named the street out front Orapax Ave. for a reason. (Actually, Louis Seretis named his restaurant after the street when he opened his confectionary in 1966, but don't try to change this good story.) The place started out selling Spam and cheese on white bread sandwiches to local longshoremen and railroad workers. Then Louie turned to pizza and started adding Greek dishes. Today, it's a casual destination restaurant filled with people who love the atmosphere and adore the food. Every meal begins with hot, fresh-baked bread and a bowl of melted butter to dip it in. Louie's pizza is still famous, and the Greek food will have you dancing in the aisles even if you can't pronounce the items on the menu.

Hamburgers/Hot Dogs/Grill

FAMOUS UNCLE AL'S HOT DOGS $
1269 North Military Hwy.
Norfolk
(757) 466-1660

See the Virginia Beach location's review on page 63. A second Norfolk location is at 155 Granby St., (757) 625-8319.

KELLY'S TAVERN $-$$
1408 Colley Ave.
Norfolk
(757) 623-3216
www.kellystavern.com

See the Virginia Beach location's review on page 64.

PHILLY STYLE STEAKS AND SUBS $
7456 Tidewater Dr.
Norfolk
(757) 588-0602
www.tidewaterdrivephillysteaks.com

These days, everybody offers a Philly chees-esteak. But there's more to the meal than some beef on a roll. At Philly Style they do it right. Why? Just look around. Those newspapers on the walls celebrating Philadelphia championships or heartbreaks aren't replicas. They've earned their yellow patina with age. The folks that run this place are from Philly. The rolls they use are too. The grill is seasoned, and never seems to stop working, like the one at Pat's on 9th and Wharton in the City of Brotherly Love. Close your eyes, and you're back in Philly downing a "cheese with." The subs are authentic enough to call hoagies, the name preferred in Philly. And for dessert, of course they sell Tastykakes. No credit cards or personal checks taken here.

VINTAGE KITCHEN $$
999 Waterside Dr.
Norfolk
(757) 625-3370
www.vintage-kitchen.com

When *The Virginian-Pilot* asked its readers who made the best burgers, they got more than 70 nominations. The test panel went out and gorged themselves, settling on the Vintage Kitchen as the winner. A lightly grilled bun, juicy beef, and really fresh dressings did the trick. Oh, yea, they also do dinner menus that have won accolades, including a Conde Nast Traveler nod as one of the nation's best new restaurants, thanks to a chef, Phillip Craig Thomason, who trained at Le Cordon Bleu.

Indian

NAWAB $$
888 North Military Hwy.
Norfolk
(757) 455-8080

See the Virginia Beach location's review on page 65.

RAJPUT INDIAN CUISINE $$
742 West 21st St.
Norfolk
(757) 625-4634

This restaurant in Ghent is another family operation that offers a variety of authentic Indian flavors. There's a vegan menu here and you can even order takeout. The Palak Tofu, a dish of spinach cooked with tofu, made *The Virginian-Pilot*'s list of best dishes. You can even take healthy cooking classes here.

Italian

FELLINI'S GOURMET PIZZA CAFE $$
3910 Colley Ave.
Norfolk
(757) 625-3000
www.fellinisva.com

The thin-crust pizzas are great, the varieties unusual (Thai chicken pizza?), the atmosphere comforting, the fireplace inviting, and the pastas excellent. How good is this restaurant? It survived the murder of its owner and founder in 1998.

REGINO'S ITALIAN RESTAURANT $$
3816 East Little Creek Rd.
Norfolk
(757) 588-4300
www.reginosrestaurant.com

This Italian landmark was founded in 1948 by a Greek sailor who spent World War II serving in Hampton Roads. His family still runs the restaurant, using the recipes that George Mazarakis Sr. developed and winning a spate of Readers' Choice awards from the local newspaper.

SIRENA CUCINA ITALIANA $$$
455 Granby St.
Norfolk
(757) 623-6622
www.sirenanorfolk.com

A few years back, Norfolk adopted the mermaid as its symbol. About then Sirena opened up on the resurgent Granby Street, using the Italian word for mermaid as its name. This is another authentic Italian restaurant and an elegant favorite for those attending the symphony or catching a show at Chrysler Hall.

VENEZIANO RESTAURANT $$
4024 Granby St.
Norfolk
(757) 625-0363

This restaurant has passed down in the same family through the generations and serves your basic family Italian menu. It's not in any fancy neighborhood; you have to go looking for it in Riverview, a few blocks beyond the zoo. But the food is worth the trek. Folks really love the meatballs and eggplant parm.

Japanese

DOMO JAPANESE RESTAURANT
AND SUSHI BAR $$
273 Granby St.
Norfolk
(757) 628-8282
www.domofriends.com

This is a favorite of downtown workers and Tidewater Community College students. You can get a wide variety of Japanese dishes here, both raw and cooked.

SAI GAI TRADITIONAL JAPANESE
STEAK HOUSE & SUSHI BAR $$
7521 Granby St.
Norfolk
(757) 423-1000

This teppanyaki hibachi grill restaurant with a sushi bar gets raves for its fresh fish. They don't take checks here, but do accept plastic.

Mexican

COLLEY CANTINA $$
1316 Colley Ave.
Norfolk
(757) 622-0033
www.colleycantina.com

The Cantina is a Ghent landmark, famous for its fish tacos. There's an outdoor patio and people tend to know each other and hang out nursing their margaritas and nachos.

EL AZTECA $
1522 East Little Creek Rd.
Norfolk
(757) 587-6016

See the Virginia Beach location's review on page 67.

EL RODEO $
5834 East Virginia Beach Blvd.
Norfolk
(757) 466-9077

This family-run restaurant was once a fast food place outside the Janaf Shopping Center, one of the first malls in Norfolk. It's authentic Mexican fare at reasonable prices. Service is usually quick, and the food is done well.

GUADALAJARA CITY CAFÉ $$
411 Granby St.
Norfolk
(757) 622-2489

See the Virginia Beach location's review on page 67.

LUNA MAYA $$
2000 Colonial Ave.
Norfolk
(757) 622-6986
www.lunamayarestaurant.com

Like to get a little adventurous with your Mexican meal? Then try Luna Maya, Mexican done with a Bolivian flair. It's another small place in a strip mall with a fervent local following. In fact, it can be downright packed, but the meal is worth the wait. And they are known for killer mojitos and margaritas.

MACHISMO BURRITO BAR $
409 West York St.
Norfolk
(757) 624-2424
www.machinsmoburritobar.com

This is a small chain where you go and build your own burrito and they claim over a billion possible creations, but I can't go that far. What you will get is fresh fixin's, a choice of six flavored tortillas, and even an option to go vegan with Boca crumbles and cheese and sour cream substitutes. The result is a huge hunk of food that tries to burst through the wrap. Get lots of napkins and dig in.

MI HOGAR MEXICAN RESTAURANT $
4201 Granby St.
(757) 640-7705
www.mihogarrestaurant.com

Fast service, authentic food, and big portions make this a favorite for nearby ODU students and others who just want a good meal at reasonable prices. The menu is the same at the Military Circle venue (471 North Military Hwy., Norfolk, 757-455-5509).

SAN ANTONIO SAM'S CAFE SALOON $$
1501 Colley Ave.
Norfolk
(757) 623-0233
www.sanantoniosams.com

Tex-Mex has been the order of the day since this Texas Grill opened in cosmopolitan Ghent. The interior is appropriately rustic, which lends to a casual atmosphere. They can be liberal in their interpretation of Mexican, though, with offerings such as Sante Fe Chicken Eggrolls, a mix of chicken, refried beans, and cheese, wrapped in a tortilla then deep-fried like an eggroll and served with duck sauce. And lots of the menu is just pure Texas, like ribs or brisket.

Seafood

456 FISH $$$
456 Granby St.
Norfolk
(757) 625-4444
www.456fish.com

Born during the Granby Street Renaissance, this restaurant has won numerous "best of" awards for its seafood and ambiance. It's right downtown, convenient for those attending shows or about to hit the clubs. Most folks love the wall of water that separates some of the tables and the old black-and-white photos of historic Norfolk on the walls. But it's the fish that keep them coming back: potato chip encrusted crab cakes, macadamia encrusted mahi, or whatever the chef has done with the fresh catch. This is a dressier atmosphere, so you'll probably be more comfortable in a sport jacket or dress.

FREEMASON ABBEY $$$
209 West Freemason St.
Norfolk
(757) 622-3966
www.freemasonabbey.com

Do you worship food? Well, why not dine in a converted church? Congregations haven't met in the historic building since 1948 when it became a meeting hall for the Independent Order of Odd Fellows. That ended in 1987 and the restaurant has been winning awards since. This is an "American Menu" kind of place famous for its lobsters, shipped fresh off the boat. They serve more than 1,000 a month here. They're also known for their she-crab soup. No personal checks are accepted here. And if you're in a hurry, they have a "lunch in a flash" menu on weekdays.

O'SULLIVAN'S WHARF $$
4300 Colley Ave.
Norfolk
(757) 961-0899
www.osullivanswharf.com

This is a favorite watering hole and seafood restaurant located away from any of the normal tourist areas, which is why it bills itself as the local's locale. It's beyond Ghent and not quite up at the Old Dominion University area, on a branch of the Lafayette River known as Knitting Mill Creek. You can dine outside by the docks when the weather's right, and there are a ton of options on the menu. There are also daily specials and, often, live entertainment to make it a one-stop night out.

SHIP'S CABIN $$
4110 East Ocean View Ave.
Norfolk
(757) 362-0060
www.shipscabinrestaurant.com

It calls itself as a gourmet Italian restaurant, but don't discount the seafood here. It's a nine-time winner of the local paper's Best of Norfolk awards. The restaurant is a landmark in Ocean View and sits right on the Chesapeake Bay. Once formal, it is now a more casual destination, with booths right on the beach for alfresco dining.

TABB'S AT RIVERVIEW $$
4019 Granby St.
Norfolk
(757) 626-0871
http://tabbsatriverview.com

The Tabb is a neighborhood favorite, one of those places where the garden clubs meet to eat. There's a Sunday lunch buffet but most go for the family atmosphere and the fried oysters.

WILLOUGHBY INN
SEAFOOD RESTAURANT $$
1534 West Ocean View Ave.
Norfolk
(757) 480-0226

It may be a hole in the wall that looks more like a bar, but the Willoughby Inn Seafood Restaurant is located right at the end of Norfolk, the perfect location for fresh seafood and hush puppies without fighting the trendy set.

Spanish/Tapas

BODEGA ON GRANBY $$
442 Granby St.
Norfolk
(757) 622-8527
www.bodegaongranby.com

The motto here is "small plates . . . big drinks." So you can pick and choose from dozens of offerings while you sip on those drinks. Or you can go with a traditional entrée, on a large plate.

EMPIRE LITTLE BAR BISTRO $$
245 Granby St.
Norfolk
(757) 626-3100
www.littlebarbistro.com
A little tapas place where folks gather to end a night on the town in Norfolk.

Steak

THE GRATE STEAK $$$
235 North Military Hwy.
Norfolk
(757) 461-5501
www.thegratesteak.com
When you talk steak in Hampton Roads you have to start with this unusual eatery. Here, more than half the customers decide to go to the cooler, pick out a hunk of prime, aged beef, and tend to it on the charcoal grill themselves. It's not that the chefs can't cook. It's just that primordial urge to hunker over your own fire that trumps the convenience of paying someone else $2 to do it. The business model has worked wonders since the place opened in 1984, with numerous "best of" awards garnered. They have all the favorite cuts here, prime rib, a giant salad bar, and seafood or chicken for those avoiding red meat.

Thai

BANGKOK GARDEN $$
339 West 21st St.
Norfolk
(757) 622-5047
See Virginia Beach location's review on page 70.

CHESAPEAKE

Barbecue

GREAT BRIDGE BBQ $
800 South Battlefield Blvd., #112
Chesapeake
(757) 546-2270
www.greatbridgebbqcatering.com
This neighborhood restaurant in the Millwood Plaza shopping strip has been serving barbecue and ribs since 2004. Now they even have a service that will bring the smoker out to your event, from corporate and civic affairs to backyard cookouts.

JOHNSON'S BARBECUE $
1903 South Military Hwy.
Chesapeake
(757) 545-6957
The smoker they use in competitions sits out in the parking lot beside this strip mall restaurant and when it's working you can follow your nose. You want local? It doesn't get much more local than this. Who goes to a barbecue restaurant for the ambiance? This is about the meat and here the meat is done right: tender pork with plenty of slaw on top of the sandwich. Folks even rave about their beans, and the hot sauce is actually hot here.

WOOD CHICK'S BBQ $
1025 North Battlefield Blvd.
Chesapeake
(757) 549-9290
www.woodchicksbbq.com
A relative newcomer, Wood Chick's has quickly made its mark hereabouts, from top prizes in state and national competitions, to a televised Throw Down victory by owner Lee Ann Whippen over Bobby Flay on the Food Network. She's also one of seven Pitmasters who were featured on The Learning

Channel's eight-part series on competitive barbecue. You might have also caught her smoking act on the *Today Show*, the *700 Club*, and *People* magazine. Remember what I said in the Close-up about local barbecue snobbery? None of it applies here. At Wood Chick's you can get pork—or beef—slow cooked and smoked for more than a dozen hours, or order the chicken and ribs dusted with the secret dry rub and smoked in apple and hickory wood until fall-off-the-bone ready. You can pick your sauce as well, from the pepper and vinegar bite of North Carolina to Virginia's unique tomatoey tang to the smoky spice of Texas. The decor is modern roadhouse. You order when you walk in and they bring it to your booth. You can buy the sauces or even your own batch of the secret "pig powder" dry rub if you have a home pit.

Deli

CITY DELI $
450 South Battlefield Blvd.
Chesapeake
(757) 482-5554
www.citydeliva.com
Open since 1990, this restaurant in Great Bridge dishes up hot pastrami and corned beef with the best of them. You can order the normal sandwich or pay extra for one that's overstuffed. They also offer wraps, soups, daily specials, burgers, and desserts.

Greek/Mediterranean/Middle Eastern

PASHA MEZZE $$
1757 Parkview Dr.
Chesapeake
(757) 361-5221
This small restaurant in a strip mall serves the tastes of Turkey, a delicate Middle Eastern fare rich with tradition. They recently opened

a larger Pasha Mezze in Norfolk's Ghent (340 West 22nd St., 757-627-1317), which is open for dinner, so this Chesapeake location is mainly a sandwich and pastry shop now, and strictly lunch.

Hamburgers/Hot Dogs/Grill

FAMOUS UNCLE AL'S HOT DOGS $
1412 Greenbrier Parkway
Chesapeake
(757) 424-5705
See the Virginia Beach location's review on page 63.

FIVE GUYS BURGERS AND FRIES $
1217 Battlefield Blvd.
Chesapeake
(757) 382-0070
See the Virginia Beach location's review on page 63.

THE GRILL AT GREAT BRIDGE $
388 South Battlefield Blvd.
Chesapeake
(757) 482-5362
The winner in the Philly cheesesteak cook-off held by *The Virginian-Pilot's* food section was The Grill at Great Bridge. This very tiny restaurant run by a husband and wife team from Philly scored the upset over Philly Style in the judge's opinion. It shouldn't be a surprise that Gary, who mans the griddle, grew up in the Philly area and takes his cheesesteaks very seriously. Really, everything he and wife Ann cook up at this breakfast and lunch outpost is outstanding. There are a few stools at the counter and a couple tables in this place right up against Battlefield Boulevard. The restroom is clean, but you have to go around back outside to get to it—that's how small this former barber shop is (but here small just means cozy and welcoming).

KELLY'S TAVERN $-$$
Chesapeake Square Mall
2400 Ring Rd.
Chesapeake
(757) 488-0500
www.kellystavern.com

See the Virginia Beach location's review on page 64. Two other Chesapeake locations can be found at Lock's Point, 136 North Battlefield Blvd., (757) 819-6567, and Greenbrier Mall, 1412 Greenbrier Parkway, (757) 523-1781.

Italian

FRANKS II ITALIAN RESTAURANT $$
200 North Battlefield Blvd.
Chesapeake
(757) 548-4243
http://franks2.webs.com

This is blue collar Italian, an authentic corner eatery where you can grab a couple slices of pizza or an eggplant Parmigiana.

Japanese

DOMO JAPANESE RESTAURANT AND SUSHI BAR $$
109 East Gainsborough Square
Chesapeake
(757) 549-7977
www.domofriends.com

See Norfolk location's review on page 76.

Mexican

EL LORO $
801 Volvo Parkway, # 14
Chesapeake
(757) 436-3415

This little family restaurant next to a super-market has a strong local following for its authentic Mexican food. It's not so much what's on the menu here that sets it apart, it's how it's executed.

EL TORO LOCO $
146 South Battlefield Blvd.
Chesapeake
(757) 482-0623
http://goeltoroloco.com

Another local favorite in Chesapeake, it's casual, quick, and super authentic. The portions are large, but be forewarned. If you order the Burrito Jalisco, a menu favorite, don't be tempted by the tortilla chips and dip. You'll never finish the foot-long entrée if you do.

PLAZA AZTECA RESTAURANTES MEXICANOS $
1249 Cedar Rd.
Chesapeake
(757) 549-8008
www.plazaazteca.com

See the Virginia Beach location's review on page 67. A second location in Chesapeake can be found at 2416 Dock Landing Rd., (757) 488-1525.

3 AMIGOS $
200 North Battlefield Blvd.
Chesapeake
(757) 548-4105

See the Virginia Beach location's review on page 67.

Thai

SIMPLY THAI $$
236 Carmichael Way
Chesapeake
(757) 204-4623

Located in a small mall across from the Hill-crest Target shopping center, this is a good neighborhood Thai restaurant. The food is authentic, the prices reasonable, and the service cheerful.

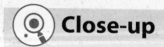

Close-up

Pierce's Famous BBQ

This technically isn't in what we normally consider Hampton Roads, but **Pierce's** (447 East Rochambeau Rd., Williamsburg, 757-565-2955, www.pierces.com; $) is the place that spawned all the others. The owners laid the cinderblock foundation and then built the small shack and huge pits. They say the special sauce is actually from a Tennessee family recipe, but there's no denying it's been adopted by Virginians as their own.

There was a time after the tiny shop opened in 1971 when the State Police constantly ticketed or towed cars that that had been abandoned on I-64 so the owners could run across the highway to get their barbecue pork sandwich fix at Pierce's.

No mere fine could end the practice, so they eventually erected a fence to discourage people from taking their chances running across the 65 mph traffic. Pierce's address may technically be in Williamsburg, but this restaurant is really in the woods along a service road between the Camp Peary and Lightfoot exits.

So what is it that builds such a fanatic following? Very slow cooked pork shoulders drenched in that signature sauce. There are three giant pits here now to meet the increased demand. The old, walk up window is gone, replaced by a bustling restaurant done in fast-food style. Governor Tim Kaine had his Inaugural Luncheon at Pierce's, not in Richmond. *Cooking with Paula Deen* featured the restaurant. *Southern Living* readers voted it a Best of the South winner in 2006. Call it a destination food trip and give it a try.

TIDA THAI CUISINE $$
1937 South Military Hwy.
Chesapeake
(757) 543-9116
See Virginia Beach location's review on page 70.

PORTSMOUTH

Barbecue

RODMAN'S BONES & BUDDYS $
3562 Western Branch Blvd.
Portsmouth
(757) 397-3900
This Portsmouth landmark is a family-run restaurant that has been serving barbecue to locals for more than three generations. Folks still come from far and wide to eat or to pack a few pounds in their suitcases to take home.

Fine Dining

BRUTTI'S RESTAURANT $$
467 Court St.
Portsmouth
(757) 393-1923
www.bruttis.com
Grand Sunday Buffet Brunch, with its waffle and omelet stations, Nova Scotia salmon, quiches, blintzes, and other edibles, has been voted the best breakfast in Hampton Roads. Of course, there's also tasty lunch and dinners here as well, and live jazz on weekends.

CAFE EUROPA $$$
319 High St.
Portsmouth
(757) 399-6652

This menu is hard to categorize since it blends the backgrounds of the two owners, Chef Michael, who is Czech, and his wife Veronique, who is French. Think of it as a trip to a European bistro, dark and intimate and romantic. The service is also Continental, so sit back and savor your meal. If you're in a hurry, consider other alternatives.

German

THE BIER GARDEN   **$$**
434 High St.
Portsmouth
(757) 393-6022
www.biergarden.com

If you love beer, or German food, or better yet the two combined, this little restaurant on High Street will seem like heaven. The Osfolk family has operated this place, with its little garden entrance and outside tables, since 1997. How many beers do they stock? Who can keep count? But the waiters know their inventory, and if you tell them what you already like, they can probably steer you to a new and even better brew. This is Old World dining, so don't come in a hurry. Each dish is prepared after you order. Relax, enjoy your brew, and when the food arrives, it will be transformational. You can order a wurst sampler or go whole hog with jagerschnitzel. (Count on a hefty bar bill. You just can't stop sampling, so have a designated driver or cab it home.)

Hamburgers/Hot Dogs/Deli

THE BARON'S PUB & RESTAURANT   **$$**
500 High St.
Portsmouth
(757) 399-4840
www.baronspubva.com

This restaurant opened on High Street in 1988 offering pub fare. The burgers are a big draw, thick, juicy, and arriving on a kaiser roll that doesn't get soggy or in the way. The nachos are just big, and there's usually live entertainment as well.

NEW YORK DELI   **$**
509 Court St.
Portsmouth
(757) 399-3354

This little restaurant in downtown Portsmouth has been serving New York style sandwiches, soups, and sides for decades. It's strictly a breakfast and lunch place, closing at 4 p.m.

SUFFOLK

American

BUNNY'S FAMILY RESTAURANT   **$**
1901 Wilroy Rd.
Suffolk
(757) 538-2325

Another place that won't win a sophistication award, Bunny's is as much a part of Suffolk as Planters' Mr. Peanut. This is where all the garden clubs and others have traditionally lunched and where, until a recent renaissance downtown, nearly everyone went to eat. This is basic Southern food, with all the requisite bacon fat for flavoring, almost like a family-run truck stop. If you want a good country breakfast, give Bunny's a try.

VINTAGE TAVERN   **$$$**
1900 Governors Pointe Dr.
Suffolk
(757) 238-8808
www.vintagetavernvirginia.com

This restaurant has been named one of the top 50 in the United States and a best in the region. You can watch the chef create his masterpieces at a demonstration kitchen. The fare is inspired by Southern traditions and based on local supplies. It's also one of the top wine bars in the region.

Caribbean

JAMMIN JERK BBQ $
148 Bennets Way, Suite 112-113
Suffolk
(757) 923-2934

A tornado destroyed Dorothy Lovell's first try at a Caribbean restaurant in Suffolk only two weeks after it opened. But after searching a decade for the perfect location, she wasn't about to let one twister do her in. The restaurant reopened at Freedom Plaza and you can drop in for some ox tails or a jammwich, a jerk pork sandwich.

Italian

PRIMO 116 BISTRO ITALIANO $$$
116 West Washington St.
Suffolk
(757) 923-0116
www.primo116.com

There was a time not that long ago that dining in Suffolk meant eating at Bunny's, not that there was anything wrong with that. It's still one of our favorite places to get comfort food. But these days, Suffolk can hold its own with any city when it comes to Italian food thanks to Primo 116. What's surprising is that it took so long. It was Amadeo Obici, after all, who put Suffolk on the map when he moved Planters Peanuts here. He'd be proud to eat at Primo's. Check out the extensive Italian seafood offerings, which makes sense since the owner, Steve Gellas, is also known as the Surfing Chef.

Mexican

PLAZA AZTECA
RESTAURANTES MEXICANOS $
1467 North Main St.
Suffolk
(757) 925-1222

See the Virginia Beach location's review on page 67.

Steaks

GEORGE'S STEAKHOUSE $$
1260 Holland Rd.
Suffolk
(757) 934-1726

Another long-time local favorite, George's is a relaxed, family-run steakhouse, where you can get a get a carnivore's rush without taking out a loan. Like most Greek steak places in the area, they also do seafood and spaghetti.

HAMPTON

American

KELLY'S TAVERN $–$$
1934 Coliseum Dr.
Hampton
(757) 313-9555
www.kellystavern.com

See the Virginia Beach location's review on page 64.

Barbecue

COUNTRY GRILL & SMOKEHOUSE $
26 East Mercury Blvd.
Hampton
(757) 723-0600
www.countrygrill.net

This is an open-pit restaurant barbecuing pork, ribs, chicken, and brisket. It also features your choice of six barbecue sauces from around the country. And you can wash it down with a vast beer selection, including 15 microbrews on tap and in bottles. And the cornbread muffins are a specialty. (They also have a restaurant in Yorktown.)

WILKES BARBEQUE $
3700 Victoria Blvd.
Hampton
(757) 722-4240

Fans lovingly describe Wilkes as a "hole in the wall" with great food and friendly service. It's Carolina style, with the vinegary sauce.

Mexican

PLAZA AZTECA
RESTAURANTES MEXICANOS $
50 Town Center Way
Hampton
(757) 826-3403

See the Virginia Beach location's review on page 67.

EL AZTECA $
2040 Coliseum Dr., Unit A-35
Hampton
(757) 838-4063

See the Virginia Beach location's review on page 67.

Seafood

OLD HAMPTON SEAFOOD KITCHEN $
124 South Armistead Ave.
Hampton
(757) 723-5777

This is a real seafood shack, with a handful of tables and some outside seating in downtown Hampton. The fare is deep fried, with fish, shrimp, and signature crab cakes. It's closed Sun and Mon.

Soul Food

QUEENS WAY SOUL CAFE $$
1144 Big Bethel Rd.
Hampton
(757) 224-7669
www.queenswaysoulcafe.com

Have a hankering for some chitterlings, pigs feet, catfish, or fried pork chops? Roger Winston and his family serves all that and more at Queens Way. And you can finish up your meal with some sweet potato pie or apple and peach cobbler. Now you know it's down home.

Thai

GAH BUA KHAM $$
2270 Executive Dr.
Hampton
(757) 838-0341

This is a family run business that offers fine food at reasonable prices. This intimate restaurant is in a small shopping center near the new Hampton City Town Center mall area. They also do takeout.

NEWPORT NEWS

American

99 MAIN RESTAURANT $$$
99 Main St.
Newport News
(757) 599-9885

This 75-seat, family-owned restaurant is located in the historic Hilton Village neighborhood of Newport News. The menu takes inventive leaps from a French classical base.

KELLY'S TAVERN $–$$
1010 Loftis Blvd.
Newport News
(757) 246-0080
www.kellystavern.com

See the Virginia Beach location's review on page 64.

Barbecue

ROCKY MOUNT BAR-B-Q $
10113 Jefferson Ave.
Newport News
(757) 596-0243
Not much to look at, this strip mall store features authentic North Carolina barbecue, sliced or minced pork with a side of slaw and fries. You can also get ribs, chicken, and other down-home meals. Or you can buy your barbecue to go.

Deli

DANNY'S DELI $
10838 Warwick Blvd.
Newport News
(757) 595-0252
Looking for a real sandwich while you're out touring the Virginia Living Museum, Mariners' Museum, or the Peninsula Fine Arts Center? Danny's is the place, and you know it's real because the sandwiches come with a real dill pickle slice.

TASTE UNLIMITED $$
702 Mariners Row
Newport News
(757) 596-8651
See the Virginia Beach location's review on page 62.

German

DAS WALDCAFE $$
12529 Warwick Blvd.
Newport News
(757) 930-1781
This long-time favorite offers up German food on a budget. Get your Rhineland favorites here, including spaetzle, rouladen, and goulash. The desserts are also homemade.

Indian

NAWAB $$
11712 Jefferson Ave.
Newport News
(757) 591-9200
See the Virginia Beach location's review on page 65.

Italian

AL FRESCO ITALIAN RESTAURANT $$
11710 Jefferson Ave.
Newport News
(757) 873-0644
www.alfrescoitalianrestaurant.com
If you're going to call your restaurant Al Fresco, you'd better have outdoor dining. There's a patio here just perfect for the situation. They're closed on Sun.

Japanese/Thai

HAYASHI SUSHI & GRILL $$$
11820 Merchants Walk
Newport News
(757) 223-5783
www.hayashisushigrill.com
This is an upscale hibachi grill/sushi restaurant in the City Center area, an offshoot of an older Japanese Steakhouse restaurant in Williamsburg. Here you will find all the usual Japanese trappings, as well as familiar and exotic sushi menus.

THAIJINDESU THAI & SUSHI BAR $$
2180 William Styron Square South
Newport News
(757) 595-8410
www.thaijindesu.us

The chef/owner trained at the Grand Hyatt Hotel in Bangkok and still personally prepares all the sushi served here. You can choose between Thai or Japanese dinner menus.

Mexican

PLAZA AZTECA RESTAURANTES MEXICANOS
12428 Warwick Blvd.
Newport News
(757) 599-6727

See the Virginia Beach location's review on page 67. A second Newport News location is located at 12755 Jefferson Ave., (757) 833-0271.

Seafood

THE CRAB SHACK ON THE JAMES RIVER $$
7601 River Rd.
Newport News
(757) 245-CRAB
www.crabshackonthejames.com

How can the food not be fresh, what with the longest fishing pier on the east coast sitting right there beside the restaurant? The shack started life as an outdoor venue with six picnic tables near the James River Bridge. Now it's able to seat 200 inside and out. Sitting here enjoying a sunset on the James River will feed your soul. The soft-shell crabs and spicy coleslaw are mainstays. It even earned a writeup in *Coastal Living* as one of "Our Favorite Seafood Dives."

Steak

SCHLESINGER'S $$$$
1106 William Styron Square
Newport News
(757) 599-4700
www.schlesingerssteaks.com

This classic chop house was named after Arthur M. Schlesinger, Jr., a Pulitzer Prize–winning author, and attempts to recreate the atmosphere of his days in the Kennedy White House. The restaurant has won *Wine Spectator* Magazine's Award of Excellence for its selection of more than 150 wines.

NIGHTLIFE

When the sun goes down, you don't have to call it a day. Hampton Roads has a number of after-dark delights geared to every age and demographic. There are the pounding clubs and the endless parade of young people down at the Oceanfront. There's another, only slightly more mature, set of watering holes off Shore Drive and the hopping new downtown at Town Center.

Norfolk is full of clubs, restaurants, and live music venues around Granby Street and Colley Avenue. Portsmouth's High Street offers a neighborhood feel to its action, and in Hampton, the new Town Center is packing them in.

Nightspots come and go fast enough to make restaurants look downright stable, so you'll want to give a call before heading to a specific club. Even if it's still there, there's a chance it has changed its M.O. or lost its mojo. Don't despair, many of the places are located in clusters. So just take a short stroll and you should find something suitable. Most clubs have dress codes. Many won't allow patrons with saggy pants or boots.

One thing to remember: Virginia has no bars, only restaurants that serve drinks. And there's a quota they have to meet to keep their food and drink revenue in balance. So you're going to find stuff to eat no matter where you go.

Let's look at what's out there.

WATERING HOLES/LIVE MUSIC

Southside

Oceanfront

The clubs tend to have a younger crowd at night, although there are places where you can go to hear live music or just relax with a cocktail. Here are a few to get you started.

ABBEY ROAD PUB AND RESTAURANT
203 22nd St.
Virginia Beach
(757) 425-6330
www.abbeyroadpub.com

Noted for a selection of 101 beers from around the world, and Beetle's memorabilia that plays to their name, Abbey Road also offers live music, sidewalk dining, free parking, and even wireless Internet if you can't sever the electronic tether.

CATCH 31
On the Boardwalk at 31st St.
3001 Atlantic Ave.
Virginia Beach
(757) 213-3474

This restaurant in the Hilton features live music and a DJ throughout the summer, but the biggest draw here is the outdoor fire pits right off the Boardwalk. Locals love to head here in the winter to cozy up to the fire and take in the beauty of the frigid Atlantic surf. Check out the breakfast buffet as well.

CHESTER'S UPPER DECK
206 16th St.
Virginia Beach
(757) 428-0048

This restaurant turns dance club every evening, with Shag and Beach music provided by local artists. It's on a second floor and you'll think you're in a time warp back to the '50s even before the Beach Blanket Bingo entertainment kicks in.

CROC'S 19TH STREET BISTRO
620 19th St.
Virginia Beach
(757) 428-5444

If you're eco-conscious, Croc's was the first restaurant in the state to be certified as Virginia Green. There's usually live music on the weekends, and the parking lot is often used as a farmers' market during the day in season. It's also just far enough from the strip that locals will venture down for a drink even in the summer.

THE JEWISH MOTHER
3108 Pacific Ave.
Virginia Beach
(757) 422-5430

The Jewish Mother is far more than a great deli. It's the area's premier blues venue; with a stage that is so cozy it feels like the acts are playing in your living room. The musicians must love the intimacy, because national acts like Tab Benoit keep coming back. The restaurant has been open since 1975 but faces an uncertain future. Urban Renewal plans are underway to raze the entire block where the Mother is located, although the timing is uncertain. The owners are looking to relocate somewhere nearby, though, so keep your eyes open. Still, the current venue, run down as it is, will be hard to top. And

on Sunday you can enjoy classical guitarist Robin Welch with your brunch.

OCEAN EDDIE'S
1506 Atlantic Ave.
Virginia Beach
(757) 425-7742
www.oceaneddiesvb.com

The address may say Atlantic Avenue, but this place is actually right on the beach at the 15th Street fishing pier. Ocean Eddie's has been going strong since 1949, growing from fishermen's snack bar to the place to eat and dance over the surf. In fact, in the early years, the dance floor was just planks, spaced like a boardwalk, and you could look down to see that ocean eddying around you. Patrons were upset when building codes required a real floor be installed. Still, there's plenty of potential ocean view.

ROCKAFELLER'S RESTAURANT
308 Mediterranean Ave.
Virginia Beach
(757) 422-5654
www.rockafellers.com

This little gem on Rudee Inlet matches its fun, casual atmosphere with excellent local seafood. It's a little off the track, but worth the trip. It's one of the rare Oceanfront places that locals will visit at the height of the summer season. There's a small, free parking lot here too.

Virginia Beach Town Center

This newly minted downtown bustles during the day, but it really shines at night, when young professionals congregate at the various bars and restaurants and take in the entertainment in the square by the water fountain. You can park your car in one of the free garages and get around the area by rickshaw cabs if walking seems like too much work.

GORDON BIERSCH BREWERY RESTAURANT
4561 Virginia Beach Blvd.
Virginia Beach
(757) 490-2739

This modern craft brewery and restaurant is as good a place as any to start. It's right on the western boundary of the area. It's part of a chain that began in California that serves up freshly brewed lagers and a full-food menu. Get your evening going with a glass boot full of one of the highlighted beers.

KEAGAN'S IRISH PUB AND RESTAURANT
244 Market St.
Virginia Beach
(757) 961-4432

This authentic Irish pub is right next door to the brewery, and the short walk takes you from Germany to Ireland. It's part of a small local chain of these pubs. The interior is all wood, handcrafted in County Kildare, and the wait staff dresses in Irish outfits.

RED STAR TAVERN
201 Town Center Dr.
Virginia Beach
(757) 473-3295

Another local hangout, this All-American-style tavern has a homey feel and gets pretty crowded on weekends as folks swing through for a drink and to meet up with old friends.

Shore Drive

This enclave around Chick's Beach has a few restaurant/bars that always seem to hop on weekends. Here, you'll find mostly locals in

the young-professional age group. But be careful. Shore Drive is a busy approach to the resort area and pedestrians who have been drinking can misgauge their chances of getting across in time. Several folks have been struck and killed around this area trying to get back to their cars after a night on the town.

HOT TUNA BAR & GRILL
2817 Shore Dr.
Virginia Beach
(757) 481-2888

Fabulous seafood combined with Top 40, high-energy dance music makes this a place that hops. There's no cover charge and plenty of free parking nearby as well. The live entertainment and DJs begin at 10 p.m. every Wed, Fri, and Sat night. Hot Tuna has been open since 1992, so it has a loyal following. And there's an open-air deck as well for when the weather is great.

SMOKEHOUSE & COOLER
2957 Shore Dr.
Virginia Beach
(757) 481-9737

This is another top-notch restaurant that morphs into a local watering hole. The owner calls it a "gastropub." You'll call it a great place to linger after some great ribs.

Norfolk

Not too long ago, Waterside was the happening place, with a series of bars that attracted a young, apparently too-boisterous crowd. The city cracked down on the owners and is in the process of revamping the offerings in this municipally owned attraction. Most of the action has spilled into other areas in the interim.

Granby Street

This small stretch of downtown between Scope and the river was once a failed pedestrian mall. For years, it was empty; then MacArthur Center mall and Tidewater Community College opened and it seemed to reach critical mass and take off. Today there are a number of restaurants where the crowd lingers long into the night. It's a place to eat before a show and to chill out afterwards. Here are a few spots to get you started.

HELL'S KITCHEN
124 Granby St.
Norfolk
(757) 624-1906

Named after New York's neighborhood, this little bar has a big-city flavor: black floors, exposed brick, and lots of deep red. There's live, edgy music here every Fri and Sat night.

TIME LOUNGE
271 Granby St.
Norfolk
(757) 623-8463

A long, elegant wooden bar, classy clientele, and DJs that keep it all moving make this a very popular place. Don't be surprised if there's a line waiting to get in.

FAHRENHEIT
437 Granby St.
Norfolk
(757) 965-8367

This fancy, small downtown lounge draws a cosmopolitan crowd. There's a college night on Thurs and a DJ spinning music Thurs, Fri, and Sat nights.

Ghent
THE BOOT RESTAURANT
123 West 21st St.
Norfolk
(757) 627-2668

The owners of this eclectic Ghent restaurant used to operate Relative Theory Records, a place where they sold vinyl and encouraged music lovers to linger and listen to the latest in live acts. Now they sell an Italian-influenced menu and still offer up cutting-edge live music. The selections are diverse, from jazz and bluegrass to indie.

COGAN'S PIZZA
1901 Colonial Ave.
Norfolk
(757) 627-6428

The pizza is almost as good as the beer selection here, with 30 varieties on tap. It's been a gathering place for young professionals for at least a generation. It is also a college hangout, with live music. Not the type of place for quiet conversations, though. It's more about fun.

TAPHOUSE GRILL
931 West 21st St.
Norfolk
(757) 627-9172

A nice beer selection and a real neighborhood bar feel make this a place where locals and Old Dominion University students old enough to imbibe share spaces at the bar. There is occasionally live music here as well.

Portsmouth

Olde Towne is the place to explore at night in this historic city, with most of the action centered around the historic center of town at High and Court Streets.

THE BARON'S PUB & RESTAURANT
500 High St.
Portsmouth
(757) 399-4840

An upscale neighborhood tavern feel and live acoustic music Wed through Fri make Baron's a place people linger long after dinner is done.

THE BIER GARDEN
434 High St.
Portmsouth
(757) 393-6022

The bar here deserves a separate review from the fantastic German restaurant. It's small and packed to the gills with every imaginable foreign and domestic brew. The selection runs between 300 and 350 varieties. But the real treats are the taps, which serve Aventinus and my personal favorite, Ayinger Brewery's Celebrator Doppelbock.

GOSPORT TAVERN
702 High St.
Portsmouth
(757) 337-0637

This new neighborhood eatery on the edge of Olde Towne also has live jazz on Wed and other live music on Fri and Sat.

Chesapeake
COURTHOUSE CAFE
350 South Battlefield Blvd.
Chesapeake
(757) 482-7077

This Great Bridge landmark has been open since 1985. (Before then, there was a cafe that was actually in the city's old courthouse.) It's busy at lunch and even busier after business hours. This is where the local lawyers and other professionals head to

mingle and meet. Folks call it Chesapeake's Cheers. There was a fire in 2008, but the place has been completely rebuilt.

Suffolk
THE BARON'S PUB & RESTAURANT
185 North Main St.
Suffolk
(757) 934-3100

Like its sibling in Portsmouth, this place has a hometown feel that makes you want to linger over a beer with friends.

JAVA 149
149 Main St.
Suffolk
(757) 923-9928

This little coffee shop in the heart of the revitalized downtown has been voted best-kept secret and best live entertainment/best hangout. Sat nights are Open Mic Musicians Night and if you love the power of words, visit on the fourth Friday of the month for Open Mic Poetry.

Peninsula

Hampton
Before the Peninsula Town Center opened up, there was the small restored Queen Street district downtown, with some nice little gathering places. They're still there and worth giving a try. Town Center has more of the bigger, chain tavern/restaurants.

GOODFELLA'S RESTAURANT & BAR
13 East Queens Way.
Hampton
(757) 723-4979

This local gathering spot is noted for bring in local, regional, and national blues artists.

THE PUB
4200 Kilgore Ave.
Hampton
(757) 838-2748
Looking for single malt scotch or an English beer on tap? The Pub at the Town Center offers it up, with wait staff clad in tartans to evoke some of that English pub atmosphere. This is part of a small chain of such restaurants and the first on the Peninsula.

TAPHOUSE GRILL
17 East Queens Way
Hampton
(757) 224-5829
With one of the best beer selections on the Peninsula, this is a sibling to the Taphouse Grill in Ghent. They rotate what's on tap here, so come back often and see how many you can sample. The food is good enough to keep pace with the bar, no easy feat.

Newport News
MANHATTAN'S N.Y. DELI & PUB
601 Thimble Shoals Blvd.
Newport News
(757) 873-0555
There's always something going on here, sort of like New York, with live entertainment every day of the week. Karaoke starts off most nights, followed by local cover bands and on Sun you can head over to watch your favorite football team or gather up your courage and try the Open Mic Night.

COMEDY CLUBS

COZZY'S COMEDY CLUB & TAVERN
9700 Warwick Blvd.
Newport News
(757) 595-2800
This venue has been operating on the Peninsula since 1991 with weekend comedy shows that have featured the likes of Tommy Chong, Nipsey Russell, Soupy Sales, and Gallagher. They even offer a Comedy School where you can learn the art of standup, Comedy Open Mic nights, and hypnotist shows.

THE FUNNY BONE COMEDY CLUB
217 Central Park Ave.
Virginia Beach
(757) 213-5555
This venue is on the national touring schedule for headline acts like Jon Lovitz, Damon Wayans, and Tom Green as well as offering a venue for up and comers and local comedy kings. It's located in Town Center and there isn't a dress code, but the owners take no responsibility if your outfit catches the attention—and the ridicule—of the act on stage. On most nights you have to be 21 to get in, so this isn't a place to take the kids. It's first-come seating, so keep that in mind if you're coming with a group. Arrive together or you'll likely sit separately. If you want to try your comic chops, they hold Clash of the Comics open mic nights where you get to perform a five-minute routine if you bring in enough guests.

SPORTS BARS

A.J. GATORS
3908 Holland Rd., Virginia Beach
(757) 340-3722
www.gatorsportsbar.com
This is a local chain of sports bars with five restaurants in Virginia Beach, two in Norfolk, and three in Chesapeake. The recipe for success has been the same: good locations, an extensive menu, plenty of TVs tuned to sports, pool tables, trivia games, and a local ownership that makes sure it all works whether it's on a city corner or at the end of

a suburban shopping strip. Visit the website for a directory of locations.

BAXTER'S SPORTS LOUNGE
500 Granby St.
Norfolk
(757) 622-9837

Baxter's is a slick, upscale sports lounge with lots of big screen TVs, including a few outside for those who prefer to sit in the small patio area. It's located right in the heart of the Granby Street's restaurant row with large glass windows that invite you inside.

R.J.'S RESTAURANT & SPORTS PUB
12743 Jefferson Ave.
Newport News
(757) 874-4246

This sports pub features 19 televisions and three wide screens to watch the action as well as seven regulation pool tables, dart boards, and video games. It's a favorite gathering place on the Peninsula on Sunday during football season.

ROGER BROWN'S RESTAURANT & SPORTS BAR
316 High St.
Portsmouth
(757) 399-5377

Roger Brown, a six-time NFL Pro Bowler, opened this huge sports bar/restaurant in 2000 in what was once a Woolworth's department store. There are more than 16,000 square feet here, with a dining room that has a fireplace and no big screen TVs for those who prefer to avoid the sports. But for most folks, sports are to be embraced, and you can certainly do that here. You have a stadium area that seats 160, with four jumbo-screen high def televisions. How big? They're 8 foot by 6 foot. There's a separate VIP room with two HD TVs, an Xbox, and Wii games. A banquet room can seat up to 90 people and a 90-foot bar with 60 stools. And if that isn't enough selection, you can bring your laptop and tap into the free Wi-Fi.

WINE BARS

EURASIA CAFE AND WINE BAR
960 Laskin Rd.
Virginia Beach
(757) 422-0184

This intimate establishment has been voted one of the region's top five restaurants. Along with a fusion menu that pairs regional foods with Asian influences, the cafe features two dozen wines by the glass and a wine shop that offers one of the largest selections in all of Hampton Roads.

PRESS 626 CAFE AND WINE BAR
626 West Olney Rd.
Norfolk
(757) 282-6234

A quaint venue in an old Ghent building with an unusual array of wines to sample and savor. The food emphasizes local ingredients. There are daily specials and 50 wines under $50, many available by the glass.

SONOMA WINE BAR & BISTRO
189 Central Park Ave.
Virginia Beach
(757) 490-WINE

Prefer your libations to be delivered by a sommelier? Then Sonoma is a great place to visit. There are 325 different wine varieties in stock here, including 70 you can sample by the glass. That doesn't necessarily mean it's cheap, though. Prices range from $4.50 to $100 for that glass. But imagine if you'd bought an entire bottle of that $100 vintage. Plus it's a fine dining establishment where they can help you match the food to the wine you like to drink.

VINTAGE TAVERN
1900 Governors Pointe Dr.
Suffolk
(757) 238-8808

This is a fine restaurant, rated one of the top 50 in the nation according to Open Table Diner's Choice Awards, that is also a top-notch wine bar. The floor-to-ceiling glass wine cabinet holds 1,300 bottles and the collection changes constantly. You can always buy a bottle or two to take with you.

GAY & LESBIAN FRIENDLY BARS/CLUBS

This area is mainly military and the services still have a don't ask, don't tell policy when it comes to homosexuality, so discretion is important.

THE GARAGE
731 Granby St.
Norfolk
(757) 623-0303

This is a men's bar with pool tables and dancing located just beyond Granby's restaurant row on the other side of Brambleton Avenue. It's an old place, but no one comes for the decor.

HERSHEE BAR
6117 Sewels Point Rd.
Norfolk
(757) 853-9842

This is a women's bar with pool tables, dancing, and food.

THE WAVE
4107 Colley Ave.
Norfolk
(757) 440-5911

A men's bar with male dancers on Wed.

COUNTRY & WESTERN DANCING/BARS

THE BANQUE
1849 East Little Creek Rd.
Norfolk
(757) 480-3600

If you love to line dance and live for country music, this is the place to go. It was voted the best nightclub with restaurant in 2009 by readers of *The Virginian-Pilot*. There's a lot of history on the two large dance floors. The Banque opened in 1973. The club is open Wed through Sat nights. They offer free dance lessons, and if you get tired of dancing, there's pool tables, Texas hold 'em, and blackjack games. And if you go see a movie, concert, opera, or anything with a ticket stub, save it and you can get into the Banque that same night free for a little after-event exercise. Belles' Dry Goods store is located inside the club with everything you might need in Western wear to cowboy up.

SADDLE RIDGE ROCK-N-COUNTRY SALOON
1976 Power Plant Parkway
Hampton
(757) 827-8100

This is a rock and country nightclub in the same building as the Cheyenne Supper Club. On this side you can listen to live country western music while you dine. On the saloon side there are free dance lessons. Thurs is ladies night with no cover and free bull rides for ladies.

DANCE/NIGHT CLUBS

CHROME SALOON, CRAZY WING CANTINA AND EAGLE'S NEST
Parkview Shopping Center
1723 Parkview Circle
Chesapeake
(757) 420-9191

This triple-named club in the shopping center off Greenbrier Parkway south of Military Highway recently changed moniker and format and is now open seven days a week. It used to be called Chevy's and was annually voted the city's best nightclub. There are still five bars, three stages, and three dance floors in the 10,000-square-foot facility you are sure to miss if you're not looking carefully. There is no cover anymore in the now, all-Country format dance bar.

GRANBY THEATER/PREMIERE NIGHTCLUB
421 Granby St.
Norfolk
(757) 961-7208

This movie palace opened in 1915 and was lovingly restored a few years ago. It hosts a Top 40 and Remix Dance Party every Fri night and on Sat the theater becomes the Premiere Nightclub for another dip into Top 40 and Remix. The interior is worth the visit alone, with original chandeliers, hand painted proscenium, and gold leaf finished trim. It has a large wooden dance floor, a dozen VIP balconies, and six VIP booths as well as a Penthouse Lounge.

JILLIAN'S OF CHESAPEAKE
1401 Greenbrier Parkway
Chesapeake
(757) 624-9100

This arcade/sports bar/billiards parlor/restaurant once was an anchor at Waterside in Norfolk. They recently moved into a large area on the first floor of the Greenbrier Mall in Chesapeake.

PEABODY'S
209 21st St.
Virginia Beach
(757) 422-6212

This is what you would expect of a beach nightclub: A giant dance floor, bikini contests, and a huge young crowd. College kids get in free on Fri. Thursday "girls" get in free if they wear a little black dress. Every Sat is a Bash at the Beach with local bands. You get the idea. It's been packing them in since 1967. This is a young venue, 18 and up for women, 21 and older for men, that gets even younger with the occasional non-alcoholic teen nights.

TRIBECA NIGHT CLUB
1000 Omni Blvd.
Newport News
(757) 873-6664

This multi-level nightclub is located in the Omni Hotel. It features live bands every Fri and a DJ on Sat.

MOVIES

The big chains, AMC, Cinemark, and Regal, have plenty of screens here in Hampton Roads so you can bet on any recent release being available at a number of locations. In addition there's the Classic Commodore Theater in Portsmouth and several Cinema Draft House locations where you can eat while you watch the film. And there are IMAX HD theaters on both the Southside and the Peninsula for those special occasions when giant isn't big enough. There are usually bargain matinees if you get in before 6 p.m. and the prices, even at night, are nowhere near New York or LA rates.

Southside

Chesapeake
CINEMA CAFE
1401 Greenbrier Parkway
(inside the Greenbrier Mall)
(757) 523-7469

If you don't mind waiting a few weeks or enjoy catching several showings, this is a great place to see a movie. The price is great: $1 on Tues, $1.75 on Fri, Sat, and Sun before 6 p.m., and just $3.75 in prime time. Best yet, you can eat a pizza or a meal and drink a brew while you watch. The seats are large and comfy and are arranged around tables so you never feel squashed.

CINEMARK MOVIES 10
4300 Portsmouth Blvd., Suite 30
(757) 465-0751

This multiplex is out by Chesapeake Square Mall. Matinees are $4, evenings $6, $4 for children and seniors 62 and older. Monday is Seniors day, any movie any time for $3.75

REGAL GREENBRIER CINEMA 13
600 Jarman Rd.
(757) 420-0105

Inside Greenbrier Mall; tickets here are $10 for adults after 3 p.m., $7.50 before.

Hampton
AMC HAMPTON TOWNE CENTER 24
1 Town Center Way
(888) AMC-4FUN

This is the movie multiplex by the new Town Center. Adult tickets here are $10 but there are some discounts available for active duty or retired military.

CINEMA CAFE
1044 Von Schilling Dr.
(757) 523-SHOW

Another in the local chain of places where you can eat, drink, and watch a film. Prices here are a little higher than in Chesapeake, because the films are more current: $7.95 on weekend evenings; $4.75 Mon through Thurs with a discount for evening shows.

IMAX VIRGINIA AIR & SPACE CENTER
600 Settlers Landing Rd.
(757) 727-0900

This is a five-story, 3D screen that offers Hollywood movies as well as scientific wonders. A full-length show costs $12 for adults, $10 for kids 3 to 18. Museum admission is separate or you can buy a combo ticket.

Newport News
REGAL KILN CREEK 20
100 Regal Way
(757) 989-5200

This is a giant multiplex showing first run features. Adults after 3 p.m. pay $10, $7.50 for matinees.

Norfolk
CINEMARK MILITARY CIRCLE MALL
880 North Military Hwy.
(757) 461-9197

Another multiplex by a mall, this one charges $6.50 for adults in the evening, $4 for matinees before 6 p.m.

NARO EXPANDED CINEMA
1507 Colley Ave.
(757) 625-6276

You're not a real city unless you have an art movie house. The Naro is Hampton Roads' place to see foreign films, independent movies, and the things you read about but that will never crack those corporate chains. It's located right in Ghent in a historic theater that has been restored. And the folks who run it also operate a video rental outlet next door where you can check out an eclectic selection of films from historic to hysterical. Pick up a schedule when you go and plan to make time to come back. Adult tickets are $9, $6.50 for matinees. Oh yeah, if you're really adventurous, come to the *Rocky Horror Picture Show* every second and fourth Fri night at 11:30 p.m. and join the cast of audience members who play along with the screen.

PHOENIX MAIN GATE MOVIES 10
1500 Mall Dr.
(757) 440-1500
This multiplex is just outside the world's largest Navy base, so it has a steady supply of customers. Tues is bargain day, with all films $5—except special engagements. Other times, it's $8.50

REGAL MACARTHUR CENTER 18
300 Monticello Ave., Suite 330
(757) 623-7800
You can usually find all the latest films at this large multiplex inside an upscale mall. Adult tickets are $10, $7.50 for matinees before 3 p.m.

Portsmouth
COMMODORE THEATRE
421 High St.
(757) 393-6962
Another of the old Movie Palaces lovingly restored. The Art Deco Commodore opened in 1945 and is on the National Register of Historic Places and the Virginia Landmarks Register. Downstairs there's fine dining at comfortable tables while you watch the show. Or if you prefer the pure movie experience, check out the nice balcony on the weekends, where you can grab some

popcorn and a soda at a small concession stand and pretend you're back in post-war Portsmouth. The actual movie experience is definitely modern, with a 41-foot screen and THX Dolby Digital Sound. You can't make reservations by phone or Internet; you have to come to the box office. Adult admission is $8; dining, obviously, is extra.

Suffolk
REGAL HARBOUR VIEW GRANDE 16
5860 Harbour View Blvd.
(757) 638-7827
Harbour View is where the population has moved, and this theater is there to serve them. It's also an easy ride for Newport News and Hampton filmgoers. Adult admission is $10, $7.50 for matinees before 3 p.m.

Virginia Beach
AMC LYNNHAVEN 18
1001 Lynnhaven Mall Loop
(888) 262-4386
This giant theater is outside the large Lynnhaven Mall.

CINEMA CAFE KEMPS RIVER
1220 Fordham Dr.
(757) 523-7469
Another one of the "eat and drink while you watch" theaters in this chain, this one features first-run films. Admission here is $7.95 on weekends, $4.75 other days or weekends before noon. Wed is considered "wacky" with all tickets $3.50 except for special engagements.

CINEMA CAFE PEMBROKE MEADOWS
758 Independence Blvd.
(757) 523-7469
This was the first of the Cinema Cafes to open. It is also a second-screening, bargain

place where tickets are $1 on Tues, $1.75 for matinees before 6 p.m. on Fri, Sat, and Sun and $3.75 for evenings.

IMAX VIRGINIA AQUARIUM & MARINE SCIENCE CENTER
717 General Booth Blvd.
(757) 385-3474
The screen is six stories high and plays Hollywood features as well as nature films that work well with the aquarium's mission. Adult admission is $10.50 for the IMAX alone, $8.50 for shorter educational films.

REGAL COLUMBUS STADIUM 12
104 Constitution Dr.
(757) 490-8181
This multiplex is right at the edge of the new Town Center. Tickets are $10 for adults, $7.50 for matinees before 3 p.m.

REGAL PEMBROKE MALL CINEMA 8
4554 Virginia Beach Blvd., Suite 500
(757) 671-7469
A movie house inside Pembroke Mall, this one also shows first run films for $10, $7.50 before 3 p.m.

REGAL STRAWBRIDGE MARKETPLACE
2133 General Booth Blvd.
(757) 563-9270
This one is in a free-standing shopping center but has the same Regal price policy.

PERFORMING ARTS

Hampton Roads is blessed with a vibrant performing arts schedule. The resident opera and orchestra companies are both nationally ranked. A number of indoor and outdoor venues annually attract some of music's top acts. In the spring, facilities come alive with the Virginia Arts Festival.

Although there really isn't a New York style theatre district in Hampton Roads, many of the region's cultural palaces are located within a few blocks in downtown Norfolk.

But the biggest acts often play under the stars at amphitheaters in Virginia Beach or Portsmouth or in the scifi–looking Scope and Coliseum stadiums in Norfolk and Hampton. Here's a breakdown of major players and the places where you can see live entertainment.

REGIONAL

VIRGINIA SYMPHONY ORCHESTRA
861 Glenrock Rd., Suite 200
Norfolk
(757) 892-6366
www.virginiasymphony.org
This orchestra played its first concert in 1921 and was once the only symphony between Baltimore and Atlanta. It is considered one of the nation's leading regional symphonies. Under maestro JoAnn Falletta, who also leads the Buffalo Philharmonic and has been called one of the finest conductors of her generation, it splits its seasons at a number of venues from Williamsburg to Virginia Beach. This is a hard working group, annually performing more than 140 classical, pops, family, and education concerts as part of an ambitious musical outreach program. It is also the orchestra playing behind the Virginia Opera, the Virginia Ballet, and for the Virginia Arts Festival. That means you have a wide range of places where you can see these master musicians, from high school auditoriums on the Eastern Shore of Virginia to the magnificent acoustics of the new Sandler and Ferguson Centers for the Performing Arts in Virginia Beach and Newport News. Falletta and the orchestra, which has been in business for eight decades, have made five nationally released CDs, performed *Peter and the Wolf* for National Public Radio, and even appeared to great reviews at the Kennedy Center and Carnegie Hall in New York City. Most of the time, though, the 70-plus-member orchestra is based at the Chrysler Center in Norfolk.

NORFOLK

VIRGINIA OPERA
160 East Virginia Beach Blvd.
Norfolk, Virginia 23510
(757) 627-9545
www.vaopera.org

This is truly the state's opera company, made so by unanimous vote of the Virginia General Assembly in 1994. As such, it takes its elaborate productions on the road to Richmond and Northern Virginia, but home is the Harrison Opera House in downtown Norfolk. The company was founded by Edythe C. Harrison in 1974 and hasn't looked back since. Led by Maestro Peter Mark, the Virginia Opera has developed a reputation for debuting new work and promising artists. Every year, the company gives 32 major performances, with four distinct operas. It also takes the music into schools and offers free performances as part of its education program, which Opera America has said reaches more students in the classroom than any other opera company in the United States. The company often offers light opera productions designed for those who want to sample the art form and Operation Opera, a free avant-garde program that brings a taste of the art form to groups of adults.

Every year, the Virginia Opera offers a Family Day, with live performances, games, activities, prizes, and food to enthrall parents and children. Past performances have included productions of *Sleeping Beauty*, *The Pirates of Penzance*, and *Pinocchio*. But the big draw is always the season's four full operas with their elaborate, often inventive sets and lavish costumes—all in the hands of some of the nation's freshest and most celebrated voices. The 2009–10 season featured Puccini's *La Boheme*, Donizetti's *The Daughter of the Regiment*, Mozart's *Don Giovanni*, and the Gershwins' *Porgy and Bess*. The Edythe C. and Stanley L. Harrison Opera House is a work of art in itself. Once a World War II USO theater, it was completely renovated in 1993. It is intimate, with just 1,632 seats, and boasts impressive chandeliers and sweeping staircases, a three-story grand lobby with floor to ceiling windows, and acoustics that enhance the entire experience.

VIRGINIA STAGE COMPANY
Wells Theatre
254 Granby St.
Norfolk
757-627-1234
www.vastage.com

This is Hampton Roads' only professional resident theater company and is another that has earned a reputation as one of the nation's best regional performing arts groups. It has debuted plays, such as the Tony Award–winning musical *The Secret Garden*, and consistently attracts top tier actors to the historic Wells Theatre. The theater itself is another marvel. Restored to its Beaux-Arts glory, it is a National Historic Landmark. The ornate theater opened in 1913 presenting such acts as Fred and Adele Astaire, Will Rogers, Billie Burke, and even a production of *Ben-Hur*, complete with teams of horses running on treadmills. It would later see duty as a burlesque house and even a porn palace, complete with attached brothel. The Virginia Stage Company moved into the theater in 1980 and completed another $35 million in restorations in 1986. The Wells was one of the first success stories for Downtown's Renaissance.

CHRYSLER HALL
215 St. Paul's Blvd.
Norfolk
(757) 664-6464

This venue annually hosts a Broadway play series. The city says the show will go on. Norfolk was negotiating with a new production company as this book went to press after Broadway Across America decided it was scaling back its touring activities and cancelled its contract with the city to provide shows.

SCOPE
201 East Brambleton Ave.
Norfolk
(757) 664-6464
www.sevenvenues.com

This flying saucer–looking concrete and glass structure next to Chrysler Hall can seat 13,600 for concerts or 8,000 for minor league hockey. It once was home to nearly all the big concerts, from the Rolling Stones to Elvis. But these days it's mostly a sports arena with the occasional performing act, like Jay-Z. Recent renovations have improved the acoustics, and this is where the Ringling Brothers Circus stops on the Southside every year. But one of the biggest events every year is the Virginia International Tattoo. That's no gathering of skin artists but a celebration of the area's military heritage as part of the Virginia Arts Festival. Tattoos evolved from a 17th-century European tradition that recognized the importance of field musicians into a festive performance of military music that emphasizes the cultures of the native countries. In Norfolk every spring, it takes the form of marching bands, massed pipes and drums, drill teams, gymnasts, Scottish dancers, choirs, and other entertainers from around the world. More than 800 performers are involved in the show, the largest of its kind in the United States.

THE NORVA
317 Monticello Ave.
Norfolk
(757) 622-2829
www.thenorva.com

So how does a small venue with so very few seats (okay, most of the 1,500 in a capacity audience actually have to stand) book big acts like the Goo Goo Dolls and B. B. King? Some credit the Jacuzzi and private basketball courts backstage for the performers. Others say it's the state-of-the-art sound system and an opportunity for artists to get close to their audience. Whatever the reason, it pays off big for Hampton Roads fans. The acts here tend to be geared to a younger crowd, but this is a venue that is rarely empty and that prides itself on diversity. So check the calendar or get on a mailing list and you might be surprised. And what about that Jacuzzi? The NorVa may have started out as a theater, but in later life it became a health club. When it was converted back to entertainment, they decided to keep the upstairs Jacuzzi and basketball court to give bored touring acts an unusual opportunity to relax.

i The NorVa's entrance is opposite the MacArthur Center, and artists often can be seen wandering the mall the afternoon before a show. Fans often gather outside the venue to wait for their favorite acts to show up in tour buses. And there's a not-so-secret trick if you want a chance to grab the rare seat or best vantage point. Attached to the NorVa on Granby Street is Jewish Mother Backstage at the NorVa. If you reserve a meal there and tell the staff you have tickets to that night's show, they'll lead you in early, through the bowels of the building and right into those precious, up against the PA speaker, vantage spots. Since everyone wants to get up close, call (757) 622-5915 as early as you buy your tickets and make those dinner reservations.

PERFORMING ARTS
TCC ROPER PERFORMING ARTS CENTER
340 Granby St.
Norfolk
(757) 822-1450
www.tcc.edu/roper
This is a former movie and vaudeville house Tidewater Community College converted to a performance venue when it moved downtown. The reclamation project restored the Loew's State Theater's gilded box seats, glass chandeliers, and other period details. These days, the venue seats up to 900 and hosts feature films, college convocations, symposia, and a variety of live acts. Among those who use the facility are the Hurrah Players, a local children's theater troupe, the Virginia Ballet Theatre, and Todd Rosenlieb Dance, a Norfolk-based modern dance company.

i Think your kid has talent? Then you might want to check out the Hurrah Players, a Hampton Roads staple for more than a quarter century that has sent scores of youngsters to careers on Broadway, in Hollywood, and on television. The school accepts students as young as five and provides instruction in tap and jazz dance, musical theater, voice, and stage production. They get to strut their stuff in the Hurrah's half dozen or so lavish stage productions every year. Visit www.hurrahplayers.com or call (757) 627-5437.

THE ATTUCKS THEATRE
1010 Church St.
Norfolk
(757) 622-4763
www.attuckstheatre.org
Once known as the Harlem of the South, Church Street was the heart of Norfolk's African-American community, and the Attucks

Theatre, named after the first patriot to lose his life in the Boston Massacre, a black man named Crispus Attucks, was its centerpiece. This is the nation's oldest theater designed, financed, and operated by African Americans. Giants such as Ethel Waters, Cab Calloway, Duke Ellington, Nat King Cole, and others performed here before it closed in the 1950s. It's been restored and reopened in 2004. Once again music and inspiration emanate from the building, officially declared a National Historic Landmark in 1977.

TED CONSTANT CONVOCATION CENTER
Old Dominion University
4320 Hampton Blvd.
Norfolk
(757) 683-4444
www.constantcenter.com
This is another large venue that does more than serve as home to the Old Dominion University Monarch and Lady Monarch basketball teams and graduation ceremonies. There is room for up to 10,000 here, which makes it a venue of choice for some large concerts. Past events have included B. B. King, comic Dave Chapelle, rock group 3 Doors Down, singer Kelly Clarkson, rockers Lynyrd Skynyrd and the Moody Blues, and even the Boston Pops Orchestra.

L. DOUGLAS WILDER PERFORMING ARTS CENTER
Norfolk State University
700 Park Ave.
Norfolk
www.nsu.edu/wilder
This 1,800-seat concert hall is named for the first African American to be elected governor of a state in America, Virginia's own L. Douglas Wilder. It features a full theatrical

103

stage that hosts not just college productions like *Porgy and Bess* but also classical and jazz programs, lectures, and educational forums.

i Like Jazz? The first Wednesday of every month, local performers take the stage at the ornate Hubert Court in the Chrysler Museum of Art in Norfolk. The music begins at 6:15 p.m. and you can even break away and take an evening tour of the galleries. Give them a call at (757) 664-6200 to see who is playing. Oh yeah, it's free. And there's an informal wine tasting that goes along with the music and Art Riffs, short explorations of selected works, to fill in when musicians take a break.

FESTEVENTS
Town Point Park and Ocean View Beach Park
Norfolk
(757) 441-2345

Every year, more than 2 million people make their way to Town Point Park to hear music or participate in festivals run by this organization. Most of the big events, like the Jazz Festival or Bayou Boogaloo, require tickets. If you'd like to turn back the clock, don't miss the regular Big Bands on the Bay programs at Ocean View Beach Park. They're free, and you can't beat the Chesapeake Bay backdrop. You can't talk about Festevents without mentioning its biggest party, the annual Norfolk Harborfest, which occurs around mid-June. See more details in the Annual Events & Festivals chapter, but it's a blast with food, music, and plenty of tall ships to ogle and tour.

THE LITTLE THEATRE OF NORFOLK
801 Claremont Ave.
Norfolk
(757) 627-8551
www.ltnonline.org

The longest running community theater in the country, Norfolk's Little Theatre is still going gangbusters. It opened in 1926 and never saw a darkened season—not even during the Great Depression or either World War. They moved into their current location in 1951. It's a completely volunteer-run troupe that presents a number of shows each season. Offerings here range from a live adaptation of the holiday classic *A Christmas Story* to the intense drama of *12 Angry Men*.

THE GENERIC THEATER
215 St. Paul's Blvd.
(down under Chrysler Hall)
Norfolk
(757) 441-2160
www.generictheater.org

Think of this as Norfolk's off-Broadway community theater. This group, founded in 1981, knows how to have fun. Their offering of *Evil Dead: The Musical*, based on Sam Raimi's cult classic film, featured wildly popular "splatter rows" where patrons were likely to get doused by flying gore from the chainsaw scene. But they also can play for impact, such as the production of *Letters for A Young Girl*, which featured the story of Anne Frank being read by a 13-year-old girl trying to endure the genocides in Darfur.

VIRGINIA BEACH

BEACH STREET USA
Various stages on the Oceanfront
(757) 491-SUNN
www.beachstreetusa.com

If you like open air concerts, it's hard to get any more open than the seven stages Virginia Beach uses along its strand to entertain tourists and locals. So what will you hear? Beach music, of course. But, mid-June through Labor Day, there is a variety of festivals to choose from: Caribbean Music, Gospel, World Drum, Latin, Rock, Funk, Italian, and the biggest draw: the Verizon Wireless American Music Festival, which has attracted such acts as James Brown, Boyz II Men, Heart, and the Black Crowes. Much of it is free, but check first. And you'll have to pay for parking down at the resort strip or risk being towed, which can spoil the best of times.

SANDLER CENTER FOR THE PERFORMING ARTS
201 Market St.
Virginia Beach
(757) 385-2787
www.sandlercenter.org

The newest venue in Hampton Roads is a jewel, specially designed so its acoustics can be adjusted from spoken word to rock concert, and all performances in between. Located in Virginia Beach's new core, Town Center, it hosts a full gamut of performances, from Broadway shows like *Menopause: The Musical* and *The Sound of Music* to music ranging from the Virginia Symphony Orchestra to Randy Travis. The center is also home to Symphonicity, the region's premier community orchestra, and the Virginia Beach Chorale. Another bonus:There's plenty of free parking nearby and a wide variety of eateries to make it a night. The Sandler also hosts lectures, comedians, ballets, and jazz.

VIRGINIA BEACH AMPHITHEATER
Intersection of Princess Anne Road and Concert Drive
3550 Cellar Door Way
Virginia Beach
(757) 368-3000

This is the biggest venue in Hampton Roads, seating 20,000 and annually attracting the largest acts. It opened in 1996 and has hosted everyone from Elton John and James Taylor to Gwen Stefani and the Warped Tour. Parking is part of the ticket price, but there are a limited number of $20 VIP spots. There is reserved and cheaper lawn seating, and concerts are a go, rain or shine.

PORTSMOUTH

NTELOS WIRELESS PAVILION
901 Crawford St.
Portsmouth
www.pavilionconcerts.com
(757) 393-8181

Sometimes it's hard to keep your eyes on the acts here. This cozy amphitheater sits right on the banks of the Elizabeth River, a working waterway where tugs and ferries, sailboats, and motor launches zip by a background of working shipyards. In fact, you can come to the concert by boat. A pedestrian ferry from Norfolk docks a few blocks away. Or you can captain your own and rent a slip at the adjacent Ocean Marine Yacht Center. The quality of the stars onstage often eclipses those in the summer sky. The Beach Boys have played here; so has Bonnie Raitt, CeCe Winans, Barry Manilow, Tony Bennett, and Harry Connick Jr. James Brown rocked the place. So did Jefferson Starship and Megadeth. And don't forget country favorites like Travis Tritt, Vince Gill, and Tricia Yearwood.

Although this is an outdoor facility, it's not cavernous, with just about 6,500 seats. You can bring a blanket or a low-slung lawn chair, or rent one when you get there and just chill. The sound is state of the art, no instruments lost to the wind here, and there are even free headsets available with reservations for the hearing impaired.

WILLETT HALL
3701 Willett Dr.
Portsmouth
(757) 393-5144
www.willetthall.com

Another often overlooked gem, Willett Hall is a small venue that offers plays, lectures, dance, and a variety of musical acts. It holds 2,000 and boasts that even the worst seat in the house is just 175 feet from the stage.

SUFFOLK

SUFFOLK CENTER FOR CULTURAL ARTS
110 West Finney Ave.
Suffolk
(757) 923-0003
www.suffolkcenter.org

What do you do with a beloved, historic high school that is no longer needed for education? In Suffolk, they turned the building into a 500-seat cultural arts center and a reason for folks to come downtown. Now people no longer travel *from* Suffolk for live entertainment. Here you can listen to highlights from *Porgy and Bess*, tap your toes to the bluegrass of Thunder Creek, or spend an educational evening with John and Abigail Adams. The center also offers classes for kids to adults in the visual to performing arts.

NEWPORT NEWS

FERGUSON CENTER FOR THE ARTS
Christopher Newport University
1 University Place
Newport News
(757) 594-7488
http://fergusoncenter.cnu.edu

Another of the new entertainment venues, the Ferguson brings the Peninsula a pair of top-drawer stages for musicals, ballets, orchestras, and other live entertainment. The Music & Theatre Hall is intimate and the larger Concert Hall exquisite, providing an opportunity for everything from magic acts to the London Philharmonic or Moscow State Radio Symphony orchestras. In 2010, the Ferguson hosted Israel Ballet's *Don Quixote* and the Moscow Festival Ballet's *Swan Lake*. From the highbrow classics of Academy of St. Martin in the Fields, to the high jinks and jokes of Jeff Foxworthy, it's all likely to wind up on the Ferguson's calendar. The Virginia Symphony Orchestra also calls Ferguson one of its many homes.

HAMPTON

THE AMERICAN THEATRE
125 East Mellen St.
Hampton
(757) 722-2787
www.hamptonarts.net

This tiny wonder got its start in 1908 as a "high class motion picture and vaudeville house." Like many such stages, it eventually hit the skids and transitioned to X-rated movies. The Hampton Arts Foundation bought the run-down building in 1997 and began a $2.9 million restoration. It reopened in June 2000 and has been bringing a wide range of entertainment to its cozy interior ever since. The 392-seat theatre is still owned by the foundation and operated by the City of Hampton's Arts Commission. If you're into eclectic, this is a place to watch. Acts in recent years ranged from the Arlo Guthrie family to *The Jackie Robinson Story*. Here, Tibetan monks descend every year and spend four days creating a magnificent sand sculpture called a mandala. The Tibetan theme is continued with monks in residence playing music and giving martial arts demonstrations. It all ends with the symbolic destruction of the sculpture. You can usually count on some fine jazz, bluegrass, world music, and dance here, with many acts, like the mandala makers, returning at the audience's request. On New Year's Eve, there's often a special show, complete with dancing afterwards in the new annex, and a champagne toast. It's a welcome alternative to the typical bar scene. Director Michael Curry, who's been at the helm since the theater opened, is always accessible. Look out for the cat named Liza who rules the place. Ticket prices here tend to be a bit more affordable than some of the bigger venues, and it's so small there really are no bad seats.

HAMPTON COLISEUM
1000 Coliseum Dr.
Hampton
(757) 838-4203 or (757) 838-5650
www.hampton.gov/coliseum
Another of the area's major concert venues, in its 4 decades the Coliseum hosted everyone from the Stones to Elvis. Jam rockers Phish loved the experience so much they began their reunion tour there in 2009. The facility also hosts the annual Hampton Jazz Festival in June, three nights of musical acts, some of which even play traditional jazz. This is where the circus annually performs for Peninsula audiences.

HAMPTON UNIVERSITY
CONVOCATION CENTER
700 Emancipation Dr.
Hampton
(757) 728-6800.
www.hamptonu.edu/convocation_center
This is mainly used for university functions, but can seat 8,000 for concerts.

MORE PERFORMING ARTS GROUPS

BALLET VIRGINIA INTERNATIONAL
http://balletvirginia.org
A professional dance academy for ages two and up, it has locations in Norfolk and Virginia Beach. It also presents several shows every year, including *The Nutcracker*.

BAY YOUTH ORCHESTRAS OF VIRGINIA
www.bayyouth.org
More than 250 student musicians are involved in the group's four performing ensembles, which appear in concert throughout the region. There's a junior string orchestra, a youth string orchestra, a youth concert orchestra, and a youth symphony orchestra.

BELLISSIMA! WOMEN'S CHORAL ENSEMBLE
www.bellissimachorale.org
An all-woman group founded in 2001, it performs music written for women's voices at a number of venues, from the Huber Court at the Chrysler Museum to local churches and concert halls. Their motto: "the most beautiful music sung by the most beautiful singers for the most beautiful audiences."

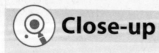

Close-up

Getting the Scoop from the Source

With so much of the population either in the military, working for it, or somehow related through blood or proximity, it's no wonder that Hampton Roads looks beyond its borders at things happening around the world.

One way we keep on top of the news is through a wonderful group of lecture series that bring to town people with insight, experience, or just good stories.

The grand poobah of the group is the Norfolk Forum, www.thenorfolkforum.org, which bills itself as the longest running community lecture series in the country. It has the cachet to bring Her Highness Queen Noor of Jordan to Chrysler Hall, as well as former president George H. W. Bush and presidential hopeful Al Gore (after his defeat but before his *An Inconvenient Truth* rally).

Every year, the Forum settles on four speakers, and it's not all politics. Recent seasons featured billionaire T. Boone Pickens; Gates Foundation global health adviser Dr. Elias Zerhouni; legendary football coach Lou Holtz, and *Newsweek* editor and author Jon Meacham.

This is a subscription series that nearly always sells out, so if you want to get in on the action, you'll want to buy a season ticket. They go fast after the final lecture every spring, when the next year's lineup is announced.

Old Dominion University is another traditional lecture powerhouse. Its President's Series is free and always thought provoking, with speakers ranging from former Attorney General Janet Reno to *Black Hawk Down* author Mark Bowden.

The World Affairs Council of Greater Hampton Roads, www.hrwac.org, is another big player, broadening the area's foreign policy perspective by bringing in speakers with insight on what is in the news. The 2010 series included a former ambassador to Iraq and Pakistan and General David Petraeus, the man commanding coalition forces there. These sessions include receptions with the speakers and dinners. The council also sponsors a Great Decisions series on Sat mornings from Jan to Mar at the Contemporary Art Center in Virginia Beach.

Finally, the Virginia Beach Forum recently moved into the Sandler Center as its resident lecture series, which feature an array of well-known writers, journalists, politicos, and the like.

BOYS CHOIR OF HAMPTON ROADS
www.boyschoirofhr.org

In the spirit of gender equity, we have to note this group founded to give the boys of Norfolk's Park Place community an opportunity to sing. It has expanded since to accept children from all over, regardless of whether they had musical training or aptitude. The goal is to foster healthy attitudes and teach life skills while imparting music theory and vocal techniques. Must be working—they've appeared at festivals and churches and even sung with the Virginia Symphony.

CANTATA CHORUS
www.cantatachorus.org

Founded in 1959, this vocal group concentrates on choral masterworks.

CHESAPEAKE CIVIC CHORUS
P.O. Box 2576, Chesapeake 23327
This group usually performs two major concerts a year, with works by Bach, Mozart, and Handel, as well as some contemporary works.

HAMPTON ROADS CIVIC BALLET
www.hrcivicballet.org
This is a pre-professional performing company based at the Academy of Ballet in Hampton since 1948 that stages two major productions every year, including *The Nutcracker*, and performs benefit concerts at art festivals, hospitals, and nursing homes.

FELDMAN CHAMBER MUSIC SOCIETY
www.feldmanchambermusic.org
This society presents nationally and internationally respected chamber artists at the Chrysler Museum Theater (not to be mistaken for the Chrysler Theatre, this is actually located in the Chrysler Museum a few miles away).

I. SHERMAN GREENE CHORALE
www.ishermangreenechorale.org
Founded by Isaac Sherman Greene, a music teacher at Norfolk's Booker T. Washington High School, the African-American chorale has been presenting recitals and concerts featuring traditional spirituals and masterworks since 1972.

NATCHEL BLUES NETWORK
www.natchelblues.org
Dedicated to promoting the blues as an American art form, this organization has been sponsoring concerts and festivals with local and national artists since 1984. The very first set the tone, featuring the legendary John Lee Hooker. Look for their Blues at the Beach festival on the Oceanfront in Sept, the free Blues on the Boardwalk acts every Thurs night in July and Aug, and workshops that have featured such stars as Taj Mahal. They also put out a bi-monthly *Blues News* and keep track of who's playing where on their website.

NORFOLK CHAMBER CONSORT
www.ncconsort.org
Founded in 1969, the consort presents chamber music from the 17th to the 21st centuries. They specialize in neglected masterpieces and works that involve voice and usually perform at the Chandler Recital Hall on the campus of Old Dominion University.

PENINSULA COMMUNITY THEATRE
www.pctlive.org
In existence since the merger of the Newport News and Hampton little theaters in the early 1950s, the all-volunteer company concentrates on musicals, comedies, and mysteries. It moved in 1994 into its current home, the Village Theatre in historic Hilton Village, converting the landmark movie theater into a performing arts center.

PENINSULA YOUTH ORCHESTRA
www.pyo-nn.org
A full symphony that began in 1960, it performs a number of concerts on the Peninsula.

SCHOLA CANTORUM
www.schola-cantorum.org
The name means choir of cantors, and the group of up to two dozen voices concentrates on choral music, from early to contemporary. They perform a series of concerts, mostly at churches throughout the region.

TIDEWATER CLASSICAL GUITAR SOCIETY

http://homepage.mac.com/dawolver/tcgs/

This nonprofit organization books prominent classical guitar artists into various venues in Hampton Roads and also has its own Classical Guitar Orchestra, a rare ensemble of nothing but nylon string instruments patterned after one in Costa Rica.

TIDEWATER WINDS

www.tidewaterwinds.org

This is a Sousa band that performs free concerts around the region.

VIRGINIA BEACH CHORALE

www.virginiabeachcorale.org

This group, founded in 1958, offers two major concerts, one in spring the other for Christmas, as well as participating in the Virginia Beach 4th of July Concert on the beach with Symphonicity and performing other concerts throughout the year.

VIRGINIA CHORAL SOCIETY

www.vachoralsociety.org

A community-based choral group with more than 100 voices, it presents three major concert series each year: fall, winter, and spring. Based in Newport News, it performs throughout Hampton Roads and was organized in 1931.

VIRGINIA MUSICAL THEATRE

www.broadwayatthecenter.com

This company is now in residence at the Sandler Center for the Performing Arts, presenting the sounds of contemporary Broadway as well as traditional American musical theater favorites with local and national performers.

ATTRACTIONS

It's impossible to miss the area's biggest attraction. Turn east and stop when you hear the breakers. You could spend an entire vacation right there and not feel cheated. But you would be missing out on so much more. Many folks look for options when the skies cloud up. Rain or shine, these gems can hold their own against the wonders of nature. Some, like Nauticus, defy easy definition but are still fun to explore. Others, like the Mariners' Museum, long ago eclipsed their origin as mere repositories and have become venerable institutions. Places like the Norfolk Botanical Gardens and the Virginia Beach Boardwalk take advantage of what nature has to offer. Others, like Mount Trashmore, artificially give nature a boost.

We have the mystic lure of Edgar Cayce's Association for Research and Enlightenment, and the religious pilgrims attracted to Pat Robertson's Christian Broadcasting Network.

And, always, there is the military.

Nearly all of these places, apart from the ones at the Oceanfront or in downtown Norfolk, offer free parking, so that shouldn't be a concern.

THE OCEANFRONT

Okay, let's acknowledge that giant gorilla in the room. Millions of people visit Hampton Roads every year to wade in the warm ocean water, ride some waves, and walk the "boards." So what is here in the tourist strip? Well, there are 35 miles of Atlantic and Chesapeake Bay beachfront in Virginia Beach alone. Folks work hard every winter replenishing the sand washed away in storms and eroded by tides, just to be sure there will be plenty of space for everyone to spread out a blanket. The beach is divided into several different areas, each with its own character. Up north, where Shore Drive meets Atlantic Avenue, it's residential and ritzy and still protected in places by grass-covered dunes. Here, there are no stores or souvenir shops reaching into your pockets. The Northend

beach is less crowded, simply because there are fewer places to park, and almost has a neighborhood feel as a result. Folks go here to enjoy the sun, not to see and be seen.

The resort area begins below the fabled Cavalier Hotel. Now you have a traditional beach community, with more than 40 hotels and motels casting their shadows on the sand and a 3-mile-long Boardwalk made of concrete packed with people and bicyclers. There are bandstands scattered through the area offering free entertainment, an amusement park at 15th Street with a Skyscraper ride, and a fishing pier right off the Boardwalk on the same block. When the kids get tired of burying each other in the sand, you can take them to a public playground right on the beach at 31st Street.

This section of the Oceanfront is busy well into the night as the crowds move from surf to Boardwalk to Atlantic Avenue.

Unlike many northern communities, you don't have to buy a tag to access the beach. Just pick a spot and walk on. The Boardwalk has restaurants and snack bars located in the beachfront motels, and one of the busiest Dairy Queens in the world at 16th Street.

Unlike the New Jersey resorts, commerce isn't really done on the Boardwalk unless you're there during one of the special festival weekends. Instead, all the traditional beach shops selling T-shirts, sandals, and sunblock are located on the first street, Atlantic Avenue. That's where you'll find the pancake houses, many restaurants, and a couple bars. There are stores and attractions as well on Pacific Avenue one more block inland, including those resort staples, miniature golf courses, at 14th, 21st and 25th streets.

The shopping gets a little tonier up by the Hilton at 31th street. The Shoppes @ 31 Ocean include boutiques, restaurants, a Harley Davidson store, and even a Starbucks coffee shop to offset that laid-back vacation vibe. But we'll get into where to shop in a separate chapter.

The Navy

If you want to get a real understanding of Hampton Roads, you have to get a feel for its biggest employer, landowner, civic partner, and income generator. The Navy is the factory in this company town. It's the reason most people first move here, and the frequent battle group homecomings are why many others come to visit. With the constant vigilance against terrorists, you can no longer just pack up the family and take a Sunday drive along the destroyer piers and board an open-house ship. But you can still get an up-close view of the world's largest Naval base on a special tour bus.

Navy personnel conduct the 45-minute tours, providing insights and answering questions as you pass aircraft carriers, destroyers, frigates, amphibious assault ships, and one of the busiest airfields in the country. You might even see them hauling a jet along one of the base streets.

The tours leave the base's **Tour and Information Center**, 9079 Hampton Blvd., in Norfolk. During the summer there are nine tours daily, fewer in spring and fall, and only one a day during the dead of winter. For information, call the center, (757) 444-0948.

i The Tour and Information Center is located about a block south of the guarded gates where Hampton Boulevard enters the base. If you're heading north on Hampton from downtown Norfolk, it will be a one-story building on your left, just past B Avenue, which is the base entrance for the destroyer piers. There's no turn lane, though, so you have to make a U-turn in a cut just beyond the building. Miss that and you're on your way to the guarded gate. Tell them where you are headed, and they'll let you turn around just inside the gates.

The Navy also has an air force and the Atlantic component of that air wing is based in Hampton Roads. Early warning radar planes and helicopter squadrons are located at the Naval Station Norfolk but the glamour guys who push fighters to their limits fly out of Oceana Naval Air Station in Virginia Beach. There are no tour buses at Oceana, but you really don't need one to see those

Super Hornets at work. Landing an aircraft on a dark deck in the middle of a heaving sea is one of the toughest assignments in the military.

You don't just head out one day and see if you have the stomach to slam down on that surging surface and snag one of those three arresting wires with your tailhook. No, it takes a ton of practice, and that occurs in places like Oceana and the Fentress Auxiliary Airfield a few miles away in Chesapeake. Pilots there do what are called "touch and go" landings, bouncing down on a runway marked to look like a carrier deck then shooting back into the sky.

They rely on the same "meatball" light system used on a carrier to get their bearings in the dark, and their attempts are graded by flight officers who help them perfect the process here, where they don't have to worry about crashing or clipping one of the planes that landed before them. Pilots have to be certified for day and night landings before they can report to a carrier.

That means there are constantly planes in the air over Oceana, and because a supersonic jet can't turn on a dime, they are always roaring over the Oceanfront as they make their big swing back to the base. Those flight patterns limit the height of the hotels at the beach and influence where malls, schools, and other gathering places are built. An actual crash is very rare. Pilots are trained to head out to sea if they have a problem and expect to have to ditch their craft. In 1986, an A-6 Intruder crashed near Oceana, killing the pilot, his navigator, and a pregnant woman in a car on the ground.

There's a monument to Naval Aviation at 25th Street and the Oceanfront that features bronze sculptures honoring Eugene Ely, the first aviator to launch from a ship; a World War II pilot and crewman rushing from a carrier hatch; modern aviators, including a female pilot; and a list of all aircraft carriers in US history.

NAUTICUS
One Waterside Dr.
Norfolk
(757) 664-1000
www.nauticus.org

When this attraction first opened, a local newspaper columnist had a lot of fun asking City Council members and other officials to describe it in one sentence. No one really could. These days, there's an official answer on the website: "Nauticus is an exciting interactive science and technology center that explores the naval, economic, and nautical power of the sea." Okay, so what does that mean, really?

Well, like the sentence says, it's a lot of things loosely tied together by water.

There are permanent exhibits on the Jamestown Exposition and the launching of the Steel Navy, and another on NOAA's National Marine Sanctuaries where you can go inside a submersible and control a robotic arm to collect samples. There are even real artifacts from the Civil War ironclad *Monitor*.

There's an exhibit on weather that allows you to touch a tornado or learn about lightning. An exhibit on the modern Navy lets you eavesdrop on sailors describing their jobs and hunt subs in a computer simulator. In "Design Chamber: Battleship X" you try to create the greatest battleship on the eve of World War II. In the Aegis Theater, you experience a simulated battle situation from a command center and see how the Navy's high-tech Aegis destroyers form a 250-mile shield around a battle group by combining advanced surveillance and firepower. And there's even a touch tank where kids of all ages can pick up starfish, hermit crabs, horseshoe crabs, and urchins.

There are also frequent changing exhibits, from a look at the real life of pirates to what it was like for servicemen taking the three-week trip to and from Vietnam.

The Navy used to make at least one of its ships available for visits every weekend. That doesn't happen anymore for security reasons. But you can still climb around on a real ship by visiting the battleship *Wisconsin* in its berth beside Nauticus. Now that the city has taken control of the *Wisconsin*, that tour is also part of the Nauticus admission and an expanded exhibit on the battleships is being created. The *Wisconsin* is one of the last and largest battleships ever made and has a long history that spanned World War II to a tour of duty against Iraq in the 1991. This is one of the most beautiful military vessels, its lines low and sleek and the three turrets full of menacing 16-inch guns just shouting power. Those guns can fire a projectile that weighs as much as a small car a distance of 24 miles. The Navy had kept the *Wisconsin* in suspended animation and allowed tours of only its teak-covered decks, but it turned the ship over to Norfolk in 2010, which plans to open up parts of the interior of the vessel to visitors.

MARINERS' MUSEUM
100 Museum Dr.
Newport News
(757) 591-5124
www.mariner.org

This is one of the largest maritime museums in the world, with more than 61,000 square feet of gallery space and 35,000 artifacts, many one-of-a-kind. It is international in scope, with vessels from all over the world represented, and was founded and funded by the son of the railroad and shipping magnate who built and ran the Newport News Shipbuilding and Drydock Company. If you have any interest in boats and nautical art, this place is a must see.

The International Small Craft Center is one of the leading collections in the world, with 150 boats from 36 countries rotating in and out of exhibits arranged by nine different themes. You can see how different cultures approached boatbuilding, the way materials influenced their vessels, and examine boats used in various competitions as well as craft used for surfing. On display are everything from racing shells to recreational yachts. You can see real Native American birch bark and dugout canoes as well as Arctic kayaks and umiaks. There are sampans and a gondola and gleaming Chris-Crafts.

As amazing as the full-sized boats are, you will be astounded by the miniatures.

The museum features a collection of elaborate models by artist/carvers August F. and Winifred Crabtree. They trace the development of boatbuilding from primitive rafts to a Venetian galleass that has 359 carved figures. Or you can wonder at the detailed model of a Chinese sampan carved from a small nut and the 33-foot-long model of the *Queen Elizabeth* that was displayed at the British Pavilion during the New York World's Fair in 1930.

Larger carvings abound throughout the museum in the form of 92 rare figureheads from the bows of sailing ships. There's also a wide range of maritime paintings and a legendary collection of navigational instruments, including a pair that may have been used by Capt. James Cook. In the days of GPS and satellite phones, it is humbling to look at a brass sundial sailors used around 1680 or the silver-coated mariner's astrolabe that dates to 1645 in Portugal. Interested in marine communications? The museum has that covered too, with an early wireless two-way radio made by the Marconi Wireless Telegraph Company.

The museum has the steering wheel used when the CSS *Virginia* battled the USS *Monitor* off Hampton Roads, and a life vest from the R.M.S. *Titanic*. Then there's the library, at nearby Christopher Newport University, a resource for anything nautical, with 1.7 million items and staff members ready to assist your research.

The museum is open Wed through Sun, and Mon when it's a federal holiday. Admission is $12; $11 for seniors, military, AAA members, and students; $7 for 6- to 12-year-olds.

USS *MONITOR* CENTER
100 Museum Dr.
Newport News
(757) 596-2222
www.monitorcenter.org
The ironclad *Monitor* sank in a storm off the coast of North Carolina after fighting the CSS *Virginia* to a standstill in Hampton Roads. Its resting place is our first National Marine Sanctuary, but parts of the ship have been removed and they are on display or being preserved at this $30 million facility run by the Mariners' Museum and NOAA next door to the museum itself. Here you can walk on a full-size replica of the *Monitor* and look at the actual turret that fired the shots in 1862 that changed marine warfare forever. It's submerged in a 20-year bath to ensure the saltwater is removed before it can eat away any more metal. In fact, one of the most exciting aspects of the center is that the folks

who are doing the preservation are in full view. You can watch as they perform their delicate dance against decay. The center uses lighting and innovative exhibits to take you back to the days of wooden warships, where decks were a dangerous place raked by broadsides with little protection for the sailors. You see a 50-foot replica of the *Virginia*'s bow, covered in iron with its massive battering ram. You learn how a designer pulled together the *Monitor* in 100 days to meet that challenge and then watch a show that recreates the battle. There's another battle that's equally exciting, the one to raise that massive turret from the ocean bottom, told in a film narrated by actor and famous film voice Sam Watterson that features interviews and the actual footage from the Graveyard of the Atlantic. Open daily, admission $12.50 for adults, $7.25 for children 6 to 17.

VIRGINIA AQUARIUM & MARINE
  SCIENCE CENTER
717 General Booth Blvd.
Virginia Beach
(757) 385-3474
www.virginiaaquarium.com
This aquarium, which opened in 1986, just keeps on growing. There are more than 800,000 gallons of tanks and live-animal habitats just a few miles south of the tourist strip. The emphasis here is on animals native to the region, but that's hardly limiting here, where the cold Labrador Current meets the warm Gulf Stream only a few miles offshore. There are two touch pools where you can see what a ray feels like or look at a horseshoe crab's mouth. And others you don't want to stick a hand in, since sharks, stingrays, and other nasty critters make places like the Norfolk Canyon Aquarium their home. Outside, there's a tank with harbor seals, a

bird aviary with 55 different species, and a marsh with river otters, seahorses, and snakes. The micro marsh magnifies plants and animals up to 10 times so you can watch them at work. And there's even a nature trail through a preserve between the aquarium buildings, with an observation tower to look over Owls Creek. A new exhibit called Restless Planet features Komodo dragons, rare crocodiles, and 110,000 gallons of aquariums designed to show how Virginia evolved into its current state. And the IMAX theater is not only 3D, it's huge—with a screen six stories tall and eight stories wide.

The aquarium also sponsors trips to watch whales in the winter and dolphins in the summer, as well as tours of Owls Creek Salt Marsh and expeditions where staff trawl the ocean floor to see what comes up. And it's home to a stranding response program that helps marine mammals and sea turtles who become beached along area coasts. Open daily 9 a.m. to 5 p.m., and until 6 p.m. in the summer. Admission is $17, $16 for seniors, $12 for children 3 to 11. IMAX is $8.50, $8 for seniors, and $7.50 for children ($2 more if it's a feature film).

CAPE HENRY LIGHTHOUSE
583 Atlantic Ave.
Fort Story
Virginia
(757) 422-9421
www.apva.org/capehenry

The Cape Henry Lighthouse is no longer operational and probably would have been torn down decades ago had the Association for the Preservation of Virginia Antiquities, which now operates the site, not stepped up in 1896 to place a tablet on it commemorating the first landing of English colonists on Virginia shores. You can climb the spiral staircase inside right to the top where the lens no longer burns. The views from there are wonderful, out over the ocean and bay and back toward the resort area. But do wear shoes and clothing fit for climbing. The octagonal structure was the first to be ordered and built by the U.S. government. It began lighting the way into the Chesapeake Bay in 1792, and was damaged by Confederate troops to keep Union troops from using it. And when cracks were discovered on six of the eight cut-stone sides in 1872, experts predicted it would soon collapse into the sea. It was closed and a new lighthouse built of cast iron rose 357 feet away. That second Cape Henry Lighthouse went online in 1881 and is still operating. The predictions of doom were unfounded, though. Congress conveyed the old lighthouse to the APVA in 1930, and the group has been letting the public in ever since. It's prominent in the City Seal of Virginia

When you visit the light, don't forget to check out the Cape Henry Cross at the nearby Cape Henry Memorial. The granite monument was erected in 1935 by the national society Daughters of the American Colonists in the spot where the English colonists presumably put up their wooden cross of thanks after making it to the new land. The inscription says: "Here at Cape Henry First Landed in America, upon 26 April 1607, those English colonists who, upon 13 May 1607, established at Jamestown Virginia, the first permanent English Settlement in America." The memorial also includes a statue of Admiral Comte de Grasse, whose French fleet kept the British Navy from coming to Lord Cornwallis' aid at Yorktown, ensuring the general's surrender that ended the war.

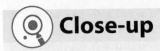 **Close-up**

Mount Trashmore!

When it opened in 1973, Mount Trashmore was an international sensation, the region's highest spot, built entirely from the area's recycled refuse. This was in the early years of environmental awareness, and it seemed a great idea to stack your trash in a place where the water table was too close to the surface to bury it.

There was a huge crowd for the park's opening, which featured a soapbox derby competition on a six-lane stretch of pavement built into the side of this artificial peak.

That 950-foot-long racetrack is gone. Kids changed and no longer were interested in hurtling down a hillside in a motor-free vehicle they had built. And the park, the city's most heavily used, was in desperate need of repair.

Workers removed the ramp, recapped the peak, and stabilized the soil in 1999. Nobody seemed to notice the track was gone. That's not to say the park was empty. People still flock here on sunny days to fly kites and climb to the top of the 60-foot-high mountain created by compacting layers of trash and soil.

It's open from 7:30 a.m. to sunset and kids are still rolling around on wheels, but it's in a skate park with a 7-foot-deep bowl and a 13.5-foot-tall vertical ramp.

There's a lake nearby where you can fish, but boating is no longer allowed. And the ever-popular Kids Cove is a wooden play area for children. Look for the Indian statue in the shaded grove in front of the Cove. It's part of a national collection, at least one in every state, carved from timber by sculptor Peter Toth, called "The Trail of the Whispering Giants." He finished this one in 1976 and came back in 2004 to spruce it up.

Beach. Open daily 10 a.m. to 4 p.m. from Nov to mid Mar and until 5 p.m. from Mar 16 to Oct 31. Admission is $4, $2 for children 3 to 12. It is on a military base, so you'll need photo ID and proof of auto ownership. And visitors have to be at least 42 inches tall to climb the 191 steps inside the light.

ASSOCIATION FOR RESEARCH AND ENLIGHTENMENT
215 67th St.
Virginia Beach
(757) 428-3588
www.edgarcayce.org/are
Virginia Beach is the international headquarters of the Association for Research and Enlightenment founded by mystic Edgar Cayce in 1931. Ever since, the center has been attracting folks who wanted to have psychic readings by Cayce or explore his extensive writings and sleep revelations. Most of his readings dealt with holistic health and the treatment of illness, but the center has identified 10,000 different topics. The library has transcripts of 14,000 Cayce readings among one of the world's largest metaphysical collections, including works on holistic health, psychic experience, psychology, and comparative religions. Its vaults also house the originals and other Cayce artifacts. There's a bookstore that sells Cayce writings and healthcare products based on his readings. The beach facility also has a Health Center and Spa, which incorporates many

of Cayce's remedies and massage therapies. And there's a massage school. The center also hosts frequent conferences.

THE CHRISTIAN BROADCASTING NETWORK
977 Centerville Turnpike
Virginia Beach
(757) 226-7000
www.cbn.com

This is the home of the international television ministry built by Pat Robertson and the studios where the syndicated *The 700 Club* is produced. Today, this charming, colonial brick campus produces programming to about 200 countries. *The 700 Club* has been on the air since 1966, one of the longest running programs in broadcast history. Regent University, a fully accredited institution with a law school, is also on the 685-acre campus CBN built. There are free, behind-the-scenes tours of the network and ministry throughout the day, and folks can join the studio audience of *The 700 Club* with an 8:30 a.m. seating. You can also eat at the Swan Terrace, a restaurant at The Founders Inn and Spa.

VIRGINIA SPORTS HALL OF FAME AND MUSEUM
206 High St.
Portsmouth
(757) 393-8031
www.vshfm.com

Virginia is not only the mother of presidents; it's the birthplace of some great athletes. This museum in downtown Portsmouth honors them. And it's a pretty impressive group, with 45 national hall of famers among the crowd and 30 of *Sports Illustrated*'s top 50 athletes of the century. In the old days, this was a pretty static place, with glass-enclosed cabinets that held a few artifacts. But when the hall of fame moved into a new building in 2005, it broke free. Sure, you can still gawk at an ancient glove, but you can also grab a ball and see how hard you can throw a fastball. There are interactive exhibits in baseball, football, soccer, and basketball. You can even take a microphone and do your own call on some of Virginia's most exciting highlights. Open daily in summer, closed on Mon Sept through May. Admission is $7, $6 for seniors, military, and AAA members.

MUSEUMS

From historic homes to living tableaus, working studios to one of the finest collections of art outside of New York, Philly, and LA, Hampton Roads has a wide variety of museums to meet every interest.

There are museums dedicated to the military and others that focus intensely on one culture. There are hands-on museums and others that are just handy. You can walk the deck of a dreadnaught or climb the winding stairs in a lighthouse. There are so many historic homes open for visits that you could specialize in that genre alone and keep busy.

You can spend months just moving from one museum to another in Hampton Roads and still not see everything. But don't get paralyzed by all the options. Just pick a type and explore. Many are free, some operate through donations, and none is expensive. Some museums, like the Mariners' Museum and the USS *Monitor* Center, have become regional attractions in their own right and will be covered in that chapter. Another don't-miss attraction is the Children's Museum of Virginia, which is covered in the Kids' Stuff chapter.

ART MUSEUMS

CHARLES H. TAYLOR ARTS CENTER
4205 Victoria Blvd.
Hampton
(757) 727-1490
www.hamptonarts.net
This building started out as Hampton's public library and now hosts a series of changing exhibitions throughout the year as well as space on the second floor for permanent collections and classes, lectures, and workshops. The emphasis here is on local artists even though the building is named for the founder and managing editor of the *Boston Globe* newspaper. He was the father of Grace Taylor Armstrong, who built the library for the city. Her estate leases it to the city to be operated by the Hampton Arts Commission. The center is free and closed on Mon.

CHRYSLER MUSEUM OF ART
245 West Olney Rd.
Norfolk
(757) 664-6200
www.chrysler.org
This is the patriarch of all area museums with a nationally recognized collection that is astounding for a region of this size. It was founded in 1939 as the Norfolk Museum of Arts and Sciences but really took off in 1971 when automobile scion Walter P. Chrysler Jr. handed the city his vast art collection. His wife was a Norfolk native, and when his collection outgrew a small museum in Provincetown, Mass., he was looking for a new place and settled on, and in, Norfolk.

Chrysler had begun collecting as a 14-year-old and always intended that his works would wind up on public view. From his first watercolor, a nude by Renoir, he eventually amassed a vast array of French and Italian paintings and some 8,000 pieces of art glass, including Art Nouveau and early American objects. He was a neighbor of Louis Comfort Tiffany and collected many of the glass master's works. He also collected rare books, many of which comprise the museum's 40,000-volume library named after his wife, Jean Outland Chrysler. And he was a fan of music, founding a Music Library and Musical Instruments Museum with 10,000 volumes and 400,000 recordings, as well as instruments.

Walter Chrysler died in Norfolk in 1988 leaving a rich legacy and a museum he was proud to have bear his name.

The museum building itself is beautiful, an Italianate structure right on a historic inlet of the Elizabeth River. Inside are nearly 40,000 objects in the permanent collection and a variety of special exhibitions that ensure you will never run out of something new to see or something to see in a new way.

There are six general areas of interest in the museum, which is basically organized by era or art form.

The collection of American Paintings and Sculpture actually predates Chrysler's involvement, but his endowment not only brought his personal collection but enticed his older sister to donate 164 folk art paintings and established the cachet for obtaining 70 marble sculptures from the renowned private James H. Ricau collection. The museum now boasts important colonial and folk painting, works by 19th-century American masters, examples of American impressionism, and those breathtaking sculptures.

Chrysler loved to collect European works, and they form the basis of one of the most distinctive collections in the United States. Here you'll see everything from delicate Renaissance panel paintings to modernist works by Henri Matisse and Georges Braque. You can spend hours staring at the works of Dutch masters or get lost in a single Degas.

The contemporary art section has continued growing since Chrysler's death. Here you can enjoy a giant Roy Lichtenstein or marvel at Georgia O'Keefe and Alexander Calder's use of color and contrast.

For those who like their art to be utilitarian, there's an emphasis on the decorative arts. Chrysler used some of the 18th-century furniture and silver now on display, then donated them when he shifted to Art Nouveau to furnish his homes. The museum also has some amazing southern furniture it had before Chrysler and a fabulous Worchester porcelain collection.

Another strength is the photography collection. Chrysler actually never collected photographs, but that hasn't stopped the museum that carries his name from becoming a leader in the field. There are more than 4,000 photos in the collection, from the earliest daguerreotypes to modern digital displays. It all began with a gift by controversial photographic artist Robert Mapplethorpe of two works in thanks for the Chrysler organizing his first museum exhibition and publishing his first catalogue. Look for the Civil War photos and those that chronicle the Civil Rights Movement in the five galleries dedicated to photography.

All that alone would make the Chrysler an amazing museum. But its ultimate distinction is in the world of glass. Chrysler, smitten by Tiffany, was one of the first to collect art glass seriously, concentrating on glass made from the early 1800s through the 20th century, including Steubens and Tiffany lamps. He loved French glass and English cameos, and the collection contains John Northwood's Milton Vase, a masterpiece in the rediscovery of the ancient Roman art form. The museum has continued to strengthen its collection by acquiring major studio and contemporary glass. The result is one of the great glass collections in America.

And if all that isn't enough, the museum offers a range of events from gallery talks by art experts to a yoga class for art lovers. And every Wed, there's a free lecture and often a concert, from jazz to classical guitar. There's a restaurant inside the museum, Cuisine & Company at the Chrysler Cafe, that stays open Wed until 8 p.m. so you don't have to rush to get to the evening event.

Admission is free. The museum is open Wed through Sun. Visiting exhibitions can have entrance fees but are always free to museum members and children five and under.

i Parking at the Chrysler Museum is free in a lot right outside the building and another just across the street. The Hague is a picturesque inlet and you can walk the park or eat a picnic lunch there or in the small outdoor garden. You can sketch using dry materials in any gallery. If you want to paint, you'll need advance permission. And you're welcome to photograph the works for personal use, so long as you don't use a flash.

CONTEMPORARY ART CENTER OF VIRGINIA
2200 Parks Ave.
Virginia Beach
(757) 425-0000
www.cacv.org

This is an art center without a permanent collection, which means it's an always-changing canvas. Recent exhibitions have included *Where the Wild Things Are: Maurice Sendak in His Own Words and Pictures*, an interactive exhibit where children were encouraged to put on costumes and slide, wild-thing-like, into a bowl of "chicken soup," and *Jenn Figg: Forest Thrall,* a composition of commonplace materials that evoke dark fairy tales in a mysterious landscape. Admission is $7 for adults, $5 for students and seniors, and $3 for kids 3 to 14. You get a $2 discount with a AAA membership and the museum is closed on Mon.

D'ART CENTER
208 East Main St.
Norfolk
(757) 625-4211
www.d-artcenter.org

This is a gallery where you not only see the finished works but also can interact with the artists as they create them. It began in 1986 in a small downtown building where 27 artists were challenged by a flood at the grand opening but soldiered on and developed a real following. They were almost too successful, helping transform an abandoned section of downtown into such prime real estate that the city eventually decided to redevelop and pushed them out. In exchange, the now 43 resident artists moved into the beautiful Selden Arcade, which opened in 1931 with a trade exposition and went on to house investment and insurance companies. The city bought the building in 2003 and it reopened as Norfolk's cultural arts center in 2005. Artists have to submit works to be reviewed by a panel before they can rent available studio space or wall locations to exhibit pieces. Here you can meet artists working in everything from painting to photography. Admission is free and the center is open every day except Mon.

HAMPTON UNIVERSITY MUSEUM
100 West Queen St.
Hampton
(757) 727-5308
www.hamptonu.edu

This is the oldest African American museum in the United States, started in 1868, and one of the oldest museums of any kind in Virginia. Its mission, like that of the school it supports, is to provide knowledge, understanding, and respect for diverse cultures and traditions.

The initial collection came from the school's founder, Gen. Samuel Chapman Armstrong, who was born and raised in Hawaii by missionary parents. The school began collecting African objects in the 1870s to augment its African Studies programs. An alumnus, William Sheppard, was the first African American to collect African art and he provided several hundred pieces of materials from the Kuba Kingdom, now the Democratic Republic of Congo.

The school was one of the first to focus on American Indian education, with 1,300 native students from 66 tribes attending between 1878 and 1923. So the museum added American Indian art. In 1894, the museum acquired two paintings by Henry O. Tanner, establishing the world's first collection of African American art, including *The Banjo Lesson*. That collection grew in 1967 with a gift of hundreds of works from the Harmon Foundation that covered the Harlem Renaissance as well as 29 works of art from the widow of Countee Cullen, the famed Harlem poet.

Today, there are more than 9,000 objects here, including traditional African, Native American, Native Hawaiian, Pacific Island, and Asian art. It also houses the largest existing collection of African American fine art by John Biggers, Elizabeth Catlett, Jacob Lawrence, Richmond Barthe, and Samella Lewis. Everywhere the school's graduates went, they brought back art for the museum. The Japanese collection features pieces from the estate of Alice Bacon, a former Hampton U. teacher who went to Japan in 1888 to teach women in the Imperial Court.

The most recent exhibit is the history collection with nearly 700 objects that illustrate Hampton's mission over the years. You can examine tools used in the agriculture program, furniture and textiles made by students, educational resources from the trade school and academic program, old nurses' uniforms, and athletic memorabilia.

The museum is in the restored Huntington Building, another former library, on the campus. Closed on Sun. Admission is free.

HERMITAGE MUSEUM & GARDENS
7637 North Shore Rd.
Norfolk
(757) 423-2052
www.hermitagefoundation.org

You'll be amazed at what is packed into this historic house museum off the Lafayette River. The place was built by William and Florence Sloane, who came from New York City to operate textile mills here.

They named their home Hermitage and expanded it to 42 rooms by 1936. The couple were art collectors, and Florence Sloane was friends with and a pen pal to many artists. They established a foundation in 1937 and donated the house and its contents, as well as the gardens, to that foundation and opened the Hermitage house museum to the public in 1942. Mrs. Sloane lived in the house until she died in 1953, and her youngest son continued living there and running the foundation until the early 1970s.

Today, there are more than 2,800 objects in the Sloane Collection on display throughout the home's hand-carved oak, walnut, and teak galleries. The range is awe inspiring, from Neolithic jade to American paintings. Even the building furthers their desire to promote the Arts and Crafts movement. The Sloanes employed an English woodcarver named Charles J. Woodsend for more than two decades to hand carve and install the interior paneling. Others came to create the furniture or carve quotations into the lintels. The art is everywhere, from the portrait of Abraham Lincoln by Douglas Volk entitled *Breasting the Winds* by the stairs, to the *Girl with a Shell* bronze fountain by Edward McCarten that highlights the 12 acres of formal gardens that are often used for wedding ceremonies. As a special bonus, there's a free playground for children on the grounds open from sunrise to sunset every day, with equipment, walking paths, and picnic tables to keep the youngsters entertained.

The museum is closed on Wed and Thurs as well as most holidays. Admission to the house is $5, $3 for college students, $2 for kids 6 to 18, and free to younger children and active duty military. A *Through the Garden Gate* guided tour is offered on some summer Saturdays for $6.

PENINSULA FINE ARTS CENTER
101 Museum Dr.
Newport News
(757) 596-8175
www.pfac-va.org
This is another museum that relies entirely on changing exhibitions with a goal of advocating for arts in the region. It also offers educational programs, a year-round studio art school, and a permanent interactive gallery for children. It's located in the Peninsula's museum district by the Mariners' Museum and is affiliated with Richmond's Virginia Museum of Fine Arts. There's a Gallery Shop where you can buy original work by regional and national artists as well as museum reproductions, jewelry, and books. A $7.50 admission ticket is good for seven days. There's a dollar discount for seniors, active duty military, students and teachers, and AAA members. Kids from 6 to 12 are $4 and those younger get in free. You can also go free on Tues, from 5:30 to 8 p.m. The gallery is closed on Mon.

MILITARY MUSEUMS

With this area's history it shouldn't be surprising that there are a number of museums dedicated to the military. Here are a few to keep you busy.

CASEMATE MUSEUM
20 Bernard Rd.
Fort Monroe
Hampton
(757) 788-3391
This museum depicting the fort's role in the Civil War opened in the 1950s with an exhibit on the cell where Confederate President Jefferson Davis was held after his arrest. These days, that cell has been joined by a number of other exhibits that tell the story of this ancient stone fort, which remains the military's only installation defended by a moat, and the Army Coast Artillery Corps. This is a military base, so you will need a valid ID and proof of ownership for your vehicle to get in. The cave-like rooms inside the walls definitely transport you to another era. If you ever wondered how Poe got so glum, realize

he was stationed here while in the Army. Also a former resident was Robert E. Lee, who was an engineer here as a young lieutenant. The quarters where he lived with his wife Mary Custis Lee and their first son was born are on a walking tour. This free museum is part of the Army's museum system and is open seven days a week.

HAMPTON ROADS NAVAL MUSEUM
1 Waterside Dr.
Norfolk
(757) 322-2987
www.hrnm.navy.mil

Located on the second floor of Nauticus on the Elizabeth River beside the Battleship *Wisconsin*, this is a free museum run by the Navy. Exhibits trace the Navy's role from the Battle off the Virginia Capes in the Revolutionary War to modern times. Many of the displays explore local naval events during the Civil War, the Jamestown Exposition, and the sailing of the Great White Fleet from Hampton Roads. Learn here how Norfolk became a Navy town, see items from the Cuban Missile Crisis, and then take the Wisky Walk that traces the history of the Battleship *Wisconsin* before visiting the actual ship.

THE MACARTHUR MEMORIAL
MacArthur Square
Norfolk
(757) 441-2965
www.macarthurmemorial.org

Remember his promise that "old soldiers never die"? Well, this is where Gen. Douglas MacArthur just faded away. This museum is housed in Norfolk's 19th-century City Hall, right across City Hall Avenue from the MacArthur Center shopping mall that bears his name. The memorial is actually four buildings in a landscaped setting. There's a

theater with galleries and a 24-minute film on the colorful general, whose mother was a Norfolk native. The separate research center is named for his wife, Jean MacArthur, and houses the library and archives. The gift shop displays the 1950 Chrysler Crown Imperial limo MacArthur used from before the Korean War until his death in 1964, shipping it from occupied Japan to New York City.

Step inside the museum itself and you see a rotunda, at the base of which the general and his wife lie interred. Banners and flags that celebrate his career surround them, and there are nine permanent and two changing galleries arranged on two levels that explore the military from the Civil War to the Korean conflict. Everywhere, though, is the spirit of the man who, when forced to evacuate the Philippines, promised "I will return." On display are everyday items like his trademark military hat, corncob pipe, and glasses as well as a large array of the medals he won, including the Medal of Honor. He and his father are the only father and son to ever win the nation's highest heroism award.

The museum is free and open seven days a week.

MILITARY AVIATION MUSEUM
1341 Princess Anne Rd.
Virginia Beach
(757) 721-7767
www.militaryaviationmuseum.org

This is one of the largest private collections of World War II and Korean War fighters, bombers, trainers, and seaplanes anywhere—all carefully restored and most still able to fly. It's located in the rural southern section of the city at the Virginia Beach Airport. They offer special events, an annual Warbirds Over the Beach air show, and frequent flight demos of planes they have restored. The aircraft come from all over the world and are returned to duty by the museum's Fighter Factory in Suffolk. There are also flying replicas of World War I planes made of wood and canvas. There's a Navy hangar, an Army Air Corps hangar, and several more being built. Open daily, 9 a.m. to 5 p.m. Admission is $10 for adults, $9 for seniors and military, and $5 for students. It's free for World War II vets.

NAVAL SHIPYARD MUSEUM
2 High St.
Portsmouth
(757) 393-8591
www.portsnavalmuseums.com
The Norfolk Naval Shipyard is the nation's oldest and largest government yard. It has been burned three times by retreating armies, was the birthplace of the ironclad CSS *Virginia* (which most incorrectly call the *Merrimack*, its name before the South converted it to an ironclad), the first battleship *Texas*, and the first aircraft carrier *Langley*. It is also home to the nation's first dry dock, still in use. All of that history is explored in this small riverfront museum. Inside are ship models, uniforms, military artifacts, and exhibits tracing the shipyard's history and the history of the city the shipyard made possible. Admission is $3, $1 for children 2 to 17, but it also covers admission to the nearby Lightship *Portsmouth*.

THE U.S. ARMY TRANSPORTATION MUSEUM
300 Washington Blvd.
Fort Eustis
Newport News
(757) 878-1115
They say an army marches on its stomach. Well, here you'll see how an army rides. From mule trains and Conestoga wagons to the latest armored personnel carriers, it's all here. The museum occupies a 50,000-square-foot building on the base as well as four outdoor parks. See how the Army standardized truck production and learn about Operation Mulberry, which created a pair of artificial harbors to support the invasion of Normandy in World War II. There are dioramas, including one with a Vietnam era gun truck, "Eve of Destruction." You can see the helicopters that ferried soldiers across that country and bikes that the Viet Cong used for transport. There are amphibious craft of all sizes, from the DUKW landing trucks to barges. The museum is free but on a military base, so have ID and vehicle owner's info. It's closed on Mon and federal holidays.

THE VIRGINIA WAR MUSEUM
9285 Warwick Blvd.
Newport News
(757) 247-8523
www.warmuseum.org
This city-run museum chronicles the U.S. military from 1775 through today in a collection of personal artifacts, weapons, vehicles, and uniforms. There's even a section of the Berlin Wall and a portion of the outer wall from the Dachau Concentration Camp and a section of a wall from a POW camp in Germany on display. There are also special galleries for women at war and African Americans in the military and a whole collection of propaganda posters. The museum has one of America's first battle tanks from World War I, a World War II American Stuart Light Tank, a Gatling gun, and a modern Iraqi anti-aircraft gun. The Fowler Gallery for Small Arms is a must see for gun enthusiasts. Admission is $6, $5 for senior citizens and active duty military, and $4 for children 7 to 19. The museum is open seven days a week.

HISTORY MUSEUMS

HISTORIC VILLAGES AT CAPE HENRY
Joint Expeditionary Base Little Creek–Fort Story
Gate 1, the north end of Atlantic Avenue at 89th Street
Virginia Beach
You don't have to drive all the way to the Historic Triangle to tour an Indian Village or see how the first settlers lived. During the summer, there are docent-led tours of this new attraction, which combines history and drama to tell the story. You can experience a young man's initiation to Algonquin warrior status and see the relationship between Native Americans and English settlers through his eyes. There's an American Indian village where you can learn about canoe building, meat curing, and other tribal practices and a 17th-century colonial outpost with a watchtower, palisade, church, and trading post. There's also a low, circular stage by the dunes where the original drama *1607: First Landing* is performed. The center is open Thurs through Sat, May 27 through Sept 4, 2 to 6 p.m. Docent tours are $8, $5 for children 6 to 15. The drama is $15 for adults, $10 for youth, which includes a free tour.

OLD COAST GUARD STATION
2400 Atlantic Ave.
Virginia Beach
(757) 422-1587
www.oldcoastguardstation.com
This museum in a historic Life Saving Service/Coast Guard Station tells the story of Virginia's coastal communities before tourism and the high-rise hotels arrived through the tales of shipwrecks and rescues. There are 1,800 artifacts and more than 1,000 photos of the services and old Virginia Beach. The 1903 building, on the Boardwalk, is on the National Register of Historic Places. The museum is open daily; admission is $4 for adults, $3 for seniors and military, and $2 for children 6 to 18.

SUFFOLK SEABOARD STATION RAILROAD MUSEUM
326 North Main St.
Suffolk
(757) 923-4750
www.suffolktrainstation.org
This tiny gem is located in the restored 1885 Suffolk Seaboard AirLine Railroad Station. It documents the city's relationship with the iron horse through an elaborate model of Suffolk that features an operating HO scale version of the Suffolk and Carolina branch of the Norfolk Southern Railroad running through a recreation of the 1907 "Birdseye View Map" of Suffolk that wanders through two rooms. The museum, owned and operated by the Suffolk Nansemond Historical Society, also has children's story times and a gift shop with railroad related items. Be sure to look at the red caboose parked next door. Open 10 a.m. to 4 p.m. Thurs through Sat and 1 to 4 p.m. on Sun.

HISTORIC HOMES

ADAM THOROUGHGOOD HOUSE
1636 Parish Rd.
Virginia Beach
(757) 385-5100
One of the oldest surviving Colonial homes in Virginia, it is open six days a week for guided tours. It was thought to date back to the 1680s, but more recent research places it in the 1720s. The city now owns and operates the home, which is built in the medieval English cottage style, complete with steep roof and massive chimneys. There are four rooms, two on each floor. The grounds overlook the

Lynnhaven River, and most historians don't believe Adam Thoroughgood, one of the region's first settlers, ever lived in the home. Rather it was probably one of his grandsons.

ENDVIEW PLANTATION
362 Yorktown Rd.
Newport News
(757) 887-1862
www.endview.org

This is a Newport News-operated house museum. The T-frame Georgian house, built in 1769, served as a Confederate hospital during the 1862 campaign. It has been restored to its appearance during the Peninsula Campaign.

FRANCIS LAND HOUSE
3131 Virginia Beach Blvd.
Virginia Beach
(757) 385-5100

It's hard to believe as you buzz down the crowded Virginia Beach Boulevard that there was once a huge plantation here. Hard until you turn onto the drive of the Francis Land House and step back a few hundred years. The home was built about 1805 and has been operated as a historic house museum since 1986. It's furnished in period antiques and docents demonstrate and educate.

HILL HOUSE
221 North St.
Portsmouth
(757) 393-0241

This four-story English basement home in historic Olde Towne was owned and occupied by the Hill family for a century and a half. It remains in its original condition, complete with the family's belongings and portraits. The home is open on weekends, 1 to 5 p.m., Apr through Dec.

HUNTER HOUSE VICTORIAN MUSEUM
240 West Freemason St.
Norfolk
(757) 623-9814
www.hunterhousemuseum.org

This home was built in 1894 and the last surviving family member created the Hunter Foundation to operate the home, donating "the furniture, decorations, paintings, and curios" as a museum and example of Victorian architecture. The home opened to the public in 1988 and offers guided tours Apr through Dec each year. It's also the headquarters of a local chapter of the Victorian Society in America, and is named for the society's founder, Eloise Dexter Hunter. They offer special programs for Girl Scout troops and individual scout visits.

JAMES A. FIELDS HOUSE
617 27th St.
Newport News
(757) 245-1991
www.jamesfieldhouse.blogspot.com

James Apostles Fields was born into slavery but escaped to freedom at Fort Monroe during the Civil War. He was in the first class of graduates from what would become Hampton University and became a teacher before graduating from Howard University law school. He would become the first black Commonwealth's Attorney in Warwick County, now Newport News, and served in the Virginia legislature in 1889-90. In 1908, he allowed four doctors to turn the top floor of the Fields house into the first hospital for African Americans in Newport News. The home went into disrepair after his death, but it has been restored and is operating as a museum to illustrate how blacks lived in Newport News at the turn of the 20th century. Open Tues through Sat, 11 a.m. to 4 p.m. Suggested donation is $3 for adults; $2 for students, seniors, and military; and free for 12 and under.

LEE HALL MANSION
163 Yorktown Rd.
Newport News
(757) 888-3371
www.leehall.org
This is the only large antebellum plantation house on the lower Virginia Peninsula. The Lee family fled the home three years after it was built when war came to the Peninsula. It became a Confederate headquarters until they were driven out of the area by Gen. George McClellan's forces. The family returned after the war, and the city of Newport News bought the home in 1996. Restored, it now documents the Peninsula Campaign of 1862. Closed on Tues all year and on Wed in the winter. Admission is $6 for adults, $5 for seniors, $4 for 7- to 18-year-olds.

LYNNHAVEN HOUSE
4401 Wishart Rd.
Virginia Beach
(757) 431-4000
This home dates to around 1725 and is an example of local architecture. Built of brick in the English bond pattern, it sits on a finger of land near the Lynnhaven River. Here you can see how a middle class planter lived.

MOSES MYERS HOUSE
Bank and East Freemason Streets
Norfolk
(757) 333-1087
This home looks at how a prosperous Jewish family lived in the late Federal period. It was one of the first brick homes built in

Norfolk after the city was burned during the Revolutionary War. It is full of original family furnishings and has been restored to its 1820 appearance. This is another of the Chrysler's historic homes; admission is free and it is open Wed through Sun.

NEWSOME HOUSE MUSEUM AND CULTURAL CENTER
2803 Oak Ave.
Newport News
(757) 247-2360
www.newsomehouse.org
This is the home of J. Thomas Newsome, a prosperous and respected attorney, journalist, churchman, and civic leader who was part of the postwar South's new black middle class. The Queen Anne home was the hub of the black community and the 1899 home is devoted to black cultural and historic themes. Open Mon through Sat, 10 a.m. to 4 p.m. A $2 donation is suggested.

NORFOLK HISTORY MUSEUM
Willoughby-Baylor House
601 East Freemason St.
Norfolk
(757) 333-1087
Capt. William Willoughby, a descendant of the man whose land would eventually become Norfolk, built this historic home in 1794. It remained in the family until 1890 and was bought in 1964 and restored by the Norfolk Historic Foundation. The home has been administered by the Chrysler Museum since 1969, and in 2005 it opened as the Norfolk History Museum. The home's exhibits examine the city's architectural, commercial, maritime, and military history using Chrysler artifacts. Admission is free and it is open Wed through Sun.

RIDDICK'S FOLLY

510 North Main St.
Suffolk
(757) 934-0822
www.riddicksfolly.org

How can't you love a home that brought its original owner, Mills Riddick, nothing but ridicule? He's got the last laugh now because his Greek Revival home keeps his name alive long after his detractors have faded away. The four-story home was built in 1837 and has 21 rooms and 16 fireplaces. It is a true mansion, with elegantly furnished double parlors and a library. Head upstairs and you can see how adults and children slept. Or you can wander the laundry, kitchen, and dining rooms and marvel at the needlepoint done by one of the young women in the family. There's a peanut museum in the basement full of information on the crop that put Suffolk on the map. Open Thurs through Sun. Admission is $4, $3 for seniors and military, and $2 for children.

SCIENCE MUSEUMS

VIRGINIA AIR AND SPACE CENTER

600 Settlers Landing Rd.
Hampton
(757) 727-0900
www.vac.org

Want to know how they put the men on the moon, or what it takes to pilot a space shuttle? Well, this museum, which serves as the visitors' center for both NASA Langley Research Center and the Langley Air Force Base, has all the answers. America's space program got its start at Langley, a NASA facility that is still on the cutting edge. The museum has exhibits tracing 100 years of flight, with more than 30 historic aircraft and unique space flight artifacts. You can even try your luck with simulators that allow you to launch a rocket, drive a shuttle, and control air traffic in a crowded corridor. The museum has the Apollo 12 Command Module that went to the moon, a meteorite from Mars, and a moon rock that's 3 billion years old. The Riverside IMAX theater shows 3D films, and there are always a variety of changing exhibits to keep it fresh. And you can take a simulated space journey to Mars in a trainer modeled after the ones NASA uses. The center is open every day of the week, but hours vary by season. Admission is $10.50 for adults, a dollar less for seniors and military, and $8.50 for kids 3 to 18. There's an additional charge for the IMAX theater or discount combo tickets.

VIRGINIA LIVING MUSEUM

524 J. Clyde Morris Blvd.
Newport News
(757) 595-1900
www.thevlm.org

This facility combines the elements of a native wildlife park, science museum, aquarium, botanical preserve, and planetarium, with exhibits and more than 245 different species that reflect all of the state's various regions. There are interactive discovery centers and galleries that take you back in time, through a limestone cave, under the sea, and in a mountain cove and cypress swamp. The museum is open 9 a.m. to 5 p.m. Mon through Sat and noon to 5 p.m. on Sun. Admission is $15, $12 for 3- to 12-year-olds ($4 more to visit the planetarium).

PARKS

Love the outdoors? In Hampton Roads you'll find everything from rustic trails, where you are likely to spook a whitetail, to wooden half-pipes just begging for a few big air tricks. Every city has its own recreational masterpiece—and a collection of smaller neighborhood green places for quicker getaways. We won't get into the neighborhood parks here. You can find them with the links to various Parks and Recreation departments in the Recreation chapter.

But there are others here that are destination parks, drawing people from across the region and even from other states and nations. Take your time and enjoy each one. Don't forget to pack your sunscreen, and especially some good insect repellant if you're going rustic.

BACK BAY NATIONAL WILDLIFE REFUGE
4005 Sandpiper Rd.
Virginia Beach
(757) 721-2412
www.fws.gov/backbay

On this 9,000-acre sanctuary, everything revolves around nature. The main mission is to provide resting and feeding areas for migrating water birds. Some 10,000 snow geese and a large variety of other waterfowl visit every fall. The refuge also is home to endangered species such as loggerhead sea turtles, piping plovers, peregrine falcons, and bald eagles. And some intruders such as feral pigs and wild ponies. There are boardwalks that lead to the beach and some other areas are open to visitors on foot. You can't swim, surf, or sunbathe here, and you have to stay on designated trails and roadways. Sections also may be closed to provide undisturbed areas for wildlife, and the refuge is only open from just before sunrise to just after sunset. Only small boats and canoes that can be hand carried to the bay's edge are permitted.

Motorboats and jet skis are banned. Two dike paths are open to bicyclists for part of the year. Both are closed for wildlife protection from Nov through Mar. There's a $5 per vehicle admission fee, or $2 per family if you hike or bike in. Those under 16 are admitted free.

BUCKROE BEACH AND PARK
End of Pembroke Avenue
Hampton
(757) 850-5134
www.hampton.gov/parks/waterfront_and_feature_parks.html

The Peninsula has it's own favorite strand, and it dates back nearly as far as First Landing. Buck Roe Plantation was set aside for public use in 1619. It was a fishing camp until after the Revolutionary War. But when the railroad arrived, so did the resort. Buckroe Beach was once segregated, like all such areas in Virginia. But there was an equally popular black beach next to it named Bay Shore Beach & Resort. The nearby Buckroe Beach Amusement Park was a popular destination but was torn down in the 1980s. Its carousel is now a highlight in downtown Hampton. The city of Hampton offers eight acres of public beachfront here, as well as a playground and picnic shelters you can reserve. You can rent beach chairs and umbrellas or, if you want to get active, kayaks and paddleboats. The beach is open from 8 a.m. to 6 p.m. and has lifeguards on duty from Memorial through Labor days. On Sun nights in the summer there's a Groovin' by the Bay concert series and on Tues nights a family movie series. There's also a new fishing pier if you'd rather watch a line than bay swells. The original was destroyed by Hurricane Isabel, which did tremendous damage to this area.

i Just above Buckroe Beach, on the Northeast corner of Hampton, is the Grandview Nature Preserve, a 475-acre refuge of salt marsh, tidal creeks, and 2.5 miles of secluded Bay beachfront perfect for a picnic or hunting for driftwood and shells. If you follow the beach you'll eventually reach the ruins of the Back River Lighthouse, which stood sentinel for much of its 127 years. A 1956 hurricane washed away what remained. Now there's just a small pile of rocks offshore. The Nature Preserve, run as part of Buckroe Beach Park, is free, but there is limited parking along State Park Drive.

FALSE CAPE STATE PARK
4001 Sandpiper Rd.
Virginia Beach
(757) 426-7128

This is one of the most unusual parks in Virginia and, as one of the least visited, one of the most vulnerable to budget cutting. There's no way to drive to this 4,321-acre

park with nearly 6 miles of beachfront on the North Carolina border. In spring and summer, a tram runs visitors through Back Bay Wildlife Refuge to the park, where they can explore for several hours before getting a ride back. There's a $2 per person fee for the tram or to travel through Back Bay from Apr through Oct. There are four primitive campgrounds here, but this is roughing-it camping. No electricity, pit toilets, no showers. The state doesn't recommend it for young children, the inexperienced, or anyone with medical conditions that might require easy access to emergency care. There are lots of ticks, mosquitoes, and biting flies. Be sure to pack plenty of repellant. And you need to watch out for poisonous eastern cottonmouth snakes. Many campers prefer to come by boat, but Back Bay is broad and shallow and can whip up to dangerous seas quickly. The state park allows motorboats and pets year round, although you'll have to ferry Fido over by boat during the months they are banned on the Wildlife Reserve.

By now, you understand why False Cape is so poorly utilized. But if you really are seeking a getaway or want to rustic camp by the Atlantic, all these warnings and hurdles mean you're likely to be left alone in your reveries. The rangers here do their best to make it memorable, offering night hikes, canoe trips, and special programs in conjunction with the Virginia Marine Science Museum, the Virginia Institute of Marine Science, and the Wildlife Refuge. The area got its name because ships often mistook this "false cape" for Cape Henry and wrecked on the shoals. The community of Wash Woods was developed here by survivors of one of the shipwrecks using cypress that washed ashore.

FIRST LANDING STATE PARK
Off Shore Drive/U.S. 60
(757) 412-2320
www.first-landing-state-park.org

Wonder what the New World looked like when Capt. Christopher Newport parked his flagship *Susan Constant* off Cape Henry? First Landing State Park in Virginia Beach will give you a pretty good idea. There are 19 miles of hiking trails here, winding through old-stand forests adorned with eerie Spanish moss (the farthest north this air plant grows).

The 2,888-acre park, largely built by African Americans with the Civilian Conservation Corps in the 1930s, begins right on the Chesapeake Bay, with a campground just behind the dune line. At First Landing you can set up a tent, park your RV, or rent one of the 20 cabins just a few miles, but another world, from the bustling Atlantic Avenue tourist strip. Be sure to make those reservations early, though, because this is Virginia's most visited state park, and there are only about 220 campsites.

The wonders continue on the other side of Shore Drive, which is where the park really goes native. Here, you'll find the park's nine hiking trails. The most popular is the Bald Cypress, a 1.5-mile trek through a cypress swamp that crosses dunes and ponds and is wheelchair-accessible. Interpreted trail walks are offered throughout the year, and trail guidebooks are available. Only one of the park's nine walking trails, the 6-mile-long Cape Henry, allows bicycles, which can be rented at the park's Baystore.

To cool off after your hike, saunter over one of the official dune crossings and take a dip in the Chesapeake.

First Landing, which used to be called Seashore State Park, is on the National Register of Natural Landmarks, because it is the northernmost location for more than just Spanish moss. It is the East Coast border beyond which subtropical and temperate plants no longer thrive together.

i The water in the Chesapeake Bay tends to be a little warmer than the Atlantic, and there are no waves to speak of. But there are also no lifeguards on duty at most bay beaches, and at times the stinging jellyfish can be abundantly painful, so take care.

There's a boat ramp in the park's southern section with access to the Chesapeake through the Narrows, between Broad and Linkhorn Bays, and it's free to overnight guests. Others will have to pay a launch fee. You can fish in the park, but you'll need a valid Virginia saltwater license. The biggest local paddle sports event of the year, PaddleFest, takes place at First Landing in mid-Sept.

The park is also home to the Chesapeake Bay Center, with a wet lab and educational displays focusing on nature and the first landing in 1607 produced in cooperation with the Virginia Aquarium and Marine Science Center.

The park also has a picnic area with a large shelter, a courtyard, gazebo, and an amphitheater that can be rented for conferences or even weddings.

LITTLE ISLAND PARK
3820 Sandpiper Rd.
Virginia Beach
(757) 426-0013
www.vbgov.com

We locals hate to give this one away, but this is where we head when we want to dip our ankles in the Atlantic. This 123-acre park sits at the southern end of the Sandbridge resort neighborhood and just outside the Back Bay National Wildlife Refuge and was once home to a Coast Guard station. Now it's a place to get away from all those tourists who flock to the resort area every summer. There's plenty of parking here, but you'll have to pay for the privilege during the season. It's $5 a day, Memorial Day through Labor Day for non-residents or $10 if you want to bring a busload. There's 2,775 feet of Atlantic beachfront and a 400-foot fishing pier ($7 a day fee from Apr to Oct. You don't need a Virginia saltwater fishing license from the pier, but you do if you stand on the beach or surf). Other amenities include: volleyball and tennis courts, a special surfing and fishing area, a playground, picnic shelters, a changing area, and showers and foot rinses for when you're ready to head home and want to get out of that itchy bathing suit. You can even walk across Sandpiper Road and fish or crab in brackish Back Bay.

The park is open from 5:30 a.m. until 11 p.m. Apr 15 through Oct 31 and 7 a.m. to 5 p.m. the rest of the year. Lifeguards are on duty from 9:30 a.m. to 6 p.m. Memorial to Labor days.

LONE STAR LAKES
1 Bob House Parkway
Suffolk
(757) 255-4308
www.suffok.va.us/parks/ls.html
Located in the Chuckatuck section of Suffolk, Lone Star is a 1,063-acre wilderness park with 11 freshwater lakes, nature trails, picnic areas, a playground, a 4-mile horse trail, an archery range, a model airplane flying field, and a fishing and crabbing pier. The park is open from sunrise to sunset. No gasoline motors are allowed on the lakes, which are part of the region's water supply

reservoirs. Like in Newport News, you'll need to complete a safety course before you can take to the archery range or the flying field. This is a freshwater fisherman's paradise, but you'll need a valid license. There's a $4 per day fishing fee, $2 to use the archery range and the flying field, and $3 per person for horseback riding access. You can also buy annual permits.

> **i** Coming soon is another environmental retreat called Paradise Creek Nature Park. The Elizabeth River Project, a nonprofit dedicated to undoing centuries of neglect and abuse of the area's waterways, has bought one of the last stands of woods on this industrial river and is building a special park in Portsmouth that will allow visitors to experience the creek, a small tributary of the Southern Branch of the Elizabeth River. Most of the waterfront in this urban city is commercial and off limits. This section will be restored and offer shorelines, wetlands, and woods to explore as well as educational exhibits. The initial phase is due to open in 2012.

MOUNT TRASHMORE
310 Edwin Dr.
Virginia Beach
(757) 473-5237
www.vbgov.com
This park is as well known for what it once was as for what it is today, the Southside's only "mountain vista." So what about the unusual name? Mount Trashmore is just that, a 68-foot-tall peak built with recycled trash. It was created by compacting 640,000 tons of solid waste amid layers of clean soil and was the first such reclamation project

in the nation, opening in 1973. Back then, it had a soapbox derby ramp and rented paddle boats. Those are gone now, for safety reasons, as is the option to sled down the region's only real slope on those odd times when the snow sticks. This is the city's most popular park, always filled with kite fliers and families.

The 165-acre park sits right off I-264 and features three large picnic shelters, five smaller shelters, three volleyball courts, horseshoe pits, and playgrounds, including Kids Cove, a play area designed and built using kids' ideas. There's a giant wooden Indian sculpture just outside Kids Cove that was carved by artist Peter Wolf Toth for the Bicentennial and which he recently gave a facelift and new lease on life. Toth erected these monuments to Native Americans in every American state, as well as some Canadian provinces, as part of his Trail of the Whispering Giants. Boating is no longer allowed on Lake Trashmore, but you can fish from shore, with a state license.

There is a 24,000-square-foot skate park featuring a street course with a 7-foot, above-ground bowl, all with a Skatelite Pro skating surface. Next-door is a competition-sized vertical ramp that's 13.5 feet tall and 40 feet wide. If you want to skate or bike on these courses you have to sign up for a free skate park pass and wear approved helmets.

MUNDEN POINT PARK
2001 Pefley Lane
Virginia Beach
(757) 426-5296
www.vbgov.com
This oasis on the water is more groomed than wild, but its views of the North Landing River are glorious, and there's a broad boat ramp where, for $6, you can launch

your yacht and set off on the Intracoastal Waterway for the Currituck Sound, the Outer Banks of North Carolina, or points beyond. This 100-acre park also offers an 18-"hole" disc-golf course, three ball fields, three basketball courts, three playgrounds, six volleyball courts, horseshoe pits, canoe and kayak rentals, and plenty of open space for picnics and kite flying. There's an intimate amphitheater that can be reserved for everything from weddings to classroom instruction. The park opens at 6:30 a.m. and closes at dusk.

i Chesapeake also has a skate park, located in Chesapeake City Park at 500 Greenbrier Parkway. It has a spine ramp, hip ramp, and a three-quarter pipe, as well as a street area that includes a series of smaller ramps, platforms, and obstacles. Skaters must wear safety equipment and obtain a Chesapeake Community Center ID card or a visitor's pass. Those IDs aren't sold at the park. They must be bought at a community center. They cost $7 per year for youths and $20 for adults who are Chesapeake residents. It's $25 and $40 for non-residents. Visitor's passes cost $5.

NEWPORT NEWS PARK
13560 Jefferson Ave.
Newport News
(757) 886-7912
www.nnparks.com/parks_nn.php
At 8,140 acres, this is not only the area's largest city park, it is the second largest municipal park in the nation and the biggest east of the Mississippi. It's hard to list everything available here, so let's start with what you can't do. There's no saltwater fishing, no fields for baseball, basketball, or

soccer, and no beach to flop on. There are two large freshwater lakes, though, where you can angle with a permit. The park is a designated stop on the official Virginia Civil War Trails Network because it has some of the best preserved fortifications, earthworks, and redoubts from that war.

You can camp here year-round. There are 188 sites spread through the natural woodlands, and most include electrical hookups, with nearby heated showers and flush toilets. The park has two famous public golf courses (see Golf chapter) with a pro shop and driving range, and it offers an 18-hole championship disc golf course. Bring your trademarked Frisbees or you can rent or buy discs there, and try to hit these links (the chain links hanging from the "holes" of course.) A $2 disc golf daily pass is needed if you're older than 12 or less than 60.

Mainly, this park is a nature lover's dream. It is home to deer, fox, otter, raccoons, and beaver, all within a short drive of shopping centers, malls, and movie houses. The park features floral gardens, including a Japanese Peace Garden with an authentic teahouse, an arboretum, and 5 miles of all-terrain mountain bike trails. If you prefer your pedaling to be less extreme, there are more than 30 miles of bike trails that wind through forest, fields, and wetlands. You can rent boats and bikes here. The park offers a Discovery Center with nature and history exhibits as well as regularly scheduled nature and history programs.

One distinctive treat is a special archery range. There's a practice area with seven shooting lanes and a 28-target course that winds throughout the woods. It's open sunrise to sunset, but you need to complete an archery safety program and pay either $2 per day or $20 a year (plus tax) if you're older than 12 or younger than 60.

i The park has a 30-acre aeromodel flying field, complete with a 400-foot paved runway, set aside for flying model aircraft. You'll need a $50 annual permit and have to be a member of the Newport News Park Radio Control Club; call (757) 591-4848 for more info.

NORFOLK BOTANICAL GARDENS
6700 Azalea Garden Rd.
Norfolk
(757) 441-5830
www.norfolkbotanicalgarden.org

Just outside Norfolk International Airport is a nonprofit museum for plants known as the Norfolk Botanical Gardens. It was begun in 1938 as a Work Progress Administration project. Some 220 African American workers, nearly all women, were paid to clear 30 acres of dense vegetation on the site. They earned 25 cents an hour for the backbreaking work. The first year, 4,000 azaleas, 2,000 rhododendrons, and several thousand shrubs and trees were planted in what was known then as the Azalea Garden, along with a hundred bushels of daffodils Today, the 155-acre garden is home to one of the largest collections of azaleas, camellias, roses, and rhododendrons on the East Coast. Spring blooms can be breathtaking. There are actually 30 distinct, themed gardens here, including winter gardens full of camellia, holly, and conifers and a tropical display house. The facility is host to 95 species of birds and 30 different kinds of butterflies. Every year, a quarter million people visit the gardens. You can just walk around or take guided tram tours. There is also a paid guided boat tour. Admission is $7 for adults, $6 for seniors and the military, and $5 for children older than two. Toddlers get in free with a parent's admission.

> **i** A pair of bald eagles annually nests in one of Norfolk Botanical Garden's tallest trees, and the world watches to see what hatches on an Internet EagleCam (www.norfolk botanicalgarden.org/e-community/ eagle-cam).

NORTHWEST RIVER PARK
1733 Indian Creek Rd.
Chesapeake
(757) 421-7151 or (757) 421-3145
www.chesapeake.va.us/services/depart/ park-rec/nwrp

Still in the mood for nature? Then head over to Northwest River Park in southern Chesapeake. This 763-acre tract is located on the banks of the wide Northwest River and is owned and operated by the city. It's open from 9 a.m. until sunset year-round and offers 70 campsites as well as two rental cabins for a quick getaway that doesn't involve sleeping on the ground. If you hike quietly, you might surprise a few whitetails on Deer Island Trail. The park has 7 miles of winding trails, all teeming with wildlife, and a portion of one is accessible to the physically disabled. One of the shortest paths leads to an elevated wooden walkway over wetlands and an observation point on the Northwest River that shouldn't be missed.

There's a ranger station loaded with information, and just outside is a fragrance garden with azaleas, camellias, honeysuckle, and other wildflowers, all under the shade of native hickory, pawpaw, oak, and buckeye trees.

You can enjoy the river by boat, and the park rents kayaks, canoes, Jon boats, and paddleboats that can be used on an enclosed 40-acre lake that runs through some of the prettiest wooded areas. The lake is stocked with bass, bluegill, crappie, and catfish. You'll need a valid freshwater license year round—and a Virginia trout license during the winter months when they put them in the lake. The park doesn't sell licenses, though, so be sure to pick one up before wetting a line.

If you want to break free, you can portage your boat to the Northwest River and paddle up Smith and Indian Creeks, which form the park's boundaries, or launch your own boat in either and circumnavigate the park.

There are plenty of picnic areas, with horseshoe courts and a children's playground. You can rent a shelter or an activity building for your group. Sometimes, there are music acts on a portable stage, and the Virginia Symphony occasionally plays a concert along the river here.

It's far enough away from the bustle and lights that every month the Back Bay Amateur Astronomers organization gathers in the park's equestrian area. Visitors are welcome and can get a primer on telescopes and what's up there in the night sky. The Sky Watch begins at dusk and runs to midnight, but bad weather can force a cancellation, so be sure to check with the park before heading down. Otherwise, the park closes to day visitors at dusk.

And that equestrian area is just that. If you have a horse, bring it to the park and ride here and on special trails. Daily passes cost $5 per person, or you can join the Equestrian Club for $15 a year, $30 for the entire family.

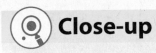 **Close-up**

A Not-So-Dismal Day Trip

Want to really get away? Take a canoe or kayak and paddle into the Great Dismal Swamp. The 3.5-mile feeder ditch opens into Lake Drummond, a giant shallow saucer that seems by satellite view to have been created by an ancient meteor strike. It is one of only two natural lakes in all of Virginia; the rest are the result of human digging or damming.

There's a public boat ramp, with a small motorized tram to get vessels under 1,000 pounds over a U.S. Army Corps of Engineers spillway. Nothing larger than 10 horsepower is allowed on the lake.

If you'd rather drive, you'll have to enter the refuge in Suffolk off White Marsh and Desert roads or Jericho Lane. Once you park, there are a number of unpaved roads for hiking and biking. You can bring your dog on a leash. This is a wildlife refuge, and there is plenty here, with one of the state's largest populations of black bear and even bobcat for the very lucky to see. Whitetail deer are common, as well as otter, raccoon, mink, fox, and squirrel. There are also three poisonous species of snakes in the refuge—cottonmouth, canebrake rattler, and copperhead—and 18 non-venomous species, so watch your step.

Or you can stay within earshot of civilization by paddling down the Dismal Swamp Canal. Surveyed by George Washington and eventually dug by slaves, it's part of the Intracoastal Waterway, which means you can paddle from Portsmouth through here to Florida, should you be super adventurous as well as fit. The canal is host to an annual Paddle for the Border event that attracts boaters from Maryland to Georgia.

Just beside the ditch, as it's called, is the new Dismal Swamp Canal Trail, an 8.2-mile multipurpose outdoor venue that used to be Virginia Route 17. When the state moved and widened that link to North Carolina, Chesapeake stepped in and took over the old roadway. It's now closed to cars and is the perfect spot to bike, run, walk, or even ride your horse. You can take the full 17-mile loop or just explore a 2-mile nature trail.

The swamp was a stop on the Underground Railroad. And it's a treat for bird-watchers every fall and spring, since many migratory birds stop here to rest before continuing their trek. More than 200 species have been spotted on the refuge, with 96 nesting here or nearby. The trail passes through a state wildlife management area and borders the Great Dismal Swamp Refuge, so there's no telling what you might see.

i Every October, Northwest River Park is home to one of the area's favorite kids' attractions, a Ghost Train that runs through a volunteer production sure to scare and enthrall the wee ones.

OCEAN VIEW BEACH PARK
300 West Ocean View Ave.
Norfolk
www.norfolk.gov/rpos/parks.asp
Another Beach access little troubled by tourist crowds is Ocean View Beach Park on the Chesapeake Bay in Norfolk. It's located on the former site of the Ocean View

Amusement Park, which was the star of the 1977 movie *Rollercoaster*. The park closed in 1978, and the historic wooden rollercoaster was destroyed as part of the 1979 ABC Movie of the Week *The Death of Ocean View Park*. Not only can you swim in the warm, gentle bay waters, but there's a large band shell for Sunday night big band shows. Lifeguards are on duty from Memorial to Labor days. There are picnic shelters, concession stands, free parking, and even a fishing pier with bait shop and tackle rentals.

DOG PARKS

With all this open land there ought to be a place where man's best friends can run free. There is actually a passel of them scattered throughout Hampton Roads. Here's a list of the various dog parks that offer fenced-in runs so animals can be turned loose to socialize and play with their own kind.

Chesapeake

Chesapeake City Park, 900 Greenbrier Parkway: There are two separate areas in this 1.5-acre facility, one for large dogs and the other for those 25 pounds and under. **Western Branch Dog Park** is a half-acre park located near Western Branch Community Center.

Hampton

Sandy Bottom Bark Park is at the corner of Hampton Roads Center Parkway and Big

Bethel Road. **Ridgway Bark Park** is at 85 East Mercury Blvd.

Newport News

Fido Field is in Riverview Farm Park, 105 City Farm Rd. There are two runs here, an acre for large dogs and 1/8 acre for those 20 pounds or less. Dogs must be registered before entering, so you'll need to bring tags and records confirming all vaccinations are current.

Norfolk

Norfolk has a dozen dog parks, in many neighborhoods of the city. Three of them are fenced. They are: **Colonial Greenway Dog Park** off Llewellyn Avenue and Delaware Street at the Colonial Greenway Playground; **Lafayette Dog Park** on Orleans Circle off Lafayette Boulevard on the Lafayette River; and **Bea Arthur Dog Park,** a one-acre park at 501 Front St. operated by PETA, People for Ethical Treatment of Animals, outside its headquarters.

Virginia Beach

Red Wing Metro Park is at 1398 General Booth Boulevard. **Woodstock Community Park** is at 5709 Providence Rd. Each one-acre park requires an on-site $10 registration along with proof of license and vaccination. Dogs get a park tag and kids have to be at least eight to get into the dog park. Children don't need a license.

RECREATION

By now you probably have an idea that we like to get out and about. How can you blame us? With so much sunshine, even in winter, there's always a nearby attraction beckoning.

If you like to golf, you will probably find good enough weather just about year-round (see the chapter on Golf). If you enjoy fishing, you'll have plenty of days to hit the water. And if you love playing team sports, there's nothing to hold you back.

That may be why Hampton Roads has produced so many fine professional athletes. Allen Iverson and Michael Vick set high-school records on the Peninsula, where each was a multi-sport star. David Wright, Ryan Zimmerman, and Mark Reynolds learned how to dominate third base on the Little League fields of Chesapeake and Virginia Beach. The Upton brothers, B. J. and Justin, were standout shortstops in Chesapeake and became the highest drafted brothers in Major League history. Justin was a number one and B. J. number two. In basketball, Joe Smith, J. R. Reid, and Alonzo Mourning all started on the Southside, and Bruce Smith, Plaxico Burress, DeAngelo Hall, Percy Harvin, and Dre' Bly dominated high-school football here.

It's gotta be the weather—or the ever-present water.

Let's tackle the temptations alphabetically. It doesn't hurt that our greatest asset is right there at the top of that list.

BEACHES

The harbor may have put us on the map, but those endless miles of inviting sand are what keep people coming back to visit Hampton Roads. You can take your pick from the pounding breakers of the Atlantic, home to the annual East Coast Surfing Championship, or the gentle swells at a Chesapeake Bay beach. But why choose only one? Virginia Beach alone has more than 35 miles of waterfront, with beaches where you can be secluded and others where you're sure to see and be seen.

In Virginia, there are no private beaches, although you'll need to locate an official public access right of way in some areas where the mansions sit right up against the

dunes. Once you hit the surf line, you can generally walk to your hearts content.

For security and safety reasons, though, the public is restricted from some of the beachfront military bases. You don't want to be caught napping as Navy SEALs storm in on a practice amphibious assault anyway.

Oceanfront

The Resort Strip

Nearly 3 million tourists visit Virginia Beach every year, and most of them never get past the resort area. This is the swath of Oceanfront that begins at Rudee Inlet and heads north to about 38th Street. The bulk of the visitors stay on this 3-mile long stretch in front of the Virginia Beach Boardwalk, a misnomer, since it is actually paved with concrete. There is a separate path for walkers and another for bikers and skaters. The parallel Atlantic Avenue is where you can buy all the typical tourist trinkets and T-shirts.

i The locals know this well, since most of us learned the hard way. The Virginia sun has no conscience. You will burn to a crisp quicker than you think. It's a combination of the southern location and the reflection off sand and sea. So pack plenty of good, waterproof, high SPF sunscreen and reapply it regularly. Nothing ruins a vacation quite like that lobster look and its accompanying pain and peeling. And that burn you prevent today could be the skin cancer you don't get down the line.

This strip is where you will find most of the resort hotels and motels, as well as a variety of restaurants and one of the world's busiest Dairy Queens. This is where those who want to enjoy the beach's social scene show up to show off. And there's a playground for the youngsters right in the sand at 31st Street.

There are lifeguards in abundance throughout this area during the season, and you can rent chairs and umbrellas, bring your own, or go local with just a towel and flip-flops. Don't tempt fate and try to find free parking here. Even in the off season it's rare, and the tow trucks are always prowling. There are plenty of public and private lots. The prices vary, even at public lots, from hourly rates of about $2 to all-day prices that range from $5 to $7 depending on the

day and the lot. Here, all day doesn't mean overnight. In most lots, if your vehicle is still there at 2:30 a.m. it's going to be towed at your expense. Some even have a midnight witching hour, so check the rules when you check in.

If you've partied too hard to drive, though, all you have to do is notify a parking cashier, hail a cop, or call (757) 385-5600, and the city will make sure you don't have to worry about the car being towed because you did the right thing.

i What may be a national first opened in May 2010 on the Virginia Beach Oceanfront between 1st and 2nd streets just north of Rudee Inlet. The city's new J.T.'s Grommet Island Beach Park and Playground for EveryBODY allows those in wheelchairs a chance to experience the sun and surf without the hassle of trying to negotiate dunes. The park is named for Josh Thompson, a local developer's surfing son who was stricken young by amyotrophic lateral sclerosis, or Lou Gehrig's disease. Beyond easy access for the disabled, the park features interactive equipment, a rubber play surface and overhead canopies. Grommet is beach slang for a young, often-obsessed surfer.

The North End

Most locals prefer to visit less crowded Atlantic beaches. The section from 38th Street to Cape Henry is known as the North End. There are no hotel strips here, just some impressive bungalows and "cottages" and a lot of fantastic, less crowded beach real estate. Parking is always a problem here unless you have a friend with a driveway. There are no public lots, just a smattering of prized on-street spots.

Make sure you don't block someone's driveway and check carefully that there are no restrictions before you lock up and cross the dunes. It's a constant battle here between landowners and visitors. Some residents have built driveways that occupy nearly all their street frontage, illegally put up their own, unofficial No Parking signs, or installed planters along the road to prevent parkers.

Croatan Beach

Another popular local getaway is located on the other side of Rudee Inlet. The area known as Croatan Beach is the 3/4-mile-long strip of public oceanfront between the inlet and the Virginia National Guard's Camp Pendleton.

This beach is a favorite for surfers, and the city has two designated surfing areas at either end of Croatan. There's a 500-car city lot and a little additional parking scattered throughout the neighborhood that is clearly marked. You can't just park in the resort area and walk the beach to Croatan because of the inlet. You have to drive there. Follow Atlantic Avenue south to where it becomes General Booth Boulevard and then turn at Croatan Road and head for the ocean. The city has public restrooms and a changing area here.

Sandbridge

The city's final stretch of Atlantic beach is in Sandbridge, which is south of the Camp Pendleton and Dam Neck military bases. This 5-mile swath is a residential colony full of beach cottages and summer rentals. It's well off the beaten path. You head south beyond Croatan Beach on General Booth Boulevard until it becomes Princess Anne Road and then drive another 7 miles on rural Sandbridge Road to Sandfiddler Road, which fronts the beach.

i Be careful swimming, especially in the ocean. Every year, people overestimate their skills and don't make it out of the water. Powerful rip currents can develop at any time and pull swimmers away from shore. Don't fight against these tides. Even Olympic swimmers would be quickly exhausted. Although often incorrectly called undertows, rip currents don't pull you under. You can always float or tread water until they weaken and, when you are able, you can escape by swimming parallel to shore. These tides are often as narrow as they are powerful. Don't get discouraged if you get caught in a wide rip. The currents always end.

Again, free public parking can be scarce, with a few spots on some side streets. The city operates a lot at the corner of Sandbridge and Sandfiddler roads that charges a maximum of $5 per day. At the southern end of Sandbridge, just before the Back Bay Wildlife Refuge begins, there is a city park called Little Island with a fishing pier and another pay-to-park lot (see entry in Parks chapter). Because this is where most visitors park, the beach by the picnic area and playground can seem crowded, by Sandbridge standards. But if you walk a few minutes north, you'll have plenty of space to spread out, even on those three-day holiday weekends.

Heading south, you'll soon encounter the refuge. There's no entry fee Nov through Mar, but pedestrians and bicyclists who visit the refuge at other times are supposed to pay $2 per immediate family or group. The refuge is open dawn to dusk.

Wildlife Refuge & False Cape State Park

The beaches on the refuge and at False Cape State Park to the south are pristine places to walk and observe nature. Neither entity encourages swimming, so there are no lifeguards. If you want to really get away from it all, you can pack in a tent and spend the night if you make reservations at False Cape (see entries in Parks chapter).

Chesapeake Bay

Chick's Beach

Other great insiders' getaways are the area's numerous Chesapeake Bay beaches.

Virginia Beach has 6 miles of Chesapeake Bay frontage, running from Little Creek Amphibious Base to First Landing State Park. You get to them off Shore Drive. One of the most popular with locals is the enclave known as Chick's Beach, which includes the strand on either side of the Chesapeake Bay Bridge-Tunnel entrance. Despite the designation, men are allowed here. Some say Chick's was named after Chic's restaurant that sold limeades and ice cream, others that it is just a contraction for Chesapeake Beach.

There are no lifeguards on duty on these beaches, which are popular for Jet Skiing, kayaking, and sailing. The only public parking is at First Landing State Park, but there are some street spots to be found.

Ocean View

Norfolk also has its own beachfront on the other side of the Little Creek amphibious base, where Shore Drive changes to Ocean View Avenue. There's been a big push in recent years to clear blight from East Ocean View and replace it with upscale housing, but the Bayfront area remains largely blue collar. There's also a city park on the beach at the end of Granby Street in West Ocean View (see the entry in the Parks chapter). Farther west is a narrow peninsula known as Willoughby Spit, which was created by a hurricane and is now home to those who love the view and can live with occasional flooding during severe storms. Although the city has spent more than $100 million redeveloping Ocean View, some of these neighborhoods are still in transition, which is a nice way of saying you'll want to lock your car and keep aware of your surroundings. Of course, that's smart no matter where you travel. The city beach park is patrolled and there are lifeguards on duty.

Buckroe Beach

Folks tend to forget that there are beaches on the other side of the Chesapeake Bay. And Peninsula locals are in no hurry to spread the news. Buckroe Beach is popular for those who just can't see fighting tunnel traffic to get to the ocean's waves. There are lifeguards on duty during the summer season on this ¾-mile resort, and places to rent chairs, umbrellas, kayaks, and paddlecraft. You get there by taking Mercury Boulevard or Mallory Street to Pembroke Avenue and following it until it turns into First Street. Nearby is the Grandview Nature Preserve with 2 ½ miles of secluded beachfront to explore. There are no lifeguards here. You reach the preserve by taking I-64 exit 263A onto Mercury Boulevard. Make a left on Fox Hill Road and another on Beach Road and, finally, State Park Drive. (See the Parks chapter for more information on both.)

BICYCLING

With no hills to speak of and a temperate climate, this is perfect bicycle territory.

Take your fat-wheeled cruiser and pedal the Boardwalk or make some skinny road tires sing in a trek through Pungo. There are also plenty of BMX and off-road opportunities to be found.

The most popular bike spot is the 3-mile Virginia Beach Boardwalk. Here bikers share a lane with skaters. There's usually a cool ocean breeze and plenty to look at. Keep alert for the pedestrian straying on the wrong track, or for kids having so much fun they don't realize they're about to get run over. The best biking is early in the morning, when it's mostly the physical fitness folks on the "boards." If you get tired, there are an abundance of benches, and plenty of places to hydrate or carb up with an ice-cream cone.

Another popular area riding place is Chesapeake's Dismal Swamp Canal Trail. Again, you won't have to worry about cars and trucks, but you'll need to watch out for those walkers and even horses. This is a much longer circuit, 17 miles round trip, but you can always turn around sooner. (See Parks entry.)

Various neighborhoods have bike trails, and there are a few bicycle commuting lanes, but it's fairly haphazard. Mostly, you'll be sharing the streets with cars and trucks and often distracted and inattentive drivers, so be wary. Be sure to wear bright colors, plus lights if you're out after dark.

The Tidewater Bicycle Association organizes mass rides throughout the year and lobbies for changes in area laws and more access and respect for bikers. For information, check out their website, www.tbarides.org.

There are also bike trails at a number of local parks (see the Parks chapter for suggestions). And you can rent a ride at various places by the Oceanfront, such as: Cherie's Bike & Blade Rental, which has a dozen locations on Atlantic Avenue or the Boardwalk, (757) 437-8888; or Boardwalk Convenience & Gift, 12th Street and Atlantic Ave., (757) 417-7307; part of a group of rental operations that also has several pick up points scattered along the strand. Call to find the one nearest you. Don't ignore those little coupon books that are available in boxes throughout the resort area. They often have bike-rental discount offers inside

BOATING

You don't need a million-dollar yacht to enjoy your water lust here, but that doesn't mean there aren't plenty around. Every spring and fall, the snowbirds from up north send their toys to warmer climes or bring them back. You can gawk at area drawbridges while you wait in traffic, or check out the marinas by Waterside or across the Elizabeth River in Portsmouth, the official mile marker 0 on the Intracoastal Waterway.

Most locals take to the bay or area rivers in smaller sailboats and power cruisers. If you don't have deep water outside your condo, there are plenty of marinas and moorings where you can tie up. If you keep your vessel on a trailer, there are public and private boat ramps scattered through the region where you can launch for a day on the water. You can even rent Jet Skis or other personal watercraft at Rudee Inlet and other locations.

i Weekends can get pretty crowded at the most popular ramps, such as Bubba's near the Lynnhaven Inlet off Shore Drive. Be prepared for a line. And if you don't want to incite an angry mob, try not to lock the keys in your truck or otherwise block that ramp.

If you love to sail, the Chesapeake and its broad tributaries can be wonderful playgrounds. The waters in summer are filled with everything from Sunfish and Hobie Cats to multi-masted yachts. If you'd like to experience life on one of those monsters, you can check out area yacht clubs. Many owners are always looking for a strong back to crew on one of the frequent regatta races. You'll also find folks windsurfing on Back Bay and other relatively calm bodies of water.

Many area waters are perfect for paddling. You can get guided tours from a number of area outfitters such as Back Bay Getaways, Chesapeake Bay Center, Chesapean Outdoors, Kayak Nature Tours, Virginia Sea Kayak Center, Surf and Adventure Company, and Wild River Outfitters Touring Company.

i Use some common sense. Big waters mean the potential for big problems. Storms can come up quickly, turning flat water into raging seas. The bigger the pond or bay, the longer the wind has to work on the surface and the larger the waves that are created. It's easy to get swamped when your Jon boat only has a foot of freeboard and a 10 horsepower motor that can't match the oncoming winds. Even on local rivers, you should stay close to shore. When a tug and barge sweeps by, it leaves a huge wake that will have your dinghy dancing. Also, commercial vessels can't stop on a dime or easily steer clear of you, if they even spot your kayak. If in doubt, don't go out.

In fact, if you have a real spirit of adventure and don't mind some narrow stretches through backyards and downed trees, you can even paddle through the heart of Virginia Beach from Chesapeake Bay to the North Carolina line on the Virginia Beach Scenic Waterway Trail. You can get a map of the trail and all waterway access sites online at www.vbgov.com by selecting the parks and recreation department and then clicking on the marinas and waterways page where there is a map link.

BOWLING

Every community has its bowling lanes, but in Hampton Roads you can still partake of duckpins, a historic competitor to the modern game. Here, the ball is small and is cupped in the hand, since it doesn't have holes. The pins are also smaller, and are more difficult to knock down. So you get three throws per turn instead of the two in traditional bowling. Once it was the most popular participatory sport in the region, but now it is limited to one location: Victory Lanes Bowling Center at 2513 Victory Blvd. in Portsmouth. By the way, it's believed no one has ever rolled a perfect game of 300 in duckpin.

If you want to use those bigger balls and go for the higher scores, there are plenty of modern AMF Bowling Centers throughout the region as well as independent lanes such as Classic Lanes in Newport News, Sparetimes and Century Lanes in Hampton, and Pinboys at the beach, as well as bowling centers on various military bases for service members and their guests.

FISHING

People travel from all over the world to fish here. There are boats and crews to be chartered to head offshore for tuna, marlin, and sailfish, or so-called head boats (they charge by the head) that you can board for a full- or half-day adventure. They furnish the rod, reel, bait, and even the fishing license for you. Many of the boats are based out of Rudee Inlet, where they have quick access to offshore waters, or in Hampton and Norfolk for bay excursions. The fishing continues year-round, with heated cabins to provide comfort, but the best action is usually spring through fall, depending on the species.

You don't have to leave terra firma to catch fish here, but if you're between 16 and 65 you'll need a Virginia Saltwater or Freshwater Fishing License, depending on where you stand. Saltwater licenses are required at the ocean, the bay, and most sections of local rivers that are tributaries of the James River. They run $12.50 for Virginians and $25 for non-residents, but if you're just visiting, you can grab a temporary license for $5, $10 for non-Virginians.

If you're fishing area ponds, lakes, reservoirs, or non-tidal stretches you'll need a freshwater license. Resident freshwater licenses cost $11 for the county or city of residence or $18 statewide. Non-Virginians have the option of a statewide license for $36 or a five-consecutive-day pass for $16. There's an additional $18 fee for fishing stocked trout waters for residents, double that for non-Virginians.

Virginians can also buy a combined freshwater and saltwater license for $30, $60 for non-Virginians. You can call (888) 721-6911 for a license, get one online at www.dgif.virginia.gov/licenses, or check out tackle shops, which often sell them.

So what's out there? Virginia sits right at the border of northern and southern species, and Hampton Roads is at the mouth of the rich Chesapeake Bay ecosystem, so there's a wide variety. Charters often focus on billfish and tuna. Head boats target spot and croaker, sea bass and flounder.

You can wade in the surf and catch everything from sharks to striped bass. Huge drum are favorite targets. And when a school of bluefish blitz, you're in for a frenzy of non-stop action.

There are also public piers all over the place; some require individual licenses, and others include it in the admission fee. Newport News, (757) 926-8000, has a trio at Denbigh Park, Peterson's Yacht Basin, and Huntington Park that require saltwater licenses. Hampton rebuilt the Buckroe Beach Fishing Pier, (757) 851-9146, after Hurricane Isabel destroyed it in 2003. Here, individuals don't need a license.

Virginia Beach operates an ocean fishing pier at 15th Street, (757) 428-2333, and at Little Island Park in Sandbridge, (757) 426-7200. Norfolk rebuilt its Ocean View Fishing Pier, (757) 583-6000, which was also destroyed by Hurricane Isabel.

There are also fishing piers off Lynnhaven Inlet, (757) 481-7071; the Chesapeake Bay Bridge-Tunnel, (757) 464-4641; and the James River Bridge, (757) 247-0364.

Don't forget the fresh water. There are countless small lakes, known around here as borrow pits because the sand from them was borrowed to build local highways. These ponds often have huge bass and pan fish. The local rivers are also home to lots of bass, and there was a time when Back Bay produced more trophy largemouth than any other body of water in the state. That fishery went into a decline but seems to be returning with an improvement in the bay's water clarity.

All of the area water reservoirs are loaded with fish. Some require special permits for anglers and restrict the size of boats and motors. Again, you can fish year-round, but things get pretty slow in the depth of winter. On summer evenings, nothing beats a fly rod and a popper for bassing excitement.

ICE SKATING

Ready to chill out? Well, there are a few places here to strap on the blades and practice your triple axels. Most are indoors, courtesy of the temperate climates. But every year, an outdoor rink opens by MacArthur Center mall in Norfolk. They use chill pipes to keep the ice hard when the weather goes above freezing, and it manages to stay open from around Thanksgiving to mid-Jan. The cost is $8 for two hours of skating, including skates. Military and their families get a discount, and there's even a kiddies' rink for the toddlers to enjoy and to keep them out of harm's way. We may all enjoy some Winter Wonderland activities, but that doesn't make us good at it. Still, there are plenty of folks who hail from colder climes who can put on a show.

Virginia Beach opened an outdoor rink in Nov 2009, that ran through mid-Feb right off the Boardwalk at Neptune's Park, 31st Street and Atlantic Avenue, The cost was $10 for two hours. It might become an annual attraction. One of the amenities planned for a beach development site at the Oceanfront is an indoor rink.

Another seasonal outdoor rink is located in Hampton. Downtown Hampton on Ice is a covered outdoor ice skating rink next to the Virginia Air and Space Center that stays open a little longer. In 2010, it ran through Feb. Admission is $6 for two hours, with $2 more for skate rentals.

As nice as those outdoor rinks can be, they're gone when the heat and humidity start to soar. Nothing beats heading to an ice rink in the summer.

In Chesapeake, you can visit Chilled Ponds Ice and Turf Sports Complex, which features an NHL-sized skating rink and is the official practice facility for the Norfolk Admirals, the top affiliate of the Tampa Bay Lightning. It's also home to a variety of youth and adult hockey leagues.

Iceland of Virginia Beach is located at 4915 Broad St., just off Virginia Beach Boulevard. It's home to the Junior Hampton Roads Admirals.

PARTICIPATORY SPORTS

You don't have to be a kid to play around here. Every city offers adult recreational leagues with softball a big favorite. Any spring evening you're likely to see a game under the lights at a variety of fields and parks. There are also different divisions, so you can start out easy or play like a pro. Recreation centers abound. And if you are a kid, there are a host of leagues and even travel teams to match your skill set.

Baseball

There are a number of leagues for kids here, from T-ball to coach pitch to semi-pro. Most cities sponsor their own youth athletic leagues and have Little League associations, as well, with spring and fall seasons. You can find a Little League team in nearly any neighborhood. There are also Pony Leagues here in Chesapeake, Portsmouth, and Virginia Beach. For information, head to the Pony League website, www.pony.org. And Hampton Roads is home to a thriving Amateur Athletic Union presence. Tryouts and registration begin as early as Feb.

If you still have the urge to chase flies yourself, Hampton Roads has a chapter of the National Adult Baseball Association.

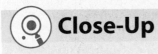# Close-Up

The Pros Know

If you want to get started on a weekend-warrior program, don't forget to check in first with your local parks and recreation department. In this area, most fields, and courts are municipally owned. The cities have a long history of sponsoring adult athletics and keep a close tab on the private parties who are using their facilities. A quick call to city hall can cut through lots of frustration and put you on track to your track and field dreams. Most Parks and Rec departments have booklets listing their leagues and other activities. You might be surprised by what's available, from softball leagues that span the gap from semi-pro to downright duffer to once exotic pursuits such as rugby and lacrosse. Here are some contact numbers:

Chesapeake	(757) 382-6411
Hampton	(757) 727-8311
Newport News	(757) 926-1460
Norfolk	(757) 441-2400
Portsmouth	(757) 393-8000
Poquoson	(757) 868-3580
Suffolk	(757) 514-7250
Virginia Beach	(757) 385-1100

Here, you'll find a dozen teams in a variety of divisions including one for those 30 and older. Check out their Website, www.home teamsonline.com/hrnaba.

Basketball

Again, there is a wealth of organized opportunities, as well as hundreds of public courts for pickup games. Check the local Parks and Recreation departments for tips, leagues, and gym locations. The local YMCAs also sponsor youth basketball leagues.

Every summer, local hoops legend Boo Williams operates an AAU summer league, sponsored by Nike, that features more than 165 teams and more than 2,000 male and female players. In addition, Williams and local investors partnered with Hampton to create the Boo Williams Sportsplex, which has eight tournament-quality basketball courts. (The facility also hosts an annual "Boo's Best" showcase tournament for sixth-, seventh-, and eighth-grade boys basketball players and a Future Stars of the Hardwood tournament for seventh-, eighth-, and ninth-grade boys.) Travel teams let the talented show off their skills to college recruiters. The Norfolk Knights, for instance, took the state United States Basketball Association title in 2009 and were national United States Specialty Sports Association champions in 2007, and 27 Knights have gone on to play college ball, including 8 at the Division 1 level.

Ice Hockey

With the Admirals a popular family draw, it was logical that local kids would want to strap on their own skates and play the game.

Of course, when it rarely dips below freezing, you have a handicap. The Hampton Roads Youth Hockey Association, www.hryha.goalline.ca, developed to fill that need. The league, with six different age divisions, plays at Iceland in Virginia Beach.

Field Hockey

The USA Field Hockey National Training Center is located in Virginia Beach next to the Sportsplex. It hosts tournaments for the country's top players in various age groups, and the U.S. Women's National Team is headquartered here. There are a number of club teams in the area, including Beach Premier in Virginia Beach, www.beachhockey.com; Focus Field Hockey in Portsmouth, www.focusfieldhockey.com; and the Thrashers in Newport News, www.thrashersfieldhockey.com. Also in the area are the Old Dominion Field Hockey Club, www.757hockey.com, and the Virginia Beach Field Hockey League, www.beachfieldhockey.com.

Football

In addition to the various municipal leagues, there are Little League football teams and others sponsoring youth tackle games, including the Virginia Beach Mustangs, www.virginiabeachmustangs.com, and several members of the Peninsula Youth Football Association www.leaguelineup.com/pyfa: the Hampton Tornados, the Poquoson Bulls, the Tidewater Wolves, and the Tri-Citi Hurricanes. There's also a Hampton Roads Flag Football League, www.hrffl.com, for those who'd rather not get involved in tackle ball. If you have game, you might try out for the Southern Virginian Trojans or the Virginia Crusaders, two semi-pro teams that play at the Virginia Beach Sportsplex.

Lacrosse

The Hampton Roads Chapter of U.S. Lacrosse, www.hrlax.com, is a clearinghouse for the sport, known as the fastest game on two feet. Games are played in Chesapeake, Newport News, Norfolk, and Virginia Beach. The Virginia Beach Lacrosse Club, the Sharks, is a men's league and member of the American Lacrosse League and won the championship in 1981. The Hampton Roads Riptide is the local women's lacrosse team. There's also an indoor adult league in the fall and winter at Chilled Ponds Arena in Chesapeake.

Rugby

The Norfolk Blues, www.bluesrugby.org, is a men's team that plays fall, spring, and summer. The Norfolk Storm, www.norfolkrugby.org, is a women's team. Both play at Norfolk's Lafayette Park. Newport News also has a rugby club, www.newportnewsrugby.com, which practices and plays at Crittenden Middle School in Newport News. Virginia Beach Rugby Football Club, the Falcons, www.virginiabeachrugby.com, practices at Lynnhaven Middle School and plays at FalconPlex, next to the Virginia Beach SPCA.

Running

You don't really need an organization to run, right? Well, if you want to race around here, you'll probably wind up joining the Tidewater Striders, www.tidewaterstriders.com. With more than 1,600 members, it's become one of the nation's largest running clubs, sponsoring more than 50 events every year. Its biggest each season is the Shamrock Marathon, which attracts world-class runners to Virginia Beach every spring. It's not the only run, though. You can try your times in the Virginia Beach Rock 'n Roll half marathon in Sept, the Armed Services YMCA Mud Run in Norfolk in Aug, or the Elizabeth River Run in Portsmouth in May. (See Annual Events chapter for details.)

Soccer

Teams from around the country regularly visit Virginia Beach to play at the Hampton Roads Soccer Complex, www.soccercomplex .org. The 75-acre facility has 19 soccer fields, 11 of them full size, so it can host the largest weekend tournaments. More than 7,000 soccer matches are played here annually, including a dozen regional tournaments. The National Collegiate Showcase is a regular. Every city has municipal leagues, and there is also the Neighborhood Youth Soccer League, www.nyslvb.org, and the Virginia Rush, www .varush.com, which fields teams from youth to adult and competes in the Virginia Soccer League and the Virginia Club Champions League.

If you'd like to avoid the elements, the Southside Indoor Soccer League, www .southsideindoorsoccerleague.com, plays its games in Virginia Beach Public Middle School Gyms.

Softball

This is probably the favorite organized outdoor activity in the area, although the amount of organization varies by league. Some are intense, with pitchers wind-milling the ball at high speeds and mashers who can put up runs in flurries. Others are low-key, lobbed-ball affairs with more giggles than aggression. There are mixed leagues, church leagues, municipal leagues, and killer leagues. The best places to start are those city Parks and Recreation departments.

If you've really got game, there are tournament teams eager to plug you into the lineup The constant movement of military in and out of the area means there are usually openings from season to season. And there are private facilities ready to help you improve your skills. The Pitch A Fit Fastpitch Training Center in Chesapeake has a link to area teams if you want to try out (www .pitchafit.com). The Hampton Roads Vipers is a girls' fast-pitch softball team and the Virginia Lady Eagles fields four teams from age 12 up to 18 and older and boasts sending nearly 100 players to college softball careers. The Tidewater Lady Tides started to give ex-college players a venue.

For the rest of us, there's always the weekend warrior route—pickup games or those organized at our office, church, or synagogue. There are a ton of venues in this area; the only problem is finding one that isn't already occupied or part of a league schedule. The sure fire method is to reserve one yourself by calling the local parks and recreation departments at the numbers listed above.

Norfolk has 125 municipal sites that can be rented for baseball, softball, soccer, football, or field hockey; six of the largest parks host various municipal league games under the lights.

Virginia Beach has 28 municipal fields with lights; 10 of them are at the Princess Anne Athletic Conference, across the street from the Virginia Beach Sportsplex. Here you'll find eight tournament-quality fields.

Portsmouth has 36 public diamonds. Chesapeake has 17 city softball fields, including 9 used for adult leagues, and Suffolk has 5 municipal fields. And in Newport News, a new five-field complex known as Stoney Run is laid out like a cloverleaf, with the home plates surrounding a snack bar/grill.

Tennis

Don't have nine friends to field a team? Take up tennis, where you only need two to tango and four makes a doubles match. The state that produced Arthur Ashe takes pride in its tennis offerings. There are leagues and clubs and schools and pros ready to give instruction. Most country clubs have well-tended courts, but there are plenty of public places to practice your serve and drop shot. For instance, Chesapeake has 51 city tennis courts, many of them under lights. Hampton has a municipal Tennis Center with a managing pro and teaching pro. Huntington Park in Newport News has 20 lit hard courts.

Volleyball

You can't have all this sand without beach volleyball. And there are plenty of places to play. Virginia Beach usually has 10 to 25 nets going on the Oceanfront at 9th Street, although league play takes over the courts after 6 p.m. June through late Aug.

Locals often set up their own nets on the sand at the North End and Chick's Beach. The Tidewater Volleyball Association, www.spike.net, is a clearinghouse for beach and traditional volleyball in the area, with indoor adult and youth leagues. It also sponsors outdoor tournaments at the beach in April.

GOLF

When you think of golf paradises, you probably imagine Palm Springs and Pebble Beach in California or Myrtle Beach in South Carolina.

Well, Virginia Beach has gone to great lengths to improve the quantity and quality of its golf courses, making it a serious contender when golf-loving families are choosing where they want to vacation.

The city has 11 top-tier golf courses, designed by the likes of Arnold Palmer, Fred Couples, and Pete Dye.

The duffer's delight doesn't end at the beach's borders. There are lots of fine, and some spectacular, courses throughout the region. They run the gamut from posh to public, devilish to delightful. Just up the road are another 15 top courses in Williamsburg that have hosted a number of PGA and LPGA tour events. Also in the mix are some military-only facilities and eight exclusive country clubs.

The country clubs include Bayville Golf Club, Cavalier Golf and Yacht Club, the Tradition Golf Club at Broad Bay, and Princess Anne Country Club, all in Virginia Beach. Greenbrier Country Club is in Chesapeake; Elizabeth Manor Golf and Country Club is in Portsmouth. Cedar Point Country Club is in Suffolk and the James River Country Club is in Newport News.

Even if you can't wrangle an invite, you can certainly find a public course that matches your ability or stretches your skills.

Here's a city-by-city rundown, starting with Virginia Beach, of the courses that welcome the public. Most have dress codes, so check before attempting to tee off in t-shirts, tank tops, jeans, or cut-offs. All require soft spikes. Many also give Hampton Roads or Virginia residents a discount, if you ask and can produce proof. The rates here were current at the time of publication and are valuable for cost comparisons, but fees change frequently, so be sure to ask when you make your reservations.

VIRGINIA BEACH

BOW CREEK MUNICIPAL GOLF COURSE
3423 Club House Rd. (Near
Lynnhaven Mall)
(757) 431-3763
www.vbgov.com

This municipal course, designed by Fred Sappenfield, plays to a par 70. It features narrow Bermuda fairways and bentgrass greens, some dogleg holes, and demanding par 3s. You can reserve tee times up to a week in advance. Like most courses, it's most expensive on weekends, $32.55 with a cart, $19.95 if you choose to walk. Fees are less during the week, for twilight golf, and for senior citizens. You can also play nine holes. Curtis Strange's father used to be the pro here when it was called White Sands Country Club, and the hall of famer grew up on this course. It's one of the least costly in the area, but well maintained and friendly. Look out for hole number 8, a par 5 over water. There's a concession area serving lunch and a cart on the greens on weekends. There's also a driving range and chipping and putting greens. The pro shop sells clubs and features two teaching pros.

CYPRESS POINT COUNTRY CLUB
5340 Club Head Rd.
(757) 490-8822
www.golfhamptonroads.net

This Bayside area 18-hole course was designed by Ault and Clark and has a par of 72. The semi-private course opened in 1987 and features rolling fairways and quick greens on its 6,541 yards. It's open every day but Christmas. The signature hole, which appears on all of its scorecards and logos, is number 17, a par 3 over water to an island green. There are four sets of tees making it attractive from beginners to intermediate golfers. The course features a driving range as well as putting and chipping practice areas. Greens fees for non-residents run from $60 weekdays to $70 weekends, from Mar 1 to Oct 15. Carts are required but included in the price. Resident, senior citizen, and military discounts are available, as are early bird specials. You can also play nine holes, although you'll have to wait until after 1 p.m. on weekends. There's a full-service pro shop and a restaurant, bar, and grill. You can take beer and wine you buy here onto the course. Liquor must stay in the bar. Reservations are recommended and taken up to one week in advance. Charles Lynn is the PGA pro here, the main hub for Hampton Roads Golf Clubs.

i State law prevents the courses from allowing bring-your-own booze, so don't try to bring in a cooler full of alcohol. Many courses will permit you to buy a beer or wine in their clubhouse and take it out on the holes with you. Virginia law also won't allow you to carry your mixed drinks or hard liquor with you.

HELL'S POINT GOLF COURSE
2700 Atwoodtown Rd.
(757) 721-3400
www.hellspoint.com

Rees Jones designed this 18-hole course that meanders through the Back Bay Wildlife Refuge. Unlike most courses these days, there are no homes either on the course or nearby, just the natural beauty of a surrounding wilderness. The course, which opened in 1982, features lakes, interesting fairway angles, challenging greens, and 61 sculptured bunkers. *Golf Digest* has tabbed it as one of America's 100 best courses. Dustin McCabe is the main pro on this par 72 course. It plays 6,766 yards from the championship tees. Signature holes include number 8, a very difficult par 3 that has sand bunkers that run from in front of the tee box to the green, and number 14, a par 5 dogleg left that goes around the lake. McCabe and general manager Mark Krause are both PGA teaching professionals. The pro shop offers repairs and sales. Although this is a semi-private course with members, it isn't a country club. This is a golf club pure and simple, and the public is always welcome. Reservations can be made up to two weeks in advance and the rounds run four hours and 15 minutes. There's a grill open sunrise to sunset, which serves sandwiches and beer. On Sat and Sun mornings, it also offers a breakfast brunch. The top rate is $69 during season on weekends, which includes the cart. You can walk the course and save $10. Prices drop during the week, and in the off season, which runs Nov 1 to Mar 31, and there are discounts for seniors.

HERON RIDGE GOLF CLUB
2973 Heron Ridge Dr.
(757) 426-3800
www.heronridge.com

This Fred Couples signature series course was built on land once inhabited by the Pungo Indians. Another par 72 offering, it features rolling fairways, and on 14 of its holes there are natural wetlands, water hazards, and lakes wrapped around tall oak, beech, and elm trees. Five sets of tees convert the course from a 5,000-yard challenge to a 7,000-yard monster. Hole number 9 is memorable. It's a par 5 with water to the left and right. In addition to being very challenging off the tee, the second shot is a difficult lay up as well if you want to make par, and the green is elevated, undulating, and protected by deep bunkers. Although this is a beach course, it has elevation changes unique to the area, with 30- to 40-foot rises on some of the holes. No holes look alike here. The course has a driving range and putting green. The pro shop offers lessons, a snack bar serving sandwiches and alcohol, and a full line of merchandise, clothing, and equipment. Reservations can be made seven days in advance by telephone or booked online 10 days in advance at www.heronridge.com. You'll have to leave your liquor at the snack bar, but beer is allowed on the course. The in-season rate is $69, seven days a week, including cart. You can walk, if you want, but the greens fees are the same. Call for twilight rates and times. And seniors get a discount. Glen Pierce, a PGA professional, is the main pro.

KEMPSVILLE GREENS MUNICIPAL
4840 Princess Anne Rd.
(757) 474-8441
www.vbgov.com

This par 70 course features a challenging back nine with numerous bunkers and water hazards and a unique view of the city skyline. Russell Breeden redesigned the 18-hole course in 1989. It plays 5,800 yards from the longest tees. Hole number 8 is a tough par 4, a full 440 yards from the back tee. Hole number 17 is probably the signature hole, though. It's a difficult par 3, covering 180 yards over water. As a municipal course with corresponding low rates, and one that plays shorter than many in the area, it's a magnet for senior and junior golfers and for a quick nine in the afternoon. The course also offers a driving range and putting and chipping greens. Tee times can be reserved two weeks in advance, but afternoons tend to be open play. A snack bar serves sandwiches and beer. Beer is allowed on the course. The dress code here is relaxed, but tank tops or T-shirts with profanity are not welcome. You can play all day with an 18-hole ticket. Off-season rates range from $31.50 to ride and $21 to walk on weekends all the way down to $9.45 to walk nine holes during the week. There are senior citizen discounts as well. Call for in-season rates. Reynolds Dawson is the PGA pro and Andrew Menk the director of golf.

HONEY BEE
2500 South Independence Blvd.
(757) 471-2768
www.golfhamptonroads.net

A challenge to the novice and expert, this 18-hole course has water on almost every hole and expansive bunkers. It's a par 70 course that was designed by Rees Jones and opened in 1988. It is operated by Hampton

Roads Golf Clubs. It plays 6,075 yards from the longest tees. Hole 17 is the most popular with a long carry over water and a dogleg to the left that can be played many ways. There's a fully stocked pro shop that does minor repairs and offers lessons and a full practice facility. There's a snack bar, grill, and banquet facility that sells a full line of alcohol, which can be taken on the course, but you can't bring your own liquor. You can make tee-time reservations seven days out. The rate for playing 18-hole rounds varies from $20 to $41 depending on season and time of day. You can also play nine for between $16 and $19. The cart is included in the greens fees, but you can walk. Ken Lake is the pro.

OWL'S CREEK GOLF COURSE
411 South Birdneck Rd.
(757) 428-2800
www.golfhamptonroads.net
This semi-private facility operated by Hampton Roads Golf Clubs is located just blocks from the resort strip. The par 62 course is often called "The Little Monster" because its 3,800 yards are interlaced with lakes, streams, hilly terrain, and undulating greens. As one course pro put it, "we may be short, but it's pretty tight and bites like a big one." You'll want to pay special attention to the 13th hole, which features an island green. There's a relaxed dress code here, which is appropriate for a beach course. You can reserve a tee time a week in advance, and you'll want to do that, especially in the summer, when the tourists descend. The pro shop sells all the necessities, repairs clubs, and offers instruction. Frank Britt, PGA apprentice, is the club pro. Not only does the course include an enclosed, heated driving range but also offers lit driving, putting, and chipping areas for night practice. The snack bar serves

sandwiches, burgers, and hot dogs and sells beer and wine, which are allowed on the course. No personal coolers are permitted. Top fees are on summer weekends and run $38, including cart, for 18 holes. You can also play nine holes on weekends for $20, which includes a cart. During the week $22 will buy you unlimited play after 2 p.m. Discounts are available for senior citizens and military, and you can walk this course.

RED WING LAKE MUNICIPAL
1144 Prosperity Rd.
(757) 437-2037
www.vbgov.com
The wide, Bermuda fairways here run between corridors of mature loblolly pines. The par 72 course, designed by George W. Cobb, was renovated in 2007. Greens were rebuilt and seeded with bentgrass, fairways were all renewed, and new wetland areas and lakes installed to add challenge. There are five different tees on the course, topping out at 7,124 yards, and it's open every day except Christmas. Hole 13 is memorable, a par 3 with big lake out to the right and a scenic community across the lake with a dock. Don't be surprised if you see deer on hole 14. No golfing in blue jeans or T-shirts is allowed here. The pro shop sells equipment and offers lessons, and Andrew Menk is the course pro. There's a driving range, as well as putting and chipping greens. Tee times can be reserved up to a week in advance. The clubhouse has a snack bar that offers sandwiches, soups, salads, and breakfasts. You can't bring a cooler through the gates, but you can purchase beer in the clubhouse and bring it on the course. There are a variety of rates depending on time of year and day of week. A non-Virginian will pay $56.70 to play 18 holes during the week, which includes a

cart. The price goes up on weekends, but there are discounts for residents, seniors, juniors, and the military.

SIGNATURE AT WEST NECK
3100 Arnold Palmer Dr.
(757) 721-2900
www.signatureatwestneck.com

This par 72 course, designed by Arnold Palmer, features 13 lakes and several natural wetlands, as well as wooded and dramatically landscaped terrain. Stonewalled bulkheads front greens on the 11th and 18th holes. The course plays 7,010 yards from the back tees, but there are five sets to accommodate various players. Hole 18 is the signature hole here, with its bulkhead and lake and the roses that surround it. There are water hazards on 13 holes. The pro shop sells clothing, clubs, and accessories and offers lessons. Head pro Roy Wickstrom is one of three PGA pros at the course. They accept tee-time reservations 8 days in advance over the phone or 10 days over the Internet at the website listed above. There's a full restaurant and bar here and you can purchase alcohol and bring it on the course. There's also a driving range, putting green, and chipping area. Prices vary widely, depending on age, residency, time of year or day, and day of the week. You can play just nine holes and you can walk the course, although there are certain times when walking isn't allowed on holidays and weekends. Don't show up in denim, and you'll need to wear a collared shirt to get on the course.

STUMPY LAKE GOLF COURSE
4797 East Indian River Rd.
(757) 467-6119
www.golfhamptonroads.net

The course was designed by Robert Trent Jones, and it sits in the midst of the woods by this large freshwater reservoir. It's a par 72 course operated by Hampton Roads Golf Clubs, with natural water hazards and bunkers scattered across its 6,846 yards. It's a golfer-friendly course without a lot of hills and undulation and no houses to worry about. It opened in 1958 but was completely renovated in 2007. The signature hole is the 18th hole, a challenging 390-yard par 4 right along the lake. Water guards the right of the fairway and the front of the green. Another challenging hole is number 13, a 540-yard par 5 over two water hazards. You can walk the course any time on weekdays and after 3 p.m. on weekends. There's a 250-yard driving range and a putting green. You'll want to reserve a tee time, especially during the season. Reservations can be made five days in advance. The course has a snack bar that sells beer, which you can bring onto the course. During the season, rates range from $28 to $32 on weekdays and $40 to $45 on weekends.

VIRGINIA BEACH NATIONAL
2500 Tournament Dr.
(757) 563-9440
www.vbnational.com

Designed for both tournament and public play, this 7,192-yard course was once known as TPC Virginia Beach and hosted Nationwide Tour's Virginia Beach Open. It's a Pete Dye design with help from Hampton Roads native and Golf Hall of Famer Curtis Strange. It's a blend of natural grasses, waste areas, rolling fairways, and tour quality greens set in the city's Sportsplex/Amphitheater area. It's a par 72, with five sets of tees to match to your skills. The final hole sums up this challenging course. It's a long, difficult par 4. This is an open course, an Americanization of the links style. You can walk it, but the cart is included in the greens fee. There's a full-service pro shop, complete with repairs and lessons, and putting, chipping, and driving areas. You can make reservations up to a week in advance. The course has a restaurant and sells alcoholic beverages. They'll even provide coolers if you want to take your drinks on the course with you. Greens fees are $75 any day of the week for non-residents, $65 on weekends, and $55 during the week for Virginians. You can play nine any time for $38 on weekends or $32 during the week, and there are discounts for twilight golf, senior citizens, juniors, and the military. Russ Dodson is the course pro.

CHESAPEAKE

CHESAPEAKE GOLF CLUB
1201 Club House Dr.
(757) 547-1122
www.golfhamptonroads.net
Another of the Hampton Roads Golf Club courses, this is a par 71 covering 6,243 yards from the longest tees. The course, which opened in 1986, winds through the Las Gaviotas neighborhood. There are tree-lined, tight fairways and small greens, as well as water hazards and sand bunkers to keep you challenged. The most difficult is hole 6, a par 5 over water. The most scenic is hole 8, a pretty par 3. The pro shop sells the necessities but not clubs. There is a pair of putting greens here. The grill has a bar and sells sandwiches, burgers, hot dogs, mixed drinks, beer, and soft drinks. If purchased here, you can take beverages onto the course. Greens fees range from $18 to $28 in the off season, but check for summer rates. Senior, military, and junior discounts are offered as well as a break for late afternoon rounds. Reservations are available up to seven days in advance,

and you can play 9 or 18 holes. You can walk anytime weekdays, but there are some restrictions on weekends. The dress code calls for collared shirts and no jeans.

CAHOON PLANTATION
1501 Cahoon Parkway
(757) 436-2775
www.cahoonplantation.com
Once flat farmland, this par 72 course models itself on the Scottish golf experience, with few trees, but plenty of gentle mounds and depressions in the middle of fairways and water, especially on the back nine, to provide challenges. It advertises itself as the only course in the region with bentgrass from tee to green. Designed by Ault, Clark and Associates, it opened in 1999. It plays 7,141 yards at longest tees, but there are five sets, with options for seniors, ladies, and three sets for men. The signature hole is number 18, a par 5 with water on both sides that comes back right up to the clubhouse. Dress code requires collared shirts; jeans are usually permitted only in the winter, and no cutoffs are allowed. The driving range is all grass and there is a putting and chipping area. One building contains a pro shop and restaurant, Plantation Cafe. Alcoholic beverages bought here can be brought onto the course. Reservations can be made up to a week in advance. Rates in season run $54 weekends and $45 weekdays. All prices include carts, but you can walk during the week if you choose. There are also discounts for seniors, juniors, and the military. The course pro Dan Shea, a PGA pro, gives lessons.

BATTLEFIELD GOLF CLUB
1001 Centerville Turnpike
(757) 482-4779
www.playthebattlefield.com

One of the area's newest courses, this is a par 70 designed by Bobby Holcomb. It has some of the highest elevations in the region, with man-made hills touching 40 feet and seven lakes. And it won't break your bank. The signature hole is number 12. The highest on the golf course, it's a dogleg par 4 that wraps around a big lake with a very small green. Only members are permitted to walk the course, and collared shirts are appreciated. There's a pro shop that offers lessons and minor repairs, but no prepared food or alcohol is sold here. The course is 6,200 yards from the back and 6,000 from the white tees. Tee-time reservations can be made two weeks out for members, one week for non-members. The course pro is Mike Waugh. Greens fees are $15 weekdays, $20 on weekends for everyone.

PORTSMOUTH

BIDE-A-WEE
1 Bide A Wee Lane
(757) 393-8600
www.bideaweegolf.com

This Curtis Strange signature course was named the state's best municipal course by *Golf Digest* magazine in 2009. The narrow fairways are lined with tall pines and open to wide greens. Rates run from $17 for Portsmouth residents in the off season to $42 for non-residents on a weekend, Mar through Nov. The course was originally opened in 1955 and the name, given by Scottish designer Fred Finlay, is slang in his native tongue for "linger a while." This was Curtis Strange's home course in his teens when he studied under local legend Chandler Harper (see Close-up) so he consulted extensively with architect Tom Clark on the $8.5 million renovation. The work involved removing many of the pines that had grown

so tall they had closed down sightlines and installing some lakes. The second hole is one of the signatures, called "The Tree" because of the monster growing in the middle of the fairway.

THE LINKS AT CITY PARK
5 Cpl. J. M. Williams Ave.
(757) 465-1500

This is a nine-hole executive golf course with a 30-station, lit driving range and natural grass putting course crafted by Ault, Clark and Associates with input from Curtis Strange. It takes an hour and a half to play through the nine holes, and par is 30. There are two sets of tees here; white covers 1,547 yards and blue 1,846. Hole 6 is the most difficult, a par 3 135-yarder you reach over water with just two yards between the water and the green. Walking is permitted. No sleeveless shirts are allowed. The pro shop offers lessons, sells golf balls and accessories, and does some club repair. No reservations are accepted here. It's strictly first come, first serve. There's no restaurant and, because it's within a city park, no alcohol is permitted or sold. Portsmouth residents can play nine holes for $10; it's $2 more for non-residents. If you want to go through twice for 18, it will cost $15 and $18. And in the summers, $10 will buy anyone unlimited play after 3 p.m. Discounts are available for seniors and juniors, and the course pro is Bob Sutter, PGA.

SUFFOLK

SUFFOLK GOLF COURSE
1227 Holland Rd.
(757) 539-6298

This 18-hole course is nestled against Lake Kilby and offers a little more elevation than most in Hampton Roads. It was designed by Dick Wilson and opened in 1952. It's a par 72 that plays 5,957 yards from the men's white tee. The most memorable hole is probably the 18th, a closing par 5 with a second shot that goes over a lake with a fountain. The front nine are fairly open, but the back winds through trees and lakes and gets a little tighter and more scenic. Walkers are permitted, with only soft spikes allowed. Collared shirts are required, but jeans are welcome. The pro shop offers three teaching pros, and sells equipment but doesn't do repairs. There's a restaurant/grill that sells beer, a driving range, and practice green. Tee-time reservations are accepted a week in advance. Greens fees for Suffolk and Portsmouth residents are $35 with cart; non-resident rate is $39 on weekends and $29 for weekdays. You can play nine any time during the week for $17 and after noon on weekends for $19. The resident PGA pro is Eddie Luke.

SLEEPY HOLE
4700 Sleepy Hole Rd.
(757) 538-4100
www.sleepyholegolfcourse.com

This 18-hole, old style course opened in 1974 and has hosted LPGA tournaments. Russell Breeden originally designed it, with improvements in 2004 by Tom Clark. It's a par 72 course with tree-lined fairways that frame every tee box. It has all the holes to test your skills, left to right, right to left, and straight, and plays 7,040 yards from the longest tees. The most popular hole is the last, which is annually voted the toughest and best finishing hole in the area. The Nansemond River is behind and to the left of this hole, and the Obici mansion, a 1920s Art Nouveau–style home built by Planters Peanuts founder Amedeo Obici, is to the right of the green. The historic mansion is being restored as a clubhouse. You can walk the course. No metal spikes or denim are allowed, and you

need a collared shirt to play here. There is a temporary pro shop and a grill that also sells beer, which you can take with you on the course. There's a driving range and putting and chipping practice areas. Reservations can be made up to seven days in advance. The greens fees are $52 on weekends and $45 on weekdays, with discounts for seniors and twilight golf. You can play nine holes anytime for $20. The course pro is J. T. Belcher.

RIVERFRONT GOLF CLUB
5200 River Club Dr.
(757) 484-2200
www.riverfrontgolf.com

This old-style course winds along riverbanks, tidal marshes, huge oaks, and rolling farmland. It was voted 4 ½ stars by *Golf Digest* and included in "40 best daily fee courses" by *Golf and Travel* magazine. It is located on the Nansemond near the mouth of the James River. The 18-hole course was designed by Tom Doak and opened in 1998. It's a par 72 that plays 6,735 yards off the back tee. The 15th hole is one to remember, overlooking the tidal marshes and bluffs at the confluence of the James and the Nansemond Rivers. Most of the holes have some kind of riverside location on one side or another, and there are tidal marshes on just about every hole. A cart is required here, and you'll need a collared shirt and won't be welcome with metal spikes or jeans. The full-service pro shop features sales, repairs, and lessons. There are putting and chipping greens and a 16-acre driving range that attracts people from all over the region. Tee-time reservations are accepted up to a week in advance. The course has a bar, lounge, and restaurant and sells beer, mixed beverages, and wine. Beer and wine are allowed on the course. Greens fees are $59 on weekdays, $69 on weekends, including the cart, with a $10 discount for Hampton Roads residents. Seniors can play Mon through Thurs for $34 and there are twilight discounts. You can also play nine holes for $27 on weekdays or $35 on weekends. The course pro is Tim Newsom.

NANSEMOND RIVER GOLF CLUB
1000 Hillpoint Blvd.
(757) 539-4356
www.nansemondrivegolfclub.com

Like to gawk when you golf? There are 3 miles of Nansemond River vistas on this course, with 14 of the 18 holes along the river. The course was designed by Thomas Steele and opened in 1999. It's a par 72 covering 7,241 yards from the back tees with the closest playing 5,173 yards. The signature hole is the 17th, an island green with little room for error on the approach shot. You can walk this course, but the cart is included in the greens fees. No blue jeans are allowed, and you must wear a collared shirt and soft spikes. The full pro shop offers equipment sales, repairs, and lessons. There's a driving range and putting and chipping greens here and a full restaurant that sells beer, wine, and mixed drinks. Only beer and wine are allowed out on the course. The most expensive round of golf here costs $55 on weekends and holidays. There are various discounts for out of season, weekdays, twilight, seniors, juniors, and the military. Tee-time reservations are available up to 7 days in advance. The club pro is Mark Lambert.

NORFOLK

LAMBERTS PONT
4301 Powhatan Ave.
(757) 489-1677
www.golfhamptonroads.net

This is a full-length, nine-hole municipal course that opened in 2005. It's a par 34 that plays 2,789 from the back tees and was designed by Lester George. The Scottish style links course runs along the Elizabeth River near Old Dominion University. The most difficult hole is number 3, a very tight 563-yard, par 5 that requires a 100-yard carry over water on the second shot. Even the green is challenging. It's very undulating and sits on the highest point of land in Norfolk. You can walk this course in soft spikes, and there is no dress code here. The pro shop sells clothing and some equipment and offers lessons. There's a double-decked, heated driving range here with 40 bays and large chipping and putting areas. The course snack bar sells beer, which you can take on the holes. You can make tee-time reservations as far as 3 months out and can play the course twice for an 18-hole experience for $27 with cart, $20 without. It costs $19 for nine holes with a cart, $15 to walk. There are also discounts for seniors, students, and military. The course pro is Michelle Holmes.

OCEAN VIEW GOLF COURSE
9610 Norfolk Ave.
(757) 480-2094
www.oceanviewgc.com

This is a par 70 course with four tees maxing at 6,011 yards. World War I veterans originally built it in 1929. Today, it is managed by Billy Casper Golf and features hybrid Bermuda greens, oak-lined fairways, and undulations and doglegs for challenge. Rates run from $21 for super twilight weekdays to $42 on weekends and holidays and include cart and taxes. Hole 13 is memorable, surrounded by water on three sides. Tiger Woods gave one of his clinics for kids here, and Arnold Palmer, Jack Nicklaus, and Sam Snead played a pro exhibition on the course. Reservations can be made a week in advance. The snack bar is open all year and sells beer. Jamie Smith is the resident teaching pro.

LAKE WRIGHT
6282 Northampton Blvd.
(757) 459-2255
www.golfhamptonroads.net

This is a par-70 course with the longest tees adding up to 6,189 yards. It was designed by Al Jamison and opened in 1966 and is operated by Hampton Roads Golf Club. The signature hole is number 5, a 214-yard, par 3 over water. In general, though, this is a pretty easy course, with wide fairways and only a few water hazards to spoil your day. You can choose to walk the course, except for weekend mornings in the summer. The pro shop sells equipment and has a teaching pro. There's a snack bar that sells beer, and you can bring it on the course. You can make reservations up to seven days in advance. Greens fees run from $18 to $35 including the cart, depending on time of year, day of week, and time of day, and discounts are available for seniors and juniors who choose to walk. The club pro is Brian Robinson.

HAMPTON

THE WOODLANDS GOLF COURSE
9 Woodland Rd.
(757) 727-1195

This 18-hole municipal course was one of the first in America, built in 1916 and redesigned by Tom Clark in 1972. But it can trace its history back to a different location in 1893. It's a par 69 par that maxes out at 5,391 yards. The most difficult hole is number 18. Why? A few years ago the leader in the Hampton Amateur took nine strokes on this par 4. Still, this is considered a very good course for seniors, who make up more than three quarters of those who play here. It is relatively short and fairly open but can be tricky. Lots of folks walk the course. You'll need collared shirts or other golf attire, but jeans are permitted. There's a full pro shop and restaurant that offers clothing and accessories and rents clubs but there is no teaching pro. You can buy wine and beer and bring it onto the course. There is a large putting green. You can make tee time reservations just 2 ½ days in advance. Greens fees are $17 to walk and $27.60 to ride weekdays; two dollars more on weekends. Seniors get a break during the week—$10 to walk and $19.54 to ride. Students can play for $5 any time, plus $10.60 if they want a cart. You can play just nine holes for $13 during the week, $14 on weekends, plus another $5.25 if you want a cart, $4.78 for seniors.

THE HAMPTONS GOLF COURSE
320 Butler Farm Rd.
(757) 766-9148
www.hampton.va.us/thehamptons

This 27-hole municipal golf course was built on a reclaimed landfill. It opened in 1989 and was designed by Dr. Michael Hurdzan. There's an 18-hole course and another 9, but golfers can play any combination of the three sections. What sets this course apart is the variety of scenery as you play through three distinct nine-hole courses. The Woods features wooded, narrower fairways and is the front nine of the main course. The Lakes is the back nine, and involves five holes where water comes into play. The other nine are called the Links, which are open and windswept. The combination of holes 10 and 11 is the most popular. Hole 10 begins the back nine with one of the longer par 4s. It has water on the right, woods on the left,

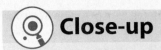 **Close-up**

Local courses spawned star

Golf Hall of Famer Curtis Strange honed his skills growing up on the courses in Hampton Roads. Curtis, named the sixth top athlete ever to emerge from South Hampton Roads, grew up on a golf course. He was the son of Tom Strange, who had played the U.S. Open and owned the White Sands Country Club in Virginia Beach. Curtis Strange started golfing at age seven and turned pro in 1976 after being named All American three times at Wake Forest on what might have been the best college team ever assembled.

He was the PGA's first million-dollar man in 1988 and the first back-to-back U.S. Open winner since Ben Hogan in 1950–51 when he won in 1988 at Brookline and the following year at Oak Hill.

Strange has a twin, Allan, who also played briefly on the PGA tour.

After their father died when he was 14, Curtis Strange was mentored by another Hampton Roads golf legend, PGA Hall of Famer Chandler Harper, polishing his game at Harper's Bide-A-Wee course in Portsmouth.

Strange won 16 of his 17 PGA Tour victories in the 1980s. He set the St. Andrews Old Course 18-hole record of 62 in 1987 during the Dunhill Cup. He was named PGA Player of the Year in 1988, winning four times as well as breaking the $1 million earnings mark. He never won a Tour event after the 1989 U.S. Open. Strange played in five Ryder Cups and was captain of the team in 2002.

He has also served as a television golf analyst for ABC and ESPN and a consultant to course designers. He was the tournament pro at Kingsmill in Williamsburg, and plays on the Champions Tour.

His mentor, Harper, competed as a pro from 1938 to 1955, winning 11 PGA Tour events, outplaying such golf icons as Ben Hogan and Sam Snead in the process. He once shot three rounds of 63 each to set a tour record. Harper founded Portsmouth's Bide-A-Wee Golf Club and was the managing pro there for 37 years. He was elected to the Hall of Fame in 1969 and died in 2004.

and the green can be challenging. Then you turn around on hole 11, which is a shorter par 4 with a carry onto a landing area and another forced carry onto the green. This all takes place around a scenic lakefront where you're likely to encounter waterfowl, deer, and maybe even a fox. The Woods and Lake combine for the 18-hole course, which is a par 71 that plays 6,400 yards from the back tees. There's a driving range, putting and chipping greens, and even a bunker practice area. The pro shop sells and rents clubs and offers lessons, but no repairs. A restaurant and bar sells beer and wine, which you can bring onto the course. Carts are only required on weekend and holiday mornings to keep play moving. There is a dress code: appropriate golf attire, no cut-offs or tank tops, and soft spikes only. The clubhouse even has a locker room and shower. You can reserve a tee time five days ahead for weekdays, and weekend reservations open up at 7 a.m. the Thurs before. This course encourages young and old golfers with greens fees as low as $5 for 18 holes for high school and under and $10 for seniors. Others will pay $19 weekdays and $21 on weekends. Carts are $10.60 for 18 holes and half that for 9. Gary Anderson is the teaching pro here.

NEWPORT NEWS

KILN CREEK GOLF CLUB AND RESORT
1003 Brick Kiln Blvd.
(757) 874-2600
www.kilncreekgolf.com
This 18-hole gem has been named one of the five best golf courses in the state by *Golf Digest*, and *Tee Time* magazine dubbed the 8th hole one of the Mid-Atlantic region's best par 4s. It's a dogleg right with bunkers all the way up the left side and water on the right you can cut off, as much as you dare, all the way to the green. The par 72 course was designed by Tom Clark and is 6,972 yards from the back tees. This is a rolly course with more than 80 sand traps to keep you honest. No denim is allowed, and collared shirts are required. The pro shop has a full line of golf merchandise, lessons, and re-gripping. There's a driving range, putting green, and a chipping green. And with all those sand traps, there's even a bunker practice area. The public can make tee-time reservations up to a week in advance. The grill is open for breakfast on weekends and for lunch daily. Alcohol is sold there, and there are beverage carts on the course as well. A cart is required and included in fees. A round of golf costs $48 on weekends, $40 on Fri, and $37 Mon through Thurs. You can also play nine holes for $22, $25 on Fri, and $27 on weekends. The course pro is Jamie Conners, a PGA pro. And if you want to stay awhile, there are 14 hotel rooms on the property.

NEWPORT NEWS GOLF CLUB AT DEER RUN
901 Clubhouse Way
(757) 886-7925
www.nngolfclub.com
Nestled in the largest municipal park east of the Mississippi are two 18-hole championship golf courses: The Cardinal and Deer Run. The facility has been rated a frugal pick and given the best value award by *Golf Digest*, which gave it four out of five stars. Deer Run, designed by Ed Ault, is the most notable course, and at 7,206 yards was once the longest in the state. The signature hole there is number 5, a par 3 over a lake. A cart is required on Deer Run. The Cardinal, at 6,645 yards, can be walked. The toughest hole here is the 8th, which is a par 5 with forced carry on both the tee and second shot. This facility is one of the last of the true woodland courses, with nature and woods on every hole. Golf attire and soft spikes are required. The pro shop offers a full range of merchandise, lessons, and club fittings. There's a driving range, and putting and chipping greens. You can reserve a tee time seven days in advance. The facility also has a full-service restaurant with catering for social or corporate events. Alcohol is sold, and beer and wine can be carried onto the course. The price for 18 holes ranges from $24.50 to $36, including cart. You can play nine for half that. There are also discounts based on age, time of day, and day of week. One unusual perk is that golfers 16 and younger get free greens fees with a paid adult. Greg Overton is the PGA pro here.

SPECTATOR SPORTS

Hampton Roads is the largest community in America without a pro sports team. It's not that we never had one. Way back in the 70s, the ABA's Virginia Squires played their seasons at Scope and people flocked to see Julius "Dr. J" Erving invent dunks and defy gravity with that funny red-white-and-blue basketball. But when the ABA melted into the NBA, the Squires were left on the outside, and Hampton Roads was once again a sports stepchild.

In the decades since, every big time sport has expanded, with major league franchises landing in less populated places like Oklahoma City, Memphis, Tampa, and Columbus. Hampton Roads sat out the early action, but in recent years it attempted to woo an expansion NHL team they were going to call the Rhinos, the NBA's Charlotte Hornets before they moved to New Orleans, and the former Montreal Expos MLB franchise that eventually settled in Washington, D.C.

In each case, league officials talked about how impressed they were with the area, then they chose other suitors. It often came down to dollars. A major league team usually looks for a lot of corporate support in the form of luxury boxes and other business buy-ins. But when your area's economic engine is the Navy, you are usually sheltered from wild fluctuations but just don't have the folks in boardrooms who can pony up for a lot of expensive luxuries.

COMPETITION & JEALOUSY

For much of our history, another problem has been the competition and jealousy within the region. Virginia Beach didn't really want to support a hockey team based in Norfolk and Norfolk had no intention of surrendering its historic leadership position to put a horse track in Virginia Beach. There's a lot more cooperation now, but there doesn't seem to be a real local passion to finally land a team.

Truth is, we sort of enjoy the sports we have here now. Our AAA baseball ballpark is one of the nicest in America. It's small, clean, and friendly, and you usually have no problems getting tickets. On top of that,

they aren't crazy expensive like seats at those new stadiums in New York City. We have pro hockey at the AAA level as well, and there, too, we can go and enjoy the sport instead of the spectacle.

Virginia and North Carolina are very much college basketball hotbeds, and we love our local teams. Even if they aren't always in anybody's NCAA pool brackets, our teams play hard and always seem to be entertaining.

Since most of us came here from someplace else, we often bring our hometown rooting interests with us. The way things are here, we can still support the teams we loved in our youth and then enjoy the sports we have right here in almost a purer form. Move to New York and you have to pick between being a Mets or a Yankees fan. Come here, and you can stay a Phillies Phanatic and still enjoy watching and rooting for the top farm team of the Baltimore Orioles.

And with all of this nature around us, we often are out doing our own thing and don't have the time or inclination to devote to true fanaticism.

So what can you see if you want to chill out and watch some sports in person?

PRO SPORTS

Baseball

NORFOLK TIDES
Harbor Park
150 Park Ave.
Norfolk
(757) 622-2222
www.norfolktides.com
This area has a long minor league history. There used to be professional teams in Portsmouth as well as in Norfolk on the Southside and another played in Hampton until a few years ago. The Norfolk Red Stockings were one of nine original teams in the Negro National League, losing the national championship in 1888 to the Cuban Giants of New York.

The Norfolk Tars were a Yankees farm team in the Piedmont League from the 1930s until 1955 and featured such baseball greats as Yogi Berra, Phil Rizzuto, and Whitey Ford. The Yankees often would play games here on their way north after spring training. For six years, the minor leagues left the area, but in 1961 the Tidewater Tides were formed in Portsmouth. They played at old Frank D. Lawrence Stadium. Some say a home run hit

there was the longest ever struck because the ball landed on a coal train running on tracks behind the stadium and kept right on going.

The Tides became a Mets affiliate in 1969 and moved to Norfolk the next year. Just about every Mets superstar since played at least some minor league games at Met Park off Military Highway. The team, renamed the Norfolk Tides, moved to Harbor Park in 1993, a stadium designed by the same architects that brought you Camden Yards and most of the celebrated retro parks that have followed. In 2008, the Orioles took over the Norfolk Tides' franchise and that's whose top farmhands are now playing at the park, which sits right on the Elizabeth River downtown and offers a fabulous view from the stands of tugs and ships plying the harbor.

The Tides are in the International League, so you also get a chance to see the top minor leaguers from another 13 major league teams.

Harbor Park has 9,000 lower deck seats, another 2,800 in the upper decks, and 24 luxury skyboxes that seat another 400 folks. There's also a picnic area overlooking left field. Basically, there isn't a bad seat in the house. And where seats at Yankee stadium can run you thousands, here the best seats are just $11—cheaper if you go with a season ticket plan.

This is a very fan friendly operation. If you can't make a game, you can exchange your season tickets for a reserved seat any other night or pay $1.50 to get replacement box seats, which is still cheaper than walking up on game day.

They let kids run on the field after most games. Players are usually willing to sign baseballs and cards and even the mascot, Rip Tide, isn't annoying. It's the kind of place you can let the kids explore on their own without worrying. The concession stands are efficient and there are plenty of large, modern bathrooms. There are parking lots around the stadium where you have to pay or you can ride the free Net bus service from most places downtown or a free shuttle lot.

i They have frequent promotion nights at Harbor Park, most giveaways designed for kids. It can get to be a madhouse though on the Turn Back the Clock nights when hot dogs, Coca-Cola products, and popcorn are only 50 cents each. Fireworks nights are always popular. The shows are elaborate, coordinated with music over the PA system, and light up the riverfront area.

Hockey

NORFOLK ADMIRALS
Scope
215 East Brambleton Ave.
Norfolk
(757) 640-1212
www.norfolkadmirals.com
Maybe it's all the northerners who have transplanted here with the Navy, but this town once went gaga over its minor league hockey. When the team was called the Hampton Roads Admirals and played in the East Coast Hockey League, the equivalent of a AA franchise, under feisty coach John Brodie, you couldn't get a seat. The infatuation seems less intense these days, but you can see even higher quality hockey now on Scope's ice. The Norfolk Admirals are the top farm club for the Tampa Bay Lightning. They entered the AHL as an expansion team in 2000–01. Like all minor league teams in any sport, the rosters and professional staffs are constantly changing to reflect needs at

the major league level. So it can be hard to develop a real relationship with players. My advice is to go to see and enjoy the sport. You'll know when a superstar is skating in front of you. At these levels that kind of talent almost seems to glow.

COLLEGE SPORTS

OLD DOMINION UNIVERSITY
43rd Street and Hampton Blvd.
Norfolk
www.odusports.com
This state commuter school's men's teams are called the Monarchs, the women are the Lady Monarchs, and there are a number of sports in which ODU teams excel. The baseball team is usually very good and has produced a number of major league talents including pitcher Justin Verlander of the Detroit Tigers. You can catch games at the Bud Metheny Baseball Complex on campus for $5.

The men's and women's basketball teams are perennial powerhouses in the Colonial Athletic Association In 2010, the men's team made it to the NCAA Tournament, upsetting Notre Dame in the first round then losing to Baylor in the second. A number of NBA players have attended the school, including Mark West, Dave Twardzik, Kenny Gattison, and Chris Gatling.

The Lady Monarchs have been an elite team in women's basketball for years, often going deep in post-season tournaments, winning national championships in 1979, 1980, and 1985 and losing the championship game to Tennessee in 1997. Nancy Lieberman, one of the first women to play pro ball, came through ODU.

Both teams now play at the 8,000-seat Ted Constant Convocation Center at 43rd Street and Hampton Boulevard.

ODU brought back football in 2009 for the first time since the sport was eliminated in 1941, and the season was a success, both in attendance and out on Foreman Field's 20,000-seat S.B. Ballard Stadium where the team finished its inaugural season 9–2.

The school also has men's and women's soccer teams and a sailing team that is nationally ranked.

NORFOLK STATE UNIVERSITY
700 Park Ave.
Norfolk
(757) 823-8600
www.nsuspartans.com

This is one of two historically black state universities in Virginia, and it offers a full range of athletics with 15 different sports. The men's teams are called the Spartans and the women are the Lady Spartans. NSU annually fields competitive teams in basketball, baseball, football, and track. The school is part of the Mid-Eastern Athletic Conference. Future NBA stars Bob Dandridge and Pee Wee Kirkland teamed up in the late '60s for an NSU basketball team that was nearly unbeatable. The basketball teams play at Joseph Echols Hall on campus. The football teams play at 30,000-seat Dick Price Stadium and the baseball team at Marty L. Miller Field.

VIRGINIA WESLEYAN COLLEGE
1584 Wesleyan Dr.
Norfolk
(757) 455-3200
www.vwc.edu

The small Methodist college on the border of Norfolk and Virginia Beach competes in Division III of the NCAA in the Old Dominion Athletic Conference. They field baseball, basketball, soccer, field hockey, and tennis teams.

HAMPTON UNIVERSITY
100 East Queen St.
Hampton
(757) 727-5641
www.hamptonpirates.com

Hampton is a private university that dates back to 1861 when a free black man was asked to teach the waves of slaves who had fled their bondage for freedom at Fort Monroe. It became the Butler School for Negro Children in 1863 and then Hampton Normal and Agricultural Institute. Booker T. Washington would be the most famous graduate, founding Tuskegee Institute in Alabama at just 25 years old. In 1929 Hampton became a college instead of a trade school. The school joined the MEAC in 1995, where it competes head to head with Norfolk State. The team is called the Pirates and it has won dozens of MEAC titles in football, men's and women's basketball, men's and women's track, and men's and women's tennis. In 2001 the men's basketball team not only made the NCAA tournament but defeated a second seeded team, one of ESPN's top 10 NCAA tournament upsets. The football team has also had a ton of success, winning the conference in 1997, 2005, and 2006 and sharing it in 1998 and 2004. The domination extends to football and tennis as well.

CHRISTOPHER NEWPORT UNIVERSITY
1 University Place
Newport News
(757) 594-7000
www.cnusports.com

In 2008–09, CNU sent 8 of the school's 22 teams to NCAA post-season tournaments. The teams, known as the Captains, annually win championships in the USA South Athletic Conference, in men's and women's basketball, football, men's and women's soccer, softball, and women's lacrosse.

HORSE RACING

COLONIAL DOWNS
New Kent County
Exit 214 of I-64
www.colonialdowns.com/

This isn't exactly in Hampton Roads—it's about halfway between here and Richmond—but it is the only place you'll see live pari-mutuel horse racing in Virginia. There is a summer thoroughbred racing season, a fall harness racing season, and some year-round special events. And there is a local connection: Colonial Downs operates eight off-track betting centers in Virginia where you can watch and wager via live satellite feeds. Two of those OTB centers are in Hampton Roads, in Chesapeake at 4301 Indian River Rd. and in Hampton at 1909 Commerce Dr.

This track boasts the nation's widest grass track on the Secretariat Turf Course and the second largest dirt track in the country that lets harness horses cover a mile with only one turn. The facility's big event is called the Virginia Derby and the $750,000, 1 ¼-mile race happens in mid July and is broadcast live on CBS Sports.

The summer season is usually Fri through Tues from mid-June through early Aug and races begin at 5 p.m. during the week, 6 p.m. on Frid, and 1 p.m. on weekends. The fall harness races begin in mid-Sept and run through early Nov. Another big event is the $100,000 Patriot Trot in mid-Oct and the $350,000 Day of Champions in early Nov.

SURFING

EAST COAST SURFING CHAMPIONSHIP
Virginia Beach Oceanfront
www.surfecsc.com

This end of summer event has been bringing surfers to the Oceanfront since 1952. Look for it around the last weekend in Aug. It goes way beyond the waves, though, with beach volleyball competitions, skimboarding, U.S. Beach Flag Football tournament, World Sand Soccer Association tournament, and even BMX extreme ramp riding and skateboarding exhibitions.

AUTO RACING

LANGLEY SPEEDWAY
3165 North Armistead Ave.
Hampton
(757) 865-7223
www.langley-speedway.com

The speedway is NASCAR sanctioned and hosts the Whelen All-American Series. It's a short track, less than 4/10 of a mile, and one of the flattest, with a maximum of just 6 degrees of banking in the corners, so it takes skill to navigate. The track opened in 1950 and currently operates the NASCAR divisions on Sat nights; Hampton Roads Kart Club races on Sun; and Wild and Wacky Wednesday races for anyone with a helmet and a street-legal car to compete. The big event is the Hampton Heat 200, a 200-lap race for the Crossroads Fuel Late Model Stock Car Division with a break at the 100-lap point to allow fueling, make setup changes, and rotate tires.

ANNUAL EVENTS & FESTIVALS

Some places have one annual party and perhaps a parade to look forward to. In Hampton Roads there's something to anticipate nearly every weekend. A lot of the crowded calendar comes from Virginia Beach efforts to lure and retain tourists and their dollars. But there are plenty of annual events scattered throughout the region—and across the year, once you get beyond the winter doldrums in January and February. As you will see, most of it is aimed at families, and is free or relatively inexpensive. And lots of it happens outdoors. Obviously, you'll want to check ahead of time because dates and prices and locations can change every year. Enjoy!

FEBRUARY

POLAR PLUNGE WINTER FESTIVAL
Virginia Beach
www.polarplunge.com
This exercise in self-torture has been going on since 1992. It's Special Olympics Virginia's largest fundraiser, drawing more than 10,000 people to the beach. Their motto: "Don't just catch any cold this winter . . . catch this cold. Take the Plunge." For this good cause, more than 3,000 normally sane folks pay $100 for the privilege of rushing into the frigid Atlantic. There's also a Boogie Down the Boardwalk Costume Parade and contest, musical entertainment, a sand sculpture, vendor displays, and giveaways. You can watch the madness for free, but if you want into the heated tent and festival area, you'll have to cough up a $5 donation. Kids can take the plunge, but a parent or guardian has to sign a waiver form.

MARCH

TASTE OF HAMPTON ROADS
Various locations
(757) 627-6599
www.tasteofhamptonroads.org
Want to sample the best of local cuisine and contribute to a good cause as well? The solution is an annual upscale social called Taste of Hampton Roads that targets corporations and individuals to raise money for the Foodbank of Southeastern Virginia. Diners get to "taste 10" of the 30 participating restaurants while dancing to live entertainment and enjoying a Vegas-style casino and live auction. The event, which began in 1989, earns the Foodbank enough money to provide a million meals to those in need. Cost is $75 per person.

ST. PATRICK'S DAY PARADE
Norfolk
(757) 587-3548
www.norfolkparade.com

It began in 1967 with a few Irish-Americans marching with trash-can lids and brooms around the tiny Ocean View headquarters of the Father Kealey Council 3548 of the Knights of Columbus. When they stopped for liquid refreshments, the leaders decided it was so much fun they wanted to launch a real parade the following spring. That little gathering has evolved into a parade up Granby Street through Ocean View that annually features nearly 200 bands, marching units, clowns, and floats and is one of the largest St. Patty's celebrations on the East Coast. There's an Emerald Ball the week before and a party immediately after the parade with live music and food.

SHAMROCKIN IN GHENT
Norfolk
http://ghentva.org

If you really want to show your Irish, head over to Ghent the Friday before St. Patty's day for what used to be called the Greening of Ghent. It's a big street party on Colley Avenue with live Irish music that involves nearly all of the restaurants and nightspots in this popular enclave. And the proceeds benefit Hope House Foundation, a nonprofit that provides independent living services to adults with developmental disabilities.

SHAMROCK MARATHON
(757) 412-1056
www.shamrockmarathon.com

This 26.2-mile race through the Virginia Beach resort area and Fort Story on St. Patrick's Day weekend is a qualifier for the fabled Boston Marathon and annually attracts some of the best national and international runners. In addition to the individual glory, there are team tests, including the Military Cup, and $25,000 in prize money. There's also a half marathon and an 8K run.

How big a deal is this? Well, *Runner's World* once dubbed it a "Cream of the Crop" and one of the top 20 marathons in America. Three world records and 32 national records have been set here since 2003 alone, and three participants have qualified for the Olympic trials.

If you're not quite in Olympic shape but still want to participate, you can even walk the half or full marathon events and they'll register your time and achievement, provided you can cover the full distance in 6.5 hours, or 4 hours for the half. No kid stuff here—you have to be at least 16 to participate in the official Shamrock, and it isn't cheap. Registration costs between $80 and $100 for the full race depending on when you sign up. But you get a lot of takeaways, earning "Best Schwag Perks and Prizes Worth Bonking For" from *Runners World*.

Elementary school students can get in on the fun by running something called the Operation Smile Final Mile. The kids cover the first 25.2 miles in advance at home or school and then run the final mile on race day, earning a goody bag, T-shirt, medal, and certificate. And for tykes six months to five years old, there's the mad dash of the Children's Marathon, which covers 26.2 yards.

APRIL

DOO DAH PARADE
Norfolk

It calls itself "Norfolk's most foolish tradition," and who can argue when you watch this wacky parade on or around April Fool's Day. Of course, when you're dealing with fools, you never know what to expect, or even if you should expect the parade to happen. Sometimes, the fools just can't work up the energy. But when they do, it can be hilarious. There have been Bed Pan Brigades, the

Wingtip and Umbrella Precision Drill Team, Marching Elvises, and even the Pooper Scooper Brigade wending their way through the financial district on Main Street.

PORTSMOUTH INVITATIONAL TOURNAMENT

Portsmouth

www.portsmouthinvitational.com

This is the place for those who really love college basketball. The PIT, which dates back to 1952, once drew the very top talent and all the NBA scouts to watch teams of college seniors, sponsored by local industries, compete for top prizes. Other tournaments, undergraduates in the NBA draft, and combines have diluted the field somewhat, but the scouts still come out in early April and turn up gems that find their way onto NBA and international rosters. The PIT alumni include Larry Brown, Scottie Pippen, Rick Barry, Earl "The Pearl" Monroe, Dave Cowens, John Stockton, Dennis Rodman, Avery Johnson, and Ben Wallace. It's a four-day tourney with a dozen games featuring 64 college seniors. There are night games for $10 each or $30 for the entire tournament, and afternoon consolation games that are free. And it all takes place in the comfy confines of Churchland High's gymnasium.

i Bring a Sharpie and plenty of things you want autographed to the Portsmouth Invitational Tournament. Not only will you have easy access to future stars, but those scouts who sit right there with you in the stands often include some of your NBA and college heroes. It's usually easiest to get to them during those free afternoon games.

AIR POWER OVER HAMPTON ROADS AIR SHOW

Hampton

www.langleyafbairshow.com

This is the first of the two military air shows that usually happen in Hampton Roads. Once there were three, the Air Force's exhibition on the Peninsula and then a pair of Navy shows, one at Chambers Field on Naval Station Norfolk and the other at Oceana. When Chambers Field was merged with Oceana, so were the Navy air shows. Although they were all popular, it put quite a strain on the military aviators. In fact, in 2010 the Air Force cancelled its Air Power show entirely because of operational demands in Afghanistan and Iraq. The show serves as Langley's premier open house, with a night show and fireworks and a pair of main shows featuring the Thunderbirds on Sat and Sun afternoons. Officials of the newly combined Joint Base Langley-Eustis promised it would resume in 2011.

EASTER SUNRISE SERVICES

Virginia Beach

www.cnic.navy.mil//jeblcfs

There are scores of sunrise services on Easter Sunday, but the one at the Cape Henry Memorial Cross on Fort Story is the grand-daddy. It began in 1927, eight years before the Daughters of the American Colonists erected the cross at the spot where the Jamestown settlers first gave thanks for a safe crossing. Here, you can actually watch the sun rise over the Atlantic as you celebrate the resurrection of Jesus on that first Easter. The base recently switched owners, from the Army to the Navy, but it's unlikely access for this traditional service will change.

NORFOLK NATO FESTIVAL
Norfolk
(757) 605-3073
www.azaleafestival.org

For more than 50 years, this end-of-April party was known as the International Azalea Festival, with annual azalea parades and an Azalea Queen chosen from the NATO country honored that year. The name was changed in 2009 to reflect what the festival was always about, recognizing the 28 NATO member and 24 Partnership for Peace nations whose staff and families live in Hampton Roads while working at NATO's Allied Command Transformation headquarters, the only NATO command on U.S. soil. This is the longest continuously running festival in the region. The Azalea Parade was renamed the Parade of Nations but still features bands, marching units, and floats. There is no longer a queen, though. In the past, that honor went to a variety of notables, including First Children Tricia Nixon, Luci Baines Johnson, Lynda Bird Johnson, Jenny Eisenhower, and Susan Ford. Now, the most honored nation provides an active duty officer, male or female, to serve as festival ambassador. Those male ambassadors are probably happy the tiara went the way of the queen title.

INTERNATIONAL CHILDREN'S
FESTIVAL
Hampton
(757) 727-8311 or (757) 727-2085
www.hampton.gov/parks/icf

This annual free event allows children and their families to experience the cultures and cuisines of far-away places without leaving Hampton's Mill Point Park. There is entertainment and educational exhibitions as well as food from more than 30 countries. The djembe drumming and local storytelling help open the minds of children and teaches them the value of diversity. There's lots of fun stuff to do, including a peek at how colonial kids played. And if you're a Girl Scout you can even earn a festival patch.

HISTORIC GARDEN WEEK
Various locations
www.vagardenweek.org
(804) 644-7776

It began during the Great Depression as an opportunity for the proletariat to visit some of Virginia's most stately gardens, homes, and historic landmarks. Sponsored by the Garden Club of Virginia, there are now three dozen historic tours from the Atlantic Ocean to the Allegheny Mountains on properties that date back to the early 17th century. Every mid- to late April, you can tour formal gardens, walled gardens, cottage gardens, cutting gardens, herb gardens, water gardens, and some "secret" gardens. It's the oldest and largest statewide house and garden tour in the nation, and proceeds benefit the restoration of historic grounds and gardens across Virginia. There's plenty to see in Hampton Roads, and the homes vary year to year, so check out the tour schedule online. You might want to travel to Charlottesville or check out plantations on the James River. Tour tickets are generally $25 ahead of time and $30 on tour day and include admission to a number of private homes as well as additional historic homes, lectures, and special events. Or you can pay $10 to get into a single site.

HAMPTON ROADS BLUEGRASS
JAMBOREE
Newport News
(757) 594-7448
http://fergusoncenter.cnu.edu

The Ferguson Center recently spawned a new annual attraction, a gathering of bluegrass giants at Christopher Newport University. If you love bluegrass, from old time to contemporary, check out the lineup at this mid-April event.

> **i** The Garden Club of Virginia puts out a guidebook every February describing the gardens and homes that are on tap that year. You can get a head start on your voyeurism by sending a $6 donation to Historic Garden Week, 12 East Franklin St., Richmond VA, 23219. Or you can wait and pick one up free at one of the tour properties.

VIRGINIA ARTS FESTIVAL
Various venues
www.virginiaartsfest.com
(757) 282-2800
Beginning on the Ides of April, this festival runs for six weeks and across 10 cities. It offers a taste of every art form, from chamber music and military bands to theater, ballet, and rock. Nearly every day during the festival, you'll find a headliner or two. Entertainers come from across the world. From a Shakespeare troupe to a Korean Army Band, classical guitarists to Russian folk dancers, it's all here.

MAY

The Virginia Arts Festival continues (see April listing).

VIRGINIA BEER FESTIVAL
Norfolk
www.festevents.org
(757) 282-2800
While the highbrows take in the rest of the Virginia Arts Festival, you can enjoy the High

Life at Town Point Park. This mid-May fest annually features the best suds from Europe and America. You can buy tasting tickets for $25 in advance, $30 at the gate, and sample the wares in your own souvenir glass. You can come by boat too, with reserved docking for $250 per vessel up to 35 feet. If your dinghy is bigger than that, so is the price. You get four tasting tickets as well as your boat slip.

CINCO DE MAYO
Norfolk
www.festevents.org
Downtown Norfolk goes Latin every May 5 as the region celebrates Mexico's Independence Day. The party at TowneBank Fountain Park on the Elizabeth River by the Waterside Festival Marketplace is free and offers music and vendors selling Mexican meals and adult beverages.

> **i** From May to October, TowneBank Fountain Park is host to a TGIF party, with free music, plenty of mingling, and a chance to start the weekend with a bite and a beer. It's a great way to let off steam and begin your weekend.

ELIZABETH RIVER RUN
Portsmouth
http://err.tidewaterstriders.com
To err is human, unless your ERR is the Elizabeth River Run, which is sublime. The 10K race, sponsored by Tidewater Striders, began in 1979 and covers a scenic course through Olde Towne Portsmouth. The race starts and finishes by the nTelos Pavilion at Harbor Center, an amphitheater right on the river that hosts a post-race party. The race is certified by USA Track & Field. Registration costs $18

for Striders, and $20 to $30 for non-members depending on how early you sign up. You can walk this course and there is a mile race and a 30-yard Children's Museum Fun Run for kids six months to six years old.

GREEK FESTIVAL NORFOLK
Norfolk
(757) 440-0500
www.norfolkgreekfestival.com
This is the area's oldest and largest ethnic festival, packed with traditional Greek cuisine, entertainment, and arts and crafts. There's even a drive-through where you can pick up some take-out Greek delicacies. The festival is held mid-May under tents on the grounds of the Annunciation Greek Orthodox Cathedral, 7220 Granby St. Grab some souvlaki, baklava, or if you're lucky, a cup of almost chewy Greek coffee (tip: don't call it Turkish coffee here, although they are essentially the same brew). Then head over to watch the church's kids do some 300 different folk dances. The proper applause here is *Opa! Opa! Opa!*

AFR'AM FEST
Norfolk
www.afram-fest.info
Held annually on Memorial Day weekend since 1983, this is the largest project sponsored by the Southeastern Virginia Arts Association, an organization that promotes the arts and culture of African Americans in Hampton Roads. The festival at Town Point Park includes fine arts exhibitions, a Children's Village with storytelling, a literary cafe, live entertainment, a marketplace, health awareness booths, and a variety of vendors. Admission is $10, but children six and under get in free with an adult.

BEACH MUSIC WEEKEND
Virginia Beach
(757) 425-3111
www.beachstreetusa.com
Nearly every weekend during the season, there are different festivals and entertainers brought to the Oceanfront by Beach Street USA. But one of the year's biggest draws is the Beach Music Weekend, a four-day series of free concerts on the beach at 30th Street. These are old-fashioned beach bands that bring their nostalgic sounds right to the surf. Rhonda can't help you stop your toes from tapping.

PUNGO STRAWBERRY FESTIVAL
Virginia Beach
(757) 721-6001
www.pungostrawberryfestival.info
Pungo's rich farmland is just perfect for growing strawberries, and every Memorial Day weekend since 1983 this rural community near the North Carolina border gathers to celebrate the magic fruit. There are strawberry shortcakes and strawberry pies. In fact, there are more than 50 different ways to sample the juicy gems. But it doesn't stop there. There's a pie eating contest, a strawberry bake-off, three stages with non-stop entertainment, a parade, livestock show and sale, pig races, youth art show, arts and craft vendors, and one of the largest carnivals on the East Coast.

i The Pungo Strawberry Festival is way out there, accessible by just a rural stretch of Princess Anne Road. Needless to say, with 120,000 visitors, traffic can back up quickly. So head out early and avoid a snarl that can take the joy out of the festivities.

GOSPORT ARTS FESTIVAL
Portsmouth
www.gosportartsfestival.com

This is a two-day juried art show around Mother's Day weekend that goes back four decades in Hampton Roads, moving to Olde Towne in 2000. There are cash awards for artists and local and regional entertainment. The festival benefits the EDMARC Hospice for Children, the first in the nation designed specifically for kids and the families that love them. You can walk down the center of historic High Street and enjoy the work and conversations with more than 150 artists in a full range of media.

STOCKLEY GARDENS ART FESTIVAL
Norfolk
www.hope-house.org
(757) 625-6161

Another of the region's long-time art festivals, this one takes over the park in Ghent's historic Stockley Gardens twice a year, in mid-May and mid-Oct. It raises funds for Hope House Foundation, which assists developmentally disabled individuals, and attracts 150 artists annually.

CHESAPEAKE JUBILEE
Chesapeake
www.chesapeakejubilee.org/

To celebrate the city's 20th birthday, the Chamber of Commerce decided to hold a big party in an open field outside the city's first mall. That was 1983 and it was the first of the city's jubilees. The venue has moved over the years to nearby City Park, but this late May fair has retained its rural flavor, with the Chesapeake 4-H livestock show and sale still a key feature even if the city has become one of the state's most populous communities. The entertainment skews towards country

and rock, with headliners such as Willie Nelson, Chuck Berry, The Commodores, Charlie Pride, and .38 Special. The jubilee hosts a barbecue cookoff for state bragging rights and a huge carnival with the largest array of traveling rides and games east of the Mississippi. There's also a Kids Korner with free fun for children, community and military displays, and one of the area's largest fireworks shows.

ℹ️ The Chesapeake Jubilee has become a park and ride affair, with shuttle buses to take you to and from your car. If you want to get close to the fireworks and avoid the festival crowd, try heading to the strip of shops on Battlefield Boulevard across from Chesapeake General Hospital. It's essentially on the backside of the park, and you can pull up and see the show from the comfort of your own car.

JUNE

HARBORFEST
Norfolk
(757) 441-2345
www.festevents.org

This is one of the area's largest and oldest public parties. Each year, half a million people attend Harborfest activities on the Elizabeth River at Town Point Park. The highlight is usually the parade of sailing ships that pull into downtown on the opening Friday afternoon as spectators watch from points all along the river. Many of these tall ships are available for public tours. Past visitors have included the Coast Guard bark *Eagle*, replicas of the *Godspeed* that brought the settlers to Jamestown, and the *Kalmar Nyckel*, a Swedish ship that brought Europeans to the Delaware Valley. Like any big street fair, there's plenty of food and beverages and lots of vendors hawking souvenirs and novelties. And there's a fireworks show here as well, billed as the biggest and best on the East Coast on Sat night. If you have a yacht and want to tie up at Waterside for the party, it can cost as much as $1,000 for boats up to 54 feet long. If yours is longer, you probably won't flinch at the additional $15 per foot fee. You can also tie up to other boats for as little as $250 with no power and limited water access. Or you can just anchor for free off Hospital Point in Portsmouth and watch the fireworks there.

BOARDWALK ART SHOW & FESTIVAL
Virginia Beach
(757) 425-0000
www.cacv.org/events/boardwalk.asp
This is a four-day event that draws not only artists from afar but patrons as well. What's not to like when you have miles of booths that back up to the blue Atlantic? The show is put on by the Contemporary Art Center of Virginia in mid-June. It began in 1952 when a group of locals held a sale to benefit an artist who had a stroke. Four years later, they started the current festival. In fact, they were holding this affair back when the Boardwalk was actually made of boards. More than 350,000 visitors annually turn out to buy some $2 million in art. The best-in-show award of $10,000 is second highest in the nation and draws top talent and the folks who collect their art.

BAYOU BOOGALOO
Norfolk
(757) 441-2345
www.festevents.org
Capture the spirit of New Orleans and Cajun country during this three-day late June festival at Town Point Park. There are three stages with national recording artists and New Orleans musicians. You can learn to cook Cajun, try your hand at crawfish and hot pepper eating contests, and enjoy the feel of New Orleans' Jackson Square. But the big draw is the food—spicy hot and authentic crawdads, jambalaya, gumbo, étouffée, alligator, and andouille sausage that fairly beg for some ice-cold beverages. The festival costs $20 in advance for a weekend pass or you can spend $10 each day.

i There's usually a free kickoff party and artist reception on the Thursday before the Bayou Boogaloo, and attendees get a free pass for Friday's admission. You can also get in free for lunch and a party preview on Friday if you enter between noon and 4 p.m.

COCK ISLAND RACE
Portsmouth
(757) 393-8481
www.portsvaevents.com
It's a can't-miss event on a Saturday afternoon every summer as some 300 sailboats in every size and shape vie to be the first to round the mystical Cock Island. Don't bother checking your charts, the island vanished like Atlantis years ago into the Elizabeth River, so the location for the race is somewhat arbitrary. It's hard to tell, anyway, whether this is a race or just an excuse to party, with live entertainment on Fri and Sat nights for the participants. Lately, the race has been held in mid-June. And there are no losers here, with prizes to first and last boats to finish as well as awards for the best themed vessel.

HAMPTON JAZZ FESTIVAL
Hampton
(757) 838-2595
www.hamptonjazzfestival.com

It began as a straight jazz festival in 1968, with a set list of immortals that included Cannonball Adderley, Count Basie, Ramsey Lewis, Wes Montgomery, and Thelonious Monk and vocalists Nina Simone, Dionne Warwick, and Muddy Waters. Over the years, a who's who of traditional jazz artists has paraded through the Coliseum the last full weekend of June: Duke Ellington, Paul Desmond, Dave Brubeck, Ray Charles, Dizzy Gillespie. As tastes changed, rhythm and blues and popular acts began to dominate the shows: Gladys Knight, Little Richard, Earth Wind & Fire, Michael McDonald. There are three different shows over the weekend, so you can usually find one that suits your tastes, from easy listening to classic jazz. Acts are announced by mid-Mar or early Apr, which is when the tickets go on sale. There's usually a lot of demand here, since it's as much a social scene and traditional friends' gathering as it is a music festival.

JULY

INDEPENDENCE DAY
Various venues

As you can expect in a military town, there's a wide array of Independence Day celebrations in Hampton Roads with fireworks shows over the Elizabeth River in Norfolk and Portsmouth, over the James in Newport News, on the Nansemond River in Suffolk, and at the Oceanfront in Virginia Beach. There are also any number of community picnics and free entertainment, including some tied to the fireworks shows. They include the 4th of July Stars in the Sky gathering at Victory Landing Park in Newport News, (757) 926-1400; the Stars & Stripes Spectacular at Constant's Wharf Park in Suffolk, (757) 514-7250; the Stars and Stripes Explosion festival at the Oceanfront in Virginia Beach, (757) 491-SUNNY; the July 4th Celebration at Mount Trashmore in Virginia Beach, (757) 385-2990; Laser Spirit at the Virginia Living Museum in Newport News, (757) 595-1900; the 4th of July Celebration at Lakeside Park in Chesapeake, (757) 382-6411; and the Great American Picnic at Town Point Park in Norfolk, (757) 441-2345.

NORFOLK JAZZ FESTIVAL
Norfolk
(757) 441-2345
www.festevents.org

What happens when you take your jazz out of a smoky club and put it under the setting sun and summer stars? It becomes a whole new experience, especially when you add in lawn chairs and lots of food and beverages to sustain your body while your soul soars. This used to be a free festival, but municipal budgets can no longer cover the entire cost, so there is an admission fee. The 12-hour festival runs over Fri and Sat evenings and nights. You can buy tickets for the entire thing or individual days. In addition to national artists, the festival usually features local and regional favorites. Past acts have included Ramsey Lewis, Pieces of a Dream, Spyro Gyra, and Arturo Sandoval.

AUGUST

NORFOLK LATINO MUSIC FESTIVAL
Norfolk
(757) 441-2345
www.festevents.org

This gathering at the end of Aug in Town Point Park is still free, with hot dancing under the stars and spicy food to match. Local, regional, and national recording artists provide entertainment.

SEAWALL ART SHOW
Portsmouth
(757) 393-8983, ext. 13
www.seawallartshow.org

This is another long-running public art show in the region. It takes place the last weekend in Aug on the Portsmouth Seawall, a long concrete promenade along the Elizabeth River. There is $9,000 in awards and an on-site student art show. You can browse booths featuring works in oils, pastels, watercolor, pencil, stained glass, pottery, photography, and metal. There's also fine jewelry and fun jewelry and free parking. The show also features free entertainment.

EAST COAST SURFING CHAMPIONSHIP AND BEACH SPORTS FESTIVAL
Virginia Beach
(757) 456-1535
www.surfecsc.com

This is the world's second oldest, continuously run surfing contest. It's an amateur and pro event sanctioned by the United States Surfing Federation and the Association of Surfing Professionals. The championship began in 1963 as the Virginia Beach Surfing Carnival, but by 1965 it had become the focal point for East Coast competitive surfing. Like all Virginia Beach festivals, this four-day party has live music, food, beverage, and souvenir sales. You can watch the wave riders on the beach at 2nd Street or walk the boards and see pros demonstrate skating and BMX tricks, take in a volleyball tournament, or watch who wins the U.S. Beach Flag Football Championship and the World Sand Soccer Association Tournament. There's also an annual swimsuit competition, and a "beach bum" triathlon.

SEPTEMBER

VERIZON WIRELESS AMERICAN MUSIC FESTIVAL
Virginia Beach
(757) 425-3111
www.beachstreetusa.com

Want to enjoy your Labor Day without a long drive? Well, if you live here in Hampton Roads you can listen to an array of rock, country, blues, and R&B artists at the largest outdoor music event on the East Coast. The shows, most of them free, fill the three-day weekend and stages all along the Oceanfront. The biggest acts appear on a 60-foot-wide, 60-foot-tall stage on the beach at 5th Street. Past stars have included the likes of 3 Doors Down, the B52s, Journey, and Charlie Daniels Band. Of course there's plenty of food and souvenirs to buy. Just remember to bring lots of tanning lotion and a comfy beach chair, and get there early if you want the best seat or, more importantly, a chance to park at the nearest lot. This is a holiday weekend, after all, at one of the nation's most popular resorts.

ROCK 'N' ROLL HALF MARATHON
Virginia Beach
http://virginia-beach.competitor.com

If you're tired of grooving and want to start moving, on Sunday morning during Labor Day weekend you can run the Rock 'n' Roll Half Marathon, the largest such race in Virginia. Our you can do a quarter marathon, 6.55 miles, in the Rock 'n' Roll Relay. The course runs along the Oceanfront and finishes along the Boardwalk. You can register online or by mail; they don't do it by telephone. This is a popular race attracting more than half its field from out of state. It is also pricy, ranging from $85 to $125 to register, depending on when you sign up. The cost includes a free ticket to Sunday night's big concert on the 5th Street Stage. You can run as young as 12, but you have to be able to do a half marathon, 13.1 miles, in less than four hours. There will be plenty of pros out there to inspire you, since the race annually attracts some of the world's best runners and now features team competitions, pitting Kenyans against Ethiopians, Europeans versus USA squads, all competing for more than $30,000 in prize money.

NEPTUNE FESTIVAL BOARDWALK WEEKEND
Virginia Beach
(757) 425-3111
www.neptunefestival.com

This annual party is the city's largest and oldest event, celebrating its nautical heritage and extending the summer tourist season to around the last weekend of the so-called shoulder month of September. Attracting more than a half million visitors to the Boardwalk—most of them from Hampton Roads—it's considered one of the nation's top 100 festivals and in the top 10 on the East Coast. What regulars learn, and locals relish, is that summer doesn't end here on Labor Day. It gets better. Afternoons remain warm, but there's less humidity, and the ocean water temperature is still usually balmy. That's why there's rarely an unbooked Oceanfront room this weekend, and more than 90 percent are repeat visitors. There are more than 35 separate events linked to the festival, including an Arts and Craft Show on the Boardwalk, but the most popular is probably the North American Sand Sculpting Championship. You'll be amazed what artists can create using just buckets, shovels, and saltwater.

SANDMAN TRIATHLON
Virginia Beach
(757) 498-0215
www.sandmantri.com

Recovered from that half marathon along the beach two weeks ago? Try our tri. All you have to do is swim a kilometer in the ocean, bike 14 miles, and then finish a 5K run in three hours or less. The Neptune Festival folks have been organizing this legal form of torture since 1982, perhaps to prove that the shoulder season isn't all sand sculptures and parades. It's a sanctioned triathlon limited to adults around the middle of September. If you're a USA Triathlon Member registration costs $60 before Aug 9, $10 more after, and you can add $10 to either figure if you're a non-member. You start out swimming either on 32nd or 16th street. These folks are teddy bears; they let you swim with the current. You get out of the ocean and onto your bike at the 24th Street Park. If the water is below 78 degrees, you can wear a wet suit and still get an award. The bike course goes up Atlantic Avenue and on Shore Drive. And the run itself is on the Boardwalk beginning and ending around 24th Street.

OCEANA AIR SHOW
Virginia Beach
www.oceanaairshow.com

Also sandwiched between the Rock 'n' Roll Festival and the Neptune Festival's Boardwalk Weekend is the Oceana Air Show, one of the most popular annual events at the beach. It's a demonstration of the world's best pilots, military and civilian, that takes place at the Master Jet Base nestled in the heart of Virginia Beach. The Blue Angels, the Navy's premier flight team, are always the highlight of the weekend. The team performs at 3 p.m. every day, Fri through Sat, but the Friday show is a practice that can only be watched by the military and invitees. Fri evening and Sat and Sun afternoons, the base is open to the public, who can thrill to aerobatics performed by biplanes, trainers, and some of the world's most advanced fighters. There's usually a parachute team exercise, and a perennial favorite is the Shockwave Jet Truck, which holds the world drag record for full size trucks at 376 miles per hour and reaches 3 Gs while accelerating across the runway. There are also static displays of military gear with service members eager to answer questions from children and adults alike. This is a free show, designed to encourage enlistments and show military prowess. But you can buy seats in the bleachers or in general and reserved sections for $4 to $14. If you want to go corporate, $60 buys you entrance to the Executive Squadron Chalet, where you can enjoy a catered lunch, unlimited beverages, and soft drinks.

i Although the best seats for the Air Show are at Oceana, the jets fly over much of Virginia Beach as they circle back to the demonstration area. They're hard to miss. Even stealth aircraft make plenty of noise when they pass directly over you. And if you are heading to the base, get there early. Traffic is always heavy, especially in the early afternoon, as people try to get there for the Blue Angels.

HAMPTON BAY DAYS
Hampton
(757) 727-1641
www.baydays.com
The party doesn't end at Labor Day on the Peninsula either. Every year since 1982, the weekend after Labor Day has been home to Hampton Bay Days, a chance for a quarter million people to visit downtown Hampton, have some fun, and learn about the Chesapeake Bay. There are interactive exhibits, entertainment, art, and activities especially for children. More than 35 groups ranging from reggae to country are offered on three outdoor stages. National acts such as Ricky Skaggs and Bruce Hornsby are part of the lineup and you can bring your lawn chair, but no coolers or glass containers. There are also artisans selling their wares, a car show, and a fireworks extravaganza.

i Really like that national act? Well, for $5 you can move ahead of the free crowd to VIP seating in the Gold Row. And it comes with a VIP refreshment area.

BLUES AT THE BEACH
Virginia Beach
(757) 425-3111
www.beachstreetusa.com
This is one of the more laid-back music festivals at the Oceanfront, as well it should be. The 17th Street Park becomes a blues paradise for three days the weekend after Labor Day, featuring national blues headliners and local talent. In addition, you can learn a few licks at instrumental workshops led by the local Natchel Blues Network and festival performers. Check out the local blues scene year-round at www.natchelblues.org.

OPERA IN THE PARK
Norfolk
(757) 441-2345
www.festevents.org
There's something special about listening to music outdoors and you rarely get a chance to enjoy classical performers, let

alone operas, alfresco. For the past couple years, the award-winning Virginia Opera has brought popular arias and Broadway melodies to TowneBank Fountain Park next to Nauticus. Bring a lawn chair and a picnic basket and enjoy this early Sept treat.

ACOUSTIC MUSIC FESTIVAL AND BOOKS IN THE PARK
Norfolk
(757) 441-2345
www.festevents.org

Another free offering in late Sept is a relatively new festival featuring eight hours of live music at Town Point Park that turns the park into three virtual coffeehouses and a literary garden. You can sample local coffee blends and buy wine, food, and other beverages, and a portion of the proceeds benefit the Great Chesapeake Schooner Race.

i Really want to feel like a local and support some good young musicians? Bring a beach chair on Saturday evenings in the summer to the little park behind the Ted Constant Convocation Center at Old Dominion and enjoy the free Music on Monarch Way series. Kids can run around while you chill out. There's usually a free snack or you can head over to the shops at the University Village and stuff yourself.

OCTOBER

POQUOSON SEAFOOD FESTIVAL
Poquoson
(757) 868-3588
www.poquosonseafoodfestival.com

Every year in mid-Oct, folks gather at Poquoson Municipal Park for the biggest seafood extravaganza in the area. There's a fishing tournament, a workboat race, and a 5K run

that honors working watermen and Poquoson's historic connection with them. You can watch blue crabs race and enter your kid in a "catch of the day" baby contest for newborns through four-year-olds. There's also plenty of live entertainment. But the big lure here is the food: crab cakes, shrimp, oysters, clams, soft shell crabs, she-crab soup, and other bounties of the bay are sold here. There's also an arts and crafts area featuring works from local and regional artisans. Admission is free, but you'll need to pay $5 for parking. Area lots can fill up fast, so there are also free shuttle buses to satellite parking. And you'll want to bring a blanket or chairs if you're heading to the Municipal Park stage for a concert. No outside coolers or pets are allowed on the festival grounds.

TOWN POINT VIRGINIA WINE FESTIVAL
Norfolk
(757) 441-2345
www.festevents.org

Since 1987, Virginia wineries have been showing their stuff along the Elizabeth River in mid-Oct. This is a very popular festival where you can not only sample the different vintages but also buy by the glass, bottle, or case. The festival also highlights made-in-Virginia foods and crafts and features live music. A tasting ticket costs $30 in advance or $35 at the gate, which includes your souvenir glass. You can bring a chair and a full picnic kit, although if it gets too crowded you may have to pick up your blanket.

FLEET WEEK
Various venues

Early every Oct, this Navy town honors the service's birthday and those who protect us with an array of Fleet Week events. This is when you'll find out who the military citizen of the year is, be able to visit an operating ship at the Nauticus Pier, and see which military team can whip up the most lethal chili concoction. It's also a great time to hear the various Navy bands.

PEANUT FESTIVAL
Suffolk
(757) 539-6751
www.suffolkfest.org
When you're the historic home of Planters, and much of your farmland is dedicated to the delicious goober, why not make the highlight of your annual schedule a festival honoring the peanut? Suffolk's first peanut festival occurred in 1941, and it included a parade, dances, and balls. The current version, though, only dates back to 1978 when it was called Harvest Fest. It was held downtown then but moved out to the municipal airport in 1981. The four-day show annually draws some 200,000 visitors who enjoy live entertainment with local and national acts, such as the Marshall Tucker Band or Wooden Nickel. This still has an all-American small town feel to it, with a midway full of funnel cakes and other treats and amusements. There's a demolition derby on Fri night, a tractor pull on Sat afternoon, and high-school bands and cloggers providing entertainment throughout the event.

i Want to know everything about peanuts? Check out the basement exhibit at the Riddick's Folly House Museum in downtown Suffolk. (See details in the Museums chapter.)

OLDE TOWNE GHOST WALK
Portsmouth
(757) 234-1416
www.oldetowneghostwalk.com
What's Halloween without a ghost story? Head over to Portsmouth and listen as the ghosts of historic Olde Towne come alive. This annual event, running since 1981, is patterned after the Jack-the-Ripper Walks in London. For your $10, you get a guided walking tour, and costumed re-enactors will tell tales of the infamous and all the haunted homes in this Colonial-era neighborhood that is on the National Register of Historic Places.

i There are a number of haunted houses and haunted forests that crop up around Hampton Roads every fall. The Ghost Train ride at Northwest River Park is an annual favorite, just scary enough but not nightmare material for most children. You need to get your tickets early. Call (757) 421-7151 or (757) 421-3145.

STOCKLEY GARDENS ART SHOW
Don't forget, there's a fall show at this Ghent location as well. For info, see the listing in May.

NOVEMBER

GRAND ILLUMINATION PARADE
Norfolk
(757) 623-1757
www.downtownnorfolk.org
The Norfolk skyline comes alive in late Nov when lights framing the buildings are all switched on to mark the start of the Grand Illumination Parade. This annual party involves floats, marching bands, giant balloons, dancers, and the arrival of Santa himself. It's part of the Holidays in the City programs in Downtown Norfolk and Olde Towne Portsmouth that salute Thanksgiving, Hanukkah, Christmas, Kwanzaa, and New Year's Eve.

MCDONALD'S HOLIDAY LIGHTS AT THE BEACH
Virginia Beach
(757) 425-3111
www.beachstreetusa.com

The full name of this event is McDonald's Holiday Lights at the Beach, Presented by nTelos Wireless, but locals usually call it the Boardwalk light show. This is likely your only chance ever to drive your car on the beach Boardwalk. As you creep from 2nd to 34th streets, you'll see a nautical and holiday themed light display. There are fish and jumping dolphins, Santa, elves, and a 40-foot-tall Christmas tree. Try to figure out the Twelve Days of Christmas figures as you drive by. Are those lords a-leaping? Some 30,000 vehicles take the trip every year between mid-Nov and New Year's Day, the vast majority likely locals. A free CD of holiday music, with some included commercials, comes with the admission price so you can get into the seasonal spirit. Southeast Tourism Society has dubbed this a "Top 20 November Event," and many hotels provide their guests with free tickets. You pay $10 per vehicle, so this is a perfect family and friends outing.

i McDonald's Holiday Lights at the Beach can get pretty busy, and folks take their time driving the boards, so the line quickly backs up. If you're short on patience or have a carful of tykes, you might want to plan this for less busy days or even take the drive on Thanksgiving night. Sometimes the police block access to Atlantic Avenue for a couple blocks. You can also buy hot chocolate from your car as you wait.

GARDEN OF LIGHTS
Norfolk
(757) 441-5830
www.norfolkbotanicalgarden.org

Want to take a different take on a driving holiday tour? Check out the Norfolk Botanical Garden's Garden of Lights. Every Nov and Dec a million lightbulbs bloom along a 2½-mile stretch of this carefully tended museum for flora. If you go during the day, there's an entirely different feel on the Yuletide Ride tram that features a narrated tour through the garden at the peak of its winter glory. Ask to see if there's a combo ticket for both the Holiday Lights and the Garden of Lights car tours.

KIDSTUFF

So you've been to the beach and hit a couple historic spots. What's left for the kids to see and do? Plenty. Hampton Roads is a young, vibrant community when you look at the demographics, and that means there are lots of kids here and businesses and attractions lined up to serve them.

There are summer camps of all sorts, and places where you can ride horses or learn to ice skate.

There's a world-class museum geared entirely for children in Portsmouth and many others that make special efforts to keep them entertained. There are city parks for adventurous tots and others for teens who love to see how much air they can get under their wheels while doing tricks on half pipes.

The resort area has its requisite amusement, water park, miniature golf, and car-track offerings. Chesapeake has its own take on water fun, with paddleboats and canoes to explore an enclosed lagoon. And in Hampton you can chill rather than thrill on the restored carousel.

The area offers children's classes in art and theater and a resident troupe that has sent graduates on to Broadway and beyond.

Then there are the less obvious excursions that are sure to please the kids, like a sightseeing trip on the pedestrian ferry between Norfolk and Portsmouth through one of the world's busiest harbors.

The options are only limited by your imagination.

Price Code

$.....................Under $6
$$ ....$6 to $10
$$$ ....Over $10

ZOO

VIRGINIA ZOOLOGICAL PARK $
300 Granby St.
Norfolk
(757) 441-2706
www.virginiazoo.org
This is the state's largest zoo with more than 350 animals housed in natural settings across its 53 acres that can be viewed and enjoyed by the entire family. There's an African exhibit called the Okavango Delta with elephants and giraffes and meerkats and a pride of lions that recently produced cubs. A prairie dog exhibit lets you look into their underground world. Also featured are a red panda, a bald eagle exhibit, a kangaroo exhibit, and Alfred, the white rhino.

The zoo began in 1892 and put its first animals on exhibit in 1900. The early days of lonely critters in metal cages are long gone. Now the animals live in large, natural enclosures and are kept challenged with a variety of toys and programs. The park participates in breeding efforts for endangered species, including African elephants and lions, Eastern bongo, fennec fox, white rhino, and red panda. In addition to the wonderful displays, the zoo has special programs just for kids. They include a spring break zoo camp, storybook times, birthday parties, classes and programs for scouts, and a summer Camp Safari, with a series of one-week half and full-day sessions for kids from 4 to 14. The zoo is also home to a collection of gardens, including a butterfly garden, herb garden, and white, blue, orange, and yellow-themed gardens.

There's a gift shop here and a restaurant, or you can pack a lunch and eat at the adjacent Lafayette Park while the kids play on the swings or other equipment. Open daily, except major winter holidays, 10 a.m. to 5 p.m.

i Outside food isn't allowed into the Virginia Zoological Park itself. And if you're heading out for lunch and want to get back in, be sure to notify the ticket booth attendant and keep your admission receipt.

MUSEUMS

Every museum here has something to offer to children, but there are a few that make the experience something special for youngsters. And one that exists just to tickle those amazing imaginations.

AIR POWER PARK   FREE
413 West Mercury Blvd.
Hampton News
(757) 727-1163
This is the place to take kids who are fascinated by flight. Throughout this 15-acre park is an array of airplanes, fighter aircraft, missiles, and rockets to explore. They include

a P-1127 Kestrel, an F-86L Sabre, a Mercury space capsule, an A-7E Corsair II, an F-101F Voodoo among the jets, and a wealth of rockets and missiles, including a NIKE SAM, a Jupiter IRBM, and a Javelin Sounding Rocket. There's also a children's playground here. Open daily from sunrise to sunset.

CHILDREN'S MUSEUM
OF VIRGINIA $
221 High St.
Olde Towne Portsmouth
(757) 393-8393
www.childrensmuseumva.com
This is that special museum, which started out in the basement of the city's main library and has been growing ever since. It is geared to kids and their imaginations and is undergoing a two-year renovation with a scheduled reopening in 2011. (Until then, there's an adjunct facility called Andalo's Clubhouse at 420 High St.—next to the Courthouse Galleries and across from the Commodore Theater. It features a series of changing exhibits as well as some old friends from the museum: Thomas the Tank Engine, and the town, with it's bank, market, and library, as well as oversized construction blocks and a series of science demonstrations that test muscles and reflexes, explain sound waves, and explore such magic as the Bernoulli Blower and Newton's Cradle and Air Cannon.)

The new facility will have an additional 12,000 square feet of space, but will retain the special, interactive character that has made this a must-go destination. The new first floor will be aimed at kids six and under and retains the make-believe town concept. Here you'll find the popular grocery store play area, only it will be expanded to a farm-to-food market. The old dentist office, where kids used to pretend to be on the other side of the drill, is growing to an entire body works area. A new exhibit will put kids into the world of a bustling port. Or they can pretend to be in a bank and count out money. Another area will let kids play vet and heal a pet. The fire engine and motorcycle that kids loved to climb will be back as will the bubble room, where you can blow giant bubbles—including one station where you pull a lever and wind up in the middle of one.

The second exhibit floor is designed for 6- to 10-year-olds. Here there will be science exhibits that make those Standards of Learning lessons fun and an environmental area called My Backyard and Beyond that uses a 1,100-square-foot house to show how to go green. The third area will be for creating art and music.

Children under 2 are always free and an adult must accompany children under 14. Open daily Labor Day through Memorial Day, Tues through Sat the remaining year. Closed most major holidays.

THE COUSTEAU SOCIETY   FREE
710 Settlers Landing Rd.
(757) 722-9300
www.cousteausociety.org
The society, founded by famed underwater explorer Jacques-Yves Cousteau, has more than 50,000 members worldwide. It picked Hampton for its headquarters in 2003 and opened the Cousteau Waterfront Gallery to the public. Here you can view models of the research vessels *Calypso* and *Alcyone*, made famous by a series of nature films; look at past and present diving equipment; watch Cousteau films and television specials; and look at a real shark cage and decompression chamber. Kids get a free copy of the society's children's publication, *Cousteau Kids*. Open Tues through Sun, 10 a.m. to 4 p.m.

LIGHTSHIP *PORTSMOUTH* MUSEUM $
420 High St.
Portsmouth
(757) 393-8393
www.portsnavalmuseums.com
The Lightship *Portsmouth* was built in 1915 and served for 48 years warning mariners about shoals or other dangerous conditions off the coasts of Virginia, Delaware, and Massachusetts. It was retired in 1964 and moved to Portsmouth, where, following tradition, it took the name of its current location. It sits in a small cutout at the foot of High Street just off the Elizabeth River. In 1989 it was designated a National Historic Landmark. You can wander through the inside and see how the crew of 15 spent months on station in all kinds of seas and weather. The admission also includes entrance to the Portsmouth Naval Shipyard Museum next door. Open Tues through Sat 10 a.m. to 5 p.m., Sun 1 to 5 p.m. Closed on most major holidays.

NAUTICUS $$$
One Waterside Dr.
Norfolk
(800) 664-1080 or (757) 664-1000
www.nauticus.org
The permanent exhibits here (see entry in Museums chapter) are kid friendly and include touch tanks, hands-on exercises, and state of the art theaters. The Battleship *Wisconsin* is berthed at Nauticus and is a must-visit while there. Entrance is included in your admission fee. They offer a Camp Nauticus here over spring break, summer, and winter. There are programs geared for kids from 6 to 15. And there are special programs in the science center for Girl Scouts and Cub Scouts, including overnight camping in the museum. Open Tues through Sat 10 a.m. to

5 p.m.; Sun noon to 5 p.m. Closed on most major holidays.

VIRGINIA AIR AND SPACE CENTER $$$
600 Settlers Landing Rd.
(757) 727-0800 or (800) 296-0800
www.vasc.org

There are a variety of permanent exhibits (see entry in Museum chapter), and many are hands-on and kid friendly. The center has special programs for Girl Scouts and Boy Scouts, home school camp-ins, and the occasional Space Adventure Overnight for children. There's a Cosmic Kids Club for 6- to 10-year-olds with special meetings, a science kit, and free museum admissions for a year for $65. There are also summer science camps here for kids from kindergarten through eighth grade. Open daily except major holidays, 10 a.m. to 5 p.m.; Sun 10 a.m. to 7 p.m.

VIRGINIA AQUARIUM $$$
717 General Booth Blvd.
Virginia Beach
(757) 385-FISH
www.virginiaaquarium.com

You'll want to schedule plenty of time, perhaps an entire day, for your family to visit this marine museum with 800,000 gallons of aquariums and live animal habitats. There are hundreds of hands-on exhibits for kids, including touch tanks throughout. After being greeted by seals that have fun with onlookers in their outdoor tank, you'll follow the walk to the entrance. Once inside, you'll find educational exhibits that will entertain everyone in the family. Outdoor trails and marshlands provide a variety of scenery, and there is a 3D IMAX theater. The Journey of Water in the Bay and Ocean Pavilion introduces young and old to the many aquatic animals and plants that are native to the state. The Restless Planet exhibit, which opened in 2009, features 6,000 animals including komodo dragons, rare crocodiles, and more. A Marsh Pavilion allows you to walk outside on an elevated deck through a half-acre bird aviary to see 55 different species of native birds. A snack bar is on the premises, and there's a gift shop with nautical and other unique items. Open daily from 9 a.m. to 5 p.m., 6 p.m. in the summer season.

VIRGINIA LIVING MUSEUM $$$
524 J. Clyde Morris Blvd.
Newport News
(757) 595-1900
www.thevlm.org

Here, you can explore Virginia's natural heritage and get up close to a red wolf, see fish with no eyes, and frogs that change colors. The museum has more than 250 living species native to Virginia. Deer, fox, bobcats, beavers, and other furry and feathered friends live in natural settings. A 62,000-square-foot educational building of galleries houses four hands-on discovery centers and an observatory. Among the permanent exhibits is an Appalachian Cove with a waterfall, a mountain stream, and a lake filled with fish. The hands-on discovery centers feature natural specimens that can be touched and handled, and there's a butterfly house in the summer months to explore. There's a wealth of activity centers for the kids, a planetarium and observatory to study the skies, an aviary, an outdoor boardwalk, and trails where you can spy animals in natural habitats. There's also an expansive gift shop. They have story time every third Saturday in the Wason Education Center that includes a live animal show that complements the tale. There are weekend safaris for families and spring break and holiday programs for younger children. And there are weeklong summer camps for children age four through fifth grade and summer field adventures for sixth and seventh graders with museum biologists in the mountains or out on vessels. Open daily, 9 a.m. to 5 p.m., noon to 5 p.m. on Sun. Closed most major holidays.

ATTRACTIONS

AMERICAN INDOOR KARTING $$$
2726 North Mall Dr.
Virginia Beach
(757) 486-3003

Here, your kids don't need a license to drive, just a helmet and one of the high-performance go-karts that can reach 35 mph. When you're done, you get a comprehensive report on your race, including your fastest lap, lap average, and how you placed in the field and among all competitors that day. Since this is real racing, with real risks, you'll have to sign a waiver and go through a safety briefing before you get behind the wheel. Obviously, a guardian must sign for any kid under 16. The place also offers an arcade, Wii and Xbox gaming systems, jousting, sumo suits, catering and in-house snack bar. Closed Mon. Open noon to 9 p.m., until 11 p.m. on Fri and Sat nights.

HAMPTON CAROUSEL $
602 Settlers Landing Rd.
In a pavilion next to the Virginia Air and Space Center
(757) 727-0900

This is art you can not only touch but can get aboard and ride. The carousel is located in Carousel Park adjacent to the Virginia Air and Space Center in downtown Hampton. It is one of only 200 antique carousels in the United States. It was built in 1920 by the Philadelphia Toboggan Company for the Buckroe Beach Amusement Park. The ride features 48 horses and two chariots carved and painted by Russian, German, and Italian immigrant artists. After the park closed, the horses were restored and the ride, with its original mirrors and oil paintings, was moved to the current location downtown. They still prance to the original band organ. There is currently a fundraising drive to give them all another sprucing up.

MOTOR WORLD OF VIRGINIA BEACH $$$
700 South Birdneck Rd.
Virginia Beach
(757) 422-4444

There are 11 go-kart tracks here, with 250 vehicles in 16 different styles to choose from. And they just opened an adult speed track if you parents want to race as well. You can also go head-to-head with the kids on a paintball course in the Splat Zone, play mini golf on a 36-hole course, or ride the bumper boats, sky coaster, Kiddie City rides, or Gravity Storm, which gives you the feeling of weightlessness. Open daily Mar through Sept, 10 a.m. to midnight, and weekends year-round.

NIGHTMARE MANSION $$
2008 Atlantic Ave.
Virginia Beach
(757) 428-FEAR

The building has a huge skeleton peeking over, and through, the roof. So you can imagine what's inside. Actually, you might not want to imagine. Just let yourself go and enjoy the terror. Probably not a great idea for young, impressionable minds unless you want to leave all the lights on at night.

OCEAN BREEZE $$$

849 General Booth Blvd.
Virginia Beach
(757) 425-1241
www.oceanbreezewaterpark.com

If the kids are bored with the ocean but still want to get wet, head to Ocean Breeze Waterpark. It's the area's water park, offering 16 waterslides, a million-gallon Runaway Bay wave pool, the Buccaneer Bay Water Playground, and other attractions. It's an easy 2-mile drive from the resort area. Here you can ride a tube through Jungle Falls, drop through Bamboo Shoots, or grab a mat and head down Kool Runnings, Pelican Falls, and Toucan Tunnel, the original slides that have been going strong for 27 years. For smaller children, there's Kiddie Caverns, where parents and tots can go together. The latest attractions are Walk the Plank, a 200-foot dark tunnel with a 50-foot drop into Davy Jones' Locker and Pirates Plummet, with a tunnel that opens just as you plunge straight down. There are private poolside cabanas as well.

VIRGINIA BEACH AMUSEMENT
PARK $$$

15th Street on the Boardwalk
Virginia Beach
www.virginiabeachamusementpark
.com/

If you're at the beach with kids, you'll eventually wind up here. It's a small amusement arcade located right on the Boardwalk opposite the fishing pier. The rides include the Skyscraper, the Hurricane, Music Express, Comic Storm, and Inverter. You pay by the ride or with all-day wristbands.

OUTDOORS

Playgrounds

FUN FOREST FREE

900 Greenbrier Parkway
Chesapeake
(757) 312-0243

This was Chesapeake's answer to Kids Cove and was built entirely by volunteers. An arsonist destroyed much of the wooden play area, but the community rallied and was in the process of rebuilding an even bigger and better facility when this book went to press.

FUN FORT FREE

361 Hornet Circle
Newport News
(757) 886-7912

On the Peninsula, a group of volunteers gathered and built their own imagination-fueled playground for kids called Fun Fort. It's located in Huntington Park, which has a wonderful view of the James River and the nearby James River Bridge. There's even a lifeguard-manned beach here with shallow water to let the kids cool off after a hard day of running through the multi-story wooden fort with its haunted castle, maze, slides, and swings. There's a concession stand and the Crab Shack restaurant is right next door.

KIDS COVE FREE

310 Edwin Dr.
Virginia Beach
(757) 473-5237

This large play area constructed of wooden timbers is located at Mount Trashmore Park. It was designed with kids' input and offers them an opportunity to let their imagination roam. There are benches in a shaded grove near a large wooden Indian sculpture where parents can relax while their kids run wild. It can get crowded here and there are lots of places to lose sight of a child, which is probably what they were hoping for when they suggested the design. The city is planning a new playground next to Kids Cove that will be wheelchair-accessible and feature a swing area, a climbing area, and a general play area. The original Kids Cove will remain open during construction.

Shredding

CHESAPEAKE SKATEPARK $
900 Greenbrier Parkway
Chesapeake
(757) 382-8878
No BMX bikes are allowed at this park within City Park, it's strictly for skating. It includes a spine ramp, a hit ramp, and a three-quarter pipe, as well as a street-skating area with smaller ramps, boxed platforms and other movable obstacles. You have to get an annual skate park pass or buy a guest pass here. You can't get them at the skate park itself, but they are sold at any community center or at the Ranger Station in City Park. Any child under 10 will need to be accompanied by an adult with a community center card. The annual youth membership is $7 for Chesapeake residents, $25 for non residents; $20 for Chesapeake adults and $40 for non-resident adults. A one-visit guest pass is $5.

MOUNT TRASHMORE
SKATE PARK   FREE
310 Edwin Dr.
Virginia Beach
(757) 473-5237
This 24,000-square-foot park opened in 2003 to give teens a place to play with their skateboards, in-line skates, and BMX bikes. There's a large street course just off an above-ground, 7-foot-deep bowl. The skating surfaces are all Skatelite Pro. You'll need to sign up for a free pass, with a parent or guardian signature, to get an admission wristband. Helmets are required and protective pads strongly recommended.

WOODSTOCK PARK
SKATE PLAZA   FREE
5709 Providence Rd.
Virginia Beach
(757) 366-4538
The other Virginia Beach city skate park, this one in the Woodstock Park, is 10,400 square feet of skate surface and another 3,200 square feet of interior greenery. It has a 5-foot-tall quarter pipe, a vertical wall, rails, hubba ledges, radial ledges, stairs, and handrails for grinding. There are even bleachers for friends and family to watch the action. Again, safety helmets are required. The same skate park pass works at Trashmore and here.

Kids Golf

JUNGLE GOLF $$
302 22nd Street
Virginia Beach
(757) 425-7240
www.junglegolf.com
This course has been around since the 1970s at the Oceanfront and has 18 jungle-themed holes; an air-conditioned game room with pool tables, air hockey, basketball, pinball, and more than 40 video games; and a food hut snack bar.

PIRATE'S PARADISE MINI GOLF
COURSE $$
2109 Pacific Ave., Virginia Beach
(757) 422-9822
www.piratesparadiseminigolf.com
A newcomer, it only opened in 2001, this is an 18-hole course with a pirate's theme. It's

open 9 a.m. to at least midnight in the summer. You play your way through a mountain cave, over footbridges, and under waterfalls.

PLAY A ROUND GOLF AND GAMES $$
10814 Warwick Blvd.
Newport News
(757) 591-2800
www.playaroundgolfandgames.com
Let the kids challenge their putting skills on 54 holes of miniature golf at three different courses, or you can head right inside to the arcade with more than 40 video or prize games. The snack bar has pizza and hand-dipped ice cream.

Outdoor Adventures

A PLACE FOR GIRLS   FREE
912 Cedar Rd.
Chesapeake
(757) 547-4405
The Girl Scout Council of Colonial Coast, which includes 16,000 girls and 6,000 adult volunteers, turned their headquarters into a destination location—a place for girls. Adults will enjoy it as well because there is a wonderful boardwalk that meanders above a pristine set of wetlands off Bells Mill Creek. You can see native plants and animals and so many bird species it's a stop on the Virginia Birding Trail. There are picnic pavilions that can be reserved and an observation tower to give you a bird's eye view over the creek. There is also a health and fitness trail here with stations to help you stretch and work out all your muscle groups.

TRIPLE R RANCH $$$
3531 Bunch Walnut Rd.
Chesapeake
(757) 421-4177
www.triplerranch.org

This is a 370-acre working ranch in southern Chesapeake that opened in 1960 as a place where kids could come and learn to ride. They still have horsemanship programs and a special equestrian program for handicapped riders. You can also come for a trail ride or hayrides year round. The ranch offers Christian summer camping experiences, an adventure retreat for 8- to 12-year-olds featuring archery, canoeing, a climbing wall, and horseback riding. There are family retreats complete with a campfire and day camps for 7- to 10-year-olds. Specialty camps for teens include a Surf Camp and a high ropes challenge course with a zip line.

INDOORS

CHESAPEAKE PLANETARIUM   FREE
312 Cedar Rd.
Chesapeake
(757) 547-0153
www.cps.k12.va.us/departments/
planetarium
This school-operated theater captures a child's imagination. The planetarium is located in the Chesapeake Municipal Center and is open to the public on Thurs nights at 8 p.m. It was the first planetarium built by a public school system in Virginia and opened nearly 50 years ago. More than 50,000 people visit annually. There's a traditional domed Sky Theater with a Spitz sky projector that reproduces the daily and annual motions of the earth so you can peek back or forward to see what things looked like or will be. The programs change regularly. Reservations are required. Children under six usually aren't ready to stay quiet long enough for such a show, so they recommend you not bring them, but if yours is particularly quiet, give it a shot. The public programs are provided as a free service of the Chesapeake Public School System.

Ice Skating

Although ice skating is always fun, it can be an amazing relief from the mid-summer heat and humidity. There is a pair of rinks in Hampton Roads, both well maintained and great for a getaway or a special birthday party.

CHILLED PONDS ICE SKATING RINK $$
1416 Stephanie Way
Chesapeake
(757) 420-4488
www.chilledponds.com
Here, you'll find an NHL-sized skating rink where the Norfolk Admirals practice. They have three levels of adult hockey here year-round and lessons for skating and sport. There are plenty of public skating sessions here as well.

**ICELAND OF VIRGINIA BEACH ICE
  SKATING RINK $$**
4915 Broad St.
Virginia Beach
(757) 490-3907
This rink is owned by the Hampton Roads Youth Hockey Association. They teach everything from figure skating to hockey moves and offer adult and youth hockey programs, including adult pickup hockey games. There's still plenty of time for public skating sessions.

Roller Skating

There are a number of roller-skating rinks around the area as well, where you can strap on your blades or traditional skates and whirl around. Some even offer roller hockey leagues. Here are a few spots to hit the hardboards.

**GREENBRIER FAMILY
  SKATING CENTER $**
1409 Stephanie Way
Chesapeake
(757) 420-0258
You can roll to Christian music here on Tues and Thurs 10 to 2 p.m., and enjoy unlimited pizza on Wed and Thurs night. Wed is family night, and Thurs is Christian music night. And on both nights the cost is $5 for skaters and $3 for non skaters.

HAYGOOD SKATING CENTER $
1036 Ferry Plantation Rd.
Virginia Beach
(757) 460-1138
They have family skating nights here with all-you-can-eat pizza for $4.99 per skater on Wed and Thurs.

**KEMPSVILLE FAMILY
  SKATING CENTER $**
5351 Lila Lane
Virginia Beach
(757) 420-9400
Family night here is on Thurs, and a family of up to 5 can get in for a month of Thursdays for $40, which includes admission, regular skate rentals, a slice of pizza and a drink.

**PENINSULA FAMILY
  SKATING CENTER $**
307 Main St.
Newport News
(757) 599-4769
Family night here is Tues, with $3.50 admission and $2 regular skate rental.

PLAZA ROLLER RINK $
1924 East Pembroke Ave.
Hampton
(757) 723-7993

This rink is closed for private parties on Mon and Wed. Thurs is family night here and an entire family can skate for $15 including rentals.

ℹ️ If you live in Virginia Beach, Norfolk, Chesapeake, or the surrounding Hampton Roads area and you have a child that loves video games, there is a local company that has the perfect party solution for him or her. The GamerBus is a 37-foot customized RV that has 16 game consoles and TVs and can have up to 16 kids or adults playing a game simultaneously in the mobile LAN. Check out more details at www.gamerbus.com or call (757) 575-1033.

Laser Tag

LASER QUEST $$$
2682 Dean Dr.
Virginia Beach
(757) 463-6300
www.laserquest.com

Laser tag combines the classic games of tag and hide-and-seek with a high-tech twist. The game is played in a large, multi-level arena featuring specialty lighting, swirling fog, and heart-pounding music. The object is to score as many points as possible with your laser while minimizing the times you get "tagged." This is one of 57 Laser Quest locations in America and 125 across the world. Open to kids from five on up. Each game lasts about a half hour.

LAZER RUSH $$$
711 Brick Kiln Blvd.
Newport News
(757) 877-0181
www.lazerrush.com

Step inside a video game where you explore an ancient Inca stone temple ruin and make your way through a jungle maze while you hunt and are hunted by other players. You wear a laser-sensitive vest and carry your own phaser. Afterwards, you get a full report on how well you did, who you hit, and how many times they hit you. It's modern warfare minus the medics. Open Tues to Thurs 5 to 10 p.m., Fri 3 p.m. to 12 a.m., and Sun noon to 8 p.m.

ART

CONTEMPORARY ART CENTER OF VIRGINIA $$$
2200 Parks Ave.
Virginia Beach
(757) 425-0000, ext. 23

The Contemporary Art Center of Virginia is more than a museum that presents works by regionally, nationally, and internationally acclaimed artists. It offers year-round Studio School classes for adults and children featuring painting, ceramics, drawing, photography, and other media. It also hosts summer Art Saturdays and a Summer Art Camp.

COLOR ME MINE $$$
1300 Colley Ave.
Norfolk
(757) 625-1666

Color Me Mine is a paint-your-own ceramics studio with birthday parties and other programs for kids. You can also tour the kiln room and learn ceramic painting techniques.

PENINSULA FINE ARTS CENTER $$
101 Museum Dr.
Newport News
(757) 596-8175
www.pfac-va.org

The Peninsula Fine Arts Center, an affiliate of the Virginia Museum of Fine Arts, is a non-profit organization dedicated to promoting art appreciation. There's a Hands On For Kids gallery designed for children and families to interact in a fun, educational environment that encourages participation with art materials and concepts. The Studio Art School offers three sessions of classes and workshops for children (ages four and up) and adults in a variety of media. Open Tues through Sat, 10 a.m. to 5 p.m., Sun 1 to 5 p.m. Closed major holidays.

i *The Atlantic Coast Kite Festival is an exciting weekend of high-flying kites and fun for families, participants, and spectators of all ages that occurs at the very end of April or beginning of May on the beach between 16th and 18th Streets. There's even a Best Kite Contest.*

SUFFOLK CENTER FOR CULTURAL ARTS $$
110 West Finney Ave.
Suffolk
(757) 923-0003
www.suffolkcenter.org

The Suffolk Center for Cultural Arts offers a variety of classes for children and adults, changing exhibits, and educational activities for visitors of all ages. There are a number of summer camps, from All The World's a Stage to Krendl's Circus Camp. Teens with a funny bone can learn improv and sketch comedy here, older children can learn to weave, and parents and kids can play with clay together, making traditional pottery. The lineup is always changing, so check it out.

SIGHTSEEING

AMERICAN ROVER $$$
Waterside in Norfolk
(757) 627-7245
www.americanrover.com

Ever wonder what it was like in the age of sail? Well, you and your kids can get a feel for life on the bounding main by taking a cruise on the *American Rover*. The schooner is 135 feet long and has three masts and an impressive array of tan bark sails that provide power. There are a number of cruises that leave from Waterside Marketplace in Norfolk every day. A 90-minute cruise around the harbor runs $16 for adults and $10 for children. The two-hour sunset evening cruise is more expensive but features a musician. And there's a moonlight cruise for adults only as well during the summer.

MISS HAMPTON II $$$
710 Settlers Landing Rd.
Hampton
(757) 722-9102
www.misshamptoncruises.com

This tour boat will take you right over the place where the *Monitor* and *Virginia* battled to a standstill. You'll travel by Fort Wool and be able to check out the warships at the Norfolk Naval Station, and the tour guides will even show your kids where Blackbeard's head was mounted on a post to discourage piracy. The harbor tour lasts about three hours and includes a stop at Fort Wool for a 30-minute walking tour of the Civil War Island Fortress. Price is $22.50 for adults and $11.50 for kids 6 to 12. Kids under six are free.

i Want to save some money or have kids who might not have the patience for a two-hour tour? Well, the *Elizabeth River Ferry* is a paddle-wheel boat that connects Norfolk and Portsmouth. You can climb aboard the pedestrian ferry at Waterside or High Street in Portsmouth and take it across the Elizabeth River. It's not a super long ride, but the scenery sure beats fighting the tunnel traffic. Get off the boat and explore what's on the other side: Olde Towne Portsmouth is one of the best-preserved historic areas in America. On the Norfolk side you have lots of shops and restaurants on Granby Street, and the upscale MacArthur Center mall is an easy stroll. Fares are $1.50 each way and you'll need exact change or have to rely on the mercy of strangers.

PERFORMANCE ART

HURRAH PLAYERS   **$$$**
420 Bank St.
Norfolk
(757) 627-5437
www.hurrahplayers.com
This quarter-century-old children's theater company offers full-length productions of musical and classical theater. In addition to the shows, the company provides training and on-stage performance opportunities in dance, vocal, music, acting, and theater. They accept students as young as five and also offer special Girl Scout workshops for Brownies, Juniors, and older girls. There's also a spring break and several summer camp sessions for 5- to 18-year-olds to learn the three Ps of theatre: producing, promoting, and performing. Hurrah graduates include Adrienne Warren of *The Dream Engine* and *Dreamgirls* and who is the vocalist with the Trans-Siberian Orchestra; Montre Burton of ABC's *High School Musical*, HBO's *Entourage*, and FX's *It's Always Sunny in Philadelphia*; and Neal Schrader, who was on Broadway with Julie Andrews in *The Boyfriend*.

THEATER FOR KIDS/TEENS   **$$$**
503 Central Dr.
Virginia Beach
(757) 425-1445
www.theaterforkidsteens.org
This is another local institution offering instruction in musical theater, acting, singing, dance, and other thespian activities. It's been in operation 16 years and the school performs musicals four times a year at Pembroke Mall.

SHOPPING

You name it; we've got it—from upscale indoor malls in Virginia Beach and Norfolk to the new outdoor ones that attempt to recreate an urban downtown in Hampton and Virginia Beach. There are flea markets and thrift stores for those on a budget and high-end fashion outlets for those who prefer custom service. Nearly every corner seems to have an auto dealership—another perk brought to you by all those sailors and soldiers returning with bulging pockets after months-long deployments.

Want to explore the outdoors? Will that be by land or sea kayak, sir? There are legendary surf shops and a wealth of marine dealers ready to sell you something a little more substantial than a boogie board.

We have a variety of grocery stores, from the big chains to those serving the area's many ethnic communities. (Thanks again to the world-traveling military.) And when the weather gets nice, farmers' markets open up around the area and growers invite you in to pick your own strawberries or other fresh favorites.

In an area so rife with history, you knew there'd be an abundance of antiques shops, and they're scattered throughout the region with a couple concentrated hot spots.

You'll also find all of the familiar big box retailers here, and the malls are crowded with the merchants you will find nearly every place in America. So let's look at it by genre.

ANTIQUES SHOPS

As you'd expect, most of these places are found in the historic cities. Portsmouth's Olde Towne has a few on High Street. Norfolk has a district in Ghent along 21st Street. Hampton has a nice group in Phoebus and Newport News has its cluster in quaint Hilton Village. Suffolk has a couple shops on Main Street, and Chesapeake, the new kid, has a line of places along Military Highway near Canal Drive that locals call Antique Alley. It's a great place to stroll through a series of converted houses and outbuildings looking for a treasure. It's virtually impossible to say what you'll find in any particular store, that's the charm of antiquing. So pick a cluster and enjoy.

Chesapeake

There is an always-changing array of antiques shops around the 3000 block of South Military Highway, the heart of Antique Alley. Just park at any of the places and wander. If you find something big down the street, you can always come back with the car to pick it up.

FLAMINGO CREEK
3020 South Military Hwy.
Chesapeake
(757) 485-0551

GRANDMA HAD ONE
3028 South Military Hwy.
Chesapeake
(757) 485-4134

THE NOW & THEN SHOP
3112 South Military Hwy.
Chesapeake
(757) 485-1383

WE HAD THAT ANTIQUES
3040 South Military Hwy.
Chesapeake
(757) 485-0551

Norfolk

on The few blocks on 21st Street between Granby Street and Colley Avenue were once an antiques shop Mecca. A combination of gentrification and recession has hit the row pretty hard. Still there are a couple of venerable operations that have weathered the storms and are worth a visit. Don't be fooled by the street frontage on some of these places. They tend to go deep with room after room just crammed full of collectables.

ANTIQUE DESIGN CENTER
240 West 21st St.

MORGAN HOUSE ANTIQUES GALLERY
242 West 21st St.

THE SWALLOWS
416 West 21st St.

More . . .
There's another small cluster of long time antique shops in Norfolk on the 2600 block

of Granby Street worth checking out, They include:

BOOBALAS IMPORTERS INC.
2600 Granby St.

HARPER'S ANTIQUES
2608 Granby St.

Portsmouth

High Street for a few blocks near the Elizabeth River in Olde Towne is where you'll find the bulk of this city's antiques shops. It's a nice place to wander, and you can catch a film at the Commodore Movie Palace or one of hundreds of imported beers at the Bier Garden afterwards.

ANTIQUE ADVENTURES
432 High St.
Portsmouth
(757) 398-8763

NEXT UPSCALE CONSIGNMENTS
607 High St.
Portsmouth
(757) 397-7173

THE QUEEN BEES ANTIQUES
425 High St.
Portsmouth
(757) 397-3939

SKIPJACK NAUTICAL WARES & MARINE GALLERY
One High St., Suite 3
Portsmouth
(757) 399-5012

WAY BACK YONDER ANTIQUES
620 High St.
Portsmouth
(757) 398-2700

Suffolk

MAIN STREET ANTIQUES
1138 Myrtle St.
Suffolk
(757) 923-4888

MAXINE'S ANTIQUES COLLECTABLES
147 North Main St.
Suffolk
(757) 539-3132

Virginia Beach

Most of the antiques action here is concentrated in two multi-dealer locations.

BARRETT STREET ANTIQUE MALL AND AUCTION CENTER
2645 Dean Dr.
Virginia Beach
(757) 463-1911

TOWNE CENTER ANTIQUE MALL
3900 Bonney Rd.
Virginia Beach
(757) 498-9191

Hampton

Historic Phoebus is the heart of this city's antiques trade. The antiques district only spans a few blocks of Mellen Street, so it's another nice park-and-wander destination anchored by a real antique auction gallery that does business worldwide.

PHOEBUS AUCTION GALLERY
16 East Mellen St.
Hampton
(757) 722-9210
www.phoebusauction.com

GRIFFIN'S ANTIQUES
34 East Mellen St.
Hampton

RETURN ENGAGEMENTS
116 East Mellen St.
Hampton
(757) 722-0617

ROBERT'S ANTIQUES
26 East Mellen St.
Hampton
(757) 722-0222

THE WAY WE WERE
32 East Mellen St.
Hampton
(757) 726-2300

BOOKSTORES

BARNES & NOBLE
MacArthur Center
300 Monticello Ave.
Norfolk
(757) 543-1982
www.barnesandnoble.com
This national chain has number of stores in Hampton Roads, so you can find one within easy driving distance no matter where you are located. Each offers free Wi-Fi service and a Starbucks Cafe. They all also offer story time readings for children. Check the individual stores for hours and days. In addition, Barnes & Noble operates the Tidewater Community College Bookstore in MacArthur Mall, which combines a traditional bookstore with the required academic offerings in a two-story retail outlet. Visit the website for a list of locations.

BIBLIOPHILE BOOKSHOP
251 West Bute St.
Norfolk
(757) 622-BOOK
This little shop in downtown features used and out-of-print volumes, as well as an inventory of first editions and rare books. Owner

Uwe Wilken will check out his network to find a favorite, even if it is out of print.

BORDERS
12300 Jefferson Ave.
Newport News
(757) 249-0480
www.borders.com
The other Goliath in bookselling has two Hampton Roads outlets, one on the Peninsula and the other in Virginia Beach (1744 Laskin Rd.; 757-425-8031). Borders stores also offer free Wi-Fi service and story times for children. Their in-store cafe serves Seattle's Best coffee.

HERITAGE STORE
314 Laskin Rd.
Virginia Beach
(757) 428-0500
www.heritagestore.com
Nestled in Hampton Roads' largest holistic health, natural food, and spiritual growth retailer is a bookstore that offers a unique selection aimed at uplifting minds and spirits. There's also a gift shop here, with everything from belly-dance items to New Age musical instruments and CDs. And there's a cafe as well with healthy offerings. A city project to improve Laskin Road is to force the Heritage to eventually move, so call before heading out.

PRINCE BOOKS
109 East Main St.
Norfolk
(757) 622-9223
www.prince-books.com
This independent bookstore has been in business downtown since 1982, with an emphasis on current events, local authors, and a personal touch that keeps readers

coming back. There's a Lizard Cafe in the bookstore, which is located in the Towne Bank Building just a block from Town Point Park. They work with local book clubs and also sell e-books here.

SMITH DISCOUNT BOOKS
961 Providence Square Shopping Center
Virginia Beach
(757) 474-9448
This is a long-time neighborhood bookstore located in the Providence Square Shopping Center.

COMIC BOOKS/COLLECTIBLES

With so many young men and women stationed in the area, it isn't surprising that Hampton Roads is a hotbed for graphic novel and comic book fans. And that means there are lots of shops for collectors to comb through looking for that missing piece that introduced your favorite hero. Here's some to get you started.

ATOMIC COMICS EMPORIUM
50 West Mercury Blvd.
Hampton
(757) 723-5003

B.T.I. COMICS
4402 Princess Anne Rd.
Virginia Beach
(757) 232-5553

COMIC CHEST
928 Diamond Springs Rd.
Virginia Beach
(757) 490-2367

COMIC KINGS
5196 Fairfield Shopping Center
Virginia Beach
(757) 467-2254

FANTASY ESCAPE COMICS AND CARDS
309 Aragona Blvd.
Virginia Beach
(757) 497-5977

HEROES & VILLAINS
1152 Big Bethel Rd.
Hampton
(757) 838-4431

LOCAL HEROES
1905 Colonial Ave.
Norfolk
(757) 383-6810

TRILOGY COMICS
5773 Princess Anne Rd.
Virginia Beach
(757) 490-2205

MALLS & SHOPPING CENTERS

CHESAPEAKE SQUARE MALL
4200 Portsmouth Blvd.
Chesapeake
(757) 488-9636
This mall is anchored by a JCPenney, Sears, Macy's, and Target and serves the Western Hampton Roads area, including Suffolk, Western Branch, and the Churchland neighborhoods of Portsmouth. A number of other retailers are located on the highways around the mall.

CITY CENTER AT OYSTER POINT
701 Town Center Dr.
Newport News
(757) 873-2020
This is a relatively new community of luxury apartments, condos, office buildings, and 230,000 square feet of retail shops and restaurants in an open-air setting. It doesn't have all of the mall regulars but does offer an Ann Taylor Loft, Banana Republic, Coldwater Creek, Jos. A. Bank, and Talbots, among other upscale retailers. There are also a number of eateries, including Aromas, Rockefeller's, and Taste Unlimited.

THE GALLERY AT MILITARY CIRCLE
880 North Military Hwy.
Norfolk
(757) 461-0777
When outdoor malls became passé, Military Circle was the area's first indoor mall. It opened around 1975 right across the street from JANAF (see entry below) and is still going strong, with more than 120 stores and a Doubletree Hotel right on the premises. The anchor stores are Macy's, Sears, and JCPenney.

GREENBRIER MALL
1401 Greenbrier Parkway
Chesapeake
(757) 424-7300
The Greenbrier Mall sprouted on farmland while the city was still largely rural. That was in the early 1980s. Chesapeake was soon one of the fastest growing cities in America, and Greenbrier was its residential and shopping center. The anchors are Sears, Dillard's, JCPenney, and Macy's.

CROSSWAYS SHOPPING CENTER
Chesapeake
1412 Greenbrier Pkwy.
The Crossways Shopping Center is one of those outdoor venues that sprout by many American malls. It offers such discount clothing retailers as TJ Maxx and Marshalls.

J.A.N.A.F. SHOPPING YARD
Virginia Beach Boulevard and Military Highway
Norfolk
(757) 461-4954

The oldest suburban shopping center in the area, and one of the first in the nation, is still in operation, but those who patronized JANAF when it first opened in 1959 probably wouldn't recognize the place. In case you're wondering, JANAF is an acronym for Joint Army Navy Air Force, picked to honor not just local men and women in uniform but the retired and active duty folks who were in the original investment group. Back then, in addition to its scads of parking and a cluster of shops, JANAF had a Norfolk public library branch and still features a post office. Now broken into five sectors, appropriately named Alpha, Bravo, Charlie, Delta, and Echo—like military units—it is a collection of outlet stores, restaurants, and other retailers.

THE SHOPS AT HILLTOP
Laskin and First Colonial Roads
Virginia Beach

This is actually three different open-air shopping centers: Hilltop North, East, and West, with 120 shops and restaurants a couple miles from the Oceanfront. Here, you'll find some of the stores that won't make it into your typical mall. Places like Blue Ridge Mountain Sports, an adventure outfitter, and Swisher Pens, a dealer in fine fountain pens and other writing implements. And across the street are the big box retailers Kmart and Target.

LYNNHAVEN MALL
701 Lynnhaven Parkway
Virginia Beach
(757) 340-9340

When Lynnhaven Mall opened in the 1980s, it set the standards for indoor shopping. It was bigger than any in the area, and it remains the largest with 180 stores, 17 restaurants, and an AMC movie theater with 18 screens. The anchors are Macy's, Dillards, JCPenney, and Dick's Sporting Goods. There's also a high-end flavor with Ann Taylor Loft, Express, Limited, New York & Company, and Sephora among the merchants. There is a large cluster of other retailers on the roads around the mall.

MACARTHUR CENTER
300 Monticello Ave.
Norfolk
(757) 627-6000

This was the first high-end mall to open in the area. It was built right in downtown Norfolk with doors that opened onto the streets to encourage people to explore the city as well as the stores. The developers scored a coup when they lured Nordstrom to be one of the key anchors. The mall also features a flagship Dillard's and an 18-screen Regal Cinema megaplex. There are 140 stores, many exclusive to this area. The parking is all indoors but there is a charge: $1 for three hours before 6 p.m., a $2 flat rate after 6 p.m., and an all-day maximum of $10 on weekdays. Weekends it's $1 before 6 p.m., $2 after 6, and $3 for the entire day.

i MacArthur Center is no teen hangout. Don't bother coming after 5 p.m. if you're under 18. Mall rules require minors be accompanied by an adult at least 21 years old after that witching hour. Security will escort you out if you can't produce valid ID.

PATRICK HENRY MALL
12300 Jefferson Ave.
Newport News
(757) 249-4305

The mall was extensively renovated in 2005, adding a Dick's Sporting Goods and Borders Book & Music. It is the only enclosed mall remaining on the Peninsula. Dillard's, Macy's, and JCPenney are the anchors among the mall's 120-plus stores.

PENINSULA TOWN CENTER
4410 East Claiborne Square, Suite 212
Hampton

This is the area's newest shopping center (opened in Mar 2010). It's one of the latest concepts in malls, open air with the feel of an old downtown. There are free parking lots around the center, but it really gets authentic if you want to park in front of a store. You'll have to have quarters to feed the meter, but the proceeds go to Peninsula nonprofits. Stores include Target, Blue Ridge Mountain Sports, Express, Chico's, H&M, JCPenney, Macy's, The Limited, and McDonald Garden Market.

PEMBROKE MALL
4554 Virginia Beach Blvd.
Virginia Beach
(757) 497-6255

This is one of the area's oldest and smallest malls located in the heart of the new downtown and across the boulevard from Town Center. It's anchored by Kohl's and Sears but also features a Stein Mart and a Regal Cinema multiplex. If you don't like crowds or needing a GPS to find your way, this is a good shopping choice.

TOWN CENTER
222 Central Park Ave.
Virginia Beach

Virginia Beach's Town Center is another of the new-style open-air shopping centers that attempts to recreate an old downtown.

It features some high-end clothiers like Ann Taylor Loft and Brooks Brothers as well as an array of dining, entertainment, and living options. The Sandler Center for the Performing Arts, which attracts national acts, is here, and the Westin Hotel & Residences building is the tallest skyscraper in the state. Parking here is free in a number of enclosed garages and surface lots.

FARMERS' MARKETS

Despite our huge population and seafaring history, Hampton Roads at heart is an agricultural community, and there are still plenty of working farms tucked into the more rural reaches of the region. That means when the crops come in you can often find the freshest selections at local farmers' markets. There are plenty to choose from—markets as well as crops—so I'll just give you a sampling here. There are also lots of farmers who sell directly. The newspapers have classified sections called "Good To Eat" that are worth checking out, especially if you like to pick your own to ensure it's from-the-field fresh. Some of these markets are year-round and that will be noted in the listings. Others are as seasonal as the products they sell and many only open a few days of the week. As always, give a call before heading out.

Southside

Norfolk
FIVE POINTS COMMUNITY FARM
 MARKET
2500 Church St.
Norfolk
(757) 640-0300
Year-Round

Chesapeake

CHESAPEAKE FARMERS' MARKET
Chesapeake City Park
900 Greenbrier Parkway
Chesapeake
(757) 382-6348

Portsmouth

OLDE TOWNE PORTSMOUTH FARMERS MARKET
Middle Street between High and Queen Streets
(757) 537-9482

Suffolk

SUFFOLK FARMERS MARKET
326 North Main St.
(757) 514-4131

Virginia Beach

VIRGINIA BEACH FARMERS' MARKET
3640 Dam Neck Rd.
(757) 385-4395
Year-Round

Peninsula

Hampton

DOWNTOWN HAMPTON FARMERS MARKET
Carousel Park
(757) 877-2933

Newport News

NEWPORT NEWS FARMERS MARKET
2801 Jefferson Ave.
(757) 247-2351
Year-Round

GARDEN SHOPS

All these farmers' markets are likely to put you in the mood to grow your own and cut that plant-to-plate time down to minutes. Again, there's a wealth of help out there for you. And if you just want to grow fescue, the local garden shops can steer you to grass varieties able to deal with our hot, often dry summers and still stay green in winter.

ANDERSON'S HOME & GARDEN SHOWPLACE
11250 Jefferson Ave.
Newport News
(757) 599-3510
This giant is one of the top 100 independent garden centers in America, according to *Nursery Retailer*. They began in the mid 1940s with a small greenhouse and opened what is now a 10-acre facility in 1953. You can find all sorts of plants and pots here, as well as outdoor furniture and garden supplies. There's even a cafe serving breakfast and lunch, using fresh herbs from their own greenhouses.

ENCHANTED FOREST NURSERY & STONE
1116 Kempsville Rd.
Chesapeake
(757) 549-9667
A boardwalk leads you through this wooded nursery, which also features koi tanks and benches and tables to just relax while you ponder your plant selection.

MCDONALD GARDEN CENTER
1139 West Pembroke Ave.
Hampton
(757) 722-7463
This outfit began in Hampton in 1945, expanding into Virginia Beach in 1980 and Chesapeake in 1992. It's open year-round with 80 percent of the plants grown locally in their own nursery. They also offer 16

Garden Markets selling annuals, perennials, edibles, trees, and garden accessories at a variety of neighborhood shopping centers. And they have a landscape design division as well. The Virginia Beach location is at 1144 Independence Blvd., (757) 464-5564, and the Chesapeake location is at 3925 Portsmouth Blvd., (757) 465-1110.

NORFOLK COUNTY FEED AND SEED
1110 Airline Blvd.
Portsmouth
(757) 397-2373
With the feel of an old country store, this place is an authentic, no-frills garden center. As the name suggests, it dates back to when there was a Norfolk County, before all this was surrounded by city. So step back in time and enjoy a visit.

SMITHFIELD GARDENS
1869 Bridge Rd. (Route 17)
Suffolk
(757) 238-2511
This center carries a large selection of trees, shrubs, groundcovers, and vines as well as annuals and perennials for your garden, and rare and unusual offerings.

WHITE'S GARDEN CENTER
3133 Old Mill Rd.
Chesapeake
(757) 487-2300
This is the retail arm of the vast White's Nursery & Greenhouses operation, a 20-acre operation that has been growing flowering plants for half a century.

GROCERY STORES

This area is served by a number of major chains, including Farm Fresh, a division of SuperValu that began here with a commitment to using local produce; Food Lion, a North Carolina based chain that focuses on value and its more upscale sibling Blooms; Kroger, the national giant, and Harris Teeter, a bit more upscale in its offerings.

Then there is Trader Joe's, a specialty retailer from California with a fanatical following. It has single stores on the Peninsula and Virginia Beach that are always crammed with customers eager to buy "Two Buck Chuck," the affectionate name given to the inexpensive and palatable store brand of wines, and special Trader Joe's frozen foods.

MEN'S CLOTHING

Hampton Roads is a casual kind of place, and most folks like to go comfortable after business hours. Still, you can pick up some finery at these stores.

BROOKS BROTHERS "346"
4554 Bank St.
Virginia Beach
(757) 497-4769
www.brooksbrothers.com
The 346 line is a little less expensive and more casual than the traditional Brooks Brothers offerings. You can even find jeans and T-shirts mixed in at this store.

BEECROFT & BULL
3198 Pacific Avenue
Virginia Beach
(757) 422-1961
www.beecroftandbull.com
A family operation that began in Newport News in 1958 and is consistently ranked by *Esquire* as one of America's top clothing stores. You can get custom clothing as well as off-the-rack tailored to fit.

DAN RYAN'S FOR MEN
1612 Laskin Rd., Suite 764
Virginia Beach
(757) 425-0660

Open since 1976, they make custom clothing as well as sell major manufacturers' lines. The sole store is located in the Hilltop North Shopping Center. They do in-office consultations and their own tailoring.

JOS. A. BANK
men's stores have three outlets in Hampton Roads, in Chesapeake near the Greenbrier Mall, in Virginia Beach at la Promenade Shops, and in Newport News at the City Center at Oyster Point.

MEN'S WEARHOUSE
4545 Virginia Beach Blvd.
Virginia Beach
(757) 518-8277
www.menswearhouse.com

The retail chain has nine outlets selling suits and accessories at discount prices.

i Flipped over a fedora or bonkers over a bowler? Well the Stark & Legum men's store in downtown Norfolk has been selling hats since 1924, when a man would feel naked without one, and is one of the nation's top hat outlets. Stop into this family-operated retailer at 739 Granby Street to browse or call (757) 627-1018 for a chapeau consult.

WOMEN'S CLOTHING

Women also like to go casual around here, but when it's time to dress up, there are some favorite places to turn.

ANN TAYLOR LOFT
701 Lynnhaven Pkwy.
(757) 631-8888
www.anntaylorloft.com

Represented here with Loft stores at Lynnhaven Mall, Town Center (221 Central Park Ave.; 757-473-9105), and MacArthur Center (300 Monticello Ave.; 757-622-4434) as well as City Center in Newport News (701 Town Center Dr.; 757-596-6290).

LILI'S OF GHENT
323 West 21st St.
Norfolk
(757) 624-9868

This store has won Best of Hampton Roads honors from *The Virginian-Pilot* readers.

LOWENTHAL OUTERWEAR BOUTIQUE
4097 Virginia Beach Blvd.
Virginia Beach
(757) 463-6017
http://lowenthatls.com

If you love furs and aren't afraid of the locally based activists from PETA, this is the place to shop.

TALBOTS
1860 Laskin Rd.
Virginia Beach
(757) 428-4442
www.talbots.com

This retail chain has stores in La Promenade Shoppes in Virginia Beach (above), at 300 Monticello Ave. in Norfolk (757-622-4334), and the City Center in Newport News (Fountain Way; 757-596-0228).

CONSIGNMENT & THRIFT SHOPS

In these days of tight dollars, it can be wise to buy pre-owned, as the luxury car dealers call their used inventory. There are a number of places around the area to grab a bargain and the entertainment value of never knowing what you might find is a bonus. And since these shops are often affiliated with a local charity, your money does some additional good. As the Children's Hospital of the King's Daughters say in their thrift shops, "Everything we sell makes another child well."

i At thrift stores inventory varies, obviously, from store to store, even within a group. If the thrift store is located in a more affluent community, you can expect to see more designer labels in the clothing and more upscale knick-knacks on the shelves. Still, you never know. Sometimes, inventory is shipped between the stores to places where that product is more likely to sell. And it's always changing. People constantly bring in bags and boxes that are quickly priced and put on shelves.

CHILDREN'S HOSPITAL OF THE KING'S DAUGHTERS THRIFT STORES
www.chkd.org/giving/thrift

This is one of the largest local outfits, all providing money for the area's prime hospital for children. There are now 22 stores throughout Hampton Roads and into North Carolina. They bring in more than $2 million a year to the institution. For a complete list of their locations in Chesapeake, Hampton, Newport News, Norfolk, Portsmouth and Virginia Beach, visit the website.

DISABLED AMERICAN VETERANS THRIFT STORE
www.davthrift.org

Sales benefit local chapters of the DAV and assist veterans with special needs. There are

stores in **Hampton** at 4209 West Mercury Blvd.; **Newport News** at 15265 Warwick Blvd.; and **Virginia Beach** at 5517 Virginia Beach Blvd. *Pilot* readers voted it the best thrift store in 2009.

ECHOES OF TIME
600 North Witchduck Rd.
Virginia Beach
(757) 428-2332

Echoes of Time is a vintage clothing store that also sells and rents costumes and accessories. It began as an antique store and morphed into this shop that has clothing from any era and wigs, masks, and other items to finish the deal.

GOODWILL INDUSTRIES OF HAMPTON ROADS
1345 Diamond Springs Rd.
Virginia Beach
(757) 248-9405

This local affiliate has nine stores in the area. Visit the website for a complete list of locations.

HOPE HOUSE FOUNDATION THRIFT SHOP
Norfolk
1800 Monticello Ave.
(757) 625-7493

Another local favorite, always has unexpected treasures. Every penny raised here goes to help people with disabilities in the community through the Hope House Foundation.

KID TO KID
Virginia Beach
539 Hilltop Plaza
(757) 271-3589

Children don't usually wear clothes out; they outgrow them. Here you can sell those still-good items or convert them into larger sizes. The store often wins Best of the Beach accolades.

SALVATION ARMY FAMILY AND THRIFT STORES

The Salvation Army's Adult Rehab centers are funded completely from proceeds from the thrift stores. There are several locations: **Chesapeake,** 901 Eden Way North, (757) 312-8598; **Hampton,** 3309 West Mercury Blvd.; **Virginia Beach,** 1136 Lynnhaven Parkway, (757) 468-0185; 5524 Virginia Beach Blvd., (757)-499-0032; and 2093A General Booth Boulevard, (757) 427-0279.

2ND ACT CONSIGNMENTS
110 West 21st St.
Norfolk
(757) 622-1533

This shop in the heart of Norfolk's antique area specializes in fine women's clothing as well as jewelry, art, and furniture.

THRIFT STORE USA
875 East Little Creek Rd.
Norfolk
(757) 588-2900

This is a huge thrift store in Norfolk that supports the local Seton Youth Shelters in Virginia Beach. There's lots of furniture here as well as clothing and other staples.

WEARS LIKE NEW STORE
501 Kempsville Road, Suite J
Chesapeake
(757) 549-9567

This store specializes in high quality designer women's and children's clothing sold on consignment.

WORTH THE WAIT CONSIGNMENT BOUTIQUE
3157 Virginia Beach Blvd.
Virginia Beach
(757) 498-9051

This is annually voted the best consignment shop in Virginia Beach as well as the best for new ladies' apparel, fashion jewelry, and handbags.

SPORTING GOODS

BASS PRO SHOPS
1972 Power Plant Parkway
Hampton
(757) 262-5200

This giant outdoors shop is part spectacle and all business. People drive long distances to shop at a Bass Pro location, and this only store in Hampton Roads is no exception. There's lots more than bass fishing gear being sold here. There's a full gun shop and a Tracker Boat Center as well. The store features a cascading waterfall and a huge bass tank where experts give outdoor skills workshops. There's a 40-foot rock climbing wall and a full archery range inside.

BLUE RIDGE MOUNTAIN SPORTS
1624 Laskin Rd.
Virginia Beach
(757) 422-2201

This is part of a small chain, mostly in Virginia, that has been operating at Hilltop for decades. Here you can find high-performance outdoor gear for hiking, camping, and paddling.

CHESAPEAN OUTDOORS
313 Laskin Rd., Suite 101
Virginia Beach
(757) 961-0447

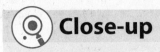# Close-up

A Perfect Blend

You might hesitate when you get to the screen door with its hand-painted "Welcome to Norfolk Coffee Co." sign. The latte-colored brick building on 18th Street just off Monticello Avenue in Norfolk sure doesn't look like much from the outside, but here **Norfolk Coffee & Tea Co. Ltd.** (212 East 18th St. Norfolk; 757-622-3950) roasts up their special blends the same way it has since the company began in 1918.

Inside, the store is frozen in time, although it's hard to pinpoint the decade. The owner's two sons, Chris and Nick Stephanitsis, craft their coffee using the same machines their grandfather and father built or modified, relying on decades of experience and the phonetically spelled instructions Dad painted everywhere in the shop. They still import their burlap bags of green beans from sources that go back generations.

The big gas roasting machine they use doesn't have a computer screen. It's about a century old, and they can tell just by color and smell when each 50-pound load is finished rolling around. The glistening beans then drop into a cooling tray and then are packed into a blending gizmo built by their father, Jerry Stephan (he shortened and Anglicized his name years ago). It looks like an old office safe suspended from diagonal corners and is rotated by a series of motors and pulleys. The result is so finely balanced that you can let it go with the door open and it will ease upright without spilling a bean.

A large coffee grinder turns their signature blends into various grinds, from coarse to Turkish (although in here, you'd do well to call it Greek-style). They once called the place and their product Aroma House, and that seems appropriate when you take it all in from beyond the small, cluttered counter.

Ground coffee goes into the top of a Willie Wonka kind of device with pistons and air hoses that hiss as cams and gears and clutches precisely measure, seal, and cut plastic packets that are perfect for a single restaurant pot of java.

It's a ballet honed over the decades. Roast one day, then give the beans some time to vent off gases that can turn it rancid before blending, grinding, and packing the next. Many of the area's top restaurants rely on Norfolk Coffee to end a gourmet meal.

The most fun, though, comes with the walk-in customers. Many are regulars who visit as much for the easy banter as the beans from all over the world, including Guatemala, Ethiopia, and Kenya—some 25 different varieties used to craft about 60 blends, and all available in caffeine-free versions. Each is roasted separately, because they cook at different rates, and then blended.

Stacked in the small space in front of the counter is an array of teas to quench any thirst. And on that counter, if you're lucky and get there early enough, are bags of fresh Virginia peanuts roasted every morning in a separate antique oven.

This local operation began in 1996 as a kayak eco-tour company, offering trips to experience bottlenose dolphins up-close near the mouth of the Chesapeake Bay. Now they also offer boat rentals and sell paddling gear and kayaks at their store one block from the beach.

DICK'S SPORTING GOODS
www.dickssportinggoods.com
This national giant has three stores in the region, at Lynnhaven Mall and Town Center in Virginia Beach, and at Patrick Henry Mall in Newport News. Here you can find gear for just about any sport, from running to golf.

17TH STREET SURF SHOP
(757) 498-3950
This retailer has been selling boards and beachwear since 1970. It's also the place to go for skate stuff and the clothing that sets you apart. There are a number of locations throughout the area, including the flagship store at 1612 Pacific Ave. at the Oceanfront (close enough to 17th Street for the name). There are also shops in the Lynnhaven Mall, Kemps River Crossing, Red Mill, Greenbrier, and Chesapeake Square shopping areas, as well as the Oyster Point retail area in Newport News.

THE SPORTS AUTHORITY
www.sportsauthority.com
This large national retailer has three outlets in Hampton Roads ready to outfit you in any participatory or outdoor venture. In Norfolk, there's a store at JANAF, 5900 East Virginia Beach Blvd., (757) 466-8107; in Virginia Beach just outside Lynnhaven Mall at 2720 North Mall Dr., (757) 498-3355; and in Hampton at 2106 Coliseum Dr., (757) 826-5033.

WILD RIVER OUTFITTERS
3636 Virginia Beach Blvd.
Virginia Beach
(757) 431-8566
If you love the outdoors, you'll probably quickly call this place a favorite. It's run by folks who are as passionate about paddling and hiking as you are. It started in 1976 from a backyard and moved into a barn, a gas station, and a small storefront in Churchland before heading to Virginia Beach. They've been at the same location now since 1990. Lillie Gilbert, one of the original partners, is still at the helm. She's not only an avid paddler, she's written a number of books and touring guides about area waters. A separate, affiliated business provides kayak and canoe instructions, trips, and tours. Anything you need for climbing, camping, hiking, or getting around on the water is likely in this shop.

WILCOX BAIT AND TACKLE
9501 Jefferson Ave.
Newport News
(757) 595-5537
In business since 1954, this is a Peninsula landmark with a full inventory of fishing tackle as well as boats, canoes, guns, ammo, archery supplies, and outdoor clothing.

DAY TRIPS & GETAWAYS

Two thirds of America's population lives within a day's drive of Virginia Beach, the visitor's bureau likes to boast. If you look at that from our end of the telescope, it means folks in Hampton Roads are the same motoring distance from many of the nation's biggest cities. The national mall in Washington, D.C., is just 200 miles up the road; Baltimore's Inner Harbor another 45; Philadelphia and its Independence Square is at 250. Even New York City's Times Square is within that 8-hour-drive window at 348 miles.

I won't waste time or ink on information about what you can do or see in such places. A couple pages here can't even touch the surface of what's going on in the nation's major metropolises. If you want a really detailed exploration, there are Insiders' Guides to Washington, Philly, and Baltimore to really scratch that itch. Instead, I'll let you in on the less chronicled locations where most of us sate our weekend wanderlust.

GETTING AWAY

When Hampton Roads residents want to get away for a day, we mostly head an hour up I-64 to the Jamestown, Yorktown, Colonial Williamsburg Historic Triangle. Or we drive another hour on the same road to visit equally historic Richmond or continue on yet another hour on I-64 to bask in the Blue Ridge glories of Charlottesville.

Ironically, since we have some of the best beaches in America right on our doorstep, many of us still enjoy heading south to experience the very different beach vibes of the Outer Banks of North Carolina. And we can't forget the freshwater paradise of the huge Lake Gaston-Kerr Reservoir to the west along the border between Virginia and North Carolina.

Then there are the less obvious excursions.

Less than an hour to the south in Gates County, N.C., you can lose yourself in a lake that seems out of the age of dinosaurs, complete with morning mist rising off cedar knobs and Spanish moss oozing from the trees, or you can take to a kayak and try to spot an alligator in the aptly named Alligator River just inland from crowded Outer Banks beaches. It's the farthest north these reptiles are known to live and reproduce.

Head about the same distance in the opposite direction and you can explore the isolated little towns on the Eastern Shore, with funny Indian names like Machipongo and Chincoteague or enjoy fresh seafood at Sting Ray's with watermen who still go to work on wooden skiffs and speak with a hint of Elizabethan brogue kept pure by generations of isolation.

There are other food-inspired trips: to Smithfield for some thinly sliced, salt cured country ham and famous peanut soup or to Wakefield for fried chicken done divinely at the Virginia Diner.

Interested in the antebellum South? Well, Plantation Row is an easy trip back in time. Rather focus on nature? The world famous Luray Caverns are within a day's drive. And if you have a hankering to barrel downhill in winter, the ski slopes at Wintergreen and Massanutten are within reach.

So let's get started.

HEADING NORTHWEST—OR THE I-64 GETAWAYS

The Historic Triangle

There's lots to see here, from living history exhibits at Colonial Williamsburg and the Jamestown Settlement to family-oriented stage shows and breathtaking rides at Busch Gardens. After your first couple visits, you'll probably want to pick up the *Insiders' Guide to Williamsburg and Virginia's Historic Triangle* to really get the inside scoop.

Colonial Williamsburg

There was a time when Colonial Williamsburg existed only in history books, back before John D. Rockefeller got up with the rector of Bruton Parish Church in 1926. Rev. W.A.R. Goodwin wanted to preserve the city's buildings, where so much of early American history took place. Rockefeller bought in and they started preserving the Colonial Capital one building at a time. Rockefeller paid for the restoration of more than 80 original buildings, the reconstruction of others, and the creation of new facilities needed to make this a tourist destination. These days, the nonprofit Colonial Williamsburg Foundation oversees a living history center that covers about 85 percent of the capital's original area.

It's a unique attraction, the largest living history museum in the United States. You can join the two million visitors who buy a ticket that entitles you to enter a variety of buildings and learn from re-enactors about life in the days of Thomas Jefferson and George Washington, or you can just park nearby and bask in the city's historic beauty as you walk up and down the cobblestone streets and enjoy the fife and drum parades for free.

Why go?

It's one thing to read about history and another to watch folks dressed in period costumes actually forging a rifle barrel or making candles. Here you not only observe but are encouraged to ask. These are not just actors but are skilled artisans who are very well versed in their trades and will answer all your detailed questions. If you rush through, you can see the place in less than a day. But if you really want to experience the 18th century, you'll want to linger and absorb. And that could take several days—or a lifetime or repeat visits. They've been doing this a very long time, so the foundation offers up several suggested itineraries you can use to plan your time efficiently. There's a First Visit version and another aimed at those more interested in colonial trades than American history.

So if history with a capital H is your interest, you want to be sure to set aside an hour to tour the Governor's Palace, where seven royal governors ruled before the Revolution. It's flash frozen to the time when Lord Dunmore, the last British ruler, held sway. (You need a special pass that costs a bit more to get inside this one, though.) Then you can mosey over to the Randolph House and Kitchen where you can see how leading politicians gathered and the way slaves worked at the time. There's the courthouse preserved as it was, and the magazine, not for reading but for storing Williamsburg's powder and guns. The itinerary also includes visits to the Printing Office, where they made what passed for the other kind of magazines in that time; the blacksmith shop to see a real forge in action; the Capitol where Virginians voted for independence; and the foundation's two museums.

While you're walking the streets, you are likely to encounter a dramatic scene or two as actors play the parts of local leaders debating their choice between war and subservience or show how the decision to go to war affected early residents.

If it's everyday life that fascinates you, try the trades tour. Here, you can peek in and pick the brains of blacksmiths, cabinetmakers, carpenters, and coopers; gunsmiths, tailors, shoemakers, and book binders; jewelers, weavers, wigmakers, and farmers; printers, apothecaries, wheelwrights, and musicians. And, these days, you can also learn how life was for the slaves who did most of the city's hardest labor.

The best part about Colonial Williamsburg is you don't have to pick one route or the other. Sit down with your free "Colonial Williamsburg This Week" publication and tailor your own trip into history. The guide lists special events, hours of operations, and other tips to help you get the most out of your day.

Getting There

It's pretty hard to miss, since this is a very well-signed destination. Take I-64 West and look for the Colonial Williamsburg signs at exit 238.

There are special blue, red, and white ribbon signs that lead you to any of the three Historic Triangle locations. The roads will lead to a Visitor's Center just outside town. You park here, buy your tickets, and then take a shuttle bus or walk a pedestrian bridge to the Historic Area. You might want to linger first to watch a film, *Williamsburg—The Story of a Patriot*, that introduces you to the 18th century. The fact that this is an international destination is brought home here by the ability to see this film in Spanish, French, German, Italian, Japanese, Portuguese, and even Russian, since Glasnost.

Lodging

It's really only an hour's drive or less from most of Hampton Roads, so you probably won't be staying over often, but there are plenty of places, either the elegant hotels right around the historic area or the motels just out of Williamsburg on Richmond Road, Virginia Route 60, if you want to get a two-day pass. Every chain you can imagine is located here.

Food

You can wander a block off Duke of Gloucester Street and encounter the real world with its modern restaurants, or give the historic taverns a try. There's a range of offerings from seafood at Christiana Campbell's Tavern, reportedly George Washington's favorite inn, to the less fancy Chowning's Tavern where you can grab a Brunswick Stew or one of those newfangled meals on bread made famous by Lord Sandwich.

Just off the path at 431 Prince George St. is a fine sandwich and coffee shop known

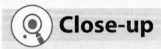

Close-up

Colonial Celebrations

Christmas may be the best time to visit Williamsburg. The summer crowds are gone, so you have the tradespeople nearly to yourself. The buildings are beautiful, each sporting a unique Colonial-style wreath, all made with natural elements, and candles flickering in every window.

The first official Christmas in Williamsburg celebration occurred in 1936 and it has been an annual tradition since.

Carolers in Colonial garb walk the streets and perform on the steps of the court-house. There's a grand illumination event that goes beyond candle lighting and includes skyrockets bursting in midair over the Governor's Palace.

And there are special seasonal shows. Local legend Dean Shostak turns his eerie glass armonica towards holiday music from Thanksgiving through New Year's at the Kimball Theatre on Merchant's Square. The armonica is an instrument invented by Benjamin Franklin, who noticed that when you rub a wet finger on a crystal glass' rim, you get a tone that varies in pitch by the size of the glass. Soon, old Ben was at work, creating a single, rotating shaft that had a course of assorted glasses attached. Shostak plays it like a concert piano, giving a history lesson as well as using crystal handbells, a glass violin, and a "cristal Baschet" to play traditional holiday tunes.

Another annual favorite are the various classical concerts offered at the Governor's Palace. Chamber music is always beautiful, but performed by candlelight in a historic setting it becomes sublime. Here, you don't have to close your eyes to be transported to another time; the place is actually part of the time machine.

You can pick up tips for your own home decorations or even buy the natural ingredients to whip up a Colonial wreath. Or you can just enjoy the holiday wassail, a traditional hot apple cider-based drink.

---

as Aromas, where William & Mary college students pack in with tourists to enjoy a quick meal. Check out the curried chicken salad sandwich, which is served on fruit and nut bread.

Other Williamsburg Destinations
SHOPPING

If history isn't your thing, there's still a reason to head to Williamsburg. On Route 60 between the city and Lightfoot are the Prime Outlets, acres of factory stores offering discounts from a wide array of major retailers. The names include Polo, Ralph Lauren, COACH, Burberry, Kenneth Cole, Chico's, and scores of others.

i The Colonial taverns get really crowded, so make reservations when you start off your day. The menus are tailored to what folks would have been eating back then, and there are often musicians playing period songs, so it's another history lesson. It can be fun to make reservations for a Colonial Thanksgiving dinner, for instance, but don't wait on something like that.

ENTERTAINMENT

Another huge lure is the Busch Gardens amusement park. They used to call it Old Country, then Busch Gardens Europe, both because it was built with a European theme. Now they just refer to it as Busch Gardens Williamsburg, because it's just 3 miles east of the city. It annually wins the award for most beautiful amusement park. There are stage shows at various locations, each reflecting the country honored in that section of the park, and concerts in the summer. There's a Sesame Street Forest of Fun for the younger visitors and animal shows for the entire family.

But the biggest lures are the roller coasters. The Big Bad Wolf, one of the first suspended roller coasters, is history now. Its top dog position has been taken by Griffon, the world's tallest and fastest Diving Machine roller coaster that drops 90 degrees from over 200 feet to a splashdown finish. The park also offers Alpengeist, Apollo's Chariot, and Grover's Alpine Express.

i There's a special deal for locals here. You can get a season's pass for the same price as a one-day admission if you buy in the spring. It's a great bargain for families looking to keep the kids entertained throughout the summer.

SeaWorld Parks and Entertainment, the parent now of Busch Gardens, also runs Water Country USA, a Williamsburg area amusement park where getting wet is part of the plan. The rides include a river rafting adventure called Big Daddy Falls; a flume ride called Aquazoid and another for older riders known as Meltdown; various water slides at Surfer's Bay pool; and other watery delights. You can buy combined passes that give you access to both. Check it all out at www.buschgardens.com.

Jamestown

There are two historic Jamestown attractions, which can sometimes be confusing.

The Jamestown-Yorktown Foundation, a state agency, runs the **Jamestown Settlement.** Here the story of the original Jamestown settlers is told through film, gallery exhibits, and living history. You can board the replicas of the three ships that originally sailed to Virginia, explore the full-sized recreation of the colonists' fort and a nearby Powhatan village, and learn about everyday life on both sides of the balustrades from costumed historical interpreters. Think of this as Colonial Williamsburg for an even earlier era. Admission is $14 for adults and $6.50 for children 6 to 12 or $19.25 and $9.25 for both centers.

Nearby is **Historic Jamestowne**, which is administered by the National Park Service and Preservation Virginia. This is the original site of the Jamestown colony where you can watch archeologists actually excavate the remains of the 1607 James Fort. Park rangers will tell you about John Smith's efforts, and while you walk amongst the ruins, you're likely to encounter a costumed character providing "eyewitness" accounts of the difficult early years. America's first attempt at industry is here, a glasshouse where you can see glass blowers practice their art. Tickets are $10 for adults and free for those 15 and younger. It's free if you have a National Park Pass or several other annual passes.

You can also buy a single ticket that gets you into both Jamestown sites and the Yorktown Battlefield and Yorktown Victory Center for $29.25 per adult.

Yorktown

This is another place with two competing but complementary historic sites.

The Yorktown Victory Center is a museum that chronicles America's battle for freedom. You can examine a rare broadside printing of the Declaration of Independence and see how the war that resulted from that document impacted the lives of 10 ordinary people who left a record of their experiences. Exhibits show the roles of different nationalities in the siege and where the various British ships were lost. The outdoor exhibits include a re-created Continental Army encampment with interpreters giving a flavor of everyday life. There's a 1780s farm that shows how rural Americans lived during the era.

The Yorktown Battlefield and Visitor Center is administered by the National Park Service. This is the location where the British Army under General Charles Lord Cornwallis was forced to surrender on Oct 19, 1781, ensuring American independence. There are ranger-guided tours that take you along the British defenses, through the town of York, and even non-firing artillery demonstrations. For $10, you get a seven-day pass to Historic Jamestowne and the Yorktown Battlefield.

GETTING HERE

The Jamestown site is linked to Williamsburg and also Yorktown by the Colonial Parkway, and there are plenty of signs off I-64 to get you there.

DINING

Jamestown is less commercial, so the only place you can grab a meal without heading back towards Williamsburg is the Jamestown Settlement Cafe. You can always pack a picnic lunch. Yorktown is a pretty little place with some restaurants and a beach picnic area along the river.

Richmond

For a few months every winter, Richmond is the center of the Commonwealth. The General Assembly, a part-time gathering of citizen legislators, meets at the Capitol and all eyes are focused on what might emerge. With them come the consultants and the lobbyists and anybody else who is looking to pass or block a law. You can't find a hotel room or a parking spot, and most restaurants are packed. The rest of the year, the machinery of state government hums along here without much legislative oversight. And Richmonders are happy for the respite. There's lots for a tourist to see in Richmond—museums that chronicle the Confederacy and science, impressive art collections, and some fun street shopping.

How to Get There

Another no brainer—just keep heading west on I-64 past Williamsburg and you'll wind up in Richmond. You take the 5th Street exit to get to downtown, the Governor's Mansion, the Capitol, and even Shockoe Bottom.

What to See
MUSEUMS

If you haven't ODed on history in Williamsburg, Jamestown, and Yorktown, there's plenty more in Richmond. Check out the **Museum of the Confederacy,** 1201 East Clay St., (804) 649-1861, www.moc.org. There are three floors of galleries containing artifacts, manuscripts, and photographs from the Confederate States of America. They have Stonewall Jackson's forage cap, J.E.B.

Stuart's pistol, and even the field tent Robert E. Lee used. A few yards away is the White House of the Confederacy, a restored mansion where CSA President Jefferson Davis lived.

Richmond is also host to the **Virginia Holocaust Museum,** 2000 East Cary St., (804) 257-5400, www.va-holocaust.com. This is a free, self-guided museum that provides an interactive experience of the ghettos, concentration camps, cattle cars, and even the refugee ship *St. Louis*. It's intense, so they don't recommend you bring kids under 9 and they suggest you check it out yourself before bringing kids between 9 and 11. You should dress for crawling through some of the 28 permanent exhibits. (There are alternate, wheelchair-accessible options.)

The museum, run by Jay Ipson, a Holocaust survivor, includes the only replica of the Nuremburg Trials Courtroom. It began in a Richmond synagogue but quickly outgrew the location. The state donated an old tobacco warehouse in historic Shockoe Bottom for the museum, which opened in 2003.

The **Valentine Richmond History Center,** 1015 East Clay St., (804) 649-0711, www.richmondhistorycenter.com, is focused on the city's individual history and also offers walking and bus tours of historic Richmond locations.

The **Children's Museum of Richmond,** 2626 West Broad St., (804) 474-7000, www.c-mor.org is a great place to bring your kids. Here, they believe play is not a waste of time. There's a Little Farm, a Town Square, a Tree Climber area, and an Art Studio to encourage creativity and imagination. There's an $8 admission fee.

Kids a little older, or are you still a kid at heart? Then take in the **Science Museum of Virginia,** 2500 West Broad St., (804)

864-1400, www.smv.org You can learn about cells and DNA, explore electricity and light, find out how solar panels and wind tunnels and geothermal sources work, or tour Virginia Tech's Solar House. They even have a game/scavenger hunt you can get on your mobile phone that sends clues, riddles, trivia, and challenges that help you interact with exhibits and films. There are always new traveling exhibits as well, and an IMAX theater. Museum admission is $10 for adults, $9 for 4- to 12-year-olds. The IMAX alone is $8.50 but you can combine the two for $15 for adults and $14 for youth.

Another popular destination is the **Museum of Edgar Allan Poe,** 1914–16 East Main St., (804) 648-5523, www.poemuseum .org.

Poe grew up in Richmond after the Allan family took him in when his mother, an actress, died in the city. The museum has the preeminent collection of manuscripts, letters, first editions, memorabilia, and personal belongings of the man who penned "The Raven" and so many other dark tales. The museum opened in 1922 and is near Poe's Richmond home. Inside you'll find his family Bible and even the walking stick he used on his last night in Richmond, two weeks before his death in Baltimore, as well as the bed he slept in as a child. In a macabre twist the author would have relished, there are a few strands of Poe's hair, cut from his brow after his death.

If you're ready to give the brain a break and just bask in beauty, head over to the **Virginia Museum of Fine Arts,** 200 North Boulevard—Yep, it's a boulevard named Boulevard but they don't call it Boulevard Boulevard, thank goodness—(804-340-1400, www.vmfa.state.va.us). Here you'll find more than 22,000 works of art, including a noteworthy collection of Art Nouveau, Art Deco, and Modern and Contemporary American art as well as French Impressionist and Post-Impressionist works, Fabergé jeweled objects, and English silver. The museum is famous for its holdings of South Asian, Himalayan, and African art.

THE CAPITOL

Since Richmond is the center of government, you can't visit without touring the **State Capitol** building. It has recently been restored. You can take a virtual tour at http://virginiacapitol.gov, but it's much more impressive in person. Although they say you should never see sausage or laws made, those who appreciate the process can head to the public gallery and watch when the Assembly is in session.

CARYTOWN

This little street is packed with shopping opportunities. The motto here is "A Mile of Style." Folks flock to explore eclectic merchants like World of Mirth, a toy store for adults as well as kids, or Plan 9 Records, a place that still has a basement full of vinyl. There are consignment stores and edgy fashions as well as excellent eateries in nearly any cuisine. A huge health food market sits on one end, and at the other is another Richmond landmark, the historic Byrd Theatre. This is a restored Grand Movie Palace that recalls the days when going to a move meant more than hitting the mall multiplex. The Byrd has one of the last working Wurlitzer theater organs, with a resident maestro who uses the keyboard as a one-man orchestra to play real instruments that are incorporated into the machinery every Sat night. They have film festivals here and often bring in stars to talk

about their classic movies. In the heart of summer, they have an annual watermelon festival where you can sample the fruit in every conceivable way and see the campy melon costumes and decorations.

MONUMENT AVENUE

This broad boulevard, called America's Most Beautiful, is a monument to the Confederate heroes from Virginia. The first statue, of Robert E. Lee astride his horse, was unveiled in 1890. Others followed, such as J.E.B. Stuart, Stonewall Jackson, and Jefferson Davis, until the final was added in 1996. Ironically, this statue at the end of the Confederate lineup is of Arthur Ashe, a Richmond native and African American tennis great and social activist. It is also the only statue on the avenue that faces away from downtown.

SHOCKOE

Shockoe Slip is just down the street from the Capitol and one of the oldest areas in all of Richmond. It became a restaurant center when several businesses moved into old Tobacco warehouses. The ad agency responsible for the Geico Gecko is located here. Just below it is Shockoe Bottom, another place famous for its nightlife. Locals call it The Bottom.

BELLE ISLE

During the Civil War, the Confederates put a POW camp on this small island in the middle of the James River. By 1863 almost 10,000 men were being held here. It's owned by the city now and a playground for folks who like to rock climb in its quarry or just hike around on trails. You get there on a suspension bridge hung below a highway high over the James. On the other side of the river, you can see Hollywood Cemetery, another favorite tourist destination since Presidents Monroe and Tyler, Jefferson Davis, and J.E.B. Stuart are interred there.

MAYMONT

This mansion, wildlife refuge, and nature park is a real Richmond secret. There are "100 acres of History, Habitats & Horticulture" here at this free park. Back in the Gilded Age of the robber barons, Richmond millionaire James Dooley built himself a Victorian country home that rivaled any lavish estate. The Romanesque mansion was finished in 1893 and filled with items James and Sallie May Dooley collected from around the world. They had no children, and when Mrs. Dooley died she left the estate to Richmond. The place was perfectly preserved when the city opened it as a public park and museum. A private nonprofit runs the facility now, with the help of donations. They suggest a $5 gift if you want to tour the mansion itself. You can also walk the wonderful gardens, take a tour of a nature center complete with a 20-foot waterfall, pet the animals at the children's farm, and enjoy wildlife exhibits, including a Birds of Prey aviary. (All of the raptors in captivity have permanent injuries that prevent them from surviving in the wild.) Maymont is adjacent to Byrd Park, and there are several entrances, including 2201 Shields Lake Dr.; 1700 Hampton St., and the corner of Spottswood Road and Shirley Lane.

Charlottesville

About an hour farther west on I-64 is Thomas Jefferson's beloved Charlottesville. It's here that he built his plantation, Monticello, and also his college, the University of Virginia. Both are worth visiting.

Monticello has been fully restored and docents there provide detailed tours of the mansion, giving a sense of the man who wrote the Declaration of Independence among other great documents of democracy and liberty. In fact, Jefferson wrote so much, and kept copies of everything thanks to a mechanical device that was called a polygraph long before the lie detector claimed that term, that his words can be used to argue both sides of many issues. This machine used a network of rods and levers to move a second quill that made an exact duplicate of whatever Jefferson was writing. The estate is owned and operated by the Thomas Jefferson Foundation, which was founded in 1923. They had lots of work to do because Tom may have been a genius but he was no businessman. He worshipped books and fine wine too much to worry about bills and other mundane matters. He died owing $107,000 and his heirs were forced to sell off his belongings and then the plantation itself.

From Monticello, Jefferson could look down and see the **University of Virginia,** an "academical village" in the heart of Charlottesville where shared learning was the way of life. Jefferson designed the university, including the Rotunda, a domed library at the head of the famous lawn.

Charlottesville is more than the museum and the mansion, though. It is a Mecca for Hollywood types who want to live the lives of landed gentry. It has been ranked one of the best places to live in America and even boasts one of the few pedestrian malls that actually *works* in downtown.

It is also the jumping off place for the Shenandoah National Park, the scenic Skyline Drive, and the Blue Ridge Parkway, a longer scenic route that begins where the

Skyline ends and that runs all the way to the Great Smoky Mountains National Park in North Carolina. The views are breathtaking, and folks plan trips to coincide with fall foliage peaks.

The Other Northwestern Attractions

You don't have to drive I-64 to head Northwest from Hampton Roads, and there are a few favorite attractions on the alternate routes.

Peanut Heaven

Take VA Route 460 and you can beat the summer traffic jams and get to Richmond in less time with less aggravation than on I-64. When you do, you'll pass the Virginia Diner in the tiny town of Waverly. Here you can buy their own brand of peanuts or just settle down for a home-style dinner. Baked Virginia ham biscuits are delicious, and there's the Brunswick stew, but most folks come for their southern fried chicken. And they serve peanut pie here.

Plantation Row

Another route that parallels the interstate is VA Route 5, which runs between Richmond and Williamsburg along the north bank of the James River. Here, in Charles City County, you can visit a row of private plantations, many of which are open to visitors. They include:

The **Sherwood Forest Plantation** was owned by President John Tyler and has been in Tyler's family ever since. It has the longest frame house in America, extended more than 300 yards. The self-guided tour of the grounds costs $10 per person. House tours are available by appointment for $35 per person. Call (804) 829-5377.

The **North Bend Plantation,** a 6,000-square-foot home on the National and Virginia landmark registers, is open to tours and you can even lodge there. Call (804) 829-5176 for reservations or visit www .northbendplantation.com.

The **Piney Grove at Southall's Plantation** also offers tours and bed-and-breakfast boarding. You can visit the gardens and grounds for $3 or for $9 you can buy a pass that also gets you onto the gardens and grounds of the **Westover, North Bend, and Edgewood Plantations.** Call (804) 829-2480 or visit www.pineygrove.com.

Evelynton Plantation, which was once part of the Westover Plantation owned by William Byrd, is no longer open to visits. The Civil War raged over this piece of land, with J.E.B. Stuart and Stonewall Jackson defending it against General George McClellan's Peninsula Campaign. The original house and outbuildings were burned and the current manor house was built in 1937 in the Georgian Revival style. Call (800) 473-5075 to see if the policy has changed.

The **Westover Plantation** was built around 1730 by Byrd, who founded Richmond, and features secret underground passageways for escape during Indian attacks and ancient boxwood hedges as well as the Georgian home's elegant proportions. The grounds are open to visitors, but the house is not.

The same family has owned the **Shirley Plantation** for over 11 generations. It was Virginia's first plantation, founded in 1613, and is the oldest family-owned business in America, dating to 1638. The mansion was begun in 1723 and finished in 1738 and is still owned and lived in by the descendants. It's still a working plantation. Admission is $11 for adults, $10 for those 60 and older, and $7.50 for 6- to 18-year-olds. Active duty military, retired service members, and their families get in for $5.

Finally, there's the **Berkeley Plantation** at Harrison's Landing, which is the site of the first official Thanksgiving in 1619 and the birthplace of Benjamin Harrison, a signer of the Declaration of Independence, and President William Henry Harrison, "Old Tippecanoe." The original Georgian mansion was built in 1726 of brick fired on the plantation. Guides in period costumes conduct tours of the mansion. Admission is $11 for adults, $6 for children 6 to 12, and $7.50 for students 13 to 16. Call (804) 829-6018 or visit www.berkeleyplantation.com.

Smithfield

In Europe, all roads lead to Rome; along the James River most head to Richmond. Another highway, this one on the south bank of the river, is Route 10. If you drive on this, you'll encounter Smithfield, famous for its pork products. In fact, the Isle of Wight County Museum, a charming local repository of county history, boasts the world's oldest edible cured ham among its collection. It dates to 1902 and was used by P. D. Gwaltney as a marketing mascot. He put a brass collar around it and called it his pet ham as a stunt to show his meat didn't need refrigeration. A flood damaged the museum a few years back, but the ham was rescued and has been returned to its place of honor near the display on the world's largest ham biscuit.

Smithfield also has a few nice antique shops along its main street and a delicious eatery, Smithfield Gourmet Bakery & Beanery, that serves meals as well as sweets. There's also an old fashioned ice cream parlor on Main Street and finer dining that includes the Smithfield Inn, Tavern and Bed & Breakfast, where you can sample real peanut soup, a savory blend of chicken stock and fresh roasted peanuts with seasoning that pulls it all together.

HEADING NORTH
The Eastern Shore

Where the trips up I-64 tend to be aimed at revisiting history, touring the land due north is more like seeing the place time forgot. Virginia's Eastern Shore is a stepchild, at the bottom of the long Delmarva Peninsula separated from the rest of the Commonwealth by the wide Chesapeake Bay. The isolation that was felt in the days of sail continued when ships turned to steam and is even palpable now in this age of hybrids and SUVs. As a result, Northampton and Accomack Counties are two of the poorest in all of Virginia. There's little industry on the Shore, as they call it, and most residents still either till the land, raise poultry, or work the water.

But the isolation also spawned independence and an easy charm you feel when you explore little towns like Exmore and Cape Charles. Lately, lots of retirees from the North have been buying up properties and settling in to enjoy the slow pace here. It's also a wonderful area to visit, or even to just take a little extra time passing through if you're heading to the big cities like Philly or New York.

Unless you have your own boat, you get to the Shore by crossing the Chesapeake Bay Bridge-Tunnel, the engineering marvel that was once called one of the Wonders of the World. It's a 23-mile-long roadway, more than half of it low-slung bridges over open water, with two tunnels set into rock islands at the mouth of the bay (see Getting Here, Getting Around for more information).

The main artery on the Shore is U.S. Route 13, which cuts right up the spine of the Peninsula. Most of the villages worth visiting, though, are a few miles off the highway, nestled either on the bay or the oceanside.

Cape Charles

This is the first little town you hit once you get off the bridge-tunnel. There's a lot of history here, since it was the northern terminus of the railroad ferry that linked the Eastern Shore with Hampton Roads. The age of rail was the golden years for Cape Charles, and many of the historic homes and buildings in the small downtown date to that era. When trucks took business from the freight trains after World War II, the town began to wither. Lately, there has been a new boom, with folks moving

i If you want to enjoy a real culinary experience, stop for a meal at the Cape Center, aka Chez Exxon. Yep, this is a fine dining establishment in the back of an operating service station. Sting Ray's Restaurant is no truck stop though. Here you'll find an extensive wine list and some of the freshest, best-cooked seafood anywhere in America. What truck stop offers up desserts like crème brûlée, death by chocolate, or a sweet potato pie drenched in Damson plum sauce? Don't just take my word for it. Framed alongside a feature I once wrote about the place are several glowing reviews by *Southern Living*. The best testimony, however, comes from the locals who flock here every day, sometimes for several meals. They especially love the chili, made from the original recipe by Ray, the former owner.

back to restore Victorian, Colonial Revival, Craftsman, and Neo-classical homes in the historic district along the waterfront.

BARRIER ISLANDS CENTER
Machipongo, 20 miles north of the tunnel on Route 13
(757) 678-5550

This is a free museum that opened in 1996 to document a time when people used to live on the windswept, frequently over-washed islands that protect the shoreline. Here, you can see exhibits that honor lifesavers who rescued watermen with special cannon-fired lines and others that show how market hunters kept pace with the demands for ducks using what amounted to small artillery pieces. You can see some of the decoys carved by legendary artisans and learn how presidents once came to bask in fancy clubs that dotted the area. The center is located in what was once the county poorhouse farm, so it also shows how Virginia's least affluent county treated its least fortunate. Out back is a shack where impoverished blacks were housed separately in the age of segregation. This is a friendly place with folks who work here related to the many families you'll read about. In fact, the museum has become a cultural anchor on the Eastern Shore, where many organizations meet and where adults bring children to get a sense of their ancestors. There's also a working farm that preserves historic farming techniques. The center is open Tues through Sat 10 a.m. to 4 p.m. and Sundays 1 to 5 p.m.

TANGIER ISLAND
www.tangierisland-va.com

This little island in the Chesapeake Bay just below the Maryland line is accessible only by boat. The town is built on fishing and crabbing, but there is a small tourist trade, with a handful of homes operating as bed-and-breakfasts and a couple little restaurants. This is a place where global warming and rising sea levels aren't open to debate. There are only a few ridges high enough to be occupied, with Main Ridge the center of today's town. They've put up a seawall to try to prevent the bay from claiming more land. You get to the island from places like Crisfield, Maryland, Reedville, and Onancock, VA. You'll have to leave your car behind, but you can rent bikes, golf carts, or just take a buggy tour on the island. If you're planning to stay over, be sure to make reservations well in advance. There's no Holiday Inn here. There's also a small airport on the island, if you prefer to fly in and out.

Chincoteague

I've skipped a lot of interesting real estate to get to Chincoteague, which is basically on the far end of Virginia's Eastern Shore. But most folks do just drive through on their way to this resort island community made famous by a children's book, *Misty of Chincoteague*, about one of the wild ponies that still make a home in the area. Every summer, folks come from around the country for the annual Pony Penning. For more than 85 years, locals have held a western-style roundup on Assateague Island at the beginning of July, herding up all the wild ponies and driving them across the shallow sound to Chincoteague where they are penned and the herd thinned enough to keep healthy by auctioning off some of the stock. The proceeds help fund the volunteer fire department, but this is far more than a fundraiser and carnival weekend. It's a tradition and a right of passage when a youngster is allowed to ride in the roundup. If you

intend to bid on one of the ponies, make sure you come with a horse trailer.

ASSATEAGUE ISLAND
NATIONAL SEASHORE
(410) 641-1441, Maryland District
(757) 336-6577, Virginia District

These days, all of the barrier islands are uninhabited and most are pretty inaccessible except by boat. Even then, the channels can be tricky and you need someone who knows the tides or you could wind up stranded on a mudflat. But there is a pristine piece of Atlantic Ocean that belongs to all of us, right over the causeway from Chincoteague village. Assateague Island actually extends into Maryland, and on that side you can camp. Most folks, though just head over the causeway from Chincoteague for a day at the beach, some surf fishing, and a chance to see one of those ponies in the wild. There are different rules in Virginia and Maryland. For instance, you can have pets on a leash in Maryland but in Virginia you can't even bring one in your car.

HEADING SOUTH

Hampton Roads sits right up against the North Carolina border, so it's no surprise that we often head to the Tar Heel state when we're looking to get away. What is a surprise is that, with our own vast array of beaches, we often choose to drive an hour or more to hit the Outer Banks' strand. Just chalk it up to a desire for variety and that old adage about the grass seeming greener—or in this case the sand finer—on the other side of the fence.

There's also a slightly different feel to a barrier island than to the more commercial offerings in Virginia Beach—at least once you get south of the more developed areas like Nags Head.

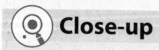

Close-up

Jurassic Park

Some trips will take you back to your youth, others to another century, but if you head to Gatesville, N.C., you can explore an earlier eon.

The name, **Merchants Millpond State Park** (71 US Highway 158 East, Gatesville, N.C., 252-357-1191), just doesn't excite the imagination the way it should. And that's great for the folks who have discovered this magic carpet just 30 miles south of Suffolk. It keeps the crowds away and the spell unbroken.

Launch a canoe or walk the paths around the pond and you'll swear you're back in the Jurassic Period. The 760-acre pond was formed 190 years ago, but it harbors long-nose gar and bowfin that haven't changed in millennia. Bald cypress and tupelo gum trees tower overhead, draped with Spanish moss. The water is dark, stained by tannins, and usually placid, as if even the wind only wants to whisper here.

Then there are the yellow cow lilies and red and green floating duckweeds and water ferns that cover the lake's surface.

Paddle awhile and you are surrounded by the thick trunks and bulging "knees" of these ancient cypresses. Mistletoe has twisted them into startling shapes. Keep going and you'll enter the more remote and even less disturbed Lassiter Swamp. Here, the frogs kick up a nightly chorus and water snakes, including the poisonous cottonmouth, are plentiful, so stay in your boat and keep an eye on overhanging branches where a stray snake might be resting and drop in for a visit.

The park has plenty of deer, and you probably won't spot the beaver but you'll see their handiwork on lodges, dams, and gnawed trees. There are also mink, bobcat, and river otter around. And when dusk comes, bats that roost in the Spanish moss dip to the pond surface to drink or to snag a mosquito or two.

The scientists say the otherworldly effect is created by the mingling of coastal pond and southern forest ecosystems. Put a kid in your canoe or just suspend a little cynicism yourself and you'll understand that there's more to this than a checklist of ingredients.

Getting there: Head south on US 17 across the North Carolina line. Make a right on US 158 West and travel about 20 miles until you hit Mill Pond Road, county route 1403. Make a left and the park entrance will be on your right.

On the Outer Banks, there are only a few north-south roads and everything is measured by mileposts that begin at the Wright Memorial Bridge, mile 0, and end at Hatteras Inlet, Milepost 72. So when you're looking for a restaurant, it will reference the nearest milepost. That is especially helpful if you want to scoot down the faster "bypass" which is what U.S. Route 158 is called by locals, rather than the Beach Road, their name for N.C. Highway 12. Keep an eye on the mileposts and then take a connecting street near your destination. It can save lots of time, since people tend to meander on the Beach Road.

Be warned that traffic can be a bear in the summer, because there are only a couple bridges to get onto and off the island and most rentals have similar check in and out times. You might want to consider leaving earlier than you have to. You can save a lot of time and aggravation that way. These days, rental companies offer a choice between properties that rent from Saturday to Saturday or Sunday to Sunday so the weekend traffic is better dispersed. But some have begun offering Friday-to-Friday rentals, which really cuts down on traffic.

Here's a little thumbnail sketch of the various communities you will encounter.

If you turn north after crossing the Wright Bridge, you hit the communities of Southern Shores, Duck, Sanderling, Corolla, and Carova.

Carova is in what is called the Four-Wheel-Drive area of the Outer Banks. This is a stretch just below the Virginia line that has no roads. You have to drive the beach to get to your cottage. You need a real off-road vehicle. Don't try it in one of those all-wheel-drive car hybrids or you're likely to be calling for a tow truck and hoping the tide doesn't arrive first. Folks who have lived here for generations actually have permits that allow them to drive the beach on the Wildlife Refuge and cut an hour or more from their trip to Virginia Beach. You can't get those anymore, though.

Corolla is next, with real roads and a lot of planned communities with pools, tennis courts, and beach shuttles. You even have grocery stores and a movie theater here.

Sanderling is just south of Corolla and is largely residential.

Duck is the next community and features a little village center.

Southern Shores is another residential community with plenty of rentals.

The Wright Bridge comes onto the island at **Kitty Hawk** and this area, plus **Kill**

Devil Hills and **Nags Head** to the south, are the heart of the traditional Outer Banks tourist experience. Here you have lots of rentals in all price and size ranges and the highways are lined with tourist shops, shopping centers, souvenir stores, and even go-cart tracks.

South of Nags Head, just beyond U.S. 64 to Roanoke Island, you get into Hatteras National Park property, a protected wild beach right up to the Oregon Inlet Bridge.

i Take 64 to Roanoke Island and you can break up the monotony of beautiful beach days. In Manteo, you'll find the Roanoke Island Festival Park, which has a replica of a 16th-century ship, the *Elizabeth II*, a working settlement site, and a docudrama about how the English changed the lives of the native Algonquin. Nearby, you can enjoy the *Lost Colony*, the first outdoor drama in the United States, which reenacts the fate of the folks who settled here and then disappeared. There's also a fine little aquarium here where you can watch sharks, feed rays, and learn about the local ecosystems. The nearby Alligator River is the most northern point in America where alligators can survive winters and reproduce. They have some of these reptiles on display at the aquarium.

North Carolina Highway 12 is the lifeblood of this area. Frequently flooded by hurricanes and other storms, it is quickly scraped clean, repaired, and put back in service so folks can have access to hospitals and other services only available on the mainland.

After you cross the Herbert C. Bonner Bridge over Oregon Inlet you are on Hatteras

Island. There are a few communities left within the Cape Hatteras National Seashore borders where people still live and rent properties—seven villages in fact.

Rodanthe, Waves, and **Salvo** are located near the center of the island, and locals call them the Tri-Villages. There are a variety of cafes and restaurants here. You have another long stretch of protected island before reaching the cluster of communities offering rentals and restaurants at the south: **Avon, Buxton, Frisco,** and **Hatteras Village.**

Buxton is located just off Cape Hatteras and is home to Cape Point, a sweeping sandbar that stretches farther into the Atlantic than any other point on the Outer Banks, making it popular for surf fishing. This is also where you'll find the Cape Hatteras Lighthouse, the tallest on the East Coast. **Frisco** has a Native American Museum near a site where an Indian village is being excavated. And Frisco is home to the Cape Hatteras Pier (which locals call the Frisco pier), the only one located south of Avon. **Hatteras Village** isn't at Hatteras Inlet or Cape Hatteras but it is the southernmost community on the island. It is also the place you catch the ferry to Ocracoke.

You can only reach **Ocracoke** by ferry, and the Cape Hatteras National Seashore owns everything except Ocracoke Village. This is the ultimate getaway for folks who don't want to be bothered. It's all bed and breakfasts and beach cottages here.

And if Ocracoke isn't remote enough for you, you can always take a trip to **Portsmouth Island** to the south from the docks at Ocracoke. The island is uninhabited now—the last two women left in 1971—and is part of the Cape Lookout National Seashore. But you can visit its beaches by boat and see what the last high tide has washed ashore. Or wander Portsmouth's ghost village, where a visitors' center and several buildings are open to the public.

Appendix

LIVING HERE

In this section we feature specific information for residents or those planning to relocate here. Topics include real estate, education, health care, and much more.

RELOCATION

People move in and out of Hampton Roads constantly, thanks to all those military families amongst us. Many only leave because they are ordered to a new station. Lots find ways to transfer between local commands and never get sent away. A huge group loves their time in the area so much they keep their homes and move back once they retire from the military, establishing a Department of Defense pension group here that's larger than a lot of small cities.

There are other reasons, though, to call Hampton Roads home, even if you aren't wearing a uniform or drawing a federal paycheck.

There's the glorious weather, the abundance of outdoor activities, and a culture that is a blend of cosmopolitan and southern comfort. Plus that resort area, the one others save up all year to enjoy in a short vacation, is yours anytime you want with just a few minutes on the road.

Then there's the economy. Buffered from wild swings in the markets by military payrolls and companies providing supplies to the services, there's usually a place here for those who want to work.

And all this comes at a relative bargain.

The cost of living in Virginia Beach, for instance, is just 70 percent of that in Washington, D.C., and if you shop around, you can probably do a lot better than that average.

Taxes here aren't oppressive, and the governments they fund tend to be efficient. The public school systems are generally good, and kids don't have to leave town to get a quality college education.

The region, long a confederation of bickering competitors, has become cooperative, and the result has been a shared water supply system as well as plans for a light rail line that will link the neighborhoods of Virginia Beach with downtown employers and the Navy bases in Norfolk. Potential spurs could reach all the way down into Chesapeake. The region also came together to back a plan that would return passenger rail service to Norfolk—without the bus ride from Newport News—and offer high-speed trips to the nation's capital.

OVERVIEW

If you've gotten this far, you know it's hard to generalize about Hampton Roads. And that's good if you're looking for a place to live. The region is huge—at more than 1,200 square miles, it's almost as big as the whole state of Rhode Island. And it is incredibly diverse.

If you like city living, you can move into a condo in downtown Norfolk or an apartment in the ersatz downtown at Town Center in Virginia Beach.

If you like quaint, you can try Ghent in Norfolk, Olde Towne in Portsmouth, or Phoebus in Hampton.

If you like lots of elbow room, there are suburban farmettes in Virginia Beach, Chesapeake, and Suffolk that will allow you to stable a horse or two, or you can go whole hog with an actual farm in the rural reaches of those same cities.

Everywhere, there are waterfront and water-view properties that command a premium but consistently hold their value. As one wag put it, "They ain't making any more waterfront these days."

That's not entirely true. Hurricanes have been known to build new landmasses, like Willoughby Spit in Norfolk. But even without a storm of the century, there are other options. Many communities are constructed along lakes that were dug out to get to the construction grade sand. They call them "borrow pits" around here. But don't let the name discourage you. These quickly become little Walden Ponds, with resident waterfowl and neighbors eager to fling bread chunks in their direction. They are also loaded with fish, with some harboring some lunker bass unbeknownst to those who just jog or sun on these suburban banks.

If you really want a water view, you might buy a boat and live aboard at one of the many marinas in the area. Be warned though: It takes a special person to walk those piers in the heart of winter, and you'd better be a minimalist because storage is at a premium on most vessels.

The cities all work hard to ensure there are affordable housing options for those just starting out without allowing areas to decay into slums—it's a difficult task that sometimes results in tough code enforcement sweeps and sometimes can end up in neighborhoods that are cleared out, demolished, and redeveloped with higher-end housing.

In this chapter, we'll look at some of the most popular neighborhoods in a range of prices and some of the leading real estate companies that can help you find your dream home, and I'll also let you know what you have to do once you move in, like getting a driver's license, registering your pet, and getting your kids immunized so they'll be ready for school.

NEIGHBORHOODS

As you can imagine, there are thousands of them spread out across the eight cities. Some of the names are so obscure even those living there don't use them. Others are iconic, and as such, are usually in high demand with a price tag to match. But if you look around, you can usually find something you love in any city and at your price range.

When my wife and I first moved here, I wasn't interested in owning. So when she asked what it would take, I created an elaborate checklist, confident it would keep us in our apartment. The mortgage had to be reasonable, and in those days of Jimmy Carter's malaise and 12 percent loans, I demanded a reasonable rate that was assumable. The home had to be fairly new, with low maintenance, and be energy efficient. There had to be a nice fireplace and a garage. It had to be in the center of the area, because I might be working at any of a number of offices my newspaper operated in the region. And, oh yeah, it had to be on water that not only was big enough to putter around in my canoe but that had a nice population of largemouth bass to keep me busy.

About four hours later, she called to say she had found such a home and arranged a visit that led to our buying a first house. I'm not guaranteeing you'll be quite so lucky. It actually took us a couple model home visits and one lucky detour to find our current house, and the one before that we stumbled on while they were building it in an adjacent neighborhood. But all three have been on water and affordable, so those requirements can slow down the process.

The first question you need to ask yourself is whether you want to live on the Southside or the Peninsula. Your job will probably be a big determinant on that, if you already have a place to work. If not, you might want to explore the employment market on both sides before settling on a home. I've known people who commute between the two areas, but it can be a bear and takes someone with lots of patience. You'll want to try it out yourself a couple mornings and evenings—especially heading back to the Peninsula on a Friday evening in the summer when traffic routinely backs up 7 or 8 miles at the tube—before you make that kind of a commitment.

The big real estate firms I list later on will be a big help in this regard. They can fill you in on the various neighborhoods. But remember, real estate, like all other purchases, is a buyer-beware business, so do your homework. You don't want to discover, as you're moving your sofa into that dream house, that your cozy getaway is just off a runway and was only quiet because you checked it out during the traditional Sunday morning break in military operations. Or that the aircraft carriers were all deployed the week you looked, and when they get back it will be hard to think over the thunder as the jets scream over your shingles.

i Real estate agents and sellers are required to inform you if you are buying into a so-called Accident Potential Zone or high noise area. The reputable ones all do. You can also get maps of the Air Installation Compatible Use Zones from the Navy or online at: www.cnic.navy.mil/oceana/programs/navalstationdepartments/flightoperations/aicuz/aicuz/index.htm. The Navy website also explains how they measure the sound, what the different levels mean, and why they fly when they do.

Crime can also be a concern when you are looking for a place to live. This region is generally safe, especially for a major metropolitan area, but there are places that can get iffy. Your real estate agent will know them, and *The Virginian-Pilot* newspaper's website has a searchable database you can use to check various neighborhoods at http://hamptonroads.com/crime. The *Daily Press* on the Peninsula offers a similar service at www.dailypress2.com/crime/nn.

If you're coming from LA or Manhattan, you probably won't be fazed by the commuter traffic. But as I point out in the Getting Here, Getting Around chapter, many roads do routinely back up, so you'll want to consider that as well when you pick a place to live.

With all the warnings out of the way, let's get to the fun stuff: finding a great place to live.

Southside

Norfolk

DOWNTOWN

There was a time when Downtown was a ghost town. Once-bustling Granby Street was a pedestrian mall through a canyon of shuttered stores. You could actually hear your footsteps echo behind as you walked on streets that were virtually abandoned. Now, it's a place where people come to play and want to live. Stores and restaurants line Granby and there are an abundance of new condos and apartments that have sprung up between Brambleton Avenue and the Elizabeth River. The economic collapse in 2008 put the brakes on some of the building, but there are still plenty of options here for elegant city living. Many of the folks moving in are empty nesters who no longer want to hassle with lawns and like the idea of walking to a mall or the movies. Nearby is Freemason, a historic neighborhood of cobblestone streets where some of the city's best-preserved relics are open for tours (see Museums chapter).

GHENT

This is another historic area, composed of what were once large suburban homes that were in disrepair before Urban Renewal efforts restored the community. It's an affluent area, inhabited by doctors, lawyers, and business people. It also has some of the area's best old apartment buildings, so it attracts a lot of young renters who enjoy walking the area and eating at the many restaurants or catching an art flick at the Naro Expanded Cinema. This neighborhood also has some of the city's best public schools, both because of its educated demographics and also because the schools themselves lure more like-minded parents to move in.

LARCHMONT

It's not just the proximity to Old Dominion University that lures the professors into this academic "ghetto" that Thomas Jefferson would be proud to inhabit. The homes are quaint to lavish. The streets are tree lined and old-fashioned. There's plenty of expensive Lafayette River waterfront here, and many of the homes have backyard piers with yachts at the ready. Of course, the prices will track the amenities and properties don't tend to stay on the market long here.

OCEAN VIEW

For years, this was Norfolk's underbelly, full of transients living in tacky motels. It was hard to understand how a neighborhood right on the Chesapeake Bay, with such breathtaking vistas, could get so down on its luck. Then the city and developers cleared out entire sections of Ocean View and built high-end communities up against the dunes. Suddenly, property values peaked, and folks were moving back in. It's still a work in progress, with run down neighborhoods a few blocks from those bayfront McMansions. But those who got in when property was cheap are enjoying the Renaissance—and everyone who lives on the water here loves the spectacular view with their morning coffee.

i Don't let the name fool you: You can't see the ocean from Ocean View. It's strictly the Chesapeake Bay here, but there's nothing wrong with that either.

Virginia Beach

NORTH END

This is where the folks with enough money to live at the Oceanfront call home. It's a place to aspire to, with the beach a block or so away and no worries about where to park your car. That also makes it the place for many of the summer "cottages" for some of

Virginia's richest folks. Million-dollar houses are the norm here, although you can grab the occasional place a few blocks off the ocean for half that. But the really prime locations can run beyond $5 million, and even they don't stay on the market long.

SANDBRIDGE

Another community right up against the dunes, this one is less residential and more weekend getaway. That's partially because it takes a lot longer to commute here, but if you have a telecommuting job, it's one heck of a place to hang out. Again, homes here run easily into the seven figures. Many are rented out, so you can get a taste of Sandbridge living before you buy, at discount prices if you're willing to leave during the tourist season. Here you can also buy homes that front Back Bay and have a sunset rather than a sunrise vantage point.

CROATAN BEACH

Nestled between Rudee Inlet and Camp Pendleton, this hidden community is another high-end getaway. Most folks live here year-round and prices run from half a million dollars to $5 million or more. There's an active community organization here.

KEMPSVILLE

This section of the city could be a city itself and was a town before merging with the county and Oceanfront village to form the city of Virginia Beach. It's a blue-collar area with roots that run back to 1775 with a wide variety of housing for nearly any price range.

TOWN CENTER

This is the new Virginia Beach downtown created from scratch in less than a decade.

Now there are condos and apartments aplenty to go with the collection of restaurants and shopping in this "urban" core to the suburban city.

KINGS GRANT

One of the older, nicer suburban areas in the northern end of the city, it's a lot like nearby Great Neck and Little Neck. Here large homes sit on mature, wooded lots. Streets are shaded and residents tend to be long-timers. There are some waterfront properties, but like anywhere, waterfront will be more expensive.

SMITH LAKE TERRACE

Here you can have a different kind of waterfront experience, nestled on one of the area's large freshwater supply lakes. Lake Smith has a number of coves and canals just begging for you to explore and even a public boat ramp. Homes here are less expensive than those looking over the ocean, but can still run $500,000 or more if you want to be right on Lake Smith.

PRINCESS ANNE

This is the area surrounding the civic center, where people still have horses, and historic homes sit side by side with custom built replicas. It's in the southern part of the city, where regulations ensure the lots are huge and the rural atmosphere will be protected. Folks still farm around here, but it's getting less common. Most of the city's agriculture is done a little farther south, in communities like Pungo and Creeds.

CHICK'S BEACH

A bayfront community, this has a very bohemian feel, with bars that jealously protect the privacy of the many Navy SEALs who call this area home. This is a neighborhood that sticks together, and newcomers are welcomed, but must earn real trust from the regulars.

THOROUGHGOOD

This quiet neighborhood between Chick's Beach and the Lynnhaven River is one of Virginia Beach's most coveted. Homes here run from $300,000 for a small rancher to more than $2 million for a place on the river with a pier to park a yacht. The Adam Thoroughgood House here gives the neighborhood its name. (See Historic Homes in the Museum chapter.)

GREEN RUN

This is one of the area's largest and earliest planned developments, with some 30 neighborhoods, 4,200 single-family homes, three condo developments, and 900 apartments in the heart of the city. There are more than 5 miles of canals and lots of green common areas that give it its name. It was begun in 1970, and the last construction finished more than 20 years ago, so the community is getting a little long in the tooth, and some of the properties have run down as the crime rate has risen, so you'll want to be careful, although there are some housing bargains here.

Portsmouth

OLDE TOWNE

This is a quaint colonial village at the heart of the original city, with a rich collection of Revolutionary-era homes and cobblestone streets. Presidents have stayed here, as well as the famous traitor Benedict Arnold, who once occupied the town with the British. There's lots of history, and you can live amongst it. Think of it as a much more affordable version of Old Town Alexandria, with a couple extra e's tacked onto the name.

CHURCHLAND

This is modern Portsmouth. It was the last piece of land annexed from the county before Chesapeake incorporated to stop the expansion, and it developed as a suburb with a full range of housing options.

STERLING POINT

Here you'll find many of the wealthiest of the city's residents with large homes overlooking the Elizabeth River on tree-lined streets and well-tended yards. The city's lawyers and doctors love this location, since it's an easy commute down High Street to downtown.

MIDCITY

Once a suburban shopping Mecca, it is full of small, blue-collar homes. The original stores closed long ago, but the area is on the comeback, with a Walmart and several other stores opening in recent years. A blighted community that went up as emergency World War II housing nearby has been eliminated, and new homes are being built there. But this is not high end.

CRADOCK

This is one of the nation's first planned communities, built for World War I workers to commute to the nearby shipyard. As a result, its homes and lots are small by today's standards, and there have been some battles with crime and blight. But the blue-collar neighborhood is tight knit and the location still convenient to those shipyard jobs.

PORT NORFOLK

Another historic neighborhood, this one sits right on the Elizabeth River, and many of the old homes have a good view of a working waterway. The nonprofit Elizabeth River Project is working hard to make its namesake a place to frolic again, but you probably wouldn't want to wade here yet. Still, the neighborhood offers waterfront living on a middle-class salary.

ELIZABETH MANOR

Today, a development on a golf course is pretty common, but Elizabeth Manor is one of the earliest stabs at golf-course living. The homes are smaller than today's link lodges, though, and the course is private, so you'll have to join to walk the links.

Chesapeake

GREAT BRIDGE

This is a historic community where the city government is based. The homes here tend to be brick, large, and well cared for. It's a place most of the old Chesapeake families call home. There are also a number of newer developments on the roads just out of Great Bridge proper that offer a full range of homes and lots.

GREENBRIER

This is a massive planned unit development with closely packed homes offset by acres of green common areas and an interconnected network of lakes and canals. Homes are available in a wide range of prices, from large custom-built properties that attract professionals to smaller, tract developments perfect for a first place. There are also a lot of apartment complexes here, just across from the large Greenbrier Mall.

SOUTH NORFOLK

One of the historic villages of old Norfolk County, it suffered through the second half of the 20th century when folks wanted bigger homes on larger lots. Most of the places here are blue collar. There are ongoing efforts to revitalize the neighborhood, starting with a trendy name, SoNo.

HICKORY

This is the name given to much of the city's rural south, a huge swath of real estate from Great Bridge down to the North Carolina border, where everything was once custom built and the rural roads are lined with small farmettes as well as large working fields. This is the place for horse lovers. New developments, such as the ones off Etheridge Road and Hillcrest Parkway, are more huge-lot suburban.

WESTERN BRANCH

This section of the city, in the horseshoe out beyond Portsmouth's Churchland suburbs, developed during the big-is-better building phase. As a result, there are many large homes on large lots mixed with some more generic suburban developments.

DEEP CREEK

This is a community in more than just a name. It's a historic village that has retained its homey feel. People here know the people you come from. It's blue collar, and many of the residents made their livings in the area shipyards. There has been some more modern development here. But it remains an enclave and the residents aren't complaining.

Suffolk

DOWNTOWN

This is the historic town of Suffolk, which used to be the heart of Nansemond County before it all became an independent city. It may seem quaint, but it has some tough urban neighborhoods surrounding the resurging Main Street district, which features a number of shops, restaurants, and nightlife. The small waterfront here along the Nansemond River is being developed with a huge hotel and marina that recently opened at Constant's Warf here.

HARBOUR VIEW

This massive development in Suffolk's north offers easy access to both the Peninsula and the Southside employment hubs. It tends to be mid- to high-end with riverfront homes along the James and Nansemond Rivers. A key selling point here is that easy commute to both Newport News and Norfolk.

BENNETT'S CREEK

Once it was way out in the boonies, a haven for those who wanted to really get away from it all or who were willing to drive long distances for a chance to live on the beautiful creek banks. But when I-664 opened, it made Bennett's Creek a more comfortable commute and opened the door to more modern developments.

CHUCKATUCK

If you really want to go rural, consider this tiny village within the city. There's not a whole lot here, but it can claim being the town that produced the great jazz guitarist Charlie Byrd and former Virginia Gov. Mills Godwin.

WESTERN AND SOUTHERN SUFFOLK

I won't list the little villages here, but the regions remain largely rural, with plenty of farmland planted in peanuts and some small residential developments both new and historic.

The Peninsula

Newport News

HILTON VILLAGE

Built for shipyard workers in 1918, it is the nation's first Federal War Housing Project, a planned community built to the recommendations of the wives of shipyard workers. It is on the National Register of Historic Places and still has a historic feel. The little downtown has shops and a theater and you can find riverfront vistas.

OYSTER POINT

This is the business-park center of the city, with housing to match. There are condos and apartments aplenty at City Center at Oyster Point and a 115-acre urban village at nearby Port Warwick. Nearby traditional neighborhoods include Harpersville and Morrison.

HUNTINGTON HEIGHTS AND HISTORIC DOWNTOWN

These neighborhoods are located south of the James River Bridge and have a full range of properties from high-rise apartments and waterfront condos to historic homes.

JAMES LANDING

This neighborhood along the James River, as well as nearby Hidenwood, Deep Creek, and Riverside are near the James River Country

Club, Christopher Newport University, and the Museum district. They are among the most affluent in the city.

KILN CREEK

There are 31 individual villages that make up this huge development with its own golf course and walking trails that extends into York County. It's right off I-64 and near local shopping centers.

CHRISTOPHER SHORES

This neighborhood has long been home to the city's middle class African American residents. Many homes here have views of Hampton Roads harbor.

Hampton

ABERDEEN

This historic area of I-64 south of Mercury Boulevard won *Neighborhoods USA*'s "Neighborhood of the Year Award." The homes here are brick and the community is close. Hazel O'Leary, President Clinton's first energy secretary, and basketball star Alan Iverson grew up in this area. It was the first of FDR's New Deal settlements built by and for African Americans and is one of the last of those New Deal communities still in existence.

BACK RIVER

This community still includes working farms. There's a boat basin and a wide range of homes from ranchers to mini-mansions. It's near the Willow Oaks shopping center and originally was military base housing.

BUCKROE BEACH

This is Hampton's beachfront resort community located on the Chesapeake Bay. There's a range of housing from modest to spacious. It is one of the oldest resort areas in Virginia, getting its start when the Chesapeake and Ohio Railway ran its tracks to the waterfront, leading to a boarding house and public bath house.

HISTORIC DISTRICT

The area goes by many names, including Acorn Point, Cedar Point, and Little England, and is surrounded by water on three sides. Victoria Boulevard is surrounded by renovated Victorian homes and it's an easy walk to downtown.

PHOEBUS

This little blue-collar community outside Fort Monroe on Hampton's East Side has a small row of shops and galleries on East Mellon Street and the American Theater at its heart. Homes here tend to be small, reflecting its history as a place for veteran soldiers, freed slaves, and new businessmen.

REAL ESTATE AGENCIES & RESOURCES

Even the most adventurous and self-reliant home shopper will have a nearly impossible time navigating all of Hampton Roads without help. There can be more than 17,000 homes up for sale at any time. Luckily this area is chock full of good real estate companies and independent agents.

It can take a good team to keep on top of this housing market. There are always new and existing homes coming on the market as people get transferred to other duty stations, move up, or simplify their lives. Even in the midst of the recent economic downturn, more than 1,200 homes sold here in June 2009. More than 100 homes sold for an excess of $1 million that year, topped by a condo in Virginia Beach's Town Center that went for more than $4 million and a series of Oceanfront places that topped $2 million.

Many agencies have people who speak other languages, if you need help. Some have new-to-the-area packets that can make your transition easier and websites where you can browse the inventory before you even get to the region.

There's no way to list every real estate agency here. You can find additional information from the Real Estate Information Network, the local multiple listing service that serves some 606 real estate offices and 6,425 agents. REIN offers a gallery of homes you can tour, including a listing of open houses and an interactive map search to narrow down your quest.

The Hampton Roads Realtors Association is the largest in the area, with more than 3,300 Realtors and 600 affiliate members. You can use their find-a-Realtor tool at www.centerforrealestate.com or call them at (757) 473-9700 for assistance.

The Virginian-Pilot's website has a real estate section with searchable databases on schools, crime statistics, and news.

CENTURY 21 NACHMAN REALTY
3220 Churchland Blvd.
Chesapeake
(757) 638-5700
www.century21nachman.com
This full-service real estate business has been operating in Hampton Roads for 50 years. It boasts 175 agents who sold more than $350

million in real estate in 2009. There are nine full-service offices in total. The website offers a wealth of information on the area as well as branch locations and links to the multiple listing service so you can have an idea about what's out there, if you'd like, before you contact them. They also manage rental units if you're looking for an apartment or home but are not ready to buy.

NANCY CHANDLER ASSOCIATES REALTORS
701 West 21st St.
Norfolk
(757) 623-2382
www.nancychandler.com
Nancy Chandler opened her small firm with a few associates in 1974 after five years of working for others and immediately sold $1.5 million in property. Nancy remains the chairperson of this company, which is now run by Web Chandler III and ranks among the largest real estate agencies in southeastern Virginia. These days, there's a relocation division and a new homes program, as well as agents who speak Spanish. A second branch is located in Chesapeake at 636 Cedar Rd. (757) 436-5500.

COLDWELL BANKER PROFESSIONAL REALTORS
1547 East Little Creek Rd.
Norfolk
(757) 583-1000
http://cb-pro.com
This national firm began in 1906, after the San Francisco earthquake, and is now a national powerhouse. They have a Military Market Specialist office in their Virginia Beach Boulevard office, (757) 222-6735. For a complete list of locations, visit their website.

HARVEY LINDSAY COMMERCIAL REAL ESTATE
999 Waterside Dr., Suite 1400
Norfolk
(757) 640-8700
www.harveylindsay.com

If you're looking for something a lot bigger than a house, you might want to give Harvey's company a call. They have been a leader in commercial real estate in Hampton Roads for more than 70 years. Harvey L. Lindsay Jr. took the reins of his father's company and built it into a powerhouse with more than 70 specialists who have been responsible for developing area malls, office buildings, and other projects that have helped reshape the area.

JUDY BOONE REALTY
809 East Ocean View Ave.
Norfolk
(757) 587-2800
www.judyboonerealty.com

Judy Boone opened up her agency in 1989 and her first act, building her office in what was considered a dying Ocean View, would send the signal that she was committed to this area. Her first day in business, she had $2 million in listings. Today she has more than 30 agents working with her, a property management division, a maintenance crew, and more than 1,200 rental units. She has continued to specialize in Ocean View, although these days there are lots more folks who believe in its potential.

LIZ MOORE & ASSOCIATES
11801 Canon Blvd., Suite 100
Newport News
(757) 873-2707
http://lizmoore.com

Liz Moore set about in 2001 to revamp how real estate was sold on the Peninsula. She opened a boutique brokerage two years later and partnered with a local attorney and area powerhouse William E. Wood and Associates to see if they could eliminate last-minute surprises for buyers and sellers. Every home sold has an independent property inspection, a market appraisal, and termite and moisture inspections done at the agency's expense. It's helped her become one of the top real estate companies on the Peninsula. There are more than 90 associates affiliated with this agency including nearly 80 Realtors.

LONG AND FOSTER REAL ESTATE INC.
(866) 677-6937

This company, based in Northern Virginia, is the largest real estate firm in the Mid-Atlantic region and the biggest privately owned real estate company in America, with more than 13,700 sales associates in 237 offices. Seventeen of them are in Hampton Roads. As can be expected, a firm of this size has experts in a wide range of foreign languages, including Arabic, German, Greek, Russian, Spanish, Filipino, Cantonese and Mandarin Chinese, French, Italian, Japanese, Punjabi, Romanian, Turkish, Urdu, Dutch, Haitian Creole, Farsi, American Sign, Indonesian, Icelandic, Korean, Cambodian, and Vietnamese.

RE/MAX PENINSULA
825 Diligence Dr., Suite 126
Newport News
(757) 873-3636
http://peninsula1.virginia.remax.com

This firm has been operating since 1991, specializing, as the name implies, in real estate north of the Hampton Roads Bridge Tunnel. The company is owned by Alfred L. Abbitt and has a staff of 36 associates, licensed assistants, and staff. The website offers tools for buying and tips for sellers.

PRUDENTIAL TOWNE REALTY
600 22nd St., Suite 500
Virginia Beach
(757) 490-6500
http://prudentialtownerealty.com

Several local real estate powers, Prudential Decker Realty of Virginia Beach, Prudential McCardle Realty of Williamsburg, and GSH Real Estate joined forces with the locally based TowneBank in 2009 to form this giant that has more than 300 years of combined management experience, 500 agents, and 50 staff members spread over 13 offices.

ROSE & WOMBLE REALTY
(800) 695-7356
www.roseandwomble.com

This regional giant has 13 offices scattered throughout the area and was recently ranked the 36th largest independent Realtor in the nation. The firm was established in 1998 when Rose & Krueth Realty Corp. and Womble Realty merged to created the largest firm in Hampton Roads. Today, there are more than 600 sales associates working in its offices. The New Home Division markets 48 new developments from Williamsburg to Elizabeth City, N.C., and the Property Management Division oversees more than 1,500 rental units.

WILLIAM E. WOOD AND ASSOCIATES REALTOR
800 Newtown Road
Virginia Beach
(757) 499-9663
www.williamewood.com

This company began in 1972 in Virginia Beach and grew quickly. It was one of the first to join a relocation network of independent real estate firms across the country. That one office has expanded to 20 locations and more than 600 full-time agents with a sales volume topping $1.4 billion. There are agents fluent in American Sign Language, Arabic, Chinese, French, German, Greek, Hebrew, Italian, Korean, Filipino, Polish, Russian, and Spanish.

S.L. NUSBAUM REALTY CO.
One Commercial Place
Norfolk
(757) 627-8611
www.slnusbaum.com

This family-operated firm began in Norfolk and has been in operation for more than a century. It specializes in commercial real estate, with more than 2 million square feet of space, and is the largest developer of community shopping centers in Virginia, managing 45 properties with more than 6 million square feet of retail space. But most folks know Nusbaum as the area's largest manager of local apartment communities. The company oversees more than 112 multi-family properties with nearly 18,000 rental units. More than 5,000 are in properties they developed or improved and still own. Although it has expanded into North and South Carolina, Florida, Georgia, Tennessee, and Maryland, most of its focus remains on Hampton Roads.

TIDEWATER BUILDERS ASSOCIATION
2117 Smith Ave.
Chesapeake
(757) 420-2434
www.tbaonline.org

If you want to go right to the source when looking for a home or find someone to build your dream house for you, the Tidewater

Builders Association is a good place to start. This group represents more than 800 companies who employ 30,000 tradespeople as well as owners and managers of more than 30,000 apartment units. On the website, you can find members, get a new homebuyers checklist, and help finding a qualified remodeler. They also sponsor the annual Homearama, a popular event where builders compete in a block or so of custom homes and buyers get to check out the latest in designs or even bid on the show homes. They also have a Green Building Council, a Remodelers Council, and a Multifamily Housing Council.

GETTING SETTLED

So you've pulled the trigger, found a place to live, and now call Hampton Roads home. What's next? As anyone who has moved to a new location can testify, the job is hardly finished when boxes are all unpacked. You need to settle in by becoming an official resident. There are cars to re-title, licenses to transfer, students to register, and even pets who need to get their official documents. Let's take them one at a time.

Transportation

Virginia gives you just 30 days to register your vehicle and get new license plates when you move here. The endeavor involves the state Department of Motor Vehicles and there are a host of DMV offices throughout the area. But be warned, it can be a long process, with lots of waiting around for your number to be called. You can find office locations at www.dmv.state.va.us. Lots of the services can be done online once you're in the state system, and you'll probably want to keep that in mind. But this first one will

require an in-person visit. Your car will need to pass a state safety inspection before you can operate it here. And you'll need some minimal auto insurance in place or they'll assess you a $500 uninsured motor vehicle fee. That doesn't buy you insurance, just the right to tags. There's a registration fee based on the weight of the vehicle and whether you want a vanity plate. (Virginia is a leader in those coded messages, but don't try to slip an off-color one through. There's a panel that reviews requests, and they don't find obscenity funny.) You'll get a pair of regular license plates right there so there's no waiting for the mail to come.

You can register to vote when you register your car, and if you're a male citizen between 18 and 25, you are required to register with the Selective Service System.

> **i** Military members and their families can keep their home-state licenses and tags no matter how long they are stationed here. So can full-time students from out of state, and temporary residents don't need to transfer anything for up to six months. Since there is no customs office registering your move to Virginia, folks have been known to peg their day of arrival or reason to be in the Commonwealth within those exceptions if stopped by an officer after the 30-day grace period.

You have 60 days to get a Virginia driver's license. If you have a valid license from another state, you should bone up on the local laws; they can ask you to take a test. You won't need to do a road test, but you'll have to pass a vision screening. Thanks to terrorists using Virginia licenses during the 9/11 attacks, you no longer can get one over the counter. It will be mailed to you in a secure process that mimics the one the feds use for passports. And if your license is suspended or revoked in another state, Virginia won't give you one until you clear up that problem.

Utilities

Unless you've chosen a log cabin, you'll need some basic services. **Electricity** in Hampton Roads is provided by **Dominion Power** (888-782-0455). Natural gas comes from two providers depending on where you live. **Columbia Gas of Virginia** (800-440-6111) serves some of the western area, and **Virginia Natural Gas** (866-229-3578) serves the greater Hampton Roads region.

Water comes from the Department of Utilities in your city: Norfolk, (757) 664-6701; Chesapeake, (757) 547-6352; Portsmouth, (757) 393-8524; Virginia Beach, (757) 385-4631; Suffolk, (757) 514-7000; and Waterworks, which serves Newport News, Poquoson and Hampton, (757) 926-1000.

Telephone service is available from a number of services now, from cell phone providers to land lines and cable providers. The big three are **Verizon Communications** (757-954-6222), **Cox Communications** (757-222-1111), and **Cavalier Telephone** (757-248-4000). They're also cable and Internet providers, along with **Charter Communications** in Suffolk (888-438-2427).

Schools

The information on the various public and private school districts is in the Education chapter. Just be aware that students must be immunized, and you'll need to prove that with an immunization certificate. You'll also need a birth certificate or the equivalent, and every child will need a federal social security number within 90 days of enrollment.

Pets

Most cities require a license for your dogs, some require cats be licensed as well, and you'll need proof of a rabies vaccination for either.

SENIOR SERVICES

SENIOR SERVICES OF SOUTHEASTERN VIRGINIA
Interstate Corporate Center
6350 Center Dr., Building 5, Suite 101
Norfolk
(747) 461-9481
www.ssseva.org
On the Southside, Senior Services of Southeastern Virginia provides a wealth of benefits to the elderly. This nonprofit works as a liaison to area agencies, delivers meals to the homebound, offers counseling on Medicare, Medicaid, and long-term care insurance. These folks drive seniors to doctors' offices and help thousands of older Virginians stay in their homes. Their I-Ride vehicle provides transportation for $1 a ride, regardless of age.

JEWISH FAMILY SERVICE OF TIDEWATER
260 Grayson Rd.
Virginia Beach
(757) 321-2223
www.jfshamptonroads.org
This nonprofit also provides services to those over 55 years old, regardless of their religious background. They include care management, home health and home care, counseling, meals on wheels, and other assistance.

MEDIA

Newspapers

There are two large daily papers serving Hampton Roads. Each keeps pretty much to its own side of the James River.

THE VIRGINIAN-PILOT
150 West Brambleton Ave.
Norfolk
(757) 446-2000
www.pilotonline.com

This is the largest newspaper in Virginia and one of the most award winning. It has been recognized repeatedly as one of the best-designed papers in the world, and its writers and photographers annually win top places in Associated Press competitions. The paper has also won three Pulitzer Prizes in its history. Two go back to the days of segregation when the editorial page took then-unpopular stands against lynching and the closing of public schools to avoid integration. A third Pulitzer Prize was awarded in 1985 for an investigation into the spending of public money by a city official in Chesapeake.

The newspaper has offices in Norfolk, Virginia Beach, Chesapeake, and Suffolk and produces local news inserts for each of the five Southside cities. It also circulates on the Eastern Shore of Virginia and into northeastern North Carolina, where it has an office as well. It is locally owned and was briefly put up for sale but pulled back.

THE DAILY PRESS
7505 Warwick Blvd.
Newport News
(757) 247-4600
www.dailypress.com

With about half the circulation of the *Pilot*, the *Daily Press* is still the fourth largest paper

in the state, part of the Tribune family of newspapers that also includes the *Chicago Tribune*, the *Baltimore Sun*, the *Hartford Courant*, and the *Morning Call* of Allentown, Pa. This paper also annually wins awards in the Associated Press competitions.

SUFFOLK NEWS-HERALD
(757) 539-3437
www.suffolknewsherald.com

This is a much smaller, Suffolk-only newspaper published Tues through Sun that keeps it very local.

NEW JOURNAL & GUIDE
974 Norfolk Square
Norfolk
(757) 543-6531
www.njournalg.com

For more than 110 years, this newspaper in Norfolk has been covering news important to African Americans. It is Virginia's oldest black weekly newspaper. It was started in 1900 by a black fraternal order known as the Supreme Lodge Knights of Gideon and was originally called the Gideon Safe Guide. It is published on Thurs and serves all of Hampton Roads.

Magazines

HAMPTON ROADS MAGAZINE
1264 Perimeter Parkway
Virginia Beach
(757) 422-8979
www.hamptonroadsmagazine.com

This is the area lifestyle magazine, with full-color, slick pages that feature stories on local trends, travel destinations, political and economic issues, gift guides, home and garden features, recreation, the arts, and fine dining.

INSIDE BUSINESS: THE HAMPTON ROADS BUSINESS JOURNAL
150 West Brambleton Ave.
Norfolk
(757) 222-5341
www.insidebiz.com

The same folks who put out *The Virginian-Pilot* newspaper publish this weekly business magazine. It has won more than 20 state and national awards in the past decade. It covers banking, commercial real estate, economic development, small business, health care, technology, maritime, and the tourism industries.

TIDEWATER PARENT
150 West Brambleton Ave.
Norfolk
(757) 222-3905
www.mytidewatermoms.com

Another in the *Pilot* family, this free monthly magazine and website offer help in raising children, from parenting tips to a calendar of places to go and things to do. You can find it at boxes and locations throughout the Southside.

TIDEWATER WOMEN
3065 Mansfield Lane
Virginia Beach
(757) 204-4688
www.tidewaterwomen.com

A free monthly aimed at local women, this has been distributed on the Southside for a decade. There are some 750 locations where you can pick up one of the 20,000 copies. It features articles on health, family, business, careers, education, and travel.

Television Stations

All three major networks plus Fox and the CW are represented here. The area also has a very strong public broadcasting presence with a PBS affiliate and two public radio stations that, using digital transmissions, actually provide six different streams of programming to those with HD radios or who listen in on their computers.

On the Dial (and on Cable and FiOs):
WTKR-TV CHANNEL 3
CBS Affiliate
20 Boush St.
Norfolk
Front Desk: (757) 446-1000
Newsroom: (757) 446-1352
www.wtkr.com

WAVY-TV CHANNEL 10
NBC Affiliate
300 WAVY St.
Portsmouth
(757) 393-1010
www.wavy.com

WVEC-TV CHANNEL 13
ABC Network
(757) 625-1313
www.wvec.com

WHRO-TV CHANNEL 15
PBS Affiliate
5200 Hampton Blvd.
Norfolk
(757) 889-9400
www.whro.org

WGNT-TV CHANNEL 27
CW Affiliate
1318 Spratley St.
Portsmouth
(757) 393-2501
http://cw27.com

WBVT-TV CHANNEL 43
Fox Affiliate
www.fox43tv.com
This is a sister station to WAVY and uses the
same contact information.

Radio Stations

This is one of the most crowded local radio
dials in America, and that means plenty of
choice. How much? Well the local public
broadcaster had to go to two stations—one,
WHRV 89.5 FM, for NPR and local news
and information and eclectic music and the
other, WHRO-FM 90.1, devoted entirely to
classical. And those are further split in their
digital stream into six distinct programs if
you have an HD receiver.

There are country stations and Spanish language stations, religious broadcasters,
and others that devote themselves entirely
to sports. Then there are the stations that
easily bleed over the North Carolina line,
offering another helping of public radio and
full time college stations at Norfolk State
and Hampton University. There's even a high
school radio station, WFOS at 88.7 FM, that
offers up a wide variety of music that commercial stations don't play—such as blues
and beach and R&B and oldies. You can
even dial in for swing at breakfast followed
by old-time radio shows on some days of
the week. And on weekend afternoons and
evenings, you can imagine yourself back at
the bandstand, with big bands, rare radio
transcriptions, and even a comedy corner.

EDUCATION

With eight different cities come eight distinct public school systems. Each has its strengths. All can provide a child with an excellent start on life. But since the U.S. Justice Department allowed the region to stop busing students across towns to enhance integration, success can often come down to that basic tenet of real estate: location, location, location.

OVERVIEW

Buying into the best neighborhoods often means getting your kids into the best schools, even if they are older facilities. Part of that is due to peer pressure and the power of a motivated home. The children of successful people generally expect success of themselves, and that establishes a culture where learning is not marginalized. Of course, rich kids can be just as bad an influence if they are lazy and unmotivated and spread that malaise like a disease. But those situations tend to be isolated, and annual test score results show the schools in more affluent areas tend to score highest on standardized measures.

Your real estate agent can guide you to the best-performing schools in your price range, or you can get a good idea by looking at the results of Virginia's Standards of Learning Exams. The local newspapers keep the SOL results on file and you can go to the state Department of Education and view "report cards" for individual schools or entire school divisions (that's what school systems are called here) that include safety measures such as weapons offenses and attacks on students or teachers. The form to begin is located at https://p1pe.doe.virginia.gov/reportcard.

The area is also blessed with some excellent private schools and academies, reaching from the youngest pre-schoolers right up through high school. Although there isn't a Manhattan-type push from birth to get your child into the right pre-school, the best can be competitive, so you won't want to delay asking about waiting lists.

The area also has its share of private schools run by a range of denominations. And it's a hotbed of home schooling, with ad hoc organizations that help parents perform this difficult job and provide a place for such students to mingle and learn their social skills.

Your children won't need to leave the area to go to college, and you might want to check out the post-secondary education offerings yourself. The area is home to Old Dominion University, Christopher Newport, and Norfolk State University, three state schools that offer a wide range of degrees. Virginia Wesleyan College, Regent University, and Hampton University are private four-year institutions, and Thomas Nelson and Tidewater Community Colleges offer two-year associate programs as well as opportunities to transfer credits to continue at four-year schools. There are also a number of colleges and universities in the area that provide flexible schedules or online options for those who need to take that route because of military or employment commitments.

There's even a free-standing medical school, Eastern Virginia Medical School, for those who want a health career, and Regent University offers an accredited law degree as well.

CHILD CARE

Before your little darlings are old enough for school—or in the hours after dismissal and when you can get home—you will probably need some child care. The Virginia Department of Social Services keeps a database of licensed childcare providers as well as some listings for those who don't require licensing. You can find the form at www.dss.virginia.gov/facility/search/licensed.cgi.

There's a wide range of options here, from commercial daycare centers to small operations run out of a neighborhood home. The state inspects licensed centers at least twice a year, but recommends you do your own homework as well before entrusting your child to anyone else.

The YMCA and the local Girl Scout Council of Colonial Coast are among many providers who offer after-school programs where children can wait safely until their parents are able to pick them up.

If you're looking for a child care provider, there are some referral services, such as the Virginia Child Care Resource and Referral Network, www.vachildcare.org, (804) 285-0846, and Hampton Roads Child Care, www.hamptonroadschildcare.net, which has an online database.

i One of the most desirable day care centers is the Old Dominion University Child Development Center where ODU graduate level education students work with lead teachers with at least a master's degree in early childhood education incorporating the latest research and methods. It's open to the community as well as faculty and staff, with admission weighted towards the academic community. As you can imagine, there is a waiting list for this kind of expert care. Call (757) 683-3320 for info and an application.

PUBLIC SCHOOL DIVISIONS

Although there are some exceptions, basically your children will go to school in the area where you live. Obviously, those areas get bigger, and the bus rides to and from potentially longer, the farther you go through the system. High schools tend to be huge and draw from large catchment zones; elementary schools are often right around the corner.

CHESAPEAKE PUBLIC SCHOOLS
312 Cedar Rd.
Chesapeake
(757) 547-0153
www.cpschools.com

Chesapeake is a large division with 39,000 students, 45 schools, and two education centers. It is the seventh biggest system in the state and second only to Virginia Beach in the area. There are seven high schools as well as an International Baccalaureate program, a Technology Academy, and one in the works to focus on medicine. In the 2008–09 academic year, 24 Chesapeake students scored a perfect 800 on the SAT tests and 26 earned National Merit Scholarship Program honors.

The division graduates almost 87 percent of its students on time, ahead of the state average of 83.2 percent, the highest rate in the region. Twenty-eight of the division's schools were certified as excellent by the state, and every school is fully accredited, with 45 in the top state category. The system has been named one of the best in the nation for music education by the American Music Conference.

NEWPORT NEWS PUBLIC SCHOOLS
12465 Warwick Blvd.
Newport News
(757) 591-4500
www.sbo.nn.k12.va.us

This division has nearly 31,000 students in 5 high schools, 8 middle schools, 26 elementary schools, and 5 early childhood centers. For five straight years, all five of the city's high schools made *Newsweek* magazine's list of the nation's top high schools, and the division has received a Technology Leadership award from the National School Boards Association. Hilton Elementary was named a Blue Ribbon School by the U.S. Department of Education in 2009, one of only 264 schools across the country and 6 in Virginia to be included.

NORFOLK PUBLIC SCHOOLS
800 East City Hall Ave.
Norfolk
(757) 628-3830
www.nps.k12.va.us

This large, urban school district has 36,000 students in 49 schools—35 elementary, 9 middle, and 5 high schools. It offers specialty programs in middle schools in world studies, technology, communications, arts, and languages and in high schools in military science, international baccalaureate, arts, medical, and engineering. Maury and Granby

High Schools are consistently excellent, both ranking among the top 5 percent of schools in the nation in *Newsweek*'s ratings in 2008. Norview High won a national Bronze Medal in 2007 from *U.S. News and World Report*, and W.H. Taylor Elementary was the only public school in the region to be named a Blue Ribbon School by the U.S. Department of Education in 2007.

POQUOSON CITY PUBLIC SCHOOLS
500 City Hall Ave., Room 219
Poquoson
(757) 868-3055
www.poquoson.k12.va.us

This tiny city serves about 2,500 students at four schools: a primary school at 19 Odd Rd.; an elementary school at 1033 Poquoson Ave.; a middle school at 985 Poquoson Ave. and a high school at 51 Odd Rd. All are state accredited.

PORTSMOUTH PUBLIC SCHOOLS
P.O. Box 998
Portsmouth 23705-0998
(757) 393-8751
http://pps.k12.va.us

This district has 15,000 students in 3 high schools, 3 middle schools, 14 elementary schools, two pre-K centers, one special education center, an alternative school, adult learning center, and a career and technology center. It's an urban system in a city with funding challenges but strives to ensure any child who wants to go to college will have the education to get there.

SUFFOLK PUBLIC SCHOOLS
100 North Main St.
Suffolk
(757) 925-6750
www.spsk12.net

The division has more than 14,000 students in 21 schools—14 elementary, 4 middle, and 3 high schools—with more likely on the way because of the city's continued growth. It has a range from very rural schools to upper class suburban and downtown urban, which makes it hard to generalize about Suffolk's offerings.

VIRGINIA BEACH PUBLIC SCHOOLS
2512 George Mason Dr.
Virginia Beach
(757) 263-1000
www.vbschools.com

This city has long prided itself on its public schools, and they continue to shine in state rankings. It is the largest school division in all of southeastern Virginia with nearly 70,000 students. There are 85 schools, including 56 elementary schools, 14 middle schools, and 11 high schools as well as specialty centers such as the Renaissance Academy, Advanced Technology Center, Technical and Career Education Center, and an Adult Learning Center. They spend almost $11,000 per student and graduate some 83 percent on time, right at the state average. In the 2008–09 school year, 63 of the 81 eligible schools earned state awards of excellence, 3 elementary schools were designated as distinguished, and 6 of the 11 high schools, Princess Anne, Frank W. Cox, Ocean Lakes, First Colonial, Kempsville, and Kellam, were ranked among the top 6 percent of high schools in the country for 2007–08 by *Newsweek*.

PRIVATE SCHOOLS

Here, you will find the gamut, from college preps to local, church-affiliated elementary schools. Approximately one third of the schools in Hampton Roads are private,

educating nearly 30,000 students. There are Christian, Jewish, and Islamic schools, and some that cater to children with learning disabilities.

The Virginia Council for Private Education represents and accredits private elementary and secondary schools in the state and maintains a list of the accredited and non-accredited schools on its website www.vcpe.org.

The Richmond Diocese administers the Catholic Schools in Hampton Roads. You can reach it at (804) 359-5661 or www.richmond diocese.org

I won't even attempt to catalog all of the private schools in Hampton Roads, but here are a few samples of what is out there. I also won't get into tuitions, but most offer some kind of scholarship programs.

College Preps

CAPE HENRY COLLEGIATE SCHOOL
1320 Mill Dam Rd.
Virginia Beach
(757) 481-2446
www.capehenrycollegiate.org

This highly competitive co-ed school was founded in an Oceanfront home in 1924. It offers pre-K through college prep high school instruction. There's a 10–1 student-to-teacher ratio among its 1,000 students who all eventually go on to mostly top-notch colleges and universities.

CHESAPEAKE BAY ACADEMY
821 Baker Rd.
Virginia Beach
(757) 497-6200
www.cba-va.org

This school focuses on smart kids who have trouble learning in normal environments. The average class size ranged from 3 to 12 students, and the student-teacher ratio is just 5–1. There are lower, middle, and upper Schools on the campus serving grades K to 12.

HAMPTON ROADS ACADEMY
739 Academy Lane
Newport News
(757) 884-9100
www.hra.org

This independent college prep on a 60-acre campus serves the Peninsula. There are about 640 students in a 10–1 ratio with teachers, and all are accepted into colleges and universities after graduating—with more than 90 percent getting into their first choice. It is the only independent, non-sectarian secondary college prep on the Peninsula and celebrated its 50th anniversary in 2009.

NORFOLK ACADEMY
1585 Wesleyan Dr.
Norfolk
(757) 461-6236
www.norfolkacademy.org

This school was chartered when Virginia was still a colony. It began in 1728, making it the eighth oldest secondary school in the nation. It boasts a challenging academic program with morning chapel, family-style lunches, and Boy and Girl of the Day awards. There are 1,220-some students in kindergarten through 12th grades.

NORFOLK COLLEGIATE SCHOOL
7336 Granby St.
Norfolk
(757) 480-1495
www.norfolkcollegiate.org

This is another of the area's top academic preps, with classes for 1st through 12th graders.

Religious-Affiliated Schools

ATLANTIC SHORES CHRISTIAN SCHOOLS
Elementary School
1861 Kempsville Rd.
Virginia Beach
(757) 479-1125
Junior and Senior High Schools
1217 North Centerville Turnpike
Chesapeake
(757) 479-9598
www.shoreschristian.org

Education at either campus is Bible-based and accredited by the Association of Christian Schools International.

BISHOP SULLIVAN CATHOLIC HIGH SCHOOL
4552 Princess Anne Rd.
Virginia Beach
(757) 467-2881
www.chsvb.org

Established in Norfolk in 1949, the school moved to a new campus in Virginia Beach in 1993. There were 451 students and 39 instructors in 2010.

HEBREW ACADEMY OF TIDEWATER
5000 Corporate Woods Dr., Suite 180
Virginia Beach
(757) 424-4327
www.hebrewacademy.net

This is a Jewish community day school for children from kindergarten through sixth grade. It is affiliated with the Strelitz Early Childhood Center for two- to four-year-olds.

PENINSULA CATHOLIC HIGH SCHOOL
600 Harpersville Rd.
Newport News
(757) 596-7247
http://peninsulacatholic.com

This is the Peninsula's Catholic High School. In 2010 it had 313 students and 29 faculty members.

TIDEWATER ADVENTIST ACADEMY
1136 North Centerville Turnpike
Chesapeake
(757) 479-0002
www.adventisteducation.com

This school began in 1918. Most students are members of the Seventh-day Adventist faith, but the school is open to all who meet basic admission requirements.

TRINITY LUTHERAN SCHOOL
6001 Granby St.
Norfolk
(757) 489-2732
www.trinityluthernannorfolk.org

This school for pre-kindergarteners through fifth graders is affiliated with Trinity Evangelical Lutheran Church.

VIRGINIA BEACH FRIENDS SCHOOL
1537 Laskin Rd.
Virginia Beach
(757) 428-7534
www.friends-school.org

This pre-K through high school was founded in 1955 to provide a Quaker education in the area. There are 235 students at the school, which has an 8–1 student to teacher ratio. You don't have to be Quaker to attend the school, which looks for diversity in the student body.

HIGHER EDUCATION

If you want to quickly take a trip through the options, check out the various colleges and universities, see what degrees are offered, compare tuition, and compare online and distance learning possibilities, there's a one-stop organization—EdUFind.org, which is a project of the Virginia Consortium for Higher Education: www.edufind.org.

HAMPTON UNIVERSITY
100 East Queen St.
Hampton
(757) 727-5000

This private, historically black school was founded in 1868 to educate freed blacks. The Emancipation Oak tree is located on the campus. It was under this giant tree that children of former slaves were taught and here that blacks gathered to hear the first Southern reading of President Lincoln's Emancipation Proclamation. Booker T. Washington was educated at Hampton. The school became Hampton Institute in 1930 and a university in 1984. Washington is just one of a long line of famous graduates, including Dr. Martin Luther King Jr's mother Alberta Williams King and Emmy Award–winning comedian Wanda Sykes. President Obama delivered the Commencement Address on May 9, 2010.

i Hampton University's Emancipation Oak has limbs that span more than 100 feet in diameter and has been designated one of the 10 Great Trees of the World by the National Geographic Society. You can see it near the entrance to the university.

CHRISTOPHER NEWPORT UNIVERSITY
1 University Place
Newport News
(757) 594-7000
www.cnu.edu

This constantly evolving university grew quickly from a local college founded in 1960 into a regional powerhouse that was named one of the 10 "up and coming" liberal arts schools in the nation by *U.S. News & World Report*'s "America's Best Colleges" guide. The university now offers 80 areas of study on its 260-acre campus stuffed with new facilities. There are 4,800 students here, some 3,000 of whom live on campus, and they have rated the dorms and apartment complexes "best in the state." The school is adjacent to the Mariners' Museum and its 550-acre wooded park.

EASTERN VIRGINIA MEDICAL SCHOOL
P.O. Box 1980
Norfolk; 23501-1980
(757) 446-5600
www.evms.edu
Every other medical school in the nation is affiliated with a university or teaching hospital. EVMS is different, born from a community desire to increase the number of quality doctors in the area. By not being tied to one organization, EVMS is able to share its wealth with many. As a result, students in the medical or health professional programs are often out working in the community. The school itself is noted for its family medicine programs, as well as research that focuses on local needs. (See entry in Health Care chapter.) The main campus is adjacent to Sentara Norfolk General Hospital and the Children's Hospital of the King's Daughters, the area's cutting-edge centers for adult and pediatric care. In 2009, the school enrolled its largest-ever medical class, 118 prospective doctors. Plans are for the school to continue growing to meet the increased needs as more people become eligible for federal health care.

NORFOLK STATE UNIVERSITY
700 Park Ave.
Norfolk
(757) 823-8600
www.nsu.edu

Founded in 1935, Norfolk State is one of the largest predominantly black institutions in the nation. It began as Norfolk Unit of Virginia Union University, and then became the independent Norfolk Polytechnic College before being forced to become a part of Virginia State College. It became fully independent again in 1969 and a university 10 years later. Today it has a College of Liberal Arts and a College of Science, Engineering, and Technology, as well as a School of Business, School of Education, and School of Social Work. There are approximately 7,000 students enrolled at the university, which has historically offered an open admission policy. In short, if you want to go to college, they'll let you try. The rest is up to you. Emmy-nominated actor, author, director, and producer Tim Reid is an alumnus.

OLD DOMINION UNIVERSITY
5155 Hampton Blvd.
Norfolk
(757) 683-3000
www.odu.edu
Old Dominion is a classic urban commuter university with 23,000 students and a wide range of fields of study among its six colleges offering 70 undergraduate, 60 master's, and 36 doctoral programs. The school is a leader in research, particularly in modeling and simulation and molecular biology.

The school began as the Norfolk Campus of the College of William and Mary and wasn't much to look at in the early years. Recently, though, there has been a massive expansion into the surrounding neighborhood with the creation of the University Village behind the new Ted Constant center. The old Field House, where basketball games were played before the Constant opened, was replaced by a huge Student Recreation

Center with 15,000 square feet of workout space, an indoor track, and even an indoor rock wall.

Football also came back to ODU and with it a renovation of old Foreman Field and a new $17 million Powhatan Sports Complex that is home to field hockey and lacrosse programs as well. (See the Spectator Sports chapter for info on ODU and other college teams.)

The school also has higher education centers in Hampton, Virginia Beach, and Portsmouth and a distance-learning network.

REGENT UNIVERSITY
1000 Regent University Dr.
Virginia Beach
(757) 352-4000
www.regent.edu
Televangelist M.G. "Pat" Robertson established this university on his Christian Broadcasting Network campus in 1978 as an academic center for Christian thought and action. The first 70 students studied for graduate degrees in communication in rented classrooms and were taught by just seven faculty members. Today, the facilities are beautiful, and the mission is clearly Bible-based. There were about 5,000 students enrolled in the spring of 2010, some 2,000 of them full time. The school awards more than 70 graduate and undergraduate degrees on campus and online. The university now includes a Robertson School of Government and a School of Divinity, as well as a School of Education, School of Communication & the Arts, and a School of Global Leadership & Entrepreneurship. It is also the only law school in Hampton Roads.

THOMAS NELSON COMMUNITY COLLEGE
99 Thomas Nelson Dr.
Hampton
(757) 825-2800
www.tncc.edu
The Peninsula's community college campus is located just off I-64. It offers more than 40 fields of study with associate degrees and professional certification. There are eight academic buildings here. It's the fourth largest community college in the Virginia system, with an enrollment of more than 15,000 students. There is also a campus in Williamsburg and a satellite site in Newport News.

TIDEWATER COMMUNITY COLLEGE
(757) 822-1122
www.tcc.edu
This school has campuses in Norfolk, Portsmouth, Chesapeake, and Virginia Beach, each providing two-year associate degree programs in a wide range of disciplines. Students can either transfer to four-year colleges, where they tend to do as well as those who started there, or they can specialize in workforce development programs designed with immediate employment in mind. The school has more than 25,000 students in the following campuses.

The **Academic Division Chesapeake,** 1428 Cedar Rd., is located just beyond the City Hall complex. The **Norfolk Campus** is located right on Granby Street across from the MacArthur Center Mall downtown. The **Portsmouth Campus** was recently relocated to 120 Campus Dr., at the corner of Greenwood Drive and McLean Street. Before, the Portsmouth Campus was actually located in Suffolk. The **Virginia Beach** campus has nine buildings, including an

Advanced Technology Center at 1700 College Crescent, which is off Princess Anne Road near Landstown High School.

VIRGINIA WESLEYAN COLLEGE
1584 Wesleyan Dr.
Norfolk
(757) 455.3200
http://ww2.vwc.edu

This small, four-year liberal arts college sits on 300 wooded acres near the junction of Norfolk and Virginia Beach. There are 1,400 students, more than half living on campus, and 38 majors are offered here. There is a deliberate desire to remain small, a college rather than a university, to keep the education intimate and personal. The school has been designated the best Southeastern college by *Princeton Review*, and one of America's Best Liberal Arts Colleges by *U.S. News & World Report*.

HEALTH CARE

The headline screamed, "She's a Cutie," announcing the miraculous birth of Elizabeth Carr at what was then Norfolk General Hospital. It was December 1981, and that 5-pound, 12-ounce product of a Petri dish put Hampton Roads on the medical map.

Carr was America's first test tube baby and the 15th in-vitro baby ever born. Her parents, Judith and Roger Carr, had been unable to conceive naturally and decided to leave the prestigious hospitals in their native Massachusetts and take their chances with the pioneering Drs. Howard and Georgeana Jones at Eastern Virginia Medical School's new in-vitro program.

The Jones Institute for Reproductive Medicine at EVMS has been going strong since. It now helps bring 3,500 babies a year into the world using cutting edge research and processes developed in their Norfolk campus.

EVMS has gone on to branch out to pioneering work in proteomics, the manipulation of proteins to identify and cure diseases as diverse as cancer and diabetes. It's also a giant in prostate cancer identification and treatment.

Hampton Roads is home to nationally certified cancer, diabetes, and heart centers. And there's an entire parallel medical world at the Naval Hospital in Portsmouth and other clinics that see people in uniform, their families, and retirees, with a separate Veterans Administration medical center in Hampton.

If treatments aren't available here, you're an easy jump to the medical centers in Charlottesville and Richmond or the Research Triangle region in North Carolina. Bottom line, if you're here, health care options really aren't a concern.

And if you need a transplant, LifeNet Health, one of the nation's biggest suppliers of such tissue, is based right here in Virginia Beach. You'll still have to get on the national waiting lists for an organ, but it's nice to know they might not have to fly it very far before your surgeon gets to use it.

MEDICAL SCHOOL

EASTERN VIRGINIA MEDICAL SCHOOL
At the Eastern Virginia Medical Center
Colley Avenue and Olney Road
Norfolk
(757) 446-7360
This is one of only four medical schools in the state and the only one in the country that is not affiliated with a university or a hospital. EVMS is a true community school and that unique status allows its teachers, researchers, and medical experts to work with every hospital, clinic, and practice in the area.

That means that new ideas hatched in EVMS labs can be quickly translated into new ways to treat folks in the field. And your private practice doctor has as much access to those ideas as those who are affiliated with the big area hospitals.

The school is a research leader and has recently put much more emphasis on trying to solve problems that are endemic to this community, such as diabetes and hypertension. It has been beefing up its research teams in those areas and working with other institutions, such as Sentara Norfolk General Hospital and the military, to test theories and get real-world results. It is a research leader in reproductive medicine, pediatrics, geriatrics, diabetes, and cancer.

The school graduated its first class of doctors in 1973 after community leaders persuaded the state to create a medical authority and raised $17 million. Now, 2,300 physicians are EVMS alumni. And true to the community's original desire to improve local medical care, 500 of them practice in Hampton Roads. In 2009, more than 5,000 applicants tried for the 118 open slots.

In addition to education, EVMS also is a center for treatment. Some 180,000 have received care here. EVMS Health Services is a nonprofit physician practice with more than 150 doctors in 20 specialties and is a pioneer in using electronic health records.

The school also offers non-MD degrees in such fields as art therapy and counseling, clinical psychology, biomedical sciences, and surgical and physician assistants.

One interesting tidbit: EVMS is a leader in standardized patients. That's not some patient that just fits a standard, it's a "patient" who is trained to simulate symptoms who uses his or her body to set standards by training medical students and assessing the quality of care in actual practices through stealth visits. EVMS standardized patients are used by institutions all over the country for training and at various medical conferences.

HOSPITALS

Bon Secours Hampton Roads Health System

This is another regional hospital power, under the auspices of the nonprofit Bon Secours group based in Maryland. Affiliated with the Catholic Church, it operates facilities in six states, although most are in Virginia and Florida.

BON SECOURS DEPAUL MEDICAL CENTER
150 Kingsley Lane
Norfolk
(757) 889-5331
This facility was founded as St. Vincent DePaul Hospital in 1856, and the current 238-bed hospital is slated to be replaced with a new, 124-bed, full service hospital by 2014. The hospital has a 30-minute service guarantee at its 24-hour emergency room.

BON SECOURS MARYVIEW MEDICAL CENTER
3636 High St.
Portsmouth
(757) 398-2449
This 346-bed hospital also includes a 54-bed Behavioral Medicine Center. It is Portsmouth's only non-military hospital and opened in 1945 to care for shipyard workers. After the war, it was dedicated to treating polio victims. The hospital has an emergency room, which also has a 30-minute guarantee.

BON SECOURS MARY IMMACULATE HOSPITAL
2 Bernardine Dr.
Newport News
(757) 886-6000

The hospital dates back to the turn of the 20th century and moved to the current location in the Denbigh area of Newport News in the 1970s. It features a birth center, an orthopedic center, outpatient surgeries, and a 115-bed St. Francis Nursing Center next door. This is another place where they guarantee that care will begin no more than a half hour after you turn up at the emergency room.

CHESAPEAKE REGIONAL MEDICAL CENTER
736 North Battlefield Blvd.
Chesapeake
(757) 312-8121

This hospital is only 30 years old and has bucked the trends by remaining independent of any national or regional health systems. There are 310 beds here, all in private rooms and arranged in special nursing units. There are nearly 600 physicians on staff and its location close to the North Carolina border makes it popular with our southern neighbors. The hospital has a Lifestyles center that offers healthy living, yoga, and tai chi classes as well as a fully equipped gym with instructors who assist those with special needs and risk factors. There's a BirthPlace, a Women's Unit, and a cancer center.

CHILDREN'S HOSPITAL OF THE KING'S DAUGHTERS
601 Children's Lane
Norfolk
(757) 668-7000

This is a health system dedicated exclusively to children. It's on the same campus as the Eastern Virginia Medical Center and connected physically to Sentara Norfolk General. It's the place where the most difficult neonatal cases are taken. It also offers special units for pediatric intensive care, rehabilitation, cancer treatment, medical and surgical care, and transitional care. The hospital combines cutting-edge medicine with child life specialists, chaplains, teachers, social workers, and parent and patient education programs. Parents can sleep in their kids' rooms here, making it easier for tots to rest. The emergency room is geared just for children and sees 42,000 patients a year. Their surgeons are specialists who know how to deal with a frightened child and tiny bodies. Waiting areas are filled with toys and video games and patients can choose how they want to get to the operating room: on a bike, in a wagon, or carried by staff.

Any specialty out there dealing with child medicine is offered here, from orthopedics to plastic surgery. EVMS pediatric residents train here, and the hospital operates a child abuse program designed to help little victims.

HAMPTON VA MEDICAL CENTER
100 Emancipation Dr.
Hampton
(757) 722-9961

This 468-bed hospital is one of the first in the VA system. It serves eastern Virginia and northeastern North Carolina, providing health care to America's military veterans. The center provides everything from primary care to extended care and rehabilitation programs. There's a spinal cord injury center here, one of the largest in the VA system, and a mental health program for post-traumatic stress disorder, depression, addictions, and even an outreach service to homeless veterans.

LAKE TAYLOR TRANSITIONAL CARE HOSPITAL
1309 Kempsville Rd.
Norfolk
(757) 461-5001

If you come out of a hospital and aren't ready to resume your life at home, you need a place like Lake Taylor. This new-style rehab center works with stroke victims and orthopedic surgery patients to get them back to or beyond where they were before their problems. This isn't a nursing home or a traditional rehab center but a long-term acute care hospital, a place for people who have a variety of illnesses perhaps, or require care of several medical specialists or who need respiratory therapists always on staff until they can be weaned from a ventilator.

RIVERSIDE REGIONAL MEDICAL CENTER
500 J. Clyde Morris Blvd.
Newport News
(757) 594-2000

Another large independent hospital, Riverside dates back to 1916. It's been in its present location since 1963. There are 570 beds at the facility, a level II trauma center that sees more than 57,000 emergencies a year and has 42 private rooms. There's a heart center, a birthing and family health center, and an intensive cancer care center.

SENTARA HEALTHCARE
Various locations
www.sentara.com

Sentara is the region's largest health care provider, operating six hospitals as well as a number of physician practices, seven nursing centers, three assisted living centers, and an adult day care center as well as several advanced imaging centers in the area. In all, Sentara operates more than 100 medical care sites, here and in Williamsburg and Woodbridge, VA.

Sentara hospitals have been listed among America's best in heart and heart surgery, diabetes and endocrine disorders, geriatric care, kidney disorders, and orthopedics. It operates the area's air ambulance, "Nightingale," and the region's solid organ transplant center, which performs heart, kidney, pancreas, and combined kidney/pancreas transplants.

This giant began in 1888 with a 25-bed Retreat for the Sick in Norfolk.

SENTARA NORFOLK GENERAL HOSPITAL
600 Gresham Dr.
Norfolk
(757) 388-3000

This is the largest of the Sentara Hospitals and home to the region's only level I trauma center and burn trauma unit. There are 543 beds here. It is consistently ranked among America's best hospitals, with top ratings in heart and heart surgery, diabetes, geriatric care, kidney disorders, and endocrine disorder treatments.

SENTARA HEART HOSPITAL
600 Gresham Dr.
Norfolk
(757) 388-3000

This is part of Sentara Norfolk General Hospital and the region's only dedicated heart hospital in a facility built specifically for cardiac care. This is a one-stop shop for everything from diagnostics to open heart surgery and transplants. There are 112 beds and 45 pre- and post-procedural rooms that offer some of the most specialized heart care in the Mid-Atlantic.

SENTARA LEIGH HOSPITAL
830 Kempsville Rd.
Norfolk
(757) 261-6000

This is considered the "country club" among the Sentara hospitals, with 250 private room beds. It specializes in orthopedic, gynecological, and urological services, plus a large outpatient wing and an emergency room. There's a Breast Cancer Center here with an all-female staff and a hyperbaric oxygen therapy unit for patients with major wounds, decompression sickness, and carbon monoxide poisoning. It was honored in 2009 as one of the top orthopedic hospitals in America by *U.S. News and World Report* and has begun a drive to enlarge and modernize patient rooms.

SENTARA BAYSIDE HOSPITAL
800 Independence Blvd.
Virginia Beach
(757) 363-6100

This 158-bed, acute care facility has a full emergency department, MRI center, and nuclear cardiology services as well as a sleep disorders center. Plans are to turn it into an outpatient campus when a new Sentara hospital opens in southern Virginia Beach in 2011. The 24-hour emergency room is scheduled to remain.

SENTARA OBICI HOSPITAL
2800 Godwin Blvd.
Suffolk
(757) 934-4000

This is a 150-bed facility that opened in 2002 in Suffolk, replacing the historic Obici Hospital. It merged with Sentara Healthcare in 2006. The hospital is expanding with a new wing slated to open in 2011. There's a full range of inpatient and outpatient services, including a 24-hour emergency room, a sleep disorder center, occupational medicine, and a women's center.

SENTARA CAREPLEX HOSPITAL
3000 Coliseum Dr.
Hampton
(757) 736-1000

This is another private-room-only hospital with Internet access and entertainment options and 200 beds. It offers specialized services in cardiac, vascular, and urologic care and a busy emergency department. It's a center of excellence in weight loss surgery and features the region's only hospital dedicated to orthopedics. There's a Sentara Center for Health and Fitness next door. It also operates an outpatient campus in Newport News.

MILITARY MEDICINE

NAVAL MEDICAL CENTER PORTSMOUTH
620 John Paul Jones Circle
Portsmouth
(757) 377-5000

When you're home to the world's largest Navy base and a concentration of other services that makes you the largest military community in the country, you need a large military health care system. The Naval Medical Center based in Portsmouth since 1830 is just that. The center and its 10 branch clinics have 6,000 military, civilian, and volunteer staffers. It's a one-stop shop for those in uniform and their dependents. This hospital has everything from pediatric oncology to in-patient psychiatry. There's a host of clinics that feed into this network, as well as the military's TRICARE insurance system to schedule appointments. There's a large military pharmacy here, with annexes at various military bases. There is also a Zachary and Elizabeth Fisher House nearby where families of seriously ill or injured patients can stay for free.

Navy Branch Health Clinics

BOONE CLINIC
Little Creek
1035 Nider Blvd., Suite 100
Norfolk
(757) 953-8351

DAM NECK ANNEX
1885 Terrier Ave., Suite 100
Virginia Beach
(757) 953-9915

NORFOLK NAVAL SHIPYARD
Building 277
Berrien St. and Mayo Ave.
Portsmouth
(757) 953-6470

SEWELLS POINT
1721 Taussig Blvd.
Norfolk
(757) 953-9000

NORTHWEST
1317 Ballahack Rd.
Chesapeake
(757) 953-6246

NORFOLK DENTAL CLINIC
1647 Taussig Blvd.
Norfolk
(757) 953-8635

NAVAL AIR STATION OCEANA
1550 Tomcat Blvd., Suite 150
Virginia Beach
(757) 953-3933

TRICARE PRIME CLINIC CHESAPEAKE
1011 Eden Way North, Suite H
Chesapeake
(757) 953-6366

TRICARE PRIME CLINIC NORTHWEST
1317 Ballahack Rd.
Chesapeake
(757) 953-6246 or (757) 953-6267

TRICARE PRIME CLINIC VIRGINIA BEACH
2100 Lynnhaven Parkway, Suite 201
Konikoff Professional Centre
Virginia Beach
(757) 953-6708

WALK-IN CLINICS

PATIENT FIRST
www.patientfirst.com
This company has 8 of its 26 centers in Hampton Roads, each open every day from 8 a.m. to 10 p.m., including weekends and holidays. No appointments are necessary and x-rays, lab tests, and prescription medications are provided on site. Most insurance plans work with Patient First, but you might want to check if you are covered. For a complete list of locations in your area, visit the website above.

PUBLIC HEALTH DEPARTMENTS

Each city has its own public health department, which ensures restaurants are sanitary, water supplies are safe, epidemics are avoided, mosquitoes and vermin are kept under control, school children are screened for potential problems and immunized, and citizens receive the care they need. This is where you'll find free testing and counseling for HIV or other sexually transmitted diseases, dental and pediatric care for poor

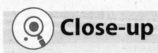

Close-up

Healing Those Who Have No Safety Net

When times get tough, business booms at **Chesapeake Care** (2145 South Military Hwy., Chesapeake, 757-545-5700), a free clinic off Military Highway that provides medical and dental services for the region's unfortunate.

Chesapeake Care, which was founded in 1992 by local surgeon Dr. Juan Montero, is dedicated to providing free medical and oral health care to the uninsured poor who don't qualify for other assistance programs.

More than 80 percent of those seen fall below the federal poverty line, and the average four-person family income of patients is $26,500. Over half the clinic's patients have jobs but don't earn enough to buy insurance.

New patient visits have more than doubled in recent years as the economy tanked. The clinic, which has a paid staff of just 14, relies on the help of 224 volunteers, including 136 licensed physicians, physician assistants, dentists, pharmacists, nurses, nurse practitioners, hygienists, physical therapists, and counselors.

Those donated hours save the Hampton Roads health care community more than $4.3 million each year, the clinic estimates.

Connie White, a Chesapeake pharmacist, has given more than 3,000 hours to the clinic over the past decade and jokingly refered to it as her second home. "It's the best way to practice pharmacy," she said. "You have the doctor, the nurse all in one building. You don't get that anywhere else." And, she pointed out, "People are here because they want to be."

The clinic provided about $2 million worth of free medications in 2008, according to Executive Director Catherine Lewis, with volunteers pursuing the drugs through pharmaceutical companies' medication access programs.

children, help with family planning, and some assistance with general medical care. Most services are based on a sliding scale depending on ability to pay.

Here's where to go for more info:

Norfolk

HEADQUARTERS
830 Southampton Ave., Suite 200
Norfolk
(757) 683-2756

CLINICS
925 South Main St.
Norfolk
(757) 494-2470

606 West 29th St.
Norfolk
(757) 683-9230

830 Goff St.
Norfolk
(757) 683-9270

207 East Little Creek Rd.
Norfolk
(757) 531-2135

Virginia Beach

HEADQUARTERS AND CLINICS
4452 Corporation Lane
Virginia Beach
(757) 518-2700

Chesapeake

HEADQUARTERS
748 North Battlefield Blvd.
Chesapeake
(757) 382-8608

CLINIC
490 Liberty St.
Chesapeake
(757) 382-2600

Portsmouth

HUMAN SERVICES CENTER
1701 High St., 1st Floor
Portsmouth
(757) 393-8585

Suffolk

DISTRICT HEADQUARTERS
135 Hall Ave., Suite A
Suffolk
(757) 514-4700

Hampton

HEADQUARTERS AND CLINICS
3130 Victoria Blvd.
Hampton
(757) 727-1172

Newport News

PENINSULA HEALTH CENTER
416 J. Clyde Morris Blvd.
Newport News
(757) 594-7305

EAST END HEALTH FACILITY
1033 28th St.
Newport News
(757) 247-2184

YORK/DENBIGH OFFICE
606 Denbigh Blvd., Suite 304
Newport News
(757) 886-2810

MENTAL HEALTH

In Virginia, the state has community services boards that are in business to provide behavioral health care and services for individuals and families affected by intellectual and developmental disabilities.

VIRGINIA BEACH COMMUNITY SERVICES BOARD
3432 Virginia Beach Blvd.
Virginia Beach
(757) 437-3608

NORFOLK
225 West Olney Rd.
Norfolk
(757) 823-1600

CHESAPEAKE
224 Great Bridge Blvd.
Chesapeake
(757) 547-9334

PORTSMOUTH DEPARTMENT OF BEHAVIORAL HEALTHCARE SERVICES
Central Intake Office
545 High St.
Portsmouth
(757) 393-5357

SUFFOLK
Suffolk Services Center
Northgate Building
Godwin Commerce Park
1000 Commercial Lane
Suffolk
(757) 942-1069

HAMPTON-NEWPORT NEWS COMMUNITY SERVICES BOARD

300 Medical Dr.
Hampton
(757) 788-0300

VIRGINIA BEACH PSYCHIATRIC CENTER

1100 First Colonial Rd.
Virginia Beach
(757) 496-6000
www.psychiatricsolutionsvbpc.com

This is a 100-bed acute psychiatric hospital that provides therapy and substance abuse services to children, adolescents, and adults. It offers a mobile assessment team that can perform crisis evaluations at local hospitals, emergency rooms, medical offices, schools, and businesses. The hospital is open for free, confidential assessments at all times.

HEALTH INSURANCE PROVIDERS

ANTHEM BLUE CROSS AND BLUE SHIELD

(800) 304-0372
www.anthem.com

Anthem is the name of the Blue Cross plans in Hampton Roads, and it provides a variety of insurance plans, including HMOs and temporary bridge protection to individuals and employers. The website also has a tool to find a doctor that takes their insurance.

OPTIMA HEALTH

(800) 741-4825
www.optimahealth.com

This is a large local provider affiliated with the Sentara Health network that offers a variety of health insurance coverage through employers or to individuals. There are plans that are fully managed and others with more control and choice of provider by the individual.

INDEX